ETHNIC MYTHS AND
PENTATEUCHAL FOUNDATIONS

THE SOCIETY OF BIBLICAL LITERATURE
SEMEIA STUDIES
Vincent L. Wimbush, Editor

ETHNIC MYTHS AND PENTATEUCHAL FOUNDATIONS
A New Approach to the Formation of the Pentateuch

by

E. Theodore Mullen, Jr.

Scholars Press
Atlanta, Georgia

ETHNIC MYTHS AND PENTATEUCHAL FOUNDATIONS
A NEW APPROACH TO THE FORMATION OF THE PENTATEUCH

by
E. Theodore Mullen, Jr.

Library of Congress Cataloging in Publication Data

Mullen, E. Theodore.
   Ethnic myths and pentateuchal foundations : a new approach to
the formation of the pentateuch / by E. Theodore Mullen.
      p. cm. — (Semeia studies)
   Includes bibliographical references.
   ISBN 0-7885-0382-0 (pbk. : alk. paper)
   1. Bible. O.T. Pentateuch—Criticism, Redaction. 2. Jews—
History—To 1200 B.C. —Historiography. I. Title. II. Series.
BS1225.2.M85 1997
222'.1066—dc21   97-23857

Printed in the United States of America
on acid-free paper

To Grace Friend Mullen, with love

TABLE OF CONTENTS

ACKNOWLEDGMENTS

The approach to the analysis of the Pentateuchal materials that this book takes is an extension of the interpretive model that was developed in my *Narrative History and Ethnic Boundaries: The Deuteronomistic Historian and the Creation of Israelite National Identity*, which was also published by Scholars Press in the *Semeia Studies* series. Though the two volumes share a common analytical approach, they are not interdependent. I am deeply indebted to Scholars Press for accepting this volume for publication, and I should like to thank Vincent L. Wimbush, editor of *Semeia Studies*, for his many helpful suggestions concerning the preparation of the manuscript.

The major research for this book was completed during a sabbatical leave granted by Indiana University Purdue University Indianapolis in the spring semester of 1994. Numerous conversations with my colleagues in the Department of Religious Studies concerning a variety of issues related to the relationships among religion, ethnicity, and social world construction have been extremely beneficial to me. Most especially I would like to express my indebtedness to my wife Grace, whose support and assistance at every stage of the completion of this work have been indispensable.

E. Theodore Mullen, Jr.
Indiana University Purdue University Indianapolis
May, 1997

1

ANOTHER STUDY OF THE PENTATEUCH:
SOME PREFATORY REMARKS

I. The Background for a New Model

Any recent survey of opinion on the status of the study of the formation of the Pentateuchal traditions and the Hebrew canon would conclude
that while there may be selected attempts to discredit the "documentary
hypothesis," that theory remains the central bulwark of modern analyses
of the formation of the initial five books of the Hebrew scriptures. Indeed,
if one consulted the article on the Pentateuch in the recently published
Anchor Bible Dictionary,[1] one would be completely unaware that the very
foundations of that theory, and its position with respect to the formation
of the other works in the Hebrew bible, have come under any criticism
from competent scholars. Additionally, the excellent handbook on the Pentateuch recently published by A. F. Campbell and M. A. O'Brien,[2] while
noting the variety of approaches available for explaining the formation
of the Pentateuch, presents an implicit defense of the classic form of that
theory as it was presented by M. Noth.[3] In short, it would not be an overstatement to say that the documentary hypothesis, with only minor variations to the basic form it took over a century ago, remains among biblical

---

[1] R. E. Friedman, "Torah (Pentateuch)," *ABD* VI, 605–622.

[2] *Sources of the Pentateuch: Texts, Introductions, Annotations* (Minneapolis: Fortress/
Augsburg, 1993).

[3] *A History of Pentateuchal Traditions*, trans. B. W. Anderson (Englewood Cliffs, N.J.:
Prentice-Hall, 1972 [German original, 1948].

Ethnic Myths

scholars the foundation for understanding the formation of the Pentateuchal materials.[4]

Yet the reconstructions of the traditions underlying the present Pentateuch, based as they may be upon extremely intricate and carefully presented argumentation, all suffer from one basic presuppositional fallacy. Each begins by assuming that the "past" recounted in these materials was not created by its authors. Now it might seem quite natural to argue that no one creates national traditions from whole cloth, though there does exist some interesting evidence to show that this does happen quite often.[5] In contrast to those who would support the diachronic development of the "traditions" contained in the Pentateuchal materials and concentrate upon their redactional development, as emphasized by all those who engage in the application of the documentary hypothesis, are those who approach those same materials from a strictly literary perspective, i.e., synchronically. From this perspective, the problems of historicity of sources or the possible processes through which they passed in obtaining their present form simply are not relevant.[6]

While it might seem that these two approaches could contain the promise of a solution to the problems associated with the study of the Pentateuch,[7] those who approach the biblical materials from one of these two

---

4 An overview of the major trends in Pentateuchal research is presented by David M. Carr, "Controversy and Convergence in Recent Studies of the Formation of the Pentateuch," *RelSRev* 23 (1997) 22–31.

5 For examples of such, see E. Hobsbawm, "Introduction: Inventing Traditions," in *The Invention of Tradition*, ed. E. Hobsbawm and T. Ranger (Cambridge: Cambridge University Press, 1983), pp. 1–14. An extremely interesting case in which an ethnic identity seems to have been invented almost devoid of any historical content is illustrated by E. E. Roosens' study of the Hurons of Quebec (*Creating Ethnicity: The Process of Ethnogenesis* [Frontiers of Anthropology, 5; Newbury Park, CA: Sage, 1990).

6 Though R. Polzin's structuralist approach to the analysis of the deuteronomistic history has not been systematically applied to the study of the Pentateuchal traditions, his vehemently negative critique of the historical critical method as applied to the deuteronomistic writings would apply equally to the use of the documentary hypothesis (*Moses and the Deuteronomist: A Literary Study of the Deuteronomic History* [New York: Seabury, 1980], pp. 1–24.

7 S. Boorer argues that the results of the two approaches should be utilized together, not as the results of separate inquiries, though few have attempted to adopt such a method ("The Importance of a Diachronic Approach: The Case of Genesis-Kings," *CBQ* 51 [1989] 195–208). While it might seem obvious to some, a fact overlooked by many investigators is that the "documents" posited by the "documentary hypothesis" do not exist, nor are they even referred to in the extant biblical materials. Despite efforts to show that there exist some parallels upon which we might base our reconstructions, such as those by J. Tigay, *et al.* (*Empirical Models for Biblical Criticism* [Philadelphia: University of Pennsylvania Press, 1985]), the fact remains that the

perspectives seem to have little to say to each other.[8] From an analytical perspective, this is quite understandable. While the documentary approach to the analysis of the Pentateuchal narratives is based upon the recognition of certain literary and stylistic criteria that may be used to differentiate among various sources,[9] the literary approach to that same corpus concentrates on incorporating those particular "criteria" into a poetics of narrative that eschews the division of the materials into a variety of disparate sources.[10] Whether the two can ever find a common ground for discussion seems open to serious doubt.[11]

If there exists such a gap between the documentary, historical critical approach to the narratives of the Pentateuch and the more purely literary approach to those materials, what might be the benefits of yet another model for interpreting those materials? This would be a highly legitimate question, for clearly the discussion seems to have divided itself into two differing

---

criteria used to reconstruct the documents that form the basis for understanding the process of the production of the Pentateuch are derived from the very theory that utilizes them to recreate its sources. The process is, unavoidably, circular. At least in the case of New Testament gospel studies and their efforts at reconstructing documents like *Quelle,* contemporary parallel gospels exist to which comparisons may be made and by which conclusions might be derived. No such contemporary or parallel materials from Israelite culture and religion exist for the study of the redactional creation of the Pentateuch, or any other biblical Hebrew text, for that matter. The possible exception might be the Hebrew texts attested at Qumran, which suggest that the final form of the biblical text was not yet established in every instance, but that such matters had, by the first century BCE, reached their concluding stages.

8 See, for example, the comments of D. M. Gunn, "New Direction in the Study of Biblical Hebrew Narrative," *JSOT* 39 (1987) 65–75.

9 The primary criteria isolated by scholars in their attempt to reconstruct the sources of the Pentateuch are enumerated by R. Friedman, "Torah (Pentateuch)," 609–618. A helpful balance to Friedman's enthusiastic endorsement of these is found in R. N. Whybray's critique of the documentary hypothesis developed in *The Making of the Pentateuch: A Methodological Study* (JSOTSup 53; Sheffield: JSOT, 1987), pp. 20–131.

10 For the classical statement of the state of literary analysis of the biblical materials, see M. Sternberg, *The Poetics of Biblical Narrative: Ideological Literature and the Drama of Reading* (Indianapolis/Bloomington: Indiana University Press, 1985).

11 As E. Greenstein has noted, "historians and synchronists ask different questions," a situation that, if correct, suggests that there exists very little possibility for the development of a unified critical approach ("On the Genesis of Biblical Prose Narrative," *Prooftexts* 8 [1988] 353). The division between these two approaches is exacerbated by the distinctively incompatible way in which "history" as a literary construct is understood by each group. An excellent discussion of these contrasting positions is provided by Regina M. Schwartz in "The Histories of David: Biblical Scholarship and Biblical Stories," in *Not In Heaven: Coherence and Complexity in Biblical Narrative,* ed. J. P. Rosenblatt and J. C. Sitterson, Jr. (Indiana Studies in Biblical Literature; Bloomington/Indianapolis: Indiana University Press, 1991), pp. 192–210.

camps, each of which is content to carry out its "normal science" in spite of the objections of the other side.[12] Yet it is too simple to divide the field of Pentateuchal studies into only two paradigms of interpretation, for a third approach, utilizing modern sociological and anthropological models, is becoming more common.[13] While such efforts add greatly to the development of an historical and sociological understanding of the cultural and social structures of "ancient Israel,"[14] the bridge between the archaeological, historical evidence and the literary remains has proved difficult to build and maintain.

The problems inherent in attempting to develop a new model for understanding the composition of the materials in the Pentateuch are compounded by the fact that many of the presuppositions employed by scholars engaged in this enterprise are theologically grounded.[15] Whether this is a

12 On the implications of the phrase "normal science" and its importance in recognizing how interpretive models might be understood, see T. Kuhn, *The Structure of Scientific Revolutions*, 2nd ed. (Chicago: University of Chicago Press, 1970), pp. 10–42. Interestingly, however, interchanges among advocates of the two approaches are infrequent. But when they do occur, they can be quite pointed. See, for example, R. Friedman's review of J. Van Seters' *Prologue to History: The Yahwist as Historian in Genesis* (Louisville: Westminster/John Knox, 1992) in *BibRev* 9/6 (1993) 12–16, and Van Seters' impassioned response (with Friedman's retort) in "Scholars Face Off Over Age of Biblical Stories: Friedman vs. Van Seters," in *BibRev* 20/4 (1994) 40–44, 54. It should be noted that in this instance, both Friedman and Van Seters are arguing from within the same historical critical model of interpretation; the disagreement comes over the arrangement of sources and their dating. The regnant paradigm, in this case the position represented by Friedman, will always tend to deprecate evidence or purported evidence cited against it.

13 An excellent example of such an approach is the work of N. P. Lemche, *Early Israel: Anthropological and Historical Studies on the Israelite Society Before the Monarchy* (Leiden: E. J. Brill, 1985). Interestingly, the application of such non-traditional approaches does not necessitate the abrogation of the older ones, as is exemplified by the work of R. Coote, who applies sociological theory to explain the emergence of Israel as a people in Canaan, departing completely from any dependence upon the traditional Hebrew narrative as an historical source (*Early Israel: A New Horizon* [Minneapolis: Augsburg/Fortress, 1990]), yet at the same time defending in its basics the traditional documentary hypothesis (e.g., *In Defense of Revolution: The Elohist History* [Minneapolis: Augsburg/Fortress, 1991]; with D. R. Ord, *In the Beginning: Creation and the Priestly History* [Minneapolis: Augsburg/Fortress, 1991] and *The Bible's First History* [Philadelphia: Fortress, 1989]).

14 On the necessities for distinguishing among "ancient Israel," "biblical Israel," and "historical Israel," and the implications of such distinctions, see P. R. Davies, *In Search of 'Ancient Israel'* (JSOTSup 148; Sheffield: JSOT, 1992; reprinted, 1995), pp. 22–46.

15 This has been amply demonstrated by the arguments of R. Oden, who proposes the adoption of an anthropological, non-theological approach (*The Bible Without Theology: The Theological Tradition and Alternatives to It* [San Francisco: Harper & Row, 1987], esp. pp. 1–39), and by J. D. Levenson, who offers an intense and fascinating critique of the Christian

positive or a negative observation, of course, depends upon how one views the discipline of theology and whether one happens to agree with the theological position adopted by a particular investigator. As Levenson notes in his quite pointed critique of the historical critical enterprise, such theological presuppositions create dividing lines which scholars with dedicated religious commitments are unable to cross.[16] What will be proposed here, then, is a model that is based upon a non-theological, secular analysis of some of the roles and functions that the particular literary traditions contained in the Pentateuchal narratives might likely have played in the development of the communities which were responsible for their final composition.[17]

This model for interpretation is based upon the one that I have developed and applied elsewhere to the development and functions of the deuteronomistic history.[18] This presentation will not attempt a complete critique of the documentary hypothesis[19] or even a review of the modern analyses of the composition of the Pentateuch.[20] Instead, it will approach the process of the composition of the Pentateuch from a perspective different from those that are presently utilized in the study of the Hebrew bible and will attempt to add a previously unaddressed dimension to the discussions concerning the development of the Pentateuch. In doing such, it will obviously address some of the major interpretive efforts pertinent to the discussion, e.g., the recent works of J. Blenkinsopp, J. Van Seters, B. Peckham, R. Rentdorff, H. H. Schmid, and D. J. A. Clines, among others.[21]

(predominantly Protestant) theological biases of the historical critical method (*The Hebrew Bible, the Old Testament, and Historical Criticism* [Louisville: Westminster/John Knox, 1993], esp. pp. 82–105.

[16] *Ibid.,* p. 104.

[17] As I shall argue in the following chapters, this process occurred sometime between the mid-fifth and mid-second centuries BCE. The reasons for this range of dates will be explained below.

[18] *Narrative History and Ethnic Boundaries: The Deuteronomistic Historian and the Creation of Israelite National Identity* (SBLSS; Atlanta: Scholars Press, 1993), esp. pp. 1–18.

[19] For one such recent analysis, see R. N. Whybray, *The Making of the Pentateuch: A Methodological Study,* and the literature cited therein.

[20] For the latter, see S. J. De Vries, "A Review of Recent Research in the Tradition History of the Pentateuch," *SBL Seminar Papers 26,* ed. K. H. Richards (Atlanta: Scholars Press, 1987), pp. 459–502, and D. Carr, "Controversy and Convergence," pp. 22–31.

[21] See J. Blenkinsopp, *The Pentateuch: An Introduction to the First Five Books of the Bible* (New York: Doubleday, 1992); J. Van Seters, *Prologue to History* and *The Life of Moses: The Yahwist as Historian in Exodus-Numbers* (Louisville: Westminster/John Knox, 1994); B. Peckham, *History and Prophecy: The Development of Late Judean Literary Traditions*

Each of these major works addresses particular problems associated with Pentateuchal analysis, and, quite admittedly, the present work is indebted to many of the insights provided by them and others. None of these treatments, however, addresses the materials contained in the Pentateuch from the perspective of the formation and maintenance of a religious community as a distinct ethnic entity. It is this emphasis that separates the approach taken here from others that are utilized in the analysis of the texts of the Hebrew bible. The model used here will not provide answers to all of the problems associated with the production of the Pentateuch, and that is not its purpose. Obviously, no single approach can do that. For example, this work will not provide any new insights into the redactional development of the Pentateuchal narratives, for from the perspective which will be elaborated in the chapters to follow, such stages remain too hypothetical to be of any real value to the present study.

The reason for this position needs to be stated at the beginning. When one surveys the variety of opinions concerning the composition of the Pentateuch, the deuteronomistic history, or any other literary collection in the Hebrew bible, one is immediately struck with the lack of explanation for the production of those works. The rationales offered for the creation of so-called Yahwistic, Elohistic, and deuteronomistic works[22] serve as excellent, and not unrelated, illustrations of this problem. As a collective whole, these provide a premier case demonstrating how certain explanations can become somewhat canonical within a field engaged in conducting its own version of "standard science."

In the case of the Yahwistic narrative, it is most confidently asserted that it was the product of the Solomonic court and that it was designed as a propaganda document supporting the establishment of a Davidic dynasty in Judah. Yet this contention leaves too many questions unanswered. For the moment we may put aside the general problem of the historicity of the stories of David and Solomon and the issues of the establishment of a dynasty

(New York: Doubleday, 1993); R. Rendtorff, *The Problem of the Process of Transmission in the Pentateuch* (JSOTSup 89; Sheffield: JSOT, 1990 [German original, 1977]); H. H. Schmid, *Der sogennante Jahwist: Beobachtungen und Fragen zur Pentateuchforschung* (Zürich: Theologischer Verlag, 1976); D. J. A. Clines, *The Theme of the Pentateuch* (JSOTSup 10; Sheffield: JSOT, 1986 [originally published 1978]).

22 This is not to suggest that there are no dissenting voices concerning the provenance of these texts or their purposes. It is simply to observe that the majority of scholars who maintain the validity of the classical documentary hypothesis offer the following explanations, or related theories, for their original composition. One need only consult the standard introductory texts or standard reference dictionaries to confirm this.

in Judah during the early tenth century BCE[23] and look at the numerous problems that such an explanation leaves unresolved. In the first instance, who, precisely, would have written this document? Clearly it would have been the members of the palace scribal and/or priestly guild, for they constituted the only known literate element of the population. Just as important is the question of audience. This is directly related to the problem of the designation of the Yahwistic material as "propaganda." Propaganda is, by definition, intentionally persuasive and manipulative. It is also designed for a target audience. The explanations of the Yahwistic narrative as a part of this genre leave unanswered the problems of audience and intention. Even if one were to posit that the audience was the general populace of Jerusalem and its immediate environs, then one must explain the manner by which this propaganda would have been disseminated. It will not suffice to suggest that since the Yahwistic materials were composed from "traditional" oral and written materials, they would have been known in their essentials to most of the populace already. Such an explanation not only begs the question, but also suggests that the particular propagandistic aspects of the materials really were inherent in their traditional forms to begin with. Without belaboring the point, it seems clear that this explanation for the composition and functional utilization of the reconstructed Yahwistic narrative must be demonstrated in some kind of concrete and realistic terms for which contemporary parallels may be adduced. Otherwise, it stands as merely a standard assertion that has become part of the ordinary explanations of the field.

Similar problems are encountered with the explanations attached to the compositions of both the Elohistic and the deuteronomistic works. The Elohistic narrative, as it were,[24] is explained as a northern Israelite counterpart to the pro-Judahite Yahwistic narrative. Hence, the parallels and

---

[23] For an overview of this problem, see T. L. Thompson, *Early History of the Israelite People: From the Written and Archaeological Sources* (SHANE, 4; Leiden: Brill, 1992), pp. 409–415.

[24] It is commonly acknowledged that the Elohistic narrative is preserved in a fragmentary form because of the purported editing by a Judahite redactor who gave priority to the Yahwistic account. As should be obvious, the reasoning here is circular, but nonetheless standard in the reconstruction of the composition of the Pentateuch. For a discussion of the reconstruction of the Elohistic narrative, see A. W. Jenks, *The Elohist and North Israelite Traditions* (SBLMS 22; Missoula, MT: Scholars Press, 1977). Other studies, such as those of J. Van Seters, have called into question the very existence of such a source, preferring to see it as a secondary redaction of the Yahwistic account (*Abraham in History and Tradition* [New Haven: Yale University Press, 1975], pp. 125–130).

differences may be explained on the basis of the difference in dynastic claims, geo-political concerns, and tribal traditions. Such an explanation leaves unanswered the same concerns as noted above with respect to the Yahwistic account. Likewise, the deuteronomistic history is commonly explained as a propaganda document supporting the reform efforts of either king Hezekiah or, more commonly, Josiah of Judah. As is the case with the Yahwistic and Elohistic works, the historical accuracy of the basic account is taken for granted,[25] and the explanations for the production of the materials are then built upon these narrative episodes.

The picture is further complicated by two difficult factors. In the first instance, it has long been noted that the deuteronomistic and Elohistic narrative style and ideological perspectives seem to be related, and each is understood as having its "roots" in northern monarchic Israel. The precise manner by which "northern monarchic traditions" were preserved after the destruction of that kingdom in 722 BCE and how they were able to become dominant elements in the narrative history of the rival "southern monarchy" are two questions that have not been satisfactorily addressed. To argue that these traditions were maintained by the "country priests," i.e., the Levites associated with shrines outside the official royal cultus in Jerusalem, does not provide an adequate answer to the how, where, when, and for what purpose that are necessary for any analytical understanding of the ways in which the materials contained in these traditions might have been utilized.[26]

The second major problem, alluded to above, is one that is raised by the very production of the Hebrew materials themselves. It is generally agreed that the Hebrew canon is the product of the Jerusalem cultus and that it was

---

25 Based on a careful literary analysis of the accounts of cultic reforms contained in the deuteronomistic work, H.-D. Hoffmann has made a strong case arguing that the account of Josiah's reform fulfills the ancient writer's idealized concept of cultic reform and that it represents little more than a possible memory of some "reforms" traditionally attributed to the time of Josiah (*Reform und Reformen: Untersuchungen zu einem Grundthema der deuteronomistischen Geschichtsschreibung* [ATANT 66; Zürich: Theologischer Verlag, 1980], pp. 250–251]). In contrast to such literary analyses of the materials, and illustrative of the debate that continues concerning the problems of the historicity of the Hebrew narrative materials and the issues of Hebrew "historiography," are the radically different treatments given the deuteronomistic materials by B. Halpern (*The First Historians: The Hebrew Bible and History* [San Francisco: Harper & Row, 1988]) and J. Van Seters (*In Search of History: Historiography in the Ancient World and the Origins of Biblical History* [New Haven: Yale University Press, 1983]).

26 An additional problem which is rarely addressed in specific terms is the reason for the incorporation of Deuteronomy into the Tetrateuchal materials, since it is generally recognized that Deuteronomy represents a work originally separate from the narrative accounts in Genesis-Numbers. This problem will be addressed below in Chapter 9.

given its present form during the Second Temple period. These two factors are related to the fourth Pentateuchal source, the Priestly materials, and involve the problem of their relationship to the pre- and post-exilic cultus.[27] While the provenance and date of the Priestly materials remain debated,[28] it is commonly agreed that the Priestly traditions were compiled in their present arrangement, i.e., as part of a narrative history as recounted in the JE epic, during the period of the Babylonian Exile. An analysis of the nature of the Priestly materials suggests that, unlike the Yahwistic and Elohistic narratives, the Priestly materials never constituted a continuous narrative source.[29] Rather, the Priestly traditions constituted a repository of cultic and Priestly sources that were incorporated as a redaction of the JE epic materials, thus completing the Tetrateuchal narrative.

As appealing as the concept of a Tetrateuch emerging from the dislocations caused by the Babylonian Exile might be, such a view must be strongly questioned. While it may be correct, it nonetheless requires some degree of "fleshing out." What mechanisms would have been in place that would have allowed for the production of these narrative and non-narrative materials during the period of the exile?[30] Who would have had the opportunity to write these materials and in what context? For whom might they have been written, and how might they have been used? How would all of this have been received by the Babylonians? What type of cultus was in opera-

---

[27] The designations pre- and post-exilic are not without their own particular problems, given that the concept of exile and the legitimacy claim of the "returning exiles" to be the "true remnant" of Israel comprise a "literary paradigm" by which the defining traditions of Israel are given their form (T. L. Thompson, *Early History of Israel*, pp. 421–422). They will be retained in the present work not as historical descriptors, but rather as internal literary designations which describe the authors' views of the idealized past that was created and incorporated into the newly emerging community associated with the Temple in the Persian and Hellenistic periods.

[28] For a discussion of the variety of problems associated with the date and origins of the Priestly traditions, see J. Milgrom, *Leviticus 1–16* (AB 3; New York: Doubleday, 1991), pp. 3–35. Milgrom dates the Priestly traditions (both P and H) to the mid-eighth to the end of the eighth century BCE. A detailed consideration of specific texts assigned to these traditions is presented by I. Knohl (*The Sanctuary of Silence: The Priestly Torah and the Holiness School* [Minneapolis: Augsburg Fortress, 1995]).

[29] F. M. Cross, *Canaanite Myth and Hebrew Epic* (Cambridge: Harvard University Press, 1973), pp. 293–325.

[30] On the scant evidence for reconstructing the life of the deportees from Judah after the destruction of Jerusalem and before the conquest of Babylon by Cyrus, see the articles on the Diaspora in *The Cambridge History of Judaism*, Vol. I, ed. by W. D. Davies and L. Finkelstein (London: Cambridge University Press, 1984), pp. 326–399.

tion during the Babylonian Exile? In order to argue convincingly that the basic form of the Tetrateuch developed while the Judahite exiles were in Babylon, such questions as these need to be addressed.

II. The Recreation of Ethnic Identity: Scripture and Ethnicity

Rather than attempt to develop answers to the questions raised above, the present analysis of the development of the Pentateuch will begin at another point. By doing so, it will attempt to address these questions, but from a very different perspective, and, in doing so, will suggest an alternative method of analysis that might serve as a type of interpretive model for those attempting to understand the social and religious functions of the narrative sources contained in the Pentateuchal materials. This approach will take as its beginning point the historical development of an ethnically distinguishable religious community and cultus in Jerusalem at the beginning of the fifth century BCE under the hegemony of the Persian government. The events associated with the Persian reestablishment of Jerusalem provide an historical context within which the composition of the Tetrateuch might be situated.[31] In a sense, this approach takes as its beginning point the concluding stage of the classical documentary hypothesis, which most commonly asserts that it was within that historical context that the Pentateuchal sources were edited into their present form. Though our evidence for precise reconstruction of the history of the period remains sketchy, it is nonetheless clear that it is within the context of the Persian and Hellenistic periods that we can trace the mechanisms by which the process of composition can be explained and for which suggestions for some of the functions of the materials might be developed.

In adopting this model, we must note one important methodological presupposition that distinguishes this approach from the standard historical critical approach to the Pentateuch and also from the literary approaches. Each of those approaches attempts an analysis of the Pentateuchal narratives as a whole, i.e., as though they were originally composed to be read/

---

31 I have argued elsewhere that the deuteronomistic history was a product of the exilic period (*Narrative History and Ethnic Boundaries*, pp. 37–47). As the following presentation will argue, the Tetrateuchal materials may be understood as supplements to the deuteronomistic narratives, thus constituting in their final form a type of "primary history" stretching from the account of the creation to the loss of the land with the demise of the Judahite monarchy. For details, see below, Chapter 3.

heard as a type of unified composition.[32] The present approach to the materials does not make this assumption. While it is clearly possible to read the Pentateuch as a whole, and while the Pentateuch came to be understood as a singular composition, I will argue that such understandings are both secondary and later developments within the understandings of these materials that arose within the varieties of Judaism that grew out of the community in which these narrative materials were originally developed. Paralleling the selected readings from the Hebrew scriptures that developed within first century CE Judaism,[33] an argument will be developed that views the collected literary corpus composing the Tetrateuch as a repository of accounts that presented numerous options for selected usage for particular didactic religious and ethnic, communal purposes.

More specifically, I will argue that the literary creation of the narrative texts composing the Tetrateuch/Pentateuch is directly related to the formation of a distinctive Judahite ethnic identity that was recreated during the Second Temple period. During this period a variety of traditions were reapplied to the community of the restoration in an effort to forge an enduring identity, the boundaries for which can be traced in the literature that came

---

[32] The issue of literacy in ancient Israel, as well as the "Israel" that was created as a new ethnic and religious community during the Persian period, remains debated. It seems clear, however, that the type of literacy necessary to read or write an extended text like that found in the Pentateuch or Tetrateuch would have been limited to a very small segment of the population who had been privileged with the advantage of a formal education. For a balanced discussion of this situation, see M. Haran, "On the Diffusion of Literacy and School in Ancient Israel," in *Congress Volume: Jerusalem 1986* [SVT 40; Leiden: E. J. Brill, 1988], pp. 81–95. Two factors in this respect that are constantly overlooked in the discussion are the very nature of the Hebrew writing system and the nature of "classical" Hebrew itself. With respect to the latter, some account must be taken of the fact that "classical" Hebrew was, in all probability, a literary construct and never an actual "living" language that was widely spoken, if it was ever spoken at all. For a consideration of this possibility, see P. Davies, *In Search of 'Ancient Israel'*, pp. 97–101. In the case of the former, the general orthographic ambiguity of the language prior to the addition of vowel indicators makes it extremely unlikely that the materials were ever intended to be read by anyone other than professional scribes and priests. A parallel situation existed in early Islam with respect to the text of the Quran. As W. Graham has argued in his work on oral and written scriptures, until the vowel points were added to the consonantal text of the Quran, some two hundred years after its composition, it could be read only by those who already knew what the text said (*Beyond the Written Word: Oral Aspects of Scripture in the History of Religion* [Cambridge: Cambridge University Press, 1987], pp. 97–98). The significance of this will be developed in the chapters to follow.

[33] See, for example, Josephus (*Ag. Ap.* 2 § 175) and the New Testament (Acts 13:15; 15:21).

to be regarded as "scripture."[34] The necessity of recreating and reconfirming the group's identity can be understood as a survival mechanism that is a predictable result of crisis-producing situations such as the exile and subsequent restoration. Such responses include structural adaptations, new leadership roles, ritual transformations, and the development of folklore traditions, all of which help to consolidate group identity and solidarity.[35]

Essential to our study is an understanding of ethnicity and of the components involved in the construction of an ethnic identity. F. Barth has noted that "ethnic group" designates a population which is predominantly biologically self-propagating, shares fundamental cultural values, constitutes a field of interaction and communication, and has a membership which identifies itself, and is identified by others, as constituting a category that can be distinguished from other categories of the same order.[36] The continuing existence of such distinguishable groups is dependent upon the formation and maintenance of boundaries, which are, of course, social constructs.[37]

As we shall argue throughout, a major part of this boundary formation, and hence social recreation and maintenance of a particular ethnic identity for the restoration community, is the creation of a narrative account of the origins and history of the group. Such "remembered history" is common to all human groups and functions in such a way as to make the past coincide with and support the self-identity of the group in its present situation.[38] To this end, the stories constituting the Tetrateuch/Pentateuch were compiled in the forms in which we presently have them, creating accounts of the origins

34 For a discussion of the various traditions that were reapplied and reinterpreted during this period, see P. D. Hanson, "Israelite Religion in the Early Postexilic Period," in *Ancient Israelite Religion: Essays in Honor of Frank Moore Cross,* ed. by P. D. Miller, Jr., P. D. Hanson, and S. D. McBride (Philadelphia: Fortress, 1987), pp. 485–508.

35 D. Smith, *The Religion of the Landless: The Social Context of the Babylonian Exile* (Bloomington, IN: Meyer Stone, 1989), pp. 74–88.

36 "Introduction," *Ethnic Groups and Boundaries: The Social Organization of Culture Difference,* ed. F. Barth (Boston: Little, Brown, 1969), pp. 10–11.

37 *Ibid.,* p. 14. At least six general characteristics of ethnic groups may be noted: (1) a past-oriented identification placing special emphasis on origins; (2) an emphasis upon cultural and social distinctiveness; (3) the relationship of the group within a broader social system of relationships; (4) a size greater than kin or local groups that extends beyond known acquaintances; (5) a differentiation of meanings for ethnic categories in different social contexts and for different individuals; and (6) an understanding that these categories have symbolic functions (A. P. Royce, *Ethnic Identity: Strategies of Diversity* [Bloomington/Indianapolis: Indiana University Press, 1982], p. 24).

38 B. Lewis, *History—Remembered, Recovered, Invented* (Princeton: Princeton University Press, 1975), pp. 11–13.

of "Israel" and the stories which would define them in a variety of ways. The very flexibility of the name "Israel" within this literature allows it to be applied as an ethnic descriptor to Israel, Judah, the whole nation, as well as to individual tribes. As these written accounts gained an authoritative status within the community which they helped to define, they began to achieve the status of "scripture." As W. C. Smith's investigation of various scriptures of world religions notes, ". . . the quality of being scripture is not an attribute of texts. It is a characteristic of the attitude of persons—groups of persons—to what outsiders perceive as texts. It denotes a relation between a people and a text."[39] When the texts constituting the Tetrateuch/Pentateuch are understood in this context, it becomes clear that they function as scripture in the ways in which they describe the relationship between "Israel" and the rest of the peoples of the world as one that is established in social terms by virtue of its special relationship with its god, Yahweh.[40]

The present model of interpretation attempts to understand the development of the Pentateuch as an initial stage in the formation of early Judaism, a term which designates that cultural and religious movement that began to develop during the Persian restoration of the Jerusalem cultus and which formed the basis for the identification of a people who claimed themselves to be the spiritual and biological heirs of Israel and Judah and who came to define themselves in relation to the shared "histories" contained in these Tetrateuchal and Pentateuchal materials.

The locus for these efforts is to be found in the developing cultus that formed the basis for the "restoration" of Jerusalem.[41] The most reasonable, if not the only conceivable, location for the production of the literature that eventually came to be considered scriptural is the Temple. The only group who would have had the ability and the opportunity to compose such materials would have been the temple staff, most particularly the scribal guilds associated with the maintenance of records. Alongside such a group might

[39] *What Is Scripture?: A Comparative Approach* (Minneapolis: Fortress, 1993), p. 18.

[40] As W. C. Smith notes, it is precisely this emphasis upon the transcendent which provides scripture with its special, authoritative status (*Ibid.*, pp. 228–233).

[41] The concept of "restoration" is one that deserves special notice. While the biblical materials make it very clear that the cultus in Jerusalem was continuous with the older monarchic cultus, any concrete evidence for such is lacking. All of the materials we have that provide any evidence for the earlier cultic activities come to us through the eyes of this "restoration" community, and their intentional biases must be so understood. No clearer indication of the ideological presuppositions of the Second Temple cultus could be found than those which guide the Chronicler's presentation of the cultus as a direct continuation of the heavenly models instituted by David and his designated heir, Solomon.

also be envisioned the professional scribes associated with the Persian governor of Jerusalem. This group would have been responsible for maintaining the records required by the Persian authorities, especially with respect to income and tribute and, like the temple staff, would have been trained in either Babylon or Persia.[42] While the literature produced by these groups would have been centered in the Temple and its cultus, and, by definition, would have had some religious implications, there is no reason to suspect that it was regarded, even by its authors, as "scriptural" from its creation. Instead, it acquired that status over a period of time and usage. It is this latter aspect that is of importance here, for it will be argued that the particular manner in which portions of these accounts provided identifying ethnic boundaries, under the aegis of religious practices, constituted a major element in their receiving the status of "scripture."

Once such a community was established by the realization and internalization of these ethnic and religious descriptors, a new status was slowly attributed to those pertinent literary formulations that provided the basis for maintaining and regulating this distinctive community. It was through a process such as this, i.e., as part of a continuing effort to define and maintain the distinctiveness of a particular community, that the "literature" was transformed into "scripture."[43] This process, with respect to the Tetrateuch and Pentateuch, might be placed between *ca.* 500–150 BCE, though it is possible that it should be extended as much as another century. It is commonly held that it was the Pentateuch that was first recognized as "scriptural," and this ascription is normally associated with the fifth century BCE and the careers of Ezra and Nehemiah. It is there that the present study will begin, concentrating in the first instance upon the identification of "Torah." While there can be no doubt that "Torah" and Pentateuch came to be identified within Judaism during the first and second centuries CE, it is not so clear that this identification should be pushed back much beyond the second century BCE. The development and significance of this identifica-

---

42 For a more complete description of the Jerusalem cultus and scribal schools, see below, Chapter 3.

43 This development of ethnic and religious distinctiveness through a model of "otherness," it must be noted, occurred in an historical context in which those who produced the literature did so from a political position of subjugation and weakness. On the significance of this "powerlessness" to the development of early Judaism, see W. S. Green, "The Difference Religion Makes," *JAAR* 62 (1994) 1200–1205. As Green notes, with the brief exception of the Maccabean period, emerging forms of Judaism were constantly marginalized politically by dominant cultures that threatened to absorb them.

tion, and its importance to the formation of identity and ethnicity, will be addressed in Chapter 3. After developing some of the ways in which the literature of the Pentateuch came to be accepted as scriptural, our study will turn to a description of the temple-based community in Jerusalem that was responsible for creating the Tetrateuch, understood as a supplement to the deuteronomistic history, forming, as it were, a "primary history" by which the community could define and maintain itself as a distinct ethnic and religious entity.

The precise ways in which these literatures were able to define the community will occupy the remainder of the study. In Chapter 4 we will investigate the "primeval history," emphasizing the manner in which "Israel"[44] reflected upon its myths of origins, especially with respect to its origins in both space and time. The following stories of the patriarchs, to be addressed in Chapter 5, build upon the "primeval" accounts to explain "Israel's" genealogy and to develop the accounts of its migrations from its place of origins to the land promised to it by its patron deity. Embedded in these accounts are the foundations for demonstrating membership in the community and for claiming ownership of the land. Each of these acts was critical in the "reestablishment" of the Jerusalem temple community.

In Chapter 6 the story of the exodus and its epic depiction of bondage and release form the background for the bonding of the people to its god by way of a covenant that requires the people to maintain a separate and distinct identity *vis-à-vis* all their surrounding neighbors. Notably, the latter have been defined in the genealogical schemata underlying the patriarchal stories. By way of allegiance to the stipulations of the covenantal demands, "Israel" would sanctify itself as a "holy people," a special possession of Yahweh. The critical element in the development and definition of the special character of this people is considered in Chapter 7. This chapter will address a variety of issues that are generally overlooked by scholars in un-

---

[44] From the perspective of the approach being adopted here, "Israel" must be understood as an ethnic descriptor which has been adapted and reapplied to a community whose actual historical connections with the national state of Israel that occupied the central Palestinian hill-country during the early centuries of the Iron Age are tenuous, at best. As such, it must be understood in symbolic terms, a factor that will become apparent in the presentation to follow. For an overview of some of the major obstacles to identifying the historical Israel with the Late Bronze-Early Iron inhabitants of the hill-country of Palestine, see K. W. Whitelam, "The Identity of Early Israel: The Realignment and Transformation of Late Bronze-Early Iron Age Palestine," *JSOT* 63 (1994) 57–87, and I. Finkelstein, "Ethnicity and the Origin of the Iron I Settlers in the Highlands of Canaan: Can the Real Israel Stand Up?" *BA* 59 (1996) 198–212.

derstanding the development of the literature of the Tetrateuch and the manner in which the "Israel" defined by these materials might have been bounded by those descriptions. This section will address the materials contained in Exodus 25–Leviticus 27, i.e., the narratives that describe the establishment of the cultic paraphernalia that were required for the proper worship of Yahweh and the priestly requirements for ritual purity that would define the holy character of this worshipping community. In order to understand the reformulation of the identity of "Israel," one must reckon with the centrality of the priesthood and temple, as well as with the requirements for sacrifice and ritual performances. There can be little doubt, in historical terms, that these matters were at the heart of the temple-centered religious community that was established in Jerusalem during the Persian period and which continued to develop around that focal point until the Great War against Rome (66–70 CE). To fail to treat seriously the importance of ritual performance to the development of early Judaism and "Israelite" ethnicity is to misunderstand the power of religious ritual in the formation of personal and communal identities. By way of ritual activities and recreations, the mythic depictions of the past are transformed into present realities. This is one of the most important, and often overlooked, properties of religious activity.

With the essential nature of the community given cultic sanction and definition, the account of the community is continued in the narratives in the book of Numbers, beginning with genealogical descriptions providing both identification and organization to the newly constructed community before it continues its journey to the land that will provide the final element in its self-understanding. The journeys and events recounted in these materials further refine the definitions of key elements of the community and provide the basis for the entry into the land of promise. In the final section, Chapter 9, the addition of the narratives of Deuteronomy and its "social manifesto" of "Israelite identity"[45] to the Tetrateuchal narratives will be discussed against the background of the formation of the restoration community in Jerusalem.[46] Such an approach to the formation of the Pentateuch

---

45 For a discussion of this description of Deuteronomy, see my *Narrative History and Ethnic Boundaries*, pp. 55–76.

46 One result of our study will be the demonstration that the materials presented in what may be called a "primary history" contain all of the motifs or elements that A. D. Smith has identified as part of a national or ethnic myth of origins and descent. According to Smith, such accounts include: myths of origin in time and in space (when and where the community was "born"); stories of ancestry; stories of migration; accounts of liberation; stories of a golden

will result in a new understanding of some of the religious functions of those narratives, which will be summarized in the concluding Postscript. Additionally, this approach will be able to emphasize the role of the cultus and ritual performance in the construction of identity and in the maintenance of a distinctive community in a world of competing values, both social and religious. Such an approach will not, in all probability, replace the documentary hypothesis, nor will it have any appreciable impact on the study of the biblical materials as literature. It will, however, draw upon both of these approaches, as well as upon modern sociological and anthropological theories, to apply a different set of questions to the Pentateuch in an effort to gain a fuller understanding of the community that might have produced it and identified itself with the stories and traditions recounted therein.

---

age; myths of decline; and myths of rebirth (*The Ethnic Origins of Nations* [Oxford: Blackwell, 1986], p. 192).

~~ 2 ~~

THE RELATIONSHIP OF TORAH
AND PENTATEUCH

I. The "Book of the Torah of Moses"

A. The absolution of vows hovers in the air, for it has nothing [in the Torah] upon which to depend.

B. The Laws of the Sabbath, festal offerings, and sacrilege—lo, they are like mountains hanging by a string,

C. for they have little scripture for many laws.

D. Laws concerning civil litigations, the sacrificial cult, things to be kept cultically clean, sources of cultic uncleanness, and prohibited consanguineous marriages have much on which to depend.

E. And both these and those [equally] are the essentials of the Torah.

(*m. Ḥag.* 1:8)[1]

What is the Pentateuch? Who wrote it? When was it written? Where was it composed? How did it function within the communities that used it? In response to these basic questions, the documentary hypothesis was developed in the mid-nineteenth century of the present era and has become the foundational model for the modern historical critical approach to biblical studies.[2] While there have been numerous attempts to challenge some of the basics of this approach, the mainstream of biblical criticism has remained firmly in support of the idea that the present Pentateuch is the

---

[1] J. Neusner, *The Mishnah: A New Translation* (New Haven: Yale University Press, 1988).

[2] For a convenient history of the development of this theory, see R. J. Thompson, *Moses and the Law in a Century of Criticism since Graf* (Leiden: E. J. Brill, 1970). For discussions of the present state of Pentateuchal research, see the works cited above, Chap. 1, n. 20.

literary result of several redactional efforts that combined originally independent narrative accounts into their present final form. It is not an exaggeration to state that few theories in the field of biblical studies have
gained canonical status comparable to that of the classical documentary
hypothesis.

It is precisely the literary analysis of scripture that allows scholars
to analyze the Pentateuchal materials without appeal to any particular religious confession or doctrine. It is the independence of the method from
any overt religious dogma that makes it an invaluable tool for the study of
the religion of the people responsible for composing this document. On one
level, then, the documentary hypothesis creates a universalistic method of
analysis that allows scholars from any or no religious persuasion to study
the texts in an objectively defensible manner. The thesis as a whole is built
upon the study of the Pentateuch in its final form, read and studied as a literary whole. The general health of the theory, as well as many of the
presuppositions associated with it, might be seen in the following excerpt
from an article on the Pentateuch from the recently published *Anchor Bible
Dictionary:*

> The Torah is the core work of the Bible. It is a work of impressive liter-
> ary artistry in its broad scope and in its small component stories. It pos-
> sesses artistry of form and depth of content, housing the ideas and values of
> a people over centuries. Not the work of any one person, it reflects a rare
> event in literary history, a literary partnership in which the works of many
> individuals were brought together into a meaningful whole that is more than
> the sum of its parts. The Torah is quintessentially a work of combination. It
> is a single work, a collection of five books, and an editorially brilliant merg-
> ing of sources.[3]

While many scholars feel that the historical critical method itself is in the
midst of a severe crisis, it is clear that such an "emergency" exists only
on the periphery of the field. As the quotation above illustrates, the documentary hypothesis remains the foundation point of the study of the Hebrew bible.

But this simple summary of a longer article also introduces us to another set of inquiries. The beginning question concerned the nature of
the Pentateuch; the summary by Friedman addresses the Torah. The documentary hypothesis simply equates the two and proceeds with its analysis. I

---

3 R. E. Friedman, "Torah (Pentateuch)," *ABD* VI, 621.

should like to challenge this approach and argue that by equating the Pentateuch with the Torah, historical biblical criticism has mixed its categories and lost sight of its own subject, the study of a particular expression of the religious life of a group in antiquity.[4] The Pentateuch is defined as the first five books of the Hebrew bible.[5] In Jewish tradition, these books came to be known as "the book of the Torah of Moses" (*sēper tôrat mōšeh;* Neh 8:1; Josh 8:31; 23:6; 2 Kgs 14:6) or " the book of Moses" (*sēper mōšeh;* Neh 13:1).

Now the question that must be addressed is whether or not this "book of Moses" or this "book of the Torah of Moses" refers to the Pentateuch.[6] A strong argument may be made that in the present form of the Hebrew scriptures, the proper internal referent for this "book" is none other than the Pentateuch. That, however, is the answer to another question, which I shall postpone until later in this work. Indeed, when historical critical studies simply equate the Pentateuch with the Torah purportedly read in Nehemiah, that story is transformed into history, and an element of that story is awarded concrete identifiable status as a known "book." I suggest that this identification is based upon an anachronistic view of the Pentateuch as a "book" that inevitably distorts the results of the inquiry.[7] It begins with the basic presupposition that "ancient Israel," "biblical Israel," and "historical

---

4 Clearly there are many ways of defining the aims of modern critical studies of the biblical materials. It is undeniable that many scholars have a personal religious agenda operating in their investigations. Some of my views on the appropriate avenues of study will be introduced below.

5 Many scholars seem to be willing to equate Hebrew bible with Old Testament, an equation that can be maintained only from a Christian perspective. Since Christianity does not form the model for the present inquiry, I shall use the term Hebrew bible throughout to refer to that collection of twenty-four "scrolls" that were adopted by Judaism as constituting the basis of its scriptures.

6 It is standard practice to equate the "book" referred to in Neh 8:1 with the first five books of the present Hebrew bible. As D. J. A. Clines states, this book "is very likely the Pentateuch as a whole in more or less its present form" (*Ezra, Nehemiah, Esther* [NCBC; Grand Rapids, MI: Eerdmans, 1984], p. 182). This equation is standard and is not a characteristic confined to conservative scholars but is accepted by the field as a whole.

7 Whether the historical critical method itself is based upon a decidedly Protestant Christian theological bias is an intriguing issue that I shall leave to those interested in theology to argue about. It seems to me that the recent article by J. Collins that critiques J. Levenson's observations as "verging on paranoia" might indeed confirm Levenson's position ("Historical Criticism and the State of Biblical Theology," *The Christian Century* 110/22 [1993], 745). Collins seems to overlook the possibility that *all* theology is confessional and particularistic by definition, though it often aims at universals.

Israel" all coincide.[8] It further assumes that the Pentateuch was completed and that it had received some type of official (or at least recognizable) status in the community prior to the times of Ezra and Nehemiah.

It is this second process, the idea of the authority that was ascribed to the book, that the present study will take as its starting point. In order to suggest some alternate approaches by which the Pentateuch might be understood, I shall place emphasis here upon some of the ways in which the traditions of the past might have functioned within the context of the communities that created and maintained them. It must be emphasized from the beginning that the critical analysis of the Pentateuchal materials as a whole, i.e., as forming a unity, both in literary and in religious terms, belongs to the domain of students and scholars, i.e., to a very small, non-representative segment of the population to which it (or portions of it) was originally addressed.

In order to investigate these issues, it is important to consider the ways in which the origins of "Judaism" as a religious tradition are reconstructed by modern scholars. Most modern reconstructions of the development of Judaism are based upon a general acceptance of the descriptions of beliefs and practices found within the biblical texts as historically accurate. Yet modern historical critical methods have made it quite apparent that the lines of continuity between the religions of "ancient" Israel and those of the restoration community of Jerusalem in the Persian period are tenuous at best. To give priority to the descriptions of the development of "Judaism" as depicted in the biblical materials with little or no attention to the rhetorical and ideological elements that fashion much of those accounts is to lose all semblance of "objectivity." In short, the historical critical method seems to fail at precisely the purpose for which it was created. It is unable to explain the development of the literature and religion of ancient Israel and early Judaism without itself participating in an acceptance of the religious ideals which it intends to investigate.

The basic problem may lie in the ways in which the questions are phrased and the model that is adopted for attempting to answer those same questions. I would suggest that an appropriate beginning point for the inquiry regarding some of the roles and functions of the Pentateuch might be to ask in specific terms how the origins of Judaism are to be explained so as to account for the common acceptance of Torah[9] among the Samaritans, the

8 See above, Chap. 1, n. 14.

9 For the moment, and for the sake of argument, I shall leave Torah undefined other than as some authoritative ideal to which a movement might appeal for guidance in its attempts to define the proper life for its adherents.

Jewish community at Elephantine, and the "restoration" community in Jerusalem during the Persian period, and later communities such as those emerging during the Hasmonean period and later. Since the "historical" periods known as "exilic" and "post-exilic" are predicated on the historical accuracy of the somewhat tendentious narratives of the Hebrew bible,[10] they should be held in some degree of suspicion.[11]

For modern scholarship, the consensus has been that such historical accuracy of the narrative portions of the Hebrew bible may and should be assumed. Hence, the common themes existing among the various ancient communities that began to emerge in the Persian and Hellenistic periods may be explained as descendants from earlier Judahite religion which is to be understood, with regional variations, as an adaptation of an even earlier (and possibly defunct) Israelite religion.[12] For the student of the Hebrew bible, nothing suggested so far is out of line with the "normal" science of the field,[13] since the special nature of the biblical materials, and subsequently the unique qualities of religious practices described in those materials, are assumed.[14] Within this paradigm for understanding the history of Judaism,[15] the similarity among the variety of Diaspora Jewish communities

[10] Anyone wanting to dispute the ideological tendentiousness of these materials need only compare the accounts of the kingdoms of Israel and Judah given by the books of Kings and Chronicles. Such a comparison makes it abundantly clear that the author(s) of each set of materials felt free enough from any constraints to change whatever materials in their "sources" might have presented something other than the vision or version of events that they desired. To suggest that the accounts in Chronicles are attempts to "correct" or to "fill out" their counterparts in Kings is to fail to perceive the issues at hand.

[11] On these issues, see especially the discussions of T. L. Thompson, *Early History of the Israelite People*.

[12] It should not be overlooked that for the period designated as the "divided monarchy," *ca.* 922–722 BCE, the only extant descriptions of northern "Israelite" religious practices are contained in the narratives of the Hebrew bible, which, in their final form, purport to have been authored by descendants of Judahite exiles. What the religion of an ancient "Israel" might have been like, and how closely it might have been paralleled by ancient "Judahite" religion, must be reconstructed on the basis of comparative materials from the ancient Near East and not solely upon the testimony of the biblical texts.

[13] See above, Chap. 1, n. 12.

[14] An interesting, and, I would add, devastating critique of the way in which comparative studies of religions give precedence to Christianity is offered by J. Z. Smith in *Drudgery Divine: On the Comparison of Early Christianities and the Religions of Late Antiquity* (Chicago: University of Chicago Press, 1990).

[15] While it is not often recognized, the study of the Hebrew bible as a religious document belongs either to the comparative study of the religions of the ancient Near East, the origins of Judaism, or the origins of Christianity. If the document is divorced from these discernible areas of critical inquiry, it becomes simply a document that has no "audience" to whom it might be understood to have been addressed and, hence, no apparent functional purpose. Using the

that may be discerned beginning with the Persian period is to be explained on the basis of their past historical connections to the Torah. Now this Torah itself is understood as a "book," a codification of materials in written form that provided the basis for the formation of Judaism and which itself came out of the period of the "divided kingdom," despite the fact that its "final" redaction might date to the Persian period.[16]

What I will argue is that if one works from a different set of premises, i.e., begins within the context of another model for understanding these materials, some radically different and highly suggestive approaches to the development of the Torah and its role in the formative periods of early Judaism[17] might be discovered. The similarities among the varieties of

document for the comparative study of ancient Near Eastern languages, while a commonly accepted area of inquiry, is not without problems, since it generally begins with the presupposition that the biblical materials reflect truly archaic traditions, a presupposition that must itself first be demonstrated before those materials may legitimately be used in a comparative manner. To demonstrate that certain motifs from selected poetic passages, such as a prophetic book or a psalm, might be similar to a 14th century BCE Ugaritic passage contained in a mythological fragment which lacks any known context requires more than simply noting the similarity of the motifs. All this demonstrates is that the writers of the biblical materials were familiar with literary and religious motifs that were also known to the scribes at Ugarit and which might have been ubiquitous among the scribal schools of the ancient world. They do not, however, tell us much of anything about the antiquity or sources for understanding the religious traditions contained in the Hebrew bible.

16 On the problems created by a literal understanding of the biblical references to "books" that fails to recognize their rhetorical implications, see the provocative essay by E. W. Conrad ("Heard But Not Seen: The Representation of 'Books' in the Old Testament," *JSOT* 54 [1992], 45–59).

17 Exactly when a movement that can be called "Judaism" began remains debatable. It is clear, at least if one accepts the evidence of the Elephantine materials as convincing, that by the late 5th century BCE there existed in Jerusalem a priesthood that was regarded as authoritative enough to be consulted on questions regarding the construction of a temple or the celebration of certain rituals. For the purposes of this study, the designation "early Judaism" will be used to refer to those religious movements associated with the Jerusalem community during the reconstruction of the province of Yehud by the Persians and continuing until the development of the variety of movements that emerged in the late Hellenistic period during the reigns of the Hasmonean rulers. In other words, early Judaism might be understood as having had a life span of some two to three hundred years, beginning with the restructuring of the Persian empire under Darius and culminating in the development of "Judaism" sometime during the middle third and early second centuries BCE. I would concur with the arguments of J. Neusner that there is "no such thing as Judaism, but only Judaisms" and that "Judaism" forms a systemic family with numerous common traits. As Neusner notes, "a system takes shape and then makes choices— in that order" ("Understanding Seeking Faith: The Case of Judaism," *Soundings* 71 [1988] 334–335). What I mean by early Judaism is the general systemic shape that emerged during the Persian period from which specific and historically discrete families of Judaism developed, based upon their communal choices.

early Jewish communities in the Diaspora might have been created during the Persian period as an "incidental" offshoot of Persian political policies. Phrased in another way, it may have been during the Persian period, and not earlier, that the Torah was created as the basis of the community and that the mode of this creation and its transmission was through the scribal schools associated with the Jerusalem priesthood as functionaries of the Persian government.[18] Further, the Torah itself was not composed as a complete narrative unit, nor was it intended to be read by "untrained" individuals. Drawing upon the analogy of the normative Judaism that developed during the first two centuries CE and is attested to by the Mishnah and related materials, I would further suggest that this written Torah never functioned apart from a tradition of interpretation.

To what then does the Hebrew bible refer when it speaks of "the book of the Torah"? While at first blush it might seem obvious that "the book of the Torah" must be the same thing as "the book of Moses" or "the Torah of Moses," when the biblical references to these "books" are studied, their concrete historical referent becomes far from clear. It must be noted from the beginning that each of the terms "torah" and "book" covers a variety of meanings. "Torah" (*tôrâ*) frequently carries the connotation of priestly ritual instructions (cf. Leviticus) as well as the broader concept of "Torah" in the sense of Yahweh's total revelation to Moses. As J. Levenson has argued, the possibility must be recognized that the biblical references to *tôrâ* may refer to a wide variety of sacred lore and not to the Pentateuch at all.[19] The manner in which "Torah" came to designate the "books" known as the Pentateuch will constitute the major portion of the discussion which follows. The word "book" (*sēper*) likewise conveys a wide variety of meanings in the Hebrew bible. The designation *sēper* may be applied to a "missive, or letter," a "legal document," a "collection of prophetic oracles," a "register," a royal "annal," a "book," a scroll," or a "law book."[20] It is clearly the latter which is germane to the present discussion.

---

[18] For a reconstruction of the possible configuration of such scribal schools during this period, see P. R. Davies, *In Search of 'Ancient Israel,'* pp. 101–107, 115–127.

[19] "The Sources of Torah: Psalm 119 and the Modes of Revelation in Second Temple Judaism," in *Ancient Israelite Religion: Essays in Honor of Frank Moore Cross,* ed. P. D. Miller, Jr., P. D. Hanson, and S. D. McBride (Philadelphia: Fortress, 1987), p. 560 and n. 7, p. 571.

[20] *BDB,* 706–707. Technically, for the period under investigation, "scroll" is the accurate designation for the form in which writing was done in ancient Israel. The codex, which probably developed as early as the first century CE, did not come into common use until the fourth century CE (E. Würthwein, *The Text of the Old Testament* [Grand Rapids, MI: Eerdmans,

When the designations *sēper* and *tôrâ* are combined to form "the book of the law" (*sēper hattôrâ*), a potentially new entity is created, at least as it is treated by biblical scholars. Modern scholars have expressed few doubts that biblical references to "books" may be treated as references to historically existent and accessible sources which may be used as evidence for reconstructing "Israel's" past. The possibility that the Hebrew bible's representations of "books" might not have been intended to convey a "simplistic historical meaning" but rather functioned to make a rhetorical claim to authority directed at the hearing audience must be seriously entertained. It is entirely possible that in this respect, "historical meaning is entirely irrelevant."[21] For the present argument, the most explicit case of identifying a biblical reference to "the book of the law" with a historical work is found in the case of the *sēper hattôrâ* which formed the basis of the "reforms" of Josiah.[22]

This designation, *sēper hattôrâ*, as having some type of binding authority on "Israel" first occurs in the context of Josiah's reforms in 2 Kings 22–23. In the Pentateuch itself, reference to such a "book" occurs only in the "editorial" frame of Deuteronomy and never in the "old core" of that book (17:18–19; 28:58, 61; 29:19, 20; 30:10; 31:11–12, 26).[23] Hence, the designation of the *sēper hattôrâ* as applied to Deuteronomy may be a "sec-

---

1979], pp. 9–10). On the production of scrolls in the ancient world, see the works cited below, n. 52.

21 E. W. Conrad, "Heard But Not Seen," pp. 47–48. A related position is further explicated in the work of S. Mandell and D. N. Freedman that insists on the recognition of the possible differences between the "real narrator" of a literary work and the "implied narrator," who is a literary creation (*The Relationship between Herodotus' History and Primary History* [South Florida Studies in the History of Judaism 60; Atlanta: Scholars Press, 1993], pp. 9–19). While such "books" would have been "real" for the "implied narrator," their historical reality remains open to question.

22 The general tendency of scholars is to treat these reforms as historical events and to understand that the "book" that was "found" during the "repairs" to the Temple was some form of the book of Deuteronomy. As E. W. Conrad notes, this identification may be traced back ultimately to Jerome (*Ibid.*, p. 49, n. 1). On the basis of careful literary analysis of the materials constituting the various "reforms" recounted in the books of Kings, H.-D. Hoffmann concludes that the accounts concerning Josiah represent the fulfillment of a literary and ideological "ideal" and that the most that might be gleaned from the account in historical terms is that some type of reform effort was associated with the rule of Josiah (*Reform und Reformen*, pp. 250–251).

23 As M. Weinfeld notes, the phrase also occurs in the "deuteronomistic history" (Josh 1:8; 8:34; 23:6; 2 Kgs 14:6; etc.; *Deuteronomy 1–11* [AB 5; New York: Doubleday, 1991], p. 17).

ondary" development itself, a fact that is especially important when one considers that Deuteronomy is the only book of the Pentateuch that is attributed to Moses (31:9). An important related fact is that the author of the account of the "reform" of Josiah is the same author who was responsible for the "editorial" frame of Deuteronomy,[24] which makes Moses the author of the book and designates it as *sēper hattôrâ*.

The references to the *sēper* "discovered" during the Temple "repairs" contain a number of interesting designations for that "book." The priest of the Temple, Hilkiah, proclaims to Shaphan, the "scribe of the Temple of Yahweh" (*sōpēr bêt yhwh;* 2 Kgs 22:3), that he has found "the book of the Torah" (*sēper hattôrâ;* 22:8). No other information is given to identify this book that has not been mentioned in the text since the days of Joshua, where it is also referred to in a variety of ways.[25] In the narrative, the contents of "the/this book" (*hassēper/hassēper hazzeh;* 22:13, 16; 23:24) receive no detailed description whatsoever.[26] Rather, the "book" constitutes "the book of the covenant" (*sēper habbĕrît;* 23:2; cf. v. 21) read by the king and entered into by the people (cf. Josh 24:26). Its contents, that is "the words of the book of the Torah" (*dibrê sēper hattôrâ;* 22:11), had previously been heard by the king and their veracity confirmed by the prophetess Huldah (22:15–16). In its narrated form, the "book" contained "the words of this covenant" (*dibrê habbĕrît hazzō'ṯ;* 23:3), i.e., "the words of the Torah" (*dibrê hattôrâ;* 23:24). It is difficult to divorce the identity of this "book" from the reference to "the Torah of Moses" (*tôrat mōšeh;* 23:25) to which conformed the "deeds" of Josiah more than those of any other king of Judah or Israel.

There are several major defining characteristics of "this book of the Torah" that may be discerned from the narrative about Josiah's "reforms." In the first instance, it is clearly presented as a "book" (*sēper*) that had been written *prior* to the events described in the account. Further, it is clear that the "book" was discovered *in* the Temple during the process of repairs. The

---

[24] For the classic statement of this position, see M. Noth, *Überlieferungsgeschichtliche Studien*, 3rd ed. (Tübingen: Max Niemeyer Verlag, 1967), pp. 27–40.

[25] In Josh 8:31 and 23:6, reference is made to the "book of the Law of Moses" (*sēper tôrat mōšeh*), while in 8:34 it is called simply "the book of the Law" (*sēper hattôrâ*). In 24:26, reference is made to Joshua's recording of the treaty made with the people of Israel at Shechem in "the book of the Law of god" (*sēper tôrat 'ĕlōhîm*).

[26] As E. W. Conrad emphasizes, only the narrator (or, better, the implied narrator) of the story knows the contents of the "book." The reading/hearing audience is completely dependent upon the materials provided by that implied narrator for its understanding of the contents ("Heard But Not Seen," pp. 51–52).

vital importance of the "book" is revealed by the consistent use of the defi-
nite article: it was not *a* "book of the Torah" but "*the* book of the Torah,"
which was immediately recognized by all the principal actors in the story
(priest, scribe, prophet, king). But none of these things reveals any information concerning the contents of "the book." Some indications are discovered in the actions attributed to the characters in the story in response
to hearing the "book" read.[27] Josiah's reaction of mourning is attributed to
hearing the curses that would befall Judah because of its failure to obey
the instructions in "this book" (2 Kgs 22:13). The assembling of the people
and the performance of a covenant ceremony, the removal of all "non-
Yahwistic" forms of worship from the land, the closing down of all the
"high places," the celebration of the festival of Passover, and the consolidation of all worship in Jerusalem complete the responses to the contents of
"the book."[28]

From these deductions concerning the contents of "the book," it becomes clear that the only such "book" included in the Hebrew bible that
contains the instructions that would lead to these actions is none other than
Deuteronomy, the one "book" ascribed to Moses. The instructions of the
Torah, then, in the account of the "reforms" of Josiah, are to be understood
as those contained in the "book of Deuteronomy," the charter expression
of the ideological basis for the "deuteronomistic history" as a whole.[29]
Hence, for the author(s) of the account of the "reforms" of Josiah, it seems
clear that the "words" of "this book of the Torah/Covenant" which were to
be associated with the authority ascribed to Moses (cf. 2 Kgs 14:6) were
presented as binding upon the people of Judah and that their failure to conform to the prescriptions of "this book" would result in their destruction
and exile. "Torah," at least from the perspective presented by the deuteronomistic author(s), was attributable to Moses, contained in "Deuteronomy,"
and covenantally binding upon all of "Judah." Likewise, it was knowable
by virtue of its public recital, required by Deuteronomy itself, which pre-
scribes the following:

---

27 Though "the book" is a focal point in the story, the dissemination of its contents is not
through publication or duplication, but rather through public and private readings. Hence, the
oral and aural aspects of a story continue to function side by side in the accounts of the use of
written "books" (see the comments of Conrad, *Ibid.*, pp. 45–59).

28 For details on these actions, see M. Weinfeld, *Deuteronomy 1–11*, pp. 80–82.

29 On Deuteronomy as a type of "social manifesto of Israelite ethnic identity," see my
work, *Narrative History and Ethnic Boundaries*, pp. 32–37.

And Moses wrote this Torah (*hattôrâ hazzō't*) and gave it to the priests, the sons of Levi who were carrying the ark of the covenant of Yahweh and to all the elders of Israel. And Moses commanded them: "At the end of seven years, at the appointed time of the year of release, at the feast of Sukkoth, when all Israel comes to appear[30] before Yahweh your god in the place which he shall choose, you shall read this Torah (*hattôrâ hazzō't*) aloud before all Israel. Assemble the people, the men, women, children, and your sojourner who is in your gates, in order that they may hear and learn and fear Yahweh your god and observe to perform all the words of this Torah (*kol-dibrê hattôrâ hazzō't*). And their sons who have not known it shall hear and learn to fear Yahweh your god all the days which you are living upon the land which you are crossing over the Jordan to inherit" (Deut 31:9–13).

For the deuteronomic writers, then, "Torah" seems to have referred to the revelation of the divine will given to Moses and recorded in the "book" that was given into the care of the Levitical priests and was to be placed in the Ark (cf. Deut 31:26; 10:2). Both the rhetorical and the ideological aspects of the role of "the book of the Torah/Covenant" in the narrative of Josiah's reforms and the ideal way in which they were binding upon "Judah" seem clearly discernible in the narratives contained in the Hebrew bible.

But clear ideology is not history, nor is "this book of the Torah" in any way connected with the Pentateuch in this narrative. The very phrase "Torah of Moses" (*tôrat mōšeh*), with which "this book of the Torah" is identified, occurs neither in the Pentateuch nor in any of the prophetic materials assigned to the pre-exilic period. Hence, if the answer to the connections between Torah and Pentateuch is to be found within the Hebrew bible, then we must look elsewhere. The second major text that refers to the public reading of "the book of the Torah" is associated with the "restoration" community and the careers of Ezra and Nehemiah.[31] According to Neh 7:72b–8:12, the Torah was read on the first day of the seventh month, and this ritual activity was followed by the celebration of the festival of Sukkoth (Neh 8:13–18; cf.

---

[30] Reading the Niphal for the Qal with the Samaritan Pentateuch (cf. *BHS*).

[31] The literary and historical problems associated with the books of Ezra-Nehemiah are outside the bounds of the present discussion. It should be pointed out, however, that there have been serious attempts recently to argue against the historical character of these narratives. See, for example, the discussions of G. Garbini, *History and Ideology in Ancient Israel* (New York: Crossroad, 1988), pp. 151–169, and of T. L. Thompson, *Early History of the Israelite People*, pp. 417–421.

Deut 31:11). These activities were focused on the reading of "the book
of the Torah of Moses which Yahweh had commanded Israel" (*sēper tôrat
mōšeh 'ăšer-ṣiwwâ yhwh 'et-yiśrā'ēl;* 8:1). In addition, the Levitical priests
read from "the book, from the Torah of God" (*bassēper bĕtôrat hā'ĕlōhîm*),
and interpreted it for the people.[32]

II. Ezra and the "Torah of Moses"

This person Ezra is described as one who had "set his heart to inquire
of the Torah of Yahweh (*lidrôš 'et-tôrat yhwh*) and to do and to teach law
(*ḥōq*) and ordinance (*mišpāṭ*) in Israel (Ezra 7:10)." That he was qualified
for such activities is indicated by his description as "a scribe diligent in the
Torah of Moses which Yahweh the god of Israel had given" (*sōpēr māhîr
bĕtôrat mōšeh 'ăšer-nātan yhwh 'ĕlōhê yiśrā'ēl;* Ezra 7:6). Under the direction of the Persian royal court, he was sent to teach this Torah to those who
did not know it (7:25). In addition to his scribal background, Ezra bears the
designation of priest (*kōhēn/kāhēn;* Ezra 7:5, 11,12, 21; Neh 8:21, 9; Neh
12:26), a further qualification for instituting and interpreting the Torah. In
the Aramaic sections, Ezra's expertise is noted as covering "the law of the
god of heaven" (*dātā' dî-'ĕlah šĕmayyā';* Ezra 7:12).[33] From the standpoint
of the narrative presentation, it seems that the Aramaic term "law" (*dāt*) is
to be equated with the Hebrew "Torah" (*tôrâ*). It seems clear, then, that this
book had achieved some "official" status from the viewpoint of the Persians
and that it represented an acceptable manner by which they might configure
the administration of the area of Judah, according to the narrative account
(cf. Ezra 7:25–26).

---

32 It remains disputed whether this means that the Levites actually translated the materials read into Aramaic, the language of the day, whether they offered expositions on the meanings of the Torah that was read, or whether they did both. According to rabbinic traditions,
this represents the beginning of the Targums, the translations of the Hebrew scriptures into
Aramaic (cf. *b. Meg.* 18b).

33 That the phrase "god of the Heavens" (*'ĕlāh šĕmayyā';* Ezra 5:11, 12; 6:9, 10; 7:12, 21,
23 (2x); *'ĕlōhê haššĕmayim;* Ezra 1:2; Neh 1:4, 5; 2:4, 20) is an indication of Persian influence
and imperial policy is a distinct possibility. It should be noted, however, that the phrase occurs
in other contexts, e.g., Gen 24:3, 7; Jonah 1:9; Dan 2:19; 37, 44; 2 Chr 36:23. It is possible,
however, that most of these references could be dated to the Persian period. For the suggestion
that this reflects Persian imperial policy, see G. Widengren, "The Persian Period," in *Israelite and Judaean History,* ed. J. H. Hayes and J. M. Miller (Philadelphia: Westminster, 1977),
p. 536.

This does not tell us much at all about the identity of "the book" that constituted the basis of the "reforms" instituted by Ezra. Indeed, the contents of the book remain nearly as nebulous as those of "the book" constituting the basis for the "reforms" of Josiah, and possibly just as historically "real." The identification of "the book" with the Pentateuch, as is standard, is based upon the same set of presuppositions as the identification of Josiah's "book" with the actual book (or portions) of Deuteronomy. Since these reforms play such a crucial role in scholars' reconstructions of the origins of Judaism, and since this "Torah" played such a critical role in the "restoration" community, it is commonly asserted that it could not have been lost. It must therefore be identifiable with some part of the present canon. The circular nature of such an argument should be apparent. Though there might be clear affinities between the reforms of Ezra and Nehemiah and the materials identified with either the "Priestly" or "deuteronomic" codes, it is simply impossible to identify "the book" referred to in those accounts with either, let alone to equate it with the Pentateuch.[34] The analytical situation is further confused by the "historicizing" of the materials resulting in positions like that taken by J. A. Sanders: "From Ezra onwards, the Torah was Judaism and Judaism was the Torah. It is impossible to understand anything that happened within Judaism from this point on without understanding this point."[35] Such a position presumes that there was a universally accepted concept of "Torah" within a unified and somewhat monolithic movement known as "Judaism."

As has been argued recently, the determination of the very status attributed to the person of Ezra is not without some serious difficulties. Tradition accords to Ezra the position of "Father of Judaism,"[36] and it is not uncommon to see evaluations like the following: "Nehemiah and Ezra, the creators of the post-exilic Jewish community in Palestine, are two of the greatest figures in Jewish history."[37] Now, there can be no dispute concerning the prominence in which these two figures are held in the traditions of later Judaism. It is the shadowy nature of Ezra, the one credited with reestablishing "the Torah of Moses" in the Jerusalem community, that

34 *Ibid.*, p. 536.

35 *Torah and Canon* (Philadelphia: Fortress, 1972), p. 51.

36 For an overview of the prominence of Ezra in the Talmudic materials, see J. Meyers, *Ezra-Nehemiah* (AB 14; New York: Doubleday, 1964), pp. lxxii–lxxiii, and J. Blenkinsopp, *Ezra-Nehemiah* (OTL; Philadelphia: Westminster, 1988), p. 59.

37 G. Widengren, "The Persian Period," p. 538.

is troubling if there was such a figure who was historically responsible for the establishment of a particular religious movement. As G. Garbini notes, apart from the books of Ezra and Nehemiah, ". . . no Jewish work, whether in the Bible or not, shows knowledge of Ezra before Flavius Josephus; and he speaks of Ezra only as a paraphrase of the biblical text."[38] Ezra is not mentioned in the book of Chronicles, nor is he included in the lengthy encomium of great religious leaders from Jewish antiquity contained in Sir 44:1–49:16, though the latter does mention Nehemiah (49:13).

However one may choose to explain the paucity of references to Ezra until after the 2nd century BCE,[39] it is clear that Ezra was remembered in the developing traditions as the official who brought to Jerusalem a copy of "the book of the Torah of Moses," which is precisely where this quest started. On the basis of interbiblical interpretation, the only other book designated in this way is the one utilized during the "reforms" of Josiah and "identified" by most with some form of Deuteronomy. In the case of Ezra, however, there is insufficient evidence to suggest even this identification. At the same time, it is worth noticing that the events associated with Ezra, i.e., the commission by the Persian royal court of a Persian-trained emissary to compile the "legal" traditions of a district and to enforce them, would be consistent with what little is known of the Persian administration of its provinces.[40] Hence, the events associated with the career of Ezra, at least

[38] *History & Ideology in Ancient Israel,* p. 152. Garbini attempts to date the story of Ezra to the time of Alcimus (1 Macc 9:54–56) and argues that it was created to support his "reform" efforts *ca.* 159 BCE. While this is an interesting proposal, as is his attempt to identify the "Law" brought by Ezra with the Temple Scroll, or something similar to it, his arguments fail to be convincing (pp. 163–169). That the Ezra story in its present form was "created" to support a particular view of the late Persian or early Hellenistic Jewish Palestinian community, however, must be seriously considered.

[39] It is important to note that at least three fragments of Ezra are attested from Cave 4 of Qumran, indicating that the book was in circulation at least by *ca.* 150–100 BCE (J. Blenkinsopp, *Ezra-Nehemiah,* pp. 70–72). The book of Nehemiah is completely missing from the texts discovered at Qumran. The significance of this fact is unclear, since, as J. Vander Kam has noted, given the particular fragments discovered, this might simply mean that Ezra and Nehemiah were already regarded as one book ("Ezra-Nehemiah or Ezra and Nehemiah?" in *Priests, Prophets and Scribes: Essays on the Formation and Heritage of Second Temple Judaism in Honor of Joseph Blenkinsopp,* ed. E. Ulrich, *et al.* [JSOTSup 149; Sheffield: JSOT, 1992], p. 62).

[40] G. Widengren, "The Persian Period," p. 515. N. Gottwald points out in conjunction with this that the initial movement of Judaism toward the canonization of selected writings must be understood as the results of political policies "imposed upon the Palestinian Jewish community by the collaboration of Persian imperial authorities and a Jewish colonial elite imported from exile to Judah" (*The Hebrew Bible: A Socio-Literary Introduction* [Philadelphia:

with respect to the institution of the "Torah of Moses" as the legally binding traditions of Jerusalem and its immediate environs (and that is all the biblical traditions associate with Ezra and Nehemiah), stand within the realm of historical possibility.

III. The Pentateuch, Early Judaism, and the "Torah of Moses"

I suggest that the quest for the origins of Judaism and of the Pentateuch begin with this historical possibility, which may at least provide some type of ideal model for imagining how early Judaism was originally constructed. The Jerusalem community, "restored" under the auspices of the Persians, became the focal point of the institution of a written set of traditions that were attributed to "Moses," allegiance to which would become the identifying characteristic of Judaism, a provincial religious tradition originating in the province of Yehud. But this constitutes only a part of the ideal, for the area that the "returnees" reestablished was one that was already inhabited. What common traditions or histories might have been shared by the variety of groups that constituted elements of this early Judaism must remain only conjecture. At the same time, there must have been enough common ground among the groups for a single set of traditions to address the cultural and religious elements to which they were to adhere. While attempting to reconstruct some of the boundaries and characteristics of early Judaism, we must remember that this entity is a pure construct, and no sooner might it be posited than it must be rejected, since this earliest Judaism immediately gave rise to a number of regional forms of Judaism, each of which would be able to make its own claims about being the remnants of the "true Israel."[41]

It is precisely the nature of this particular type of religious claim that indicates the ethereal nature of any reconstructed ideal original, for whatever the "reconstituted" community in the Persian province of Yehud might have been, it was most emphatically not the only direct heir to the religion

---

Fortress, 1985], p. 437). For a discussion of the effects of Persian imperial policy on the reformation of Israelite ethnic identity, see below, pp. 71–73.

[41] During the past decade and a half, scholarship has come to understand that the old view that Jewish religious belief and practice in the ancient Mediterranean world were generally uniform and highly consistent among populations can no longer be maintained. Rather, the evidence available to us would seem to indicate that between 330 BCE and 200 CE Judaism was characterized by diversity and variety, and each form of it seems to have constituted its own particular system (J. A. Overman and W. S. Green, "Judaism [Greco-Roman Period]," *ABD* III, 1038).

of "ancient Israel." Further, and this is admittedly a minimalist view, we know almost nothing about the religion of "ancient Israel." What little we do know derives from the scriptures composed by the scribal schools of Persian and Hellenistic "Yehud," whose historical connections with the ancient national state of "Israel," which ceased to exist after 722 BCE, are tenuous at best. The "true Israel" to which Judaism appeals as its foundation block must be understood as religious, cultural, and ethnic retrogressions that attempt to address situations in the present, not historical events from the past.[42] At precisely what historical point in time the traditions concerning this "ancient Israel" were consolidated remains conjectural, but there does seem to be a common element in the final form given to these traditions, especially those concerning the Torah, and that common element is Moses.

Again the question must be asked: "What is the relationship of this 'Torah of Moses' to the Pentateuch?" In the traditions concerning the origins of "Israel," Moses is the dominant character from the beginning of the "bondage in Egypt" until the eve of the "conquest of the land." All of the narrated accounts concerning "Israel's" past contained in Exodus through Deuteronomy revolve around the figure of Moses, the divinely appointed leader and the sole mediator of Torah on Sinai/Horeb.[43] Based upon the materials surveyed to this point, it seems obvious that Moses is intimately connected to Torah and that Moses dominates in the Pentateuch, except in Genesis. What, however, are the roles of Moses and the traditions of the Pentateuch in the non-Pentateuchal materials of the Hebrew bible?[44]

---

42 For examples of this cultural phenomenon, see E. Hobsbawm, "Introduction: Inventing Traditions," in *The Invention of Tradition*, pp. 1–14.

43 As is commonly recognized, the traditions concerning the revelation of the Torah to Moses are divided as to the place of those revelations. According to the standard source divisions of the documentary hypothesis, the name Sinai is associated with both the "Yahwistic" and the "Priestly" sources. In the "Elohistic" and "deuteronomic" materials, the name of the mountain is Horeb. In Exodus, there seems to be an attempt to harmonize these two traditions by identifying them with "the mountain of god" (*har hā'ĕlōhîm;* Exod 3:1; 4:27; 18:5; 24:13).

44 It must be emphasized that the methodologies employed in the study of the Hebrew bible to distinguish among periods in which texts were produced, e.g., pre-exilic, exilic, post-exilic, etc., are all dependent to one degree or another upon the general acceptance of the history of Israel and Judah depicted in that very literature. Further, if one admits to the probability that *all* of the texts of the Hebrew bible have passed through the hands of redactors and have been susceptible to a variety of changes until the general standardization of the textual traditions, then it becomes quite difficult to argue that any of the "traditions" are historically early. Though it remains debated, especially since many of the major biblical manuscripts from Cave 4 of Qumran remain unpublished, the textual traditions which can be reconstructed on the basis of the available evidence seem to have been undergoing the process of standardization

This is, as one might guess, a debated issue. If one brackets the Pentateuchal references to Moses and concentrates on the Hebrew materials generally claimed to be pre-exilic, one discovers that Moses and the traditions relating to the ancestors are strikingly absent from the pre-exilic prophetic materials. According to H. Vorländer,[45] who compiled lists of the Pentateuchal motifs and allusions to them in the non-Pentateuchal materials, there are *no* references to the Pentateuchal stories in any pre-exilic text. While most scholars would not be willing to follow Vorländer this far, many would agree with the conclusions of N. P. Lemche's critique of Vorländer's work, which concludes:

> These narratives are not the free inventions of the late period. On the other hand, there is no doubt that these traditions were first collected and adapted for theological purposes at a very late point in the history of Israel. It accordingly seems possible provisionally to state that the traditions concerning early Israel until the introduction of the monarchy were only slightly known if they played any role at all in Judah prior to 722. Also, it seems certain that the Northern Kingdom was familiar with these traditions before the catastrophe of 722. Unfortunately it will hardly be possible to say anything definite about the contents and the extent of their traditions.[46]

Abraham is not mentioned in the pre-exilic prophets at all, and there are only two texts which *might* be pre-exilic that do mention him.[47] Likewise, Jacob occurs in the pre-exilic prophets only in Hos 12:3–5, 13–14. That these references reflect the same traditions as those in the Pentateuch is questionable. With regard to Moses, it is notable that all of the references to him outside the Pentateuch, excepting Hos 12:14 and, possibly, Mic 6:4 and

---

by the mid-third to mid-second centuries BCE. This is confirmed by the biblical manuscripts from Cave 4 that are now available for study. For the more important biblical texts, see E. Ulrich, *et al.*, *Qumran Cave 4: VII: Genesis to Numbers* (DJD XII; Oxford: Clarendon, 1994); E.Ulrich, *et al.*, *Qumran Cave 4: IX: Deuteronomy, Joshua, Judges, Kings* (DJD XIV; Oxford: Clarendon, 1996); and, E.Ulrich, *et al.*, *Qumran Cave 4: X: The Prophets* (DJD XV; Oxford: Clarendon, 1997).

[45] *Die Entstehungszeit des jehowistischen Geschichtswerkes* (Europäische Hochschulschriften: Reihe 23; Theologie; Bd. 109; Frankfurt am Main: Verlag Peter Lang, 1978). The major results of his study are discussed by N. P. Lemche in *Early Israel*, pp. 357–385.

[46] *Early Israel*, p. 375.

[47] In 1 Kgs 18:36, Elijah addresses God as "Yahweh, god of Abraham, Isaac, and Israel," while Israel is called the "people of the god of Abraham" in Ps 47:10 (N. Whybray, *The Making of the Pentateuch*, p. 103). Whybray reads Jacob for Israel in 1 Kgs 18:36 and gives no reason for having changed the text.

Isa 63:11, as well as the genealogical notices concerning him in Judg 1:16; 4:11; 18:30 and 1 Chr 23:14–15, seem to be dependent upon the Pentateuchal traditions.[48] Of these, only Hosea 12:14 has any real probability of being pre-exilic. These factors, along with the datum that reference to "the Torah of Moses" occurs neither in the Pentateuch nor in the pre-exilic prophets, would weaken the identification of Torah and Pentateuch, at least within the context of the texts of the Hebrew bible.

Whatever roles the traditions about Moses or the "Torah of Moses" might have played in the lives of the people of Israel or Judah prior to the exile, it is clear that neither finds a dominant position in the pre-exilic non-Pentateuchal accounts. If the "Torah of Moses," the basis of the reconstituted Jerusalem and Judah according to the traditions contained in Ezra and Nehemiah, is not equated with the Pentateuch, then with what is it to be identified? Obviously, any answer here must be conjectural. Is it to be identified with an existing biblical text? If so, which is the most likely? Clearly, it would seem that the most likely text to identify with the "Torah of Moses" would be some form of the book of Deuteronomy, possibly what is commonly referred to as the "old core" (4:44–28:26).[49]

At the same time, there is no empirical reason to make this connection. If some of the more recent analyses of the Josianic "reforms" and the Ezra accounts are taken seriously, then each of these may be understood as politico-religious propaganda which attempts to establish the legitimacy of a particular ruling elite by appealing to its efforts to "reestablish" the "traditional" religious status by virtue of cultic reforms.[50] Taking the implications of these conclusions seriously, one might be led to conclude that the most that the Hebrew bible will allow *vis-à-vis* the identification of "the Torah of Moses" is that the particular groups producing the accounts of Josiah and Ezra envisioned some form of the deuteronomic materials (with probable supplements) to be accepted as the basis for the "reforms" which they themselves evidently supported. Whether or not the accounts of either Josiah or

48 M. Greenberg, "Moses," *EncJud* 12: 378.

49 The precise limits of the deuteronomistic editing of the "older" deuteronomic materials, while agreed upon in general, remain debated in terms of specifics. For examples, see the discussions of A. D. H. Mayes, *Deuteronomy* (NCBC; Grand Rapids, MI: Eerdmans, 1981), pp. 41–55, or of M. Weinfeld, *Deuteronomy 1–11*, pp. 9–14.

50 As noted by T. L. Thompson, the religious "policies" of Cyrus of Persia, following as he has suggested the variety of "reforms" claimed by Nabonidus of Babylon, present an excellent conceptual background for understanding such claims (*Early History of the Israelite People*, pp. 416–417).

Ezra, along with their appeal to a particular extant "book of the Torah," can be taken as historically accurate must be bracketed until such time as there exists sufficient evidence to answer the question one way or another.[51]

What can be said with some confidence, however, is that particular scribal and/or priestly groups did indeed produce these accounts that appealed to the "Torah of Moses" for their authority.[52] Given the contents of these accounts, it seems clear that the focus of the community producing these texts is to be found in the Temple in Jerusalem, for it is in conjunction with this institution that each of the "reforms" based on the "Torah of Moses" is promulgated. Likewise, it is the priesthood that plays the essential role in both the "discovery" and the "exposition" of this "Torah," whether it be the same in each case or not. But, despite the variety of religious claims to continuity between the pre-exilic Judahite temple cultus and the restoration Jerusalem Temple of the Persian period,[53] there are several critical historical changes that must be noted. The "original" Temple of the pre-exilic period served as a dynastic shrine for the ruling monarchic family. As such, it was a part of the palace complex, and the cultus associated with it was designed to support and legitimate the worship of the ancestral deity of the dynasty. In the "restoration" Jerusalem Temple, there

[51] The numerous attempts to identify this "Torah" with Deuteronomy, parts of the Priestly code, or the Holiness code all encounter a similar problem: the evidence from Ezra-Nehemiah and Chronicles is mixed. Sometimes one can detect direct dependence upon the deuteronomic code, the Priestly code, or the Holiness code. At other times, there seems to be the reflection of traditions not contained in any of the biblical codifications of ritual practice. It might be best to conclude on the evidence adduced for identifying this "Torah" that we do not possess the particular rendition of it that is reflected in these accounts. For a review of the various systems reflected in Chronicles, Ezra, and Nehemiah, see J. Blenkinsopp, *Ezra-Nehemiah*, pp. 153–157.

[52] Despite the prevailing, yet generally not admitted, presupposition that the accounts contained in the biblical materials represent commonly held, popularly acknowledged traditions, there is really no evidence to which one might appeal for support. Writing, and hence the production of texts in the ancient world (apart from graffiti or crude lists), fell under the purview of the professionally trained, urban elite (see above, Chap. 1, n. 32). That the traditions they chose to record, copy, and propagate were identical to those of the outlying peasantry is clearly open to debate. For an extended discussion of writing practices in ancient Israel and the actual production of scrolls, see the following works by M. Haran: "Book-Scrolls in Israel in Pre-Exilic Times," *JJS* 33 (1982) 161–173; "Book-Scrolls at the Beginning of the Second Temple Period: The Transition from Papyrus to Skins," *HUCA* 54 (1983) 111–122; and "More Concerning Book-Scrolls in Pre-Exilic Times," *JJS* 35 (1984) 84–85.

[53] For an analysis of the role of the Temple in the political structuring of the Persian period, see J. Blenkinsopp, "Temple and Society in Achaemenid Judah," in *Second Temple Studies: 1. Persian Period*, ed. P. R. Davies (JSOTSup 117; Sheffield: JSOT, 1991), pp. 22–53.

is a clear change, for there is no longer a Judahite monarchy, and hence no dynasty to associate directly with the deity.[54] Rather than being a visible religious symbol of native rule, the Temple of the Persian period became the symbolic focus of foreign domination, and those who were in charge of the Temple and its cultus performed as functionaries to the Persian court.

As such, they would have been charged with the production and promulgation of a law acceptable to their Persian overlords. While the "law" instituted by these delegates of the Persian government may have received a "religious" interpretation, at the most basic level it was a political document designed to provide ethnic and political boundaries to a particular province of the empire. Whatever the exact nature of the "law" that was instituted by the Persians, there could be little doubt that it was written. At the same time, as with any legal code, there is also the certainty that it required interpretation in order to be applied. Hence, there developed a need for a trained scribal guild, not only in charge of maintaining the written code, but also of continuing its "tradition" of interpretation.[55] To build upon this concept, it seems undeniable that whatever the precise nature of this "law," and despite whatever claims to continuity with past Judahite codifications might have been made about it, its origins were with the returning "Judahite" officials who had been separated from Judah and Jerusalem for their entire lives. To the best of our knowledge, none of the original "exiles" from Judah returned from Babylon. This means that those who returned in accord with the "decree of Cyrus" would have been born, reared, and educated in "exile," i.e., in Babylon and its provinces.[56] Likewise, if one accepts the

---

54 The "messianic" hopes attached to the prince Zerubbabel, as reflected in Haggai and Zechariah 1–7 in association with the rebuilding of the Temple, and their failures serve to illustrate this shift of emphasis. Zerubbabel was replaced in the enthronement narrative of Zech 6:9–15 by none other than the priest, Joshua. It was this same change in the political structure of the community that may have led to the shift in emphasis away from the role previously attributed to the prophet.

55 The concept of "tradition," especially as it is used within the study of religions, is often misunderstood. Just because something becomes a "tradition," it does not mean that it was not recently invented or created. Now this latter possibility is often shied away from on the basis that it implies some degree of manipulation on the part of an officially franchised class of people, i.e., the politically and religiously empowered. What must not be overlooked is that it is the effectiveness of the *claim of antiquity* which is much more important than the actual historical antiquity of a "tradition" that empowers it for a community, either ancient or modern.

56 This assumes that the "decree of Cyrus" (cf. Ezra 1:1–4; 6:3–5) reflects some degree of historical reality. Based upon parallel claims of religious restoration, admittedly propagandistic as they are, such as those of the "Cyrus Cylinder" (*ANET*, pp. 315–316), some such "edict" seems to be within the realm of historical probability.

general outlines and chronology of the "reforms" attributed to Ezra and Nehemiah, then the major figures determining the shape of this official Jerusalem Judaism were no less than third- or fourth-generation descendants of those original Judahite exiles. Their training would have been in the Persian scribal schools where they would presumably have been allowed to retain their own scribal traditions, whatever those might have been in their historical contexts, while being trained in the appropriate Persian administrative manners and matters.

Now all of this is, admittedly, a house of cards, for there are few more poorly documented periods in the history of the development of Judaism than the Persian and early Hellenistic eras. And, as is known within the scholarly world, it is precisely within this period that the basic shapes of the variety of forms that Judaism would take began to develop. But it is precisely here that care must be taken in the attempt to conceive of Torah and its relationship to Pentateuch, as well as the relationship of each of these to early Judaism and its divergent forms. It might be appropriate at this point to attempt to define what "Torah" might mean, within the context of early Judaism and within the variety of forms that diverged from it. In the most simple of terms, "Torah" designates the instructions of Yahweh for his people, received by Moses at Sinai/Horeb. This, at least, seems to be the meaning given to it within the Hebrew bible. But, as M. Smith has pointed out, ". . . the Hebrew Bible, as we have it, is primarily evidence of the interests of the Pharisees and their successors, who not only selected and interpreted the books but also carefully determined and corrected their texts," and, as such, represents the end product of numerous partisan revisions.[57] Hence, by Pharisaic times, i.e., by the late Hellenistic period (*ca.* 150 BCE), "Torah" would seem to carry a clearly religious meaning. But "Torah," in Pharisaic and later rabbinical Judaism, was very much like the concept of "law" noted above: it was two-fold, written and oral. For the particular brand of Palestinian Judaism that survived the destruction of the Temple in 70 CE and which has come to be thought of as normative for Judaism in general, this dual Torah represented the whole of Yahweh's revelation to his people. As suggested by the passage from the Mishnah with which this chapter began, the relationship between the two could often be very loose. This "oral Torah" was put into written form by the sages of

---

[57] *Palestinian Parties and Politics that Shaped the Old Testament* (London: SCM Press, 1987), pp. 7–8.

Judaism between the second and seventh centuries CE[58] and became the foundational scriptures for all the varieties of Judaism that have developed subsequently.

Problematically, these scriptures which provide particular parameters to the varieties of Judaism that can be traced historically date in their final form some five hundred to one thousand years after the time to which the formation of the Jerusalem community under the Persian emissary Ezra occurred. How might the role and function of Torah be described during this period? What indicators are there that Torah was identified with Pentateuch prior to the codification of the "oral Torah" in the forms of the Mishnah and the Talmud? Just as importantly, how does one account for the problem that not only did these different varieties of Judaism read "scripture" in different ways, both textually and linguistically, but they also read different "scriptures." Prior to *ca.* 200 CE then, one might argue that each of these forms of Judaism represented a discrete system.[59] To the best of our historical knowledge, and this suffers from quite a number of significant gaps, all of these expressions of Judaism share the concept of "Torah" in common. But, it must be cautioned, a common allegiance to "Torah" does not mean a common definition of "Torah," or even a common "Torah." At what point prior to *ca.* 200 CE such a common definition might have been reached remains to be investigated.

One of the most important (and also most frequently dismissed) expressions of Judaism comes from the military colony of Elephantine in Egypt. A number of Aramaic papyri dating from the fifth century BCE reveal that the inhabitants of that fortress, located opposite Aswan and to the north of the first cataract of the Nile, claimed descent from Judah and Israel and identified themselves closely with the communities in Persian Yehud and Samaria.[60] Yet, when their religious practices are compared with those that are associated with scholarly conceptions of "normative" Judaism, they

58 Both the Hebrew scriptures and the Mishnah probably took their final written form by 200 CE. The Tosefta, a collection of sayings supplementing the Mishnah and the Talmud Yerushalmi, a systematic commentary on the Mishnah, were completed *ca.* 400 CE. The Babylonian Talmud, another systematic exposition of the Mishnah, was completed between 500–600 CE (J. Neusner, *Scriptures of the Oral Torah* [San Francisco: Harper & Row, 1987], pp. 5–6). As we shall show below, the Talmud clearly identifies Torah with Pentateuch, but this is not central to the progression of the argument at this point.

59 J. A. Overman & W. S. Green, "Judaism (Greco-Roman Period)," *ABD* III, 1039.

60 For reconstructions of the major periods when the establishment of a garrison in Egypt by emigrants from Israel or Judah might have been most likely, see B. Porten, *Archives from Elephantine* (Berkeley: University of California Press, 1968), pp. 8–16.

appear to have been a peripheral group. Two of the major religious differences from the "norm" that the Elephantine group displays are the existence of a temple to Yahweh (*Yhw*), where sacrifices were offered, and the invocation of a variety of deities, e.g., the goddess Anatyahu, in legal oaths.

From the standpoint of deuteronomic legislation, neither of these practices should be tolerated. The worship of other gods, not to mention goddesses, would lead to expulsion from the land. Likewise, no temple could be permitted outside of Jerusalem (Deuteronomy 12), nor could sacrifices be offered elsewhere. If Deuteronomy formed the core of the Torah as perceived by the Jewish colonists of Elephantine, they clearly chose to reinterpret it or to ignore it. On the other hand, it is entirely possible that their concept of "Torah" did not include such legislative positions, or that they had a tradition by which they were able to reapply the deuteronomic ideals, as were the Samaritans. If, as the correspondence with Jerusalem indicates, the colony was founded prior to the Persian period and the temple there was built before the Persian conquest of Egypt in 525 BCE,[61] then one might surmise that whatever the extent of the legal restructuring that took place under Ezra, it did not extend to this Jewish colony.[62] This clearly indicates the possibility that whatever the written or oral traditions to which "Torah" might be traced at this period, they did not specify the exclusivity of the Jerusalem Temple and the prohibition against any other, nor did they restrict sacrifices to the Jerusalem cultus. Or, if they did, the colony at Elephantine simply chose to ignore them.

At the same time, it is clear that this colony perceived itself to be closely related to the Judaism established in Jerusalem. Both the Passover and the Sabbath were celebrated by this group, though the precise manner in which this was done is ambiguous.[63] With respect to the Sabbath, it is unclear from the evidence how stringently it was observed in Egypt, though references to the day in the extant materials and the evidence of the per-

---

61 For the text (#32), see A. Cowley, *Aramaic Papyri of the Fifth Century B.C.* (Oxford: Clarendon, 1923), pp. 122–124.

62 It should also be remembered that this is not the only reference to a Jewish temple that was constructed outside of Jerusalem. At least three other Jewish temples outside of Jerusalem are attested: the Samaritan temple on Mt. Gerizim, the Transjordanian temple of Hyrcanus at Araq el-Emir, and the temple of Onias IV at Leontopolis in Egypt. For a description of these temples, see B. Porten, "The Jews in Egypt," in *The Cambridge History of Judaism, I: Introduction; The Persian Period,* ed. W. D. Davies and L. Finkelstein (Cambridge: Cambridge University Press, 1984), pp. 186–187.

63 For a discussion of the pertinent materials, see B. Porten, *Archives from Elephantine*, pp. 122–133.

sonal name *Shabbatay* indicate a familiarity with the practice. It is also
clear that the Passover was celebrated by this group and, to judge from the
references to it in a letter written *ca.* 419 BCE, had been for some time. Interestingly, this letter, written from one Hananiah to Yedoniah and the
Jewish garrison, seems to be an answer to a request concerning the precise
time for the celebration of the Passover by the Elephantine community.[64]
While the exact identity of Hananiah remains debated, it is possible that he
was a Persian official in Jerusalem.[65] If this view is correct, then it is clear
that the two Jewish communities recognized some relationship between
their religious identities and practices.

A second series of letters also suggests that the Elephantine community
viewed itself as related to the community in Jerusalem. After their temple
was destroyed by the priests of Khnum, the community wrote to Arsham,
the Persian satrap in Egypt, requesting that its temple be rebuilt (*ca.* 410
BCE).[66] Later, *ca.* 408 BCE, Yedoniah, head priest of the Elephantine community, wrote to Bagohi (Bogoas), the Persian governor of Judah, requesting permission to rebuild its temple (#30–31). They also forwarded their
request to Delaiah and Shelemiah of Samaria, which suggests that they
may have been unaware of any Jerusalem/Samaritan schism, had one even
occurred by this point. In response, Bagohi of Judah and Delaiah of Samaria
wrote to Arsham, satrap of Egypt, instructing that the "altar house of the god
of heaven" (*bêt madbĕḥāʾ zî ʾĕlāh šĕmayyāʾ;* #32.3–4) be rebuilt, but did
not give permission for the resumption of the sacrificial cultus.[67] All of this
correspondence suggests that whatever the nature of the Torah that was
understood as defining the Judaism of the province of Yehud, and whatever
control or influence that provincial religious tradition might have had over
other Jewish communities, it was not identical with the Torah that eventually emerged to give priority to the Temple in Jerusalem alone and that
required the exclusive worship of Yahweh alone. While modern scholarship
tends to see Elephantine Judaism as somewhat aberrant, it must be remembered that it can be understood as such only by comparison to a norm.
I suggest that no such standard yet existed within the Judaism that was
emerging in the Levant during the late fifth century BCE.[68]

---

64 Cf. A. Cowley, *Aramaic Papyri*, #21, pp. 60–65.

65 B. Porten, *Archives from Elephantine*, p. 130.

66 Cf. A. Cowley, *Aramaic Papyri*, #27, pp. 97–103.

67 B. Porten, "Elephantine Papryi," *ABD* II, 449.

68 According to most reconstructions of the fate of the community at Elephantine, it
seems that the garrison remained loyal to the Persian authorities and, as a result of the successful Egyptian rebellion against Persia that began *ca.* 405 BCE, was destroyed *ca.* 400 BCE.

Before continuing with a consideration of some of the historical materials that may provide further evidence of the ways in which Torah functioned in various communities, it is important to look at a particular aspect of Torah that conditions the manner in which it is conceived and the materials with which it is often identified. As it develops in the "whole" of the dual Torah which took final form between the second and sixth centuries CE, Torah contains two components: *halakah* (*hălākâ*) and *haggadah/aggadah* (*haggadâ/ʾaggādâ*). *Halakah* refers to the legal discourses of the rabbinic Torah which are regarded as binding, while *haggadah/aggadah* refer to those non-legal materials, e.g., stories, expositions, etc., that are not perceived as mandatory. In its final form, Torah was clearly perceived to include both the "instructions" and the "exposition" on those divine directives. However, the question must be asked whether or not *haggadah/aggadah* constituted parts of the "Torah of Moses" which formed the basis of the legal reconstitution of the district of Yehud under the Persian authorities. On the basis of the materials contained in Ezra-Nehemiah, and reflected in the Elephantine materials, the relationship of *halakah* and *haggadah* is unclear. That this "Torah" might have contained both could be suggested by the custom of public reading and interpretation of "Torah" reflected in Neh 8:3–8.

Further evidence in support of this might be found in the materials related to the Samaritan sect and the Samaritan Pentateuch. One indicator of the prominence attained by the development of the early Judaism that might have been generated with public and political propagation of a Judahite/Persian "Torah/law" that found its position as the basis of Jerusalem Judaism might be found in the relationship that developed between this Jerusalem Judaism and the sectarian movement that is associated with the Samaritans.[69] According to Samaritan sources, the Samaritans themselves traced their lineage back to Ephraim and Manasseh and claimed to have occupied their own territories peacefully until Eli moved the cultus from Shechem to Shiloh. Hence, they viewed themselves as a distinct religious group from the time of Eli, through the period of the kings, and into the Babylonian, Persian, Hellenistic, Roman, and Arab periods. Likewise, they did not refer

---

[69] Two factors related to this issue require clarification. In the first instance, it is notable that as soon as one posits the existence of an early Judaism as a matter of public religious/political activity, one must abandon the concept and move to specific appropriations of that "ideal"—hence, Jerusalem Judaism. Secondly, the application of the term "sectarian" to any of the forms of Judaism is admittedly anachronistic, implying as it might that there existed at this point some normative elaboration of the religious tradition, which is exactly the opposite of what is argued here.

to themselves as "Samaritans" (*šōměrōnîm*), but as "keepers, observers" (*šāměrîm*) "of the truth" (*'al hā'ěmet*).[70] From the perspective of the Judahite materials that became the Hebrew scriptures, the Samaritans were the remnants of the populace of the destroyed Israel, which had been repopulated by Assyrian and other non-Israelite elements and constituted a highly syncretistic religion that was completely out of line with the requirements of the Jerusalem cultus (cf. 2 Kgs 17:24–34). Ethnic, political, and religious ascription are clearly at work in such identifications. In short, the historical origins of the Samaritan group remain obscure to us, as does the precise time when such a schism might have occurred.

What is known is that the two movements differed radically on three points: priesthood, sanctuary, and scriptures. With respect to the priesthood, the Samaritans constructed a priestly genealogy that was descended directly from Phinehas and Eleazar, descendants of Aaron, but that did not form a collateral line with the Zadokite line of Jerusalem.[71] Such claims must be understood as attempts to legitimize the Samaritan priesthood over against the counter-claims of the Jerusalem cultus. Just as important as the claim legitimizing the priesthood was the sanctuary built on Mt. Gerizim, overlooking the city of Shechem. While much remains unclear about the history of the sect and its temple, it is clear that under the Persians, the district of Samaria was configured as a province, like Yehud.[72] Likewise, it seems that either in the late Persian or early Hellenistic period, this group erected its own sanctuary on Mt. Gerizim, which stood for over two hundred years until its destruction by the Hasmonean John Hyrcanus in 128 BCE.[73]

One of the most intriguing aspects of this sanctuary is the foundational document by which it is legitimated: the Samaritan Pentateuch. For this

---

70 A. Loewenstamm, "Samaritans," *EncJud* 14:727–728. Much remains debated about the origins of this sect. They are often identified with the opponents of Nehemiah and his efforts to rebuild the Temple and walls in Jerusalem (Ezra 4:2–5, 17–24; Neh 2:19; 4:2–3), but the identification is tenuous, since the opponents are not explicitly named.

71 J. D. Purvis, "The Samaritans," *The Cambridge History of Judaism, II: The Hellenistic Age*, ed. W. D. Davies and L. Finkelstein (Cambridge: Cambridge University Press, 1989), pp. 611–613.

72 For a discussion of the number of smaller districts that composed the areas of Yehud and Samaria during the Persian age, see E. Stern, *Material Culture of the Land of the Bible in the Persian Period: 538–332 B.C.* (Warminster/Jerusalem: Aris & Phillips/Israel Exploration Society, 1982), pp. 244–249. The governor of Samaria, Sanballat, is depicted as one of the enemies of Nehemiah in Neh 2:10, 19; 4:1. His sons, Delaiah and Shelemiah, also governors of that district, have already been mentioned above, in the context of the Elephantine request for help in rebuilding their sanctuary.

73 Josephus, *Ant.* 13 § 254–256.

segment of Judaism, its version of the Pentateuch constituted the whole of its written scriptures.[74] Discovered at Qumran were a number of texts, e.g., 4QPaleoExm, 4Q158, etc., which display many of the harmonizing tendencies that characterize the Samaritan Pentateuch and are thus categorized as proto-Samaritan.[75] Hence, there is some evidence of the formation of a textual tradition like that found in this sectarian version that can be dated to *ca.* 150 BCE–68 CE. This textual tradition represents a distinct movement from the proto-Masoretic and proto-LXX traditions attested at Qumran and indicates that the Samaritan tradition represents an ancient, pre-Masoretic tradition.[76] These data would suggest that the final Samaritan Pentateuchal recension was completed sometime during the Hasmonean period, i.e., during the late second century BCE. In its present shape, the Samaritan Pentateuch has been adapted to defend the Samaritan concept of Mt. Gerizim as the only legitimate place for the worship of Yahweh.[77]

While this may not reveal much about the Samaritan concept of Torah, it does make one very important point: the final text of the Pentateuch was not yet formally established within the varieties of Judaism in Palestine until the end of the third or the beginning of the second century BCE.[78] By the time we have actual textual evidence for the Pentateuch, and that Pen-

---

[74] Regrettably, we know virtually nothing concerning the Samaritan concept of Torah. Despite the temptation to equate Torah with Pentateuch in this instance, any empirical evidence for such is lacking.

[75] E. Tov, "Textual Criticism (OT)," *ABD* VI, 401.

[76] J. D. Purvis, *The Samaritan Pentateuch and the Origins of the Samaritan Sect* (HSM 2; Cambridge: Harvard University Press, 1968), p. 78.

[77] B. Waltke, "Samaritan Pentateuch," *ABD* V, 938. Waltke's suggestion that the limitation of the Samaritan scriptures to the Pentateuch might be attributed to the fact that in the non-Pentateuchal materials Jerusalem/Zion serves as an object of praise, while the Pentateuch is relatively silent on the matter, seems to presuppose that there was at this time an active concept of an exclusive canon emerging.

[78] This fact is clear from the radically different chronologies present in the Pentateuch among the Samaritan, Septuagint, and Masoretic versions. For a discussion of the chronological differences between the Septuagint and Masoretic texts, see G. Larsson, "The Chronology of the Pentateuch: A Comparison of the MT and LXX," *JBL* 102 (1983) 401–409. Larsson concludes that the chronology of the MT is original when compared to the LXX and that the chronological system in the MT is no earlier than the late third century BCE. Further, since all of the chronological differences are confined to what is commonly designated as the Priestly source, Larsson argues that "P never existed as an independent unity but rather *is* the final collection of older and newer source material of the Pentateuch, supplemented with new-written texts and formed into a work of unique consistency and importance" (p. 408). For a comparison of these chronologies with that of the Samaritan Pentateuch, see J. Skinner, *Genesis,* 2nd ed. (ICC; Edinburgh: T. & T. Clark, 1930), p. 134.

tateuch is envisioned as containing some form of the earlier Torah, then Torah, in its written form, included both *halakah* and *haggadah*. This factor is further illustrated by the emergence of a third textual tradition, represented by the Septuagint, which may now be traced in general terms. The earliest extant papyri containing portions of the Greek translations of the Pentateuchal materials come from the second century BCE, and fragments of several Greek manuscripts were discovered among the materials at Qumran. It is generally maintained that the earliest Greek translations were of the Pentateuch only and that other writings were translated from Hebrew at a later period. The origins of the Septuagint translation, however, remain somewhat obscure, but nonetheless critical to the present discussion. Since the Septuagint itself represents another traditional text that differs from both the Hebrew of the proto-Masoretic tradition and the Samaritan Pentateuch, it is clear that it represents the scriptures of yet another text of the Pentateuch that reflects the needs of a particular community.[79]

If the traditions contained in the story of Aristeas have any historical validity, and many scholars do credit them with some, then the translation of the Pentateuch, or at least portions of it, began in Alexandria, Egypt at the command of Ptolemy (II Philadelphus [*ca.* 285–247 BCE]). According to this account, Demetrius, the king's librarian, made a worldwide collection of books for the king's library at the request of his master (vv. 1–8). "The laws of the Jews" (*tōn Ioudaiōn nomima;* v. 10) were desired as an addition to the library, so a communiqué was sent to the priests in Jerusalem, who agreed to dispatch six delegates from each of the twelve tribes to translate "the law of the Jews" into Greek.[80] Regrettably, the lengthy "defense" of the Law that is contained in vv. 121–171 of the letter concentrates on monotheism, clean and unclean animals, and sacrifice. It gives no indication of the extent of the "Torah" with respect to the non-halakhic aspects of the contents.[81] It does indicate, however, the significance of the role of

79 Whether these three traditions of the biblical texts should be understood as separate texts or as different recensions or text types of an earlier "Urtext" remains debated among text critics. What is clear, however, is that whether one talks of Septuagintal texts or of Egyptian text types, the texts themselves remained adaptable in their basic form to address the ongoing needs of the communities.

80 For a summary of this letter that purports to be from Aristeas, an Alexandrian Jew, to his brother Philocrates, see R. J. H. Shutt, "Aristeas, Letter of," *ABD* I, 380–381.

81 An interesting aspect of the contention that the Septuagint translation originally pertained to the Pentateuch and was subsequently identified with the Torah is the translation of a line in §30 of the Letter of Aristeas, commonly rendered "the books of the Law of the Jews." The article is normally supplied by translators, since the text itself reads simply (certain/some?) "books of the Law of the Jews" (*tou nomou tōn Ioudaiōn biblia*).

Jerusalem and the temple priesthood there in the maintenance of some "center" around which different appropriations of Judaism revolved. In all probability, this was due to the continuation of the temple-oriented form of governance that was established during the Persian period. In the case of the administration of Judah, the Temple itself seems to have been the focus of the administrative personnel, making the province of Judah a "temple-community" not unlike others established by the Persian authorities.[82] It would be within this temple-community context that the scribal guilds, along with whatever archives might have existed, would have been situated, creating a highly specialized and socially privileged group that was separated from the remainder of the society of the district,[83] and who would have been responsible for the formulation and maintenance of the Torah.

Still, the manuscript evidence from Qumran that includes several fragments of Greek translations of the Pentateuch, along with fragments from every biblical book except Esther, indicates that by the middle of the second century BCE, the Pentateuch had obtained its basic form in which the legal/halakhic materials were accompanied by narrative accounts that seemingly provided an interpretive frame for the *halakot*. But the question still remains as to whether or not Pentateuch was to be equated with Torah at Qumran. A related question focuses on the nature of the non-halakhic materials in the Pentateuch. Unlike rabbinic *haggadah*, the narratives of the Pentateuch do not hold any direct relationship to the halakhic materials for which they seem to form a narrative frame.[84] But like those didactic narratives, the stories of the Pentateuch provide an instructive background by which the nature of the community is both founded and bounded, encircling

---

[82] J. Blenkinsopp, *A History of Prophecy in Israel: From the Settlement in the Land to the Hellenistic Period* (Philadelphia: Westminster, 1983), p. 227. For a more detailed discussion of the type of economy that may have accompanied this political and social form, see Blenkinsopp's discussion in "Temple and Society in Achaemenid Judah," in *Second Temple Studies*, pp. 22–53.

[83] P. R. Davies, *In Search of 'Ancient Israel'*, p. 81. Davies notes that the evidence for such a division is to be found in the terms *qĕhal haggōlâ* and *bĕnê haggōlâ*, which occur in the book of Ezra (Davies mistakenly designates this as Nehemiah, where neither of these terms occurs).

[84] Clearly the issue of the manner of the formation of the Pentateuch is one which cannot be directly addressed in this chapter. It is important to note that the overwhelming majority of *halakot* are derived from the materials contained in the writings associated with Sinai and in portions of Deuteronomy. One might venture to suggest, as has been done by others, that the stories of the Pentateuch were written as supplements to the general materials presented in Deuteronomy and functioned as the basis for the development of a fuller, more discernible national and ethnic mythography. These issues will be addressed in the remaining chapters.

the *halakot* and thus supporting them. By the late third century BCE, and possibly earlier, the Pentateuch had achieved its basic shape. But, again, was it equated with Torah?

There is no doubt that Torah played a critical role in the conception of the Jewish community that is associated with the "Dead Sea Scrolls." In the "Rule of the Community" (1QS), this is noted quite explicitly:

> And where there are ten (members) there must not be lacking there a man who studies the Torah day and night continually, each man relieving another. The Many shall spend the third part of every night of the year in unity, reading the Book, studying judgment, and saying benedictions in unity (1QS 6.6–8).[85]

Given the presence of Pentateuchal manuscripts at Qumran, especially those which were preserved in paleo-Hebrew script,[86] along with the fact that the study and interpretation of Torah clearly plays a significant role in the sectarian group that produced these documents, it is especially tempting to suggest that by the time of Qumran, Pentateuch had come to be understood as equal to Torah.

Two major manuscripts from Qumran seem to suggest that the entire concept of Torah itself was open to some degree of debate and change. It is commonly asserted that by the time of ben Sirach (*ca.* 135–110 BCE), two portions of the Hebrew scriptures had been formally adopted and were closed to further change. The prologue to ben Sirach refers directly to "the law, the prophets, and the other writings of our ancestors" (ll. 8–10; *tou nomou kai tōn prophētōn kai tōn allōn patriōn bibliōn*). But both the "Temple Scroll" (11QTemple; *mĕgillat hammiqdāš*)[87] and the halakhic letter called 4QMMT (*miqṣat ma'ăśê hattôrâ*)[88] suggest that the written Torah was

---

85 For translation and text, see J. H. Charlesworth, *et. al.*, *The Dead Sea Scrolls: Hebrew, Aramaic, and Greek Texts with English Translations, Vol. 1: Rule of the Community and Related Documents* (Tübingen: Mohr/Louisville, KY: Westminster/John Knox, 1994), pp. 26–27.

86 The precise "honor" that this special script might suggest is unclear given the fact that the book of Job is also attested from Qumran with this same orthographic peculiarity.

87 On the Temple Scroll, see Y. Yadin, *The Temple Scroll,* 3 vols. (Jerusalem: Israel Exploration Society, 1983), and J. Maier, *The Temple Scroll* (JSOTSup 34; Sheffield: JSOT, 1985).

88 This recently published text, which is in fragmentary form, has been the object of much recent controversy. While the exact form and function of these fragments remain debated, it is clear that the context in which it was produced was one that reflects some type of controversy between groups concerned with interpreting Torah. For a presentation of the text and attempts at its interpretation, see E. Qimron and J. Strugnell, *Qumran Cave 4.V, Miqṣat Ma'ase HaTorah, DJD 10* (Oxford: Oxford University Press, 1994). The text and translation

not yet in a universally accepted form and that it was possible for portions of it to be rewritten.

The purpose of the Temple Scroll, which is dated to *ca.* 100–85 BCE, seems to have been "to provide a system of law for the pre-messianic temple."[89] In other words, it presents the halakhic system by which the purity of the Jerusalem Temple was to be insured in the period prior to the manifestation of the messiah. As such, it represents a sectarian effort to present the "correct" interpretation of Torah, which, by implication, means that there were competing concepts of Torah at that time.[90] There are two extremely interesting aspects of the texts that this scroll cites as authoritative. First, when the Temple Scroll recounts direct revelations from God, it changes biblical passages from the third to the first person, especially with respect to materials from Deuteronomy, thus avoiding any appearance of indirect mediation of the Torah. Second, biblical quotations appear in the scroll in expanded, abbreviated, and conflated forms, demonstrating that the writers felt free to combine different texts to create their own.[91] Of equal importance is the fact that this document treats extrabiblical laws as if they had been derived from the primary revelation at Sinai, i.e., as actual Torah.[92] This suggests that by the second century BCE, Torah was *not* interpreted or understood as restricted to the Pentateuch, at least by all Jewish groups.

A similar understanding might be gained from a consideration of 4QMMT.[93] At least six incomplete manuscripts of this document have been identified among the fragments from Cave 4 at Qumran. It is a clearly sectarian document of approximately 190 lines in length. Regrettably, the beginning is lost. It is possible that it is a letter from the sectarians to a group with whom they are in severe disagreement concerning particular *halakot,* most of which pertain to the Temple in Jerusalem. On the basis of what has been reconstructed for this letter, over 20 different *halakot* peculiar to this group, some of which are known from the Temple Scroll, may

---

have been reproduced by H. Shanks in *BARev* 20/6 (1994) 51–61, in an article entitled "For This You Waited 35 Years: MMT as reconstructed by Elish Qimron and John Strugnell."

89 L. Schiffman, "Temple Scroll," *ABD* VI, 349.

90 Evidence of this might be found in the phrase *sēper hattôrâ haššēnît,* "the book of the other/second Torah" (4Q177:14), which may refer to a copy of a "non-canonical Torah" (M. Weinfeld, "Deuteronomy, Book of," *ABD* II, 169).

91 J. Maier, *The Temple Scroll,* p. 3.

92 L. Schiffman, "Temple Scroll," 350.

93 The following description of the contents of 4QMMT is based on the materials presented by Qimron in "Miqṣat Maʿase Hatorah" in *ABD* IV, 843–844.

be reconstructed. The abbreviation MMT is derived from the phrase, "some precepts of the Torah" (*miqṣat maʿăśê hattôrâ*), which is a phrase contained in the letter itself. What is intriguing about these *halakot* is that they deviate from what is known concerning "normative Pharisaic Judaism," the ancestor of the rabbinic movement that would become "normative," for scholars at least. The letter attempts to persuade the addressees to adopt the writer's (or writers' [?]) halakhic views rather than the ones which they had been following. Naturally, none of the parties is named in the letter. According to Qimron's interpretation of this letter, it was written by the founder of the sect at Qumran, "The Teacher of Righteousness," was addressed to "The Wicked Priest," and outlined the reasons for the Qumran group's splitting away from the Temple in Jerusalem.[94]

IV. Torah and Canon

What the materials investigated to this point suggest is that the modern historical critical investigation of the Hebrew bible, most specifically of the Torah, has lost sight of its own subject. It has modified in radical ways the basic nature of the very thing it intended to study and has made Torah into an unchanging historical and literary phenomenon. It has failed to recognize that from the traceable beginnings of Torah in the Persian period, down to its "official" codification with the completion of the Mishnah and Talmud (Yerushalmi and Bavli) between the late second and early seventh centuries CE, Torah was *never* understood as being delimited by a single written text. While the heart of all Judaism is Torah, that is not in any way to equate Judaism with a book, or even a collection of books.[95] Torah, as used by the variety of forms of Judaism known to scholars, refers to a system of organizing the religious life and identity of a community. As such it has two aspects, the written Torah (*tôrâ šebbiktāb*) and the oral Torah (*tôrâ šebbeʿal peh*). It is the understanding of the biblical injunctions, which were understood to be 613 in number,[96] as interpreted and applied in a religiously

94 If the "Wicked Priest" is identified as Jonathan the Prince, then 4QMMT may have been written *ca.* 150 BCE.

95 On the inadequacy of understanding Judaism as a "book religion," see the comments by W. S. Green in "Writing with Scripture," in *Writing with Scripture,* by J. Neusner (Philadelphia: Fortress, 1989), pp. 7–10.

96 According to R. Simlai, a Palestinian teacher, these 613 commandments, 365 of which were prohibitions corresponding to the number of days in a solar year, and 248 of which were mandates, equaling the number of limbs of the human body, were all given to Moses at Sinai (*b. Mak.* 23b; A. H. Rabinowitz, *EncJud* 5:760).

binding manner, that constituted the complete Torah. It was this complete Torah that provided the common shared "history" and understanding of community that defined what it was to be Jewish.

At the same time, however, it is clear that within Jewish tradition, the Pentateuch did come to be equated with the *written* portion of Torah. From the perspective of normative rabbinic Judaism, however, the written Torah could never be considered apart from the oral application of that Torah.[97] For the normative rabbinical interpretation of Torah, the written Torah can have no real existence apart from the oral, and the oral Torah itself is inherent in the very character of Torah.[98] It is within the writings of the Talmud, however, that we can finally confirm the identification of the written Torah with the Pentateuch. There we find references to the "five books of the Torah" (*hămēšet siprê hattôrâ/hămiššâ siprê hattôrâ*) or the "five fifths of the Torah" (*hămiššâ homšê hattôrâ*).[99] That these designations occur in the Talmud Yerushalmi shows that this identification had occurred sometime before *ca.* 400 CE.

This probably may be pushed back at least a century, or possibly even more, when the evidence from Christian lists of canonical books is consulted. In lists dating from the late third and early fourth centuries CE, reference is made by Eusebius, quoting Melito (*ca.* 175 CE), to the "five (books) of Moses" (*Mōuseōs pente*). Later, in a list attributed to Cyril of Jerusalem (4th century CE), the Pentateuch is referred to as "the first five books of Moses" (*hai Mōseōs prōtai pente bibloi*). In a list attributed to Epiphanus (4th century CE), we encounter the term "Pentateuch" (*pentateuchos*) as a designation of the first five books of the canon.[100] There is little reason to doubt that Christianity borrowed this designation from Judaism in the process of the formation of Christianity's canon.[101]

---

97 Even the Qaraites (*qārā'îm; ba'ălê hammiqrā'*; "the reciters"; "masters of the written word"), who emerged in the eighth century CE and who rejected the talmudic traditions, maintained a tradition of interpretation known as the "yoke of inheritance" (*sebel hayrûšâ*) (S. Hofman, "Karaities," *EncJud* 10:761).

98 Indeed, according to rabbinic tradition, "the statutes of the written Law could not have been fulfilled literally even in the generation in which they were given, since 'that which is plain in the Torah is obscure, all the more that which is obscure' (Judith Halevi, *Kuzari*, 3,35; cf. Moses of Coucy in *Semag*, introduction: 'For the verses contradict and refute each other,' and 'statements in the Written Law are vague'" [M. D. Herr, "Oral Law," *EncJud* 12:1439]).

99 For references, see N. M. Sarna, "Bible," *EncJud* 4:820.

100 For details of these canonical lists, see H. B. Swete, *An Introduction to the Old Testament in Greek* (New York: KTAV, 1968 [first printed, 1902]), pp. 203–204.

101 Readings of selected portions of the Pentateuch became a major part of the synagogue service. According to *b. Meg.* 29b, "in the West" (Palestine), the reading of the Torah

More difficult to determine is the precise point at which the biblical materials themselves were divided into "books," most specifically, into a collection of five, i.e., a Pentateuch.[102] It is clear that this division had occurred by the end of the first century CE, for Josephus notes that five of the twenty-two books comprising the sacred writings of Judaism are "the five books of Moses" (*pente men esti ta Mōuseōs*), which contained both the laws and traditions from the creation until the death of Moses.[103] This would suggest that they coincided with the present books of the Pentateuch. The Damascus Document refers to "the books of the Torah" (*siprê hattôrâ;* VII. 15), suggesting that such a division into five books may have occurred as early as the second century BCE.[104] While such a division into books may well have occurred by this time, it is important to note that the additional materials from Qumran noted above suggest that Torah was not limited to the materials contained in such a Pentateuch.

It is precisely here, where Christianity borrows the designations of the Torah as Pentateuch, that a very basic misappropriation occurs. The history of this appropriation remains obscure and belongs to the process of the formation of the Christian canon, a process which has been secondarily projected onto the Jewish concept of scripture. The following general outlines might be sketched as a background for substantiating this position.[105] In the first place, the scriptures adopted by Christianity were the Greek Septuagintal versions of the Jewish writings, not the Hebrew. This is most clear from the quotations contained in the Pauline corpus. This very fact suggests

---

was completed every three years; in Babylon and other areas outside Palestine, the Torah was read on an annual cycle (L. Jacobs, "Torah, Reading of," *EncJud* 15:1248). Earlier, both the NT (Acts 13:15; 15:21) and Josephus (*Ag. Ap.* 2 § 175) refer to the practice of Torah reading, but the extent or regularity of such is not at all clear. Specific readings are noted for special dates in *m. Meg.* 3, 4, which, most interestingly, specifies certain passages that are *not* to be translated after their presentation in Hebrew.

102 On the problem of the relationship of the Tetrateuch, Pentateuch, and the Former Prophets, see the following chapter.

103 *Ag. Ap.* 1 § 39.

104 For a discussion of the additional materials supporting this dating, see J. Blenkinsopp, *The Pentateuch: An Introduction to the First Five Books of the Bible* (Anchor Bible Reference Library; New York: Doubleday, 1992), pp. 42–45. The contention by S. Mandell and D. N. Freedman that the division of Primary History (Genesis-Kings) into books occurred prior to 560 BCE goes completely beyond the evidence at hand and is based on their particular reconstruction of the formation of the Pentateuch (*The Relationship between Herodotus' History and Primary History,* p. 121).

105 The following sketch is based on the treatment of the formation of the NT canon by H. Y. Gamble, "Canon (New Testament)," *ABD* I, 853–861.

a distinct break between the emerging rabbinical movement associated with the oral Torah from the very beginning of the spread of Jesus-centered Judaism outside its Palestinian homeland. Additionally, Christian appeals to the writings of Judaism were highly selective, both in terms of content and interpretation, and were most commonly used to support teachings associated with either Jesus or his apostles.

One of the most significant factors in this process which is often overlooked is the basic change that occurred in this Palestinian Jesus-centered Judaism within less than a half-century after the death of its founder. When this movement broke with the Jerusalem cultus,[106] and this process seems to have been under way by the time of the destruction of the Temple in 70 CE, and began to focus on recruiting Gentile members, then it severed, once and for all, the concept of Torah which provided the basis for the Judaism of the Diaspora from which it had originally emerged. If the concept of Torah that has been suggested throughout this argument is accurate, then Torah never existed, nor could it ever exist, apart from its functional application.[107] In other words, in the religious world in which it was created (and which created it), Torah functioned to define Judaism as a living part of culture. To be Jewish was to be separated from other cultural groups by certain ascribed boundaries, created by the application of Torah to community life. By moving into the Gentile world and by breaking from the application of Torah, Jesus-centered Judaism was transformed into Christianity, which developed into a non-Jewish movement. The roots of this shift are reflected in the Pauline presentations in the letters to Galatia and Rome, where Paul clearly rejects the applicability of Torah to Gentile followers of the movement. Rejection of part of the Torah quite naturally transformed the movement's conceptions of the whole.

Christianity's decisions to adopt the Greek version of the Hebrew scriptures as its "Old Testament" allowed it to make particular sets of claims concerning its own integrity as a religious tradition in the Roman empire where antiquity was always viewed as an important legitimating factor.

---

[106] An interesting point to ponder is whether or not the Jerusalem cultus ever really recognized this Jesus-centered movement as an actual movement. Had it not been for the Constantinian elevation of Christianity in the fourth century CE, almost all of our information about this movement might have been lost as it has been with so many of the competing mystery religions of that time.

[107] Much of what is being suggested here is also true of modern Judaism, each form of which is characterized by the ways in which it has chosen to appropriate Torah to the modern world. The past tense is used here for the sake of historical specificity and does not imply anything about the vitality of Judaism in more recent times.

But what Christianity adopted was Pentateuch, *not* Torah. In officially adopting its own canon, an idea only implicit in the Jewish scriptural tradition, Christianity projected its own model onto Judaism, which never really officially designated a particular canon.[108] The contents of the *TANAK,* or threefold division of the Hebrew scriptures, were determined by usage in the formulation of the oral Torah.[109] As far as canon is concerned, in rabbinic Judaism *TANAK* cannot be separated from the complete Torah, which includes the whole of the oral traditions. This may seem minor, but it has had important implications for the history of the development of the historical critical study of the Hebrew bible.

As the historical critical method developed in the post-Enlightenment era,[110] it was adopted mainly by Protestant scholars.[111] In conjunction with the development of the academic study of religions,[112] the practitioners of this method began to apply it to the study of the Hebrew bible and attempted, at the same time, to place their studies on theologically and religiously neutral grounds. What the method was developed to study was the formation and application of a religious document, the Hebrew bible, within the life of a religious community, developing Judaism and its descendants. But it has not been applied to this. Instead, the historical critical method has concentrated on the Pentateuch, i.e., a literary collection that it has divorced from the life of the community that produced it. Perhaps this was an inevitable development, since the community that produced these materials was very different in religious background from those who were and are engaged in this type of study.

108 One of the most common pieces of "disinformation" in the field of biblical studies is the canonical council of Jabneh in *ca.* 90 CE that is commonly cited. The evidence for such a meeting that purportedly set the extent of the Jewish canon is nonexistent. For the development of the idea of such a council, see D. E. Aune, "On the Origins of the 'Council of Javneh' Myth," *JBL* 110 (1991) 491–493.

109 This acronym reflecting such a three-fold division occurs frequently in the Talmudic materials. Often the rabbis would offer verses from each of the three sections in support of their arguments. For references, see "Tanakh," *EncJud* 15:790.

110 A description of the development of this method may be found in J. H. Hayes, *An Introduction to Old Testament Study* (Nashville: Abingdon, 1979), pp. 83–120.

111 On the decidedly Protestant nature of the historical critical method, see the comments of J. Levenson, *The Hebrew Bible, the Old Testament, and Historical Criticism,* esp. pp. 82–105.

112 For a challenging treatment of the development of the "scientific" study of religions, see J. S. Preus, *Explaining Religion: Criticism and Theory from Bodin to Freud* (New Haven: Yale University Press, 1987).

Perhaps the solution is to recognize that the subject of the study of the Hebrew bible is the Hebrew bible *and* the community which used it to define and structure its religious and ethnic identity among competing claims of a variety of cultural and ethnic competitors. At some point in the Persian period, the scribal authorities of Jerusalem, functionaries of the Persian government and connected directly to the temple cultus, were responsible for the formulation of the "Torah of Moses" that was applied to Jerusalem and its environs as the "restoration" cultus granted by the Achaemenid rulers. With this began early Judaism. As this "Torah of Moses" was applied through the auspices of the temple priesthood, it was supplemented with didactic haggadic materials until the Pentateuch took written form sometime in the late fourth or early third century BCE. But this collection of books never stood alone, nor was it ever understood in the forms of Judaism that emerged from this early movement as complete or freestanding apart from the accompanying applications which were preserved in oral form until their commitment to writing between the second and sixth centuries CE. At every point in their development, the accounts contained in the books attributed to Moses were understood as functioning actively in the daily life of those who adopted them. They were not history books—they are the traditions containing the mythographic foundations of Judaism throughout its history.

The historical critical method has lost this insight, and thus lost connection with its own subject. Instead, reified discussions of the composition of the Pentateuch concern themselves with matters of assigning portions of verses to various hypothetically reconstructed sources without ever asking how these matters might have anything to do with the study of religions, let alone with the understanding of human culture. They possibly bear some relevance to the study of how a particular text might have developed within a temporal continuum, but this can apply only to the Pentateuch as understood from a decidedly neutral perspective. Likewise, modern literary interpretations of the Hebrew bible have succeeded in applying modern and post-modern literary theories to the reading of the Hebrew texts, thus making it an interesting text for literary theorists, but divorcing it completely from any functional application it might have had for the communities producing it. Religions are never neutral. The failure to recognize this has led the modern study of the Hebrew bible to misunderstand its own subject.

—— ℬ 3 ℭ ——

TETRATEUCH, PENTATEUCH, PRIMARY HISTORY: IDENTIFYING THE SUBJECT OF STUDY

The connecting link between old and new, between Israel and Judaism, is everywhere Deuteronomy.[1]

I. The Concept of a "Primary History"

The recognition that the identification of the Torah with the Pentateuch is a relatively late phenomenon in the development of the scriptures of emerging Judaism in the Persian and Hellenistic eras necessitates a reconsideration of the narrative materials that presently compose the Tetrateuch and Pentateuch. Further, it requires that some consideration be given to the ways in which those narrative materials might be related to the stories in Joshua through Kings. In their present canonical arrangement, the narratives beginning in Genesis and extending through the book of Kings constitute an account of the origins, development, and history of the people known as "Israel" from their patriarchal beginnings with Abram until their exile from their ancestral land with the defeat of Judah by Babylon. Even the emergence of the patriarch Abram is placed into a larger conceptual background by the "primeval history" in Genesis 1–11, which constructs both a theological and an "historical" background for the creation of both cosmos and ethnos. This "primary history,"[2] as reconstructed by modern scholar-

---

[1] J. Wellhausen, *Prolegomena to the History of Ancient Israel* (Cleveland and New York: World Publishing Co., 1957), p. 362.

[2] This term, "primary history," as a designation for the literature encompassing Genesis through Kings, is adapted from the theory concerning the formation of the biblical corpus advanced by D. N. Freedman ("The Law and the Prophets," *VTSup* 9 [Leiden: E. J. Brill, 1963],

ship, was created when the materials forming the Tetrateuch (Genesis-Numbers) were combined with Deuteronomy and the "Former Prophets" (*hannĕbî'îm hārī'šōnîm;* cf. Zech 1:4).[3] In the field of modern biblical research, however, little beyond this general outline commands a consensus.

While the composite nature of the materials contained in the "primary history" seems beyond dispute in the discipline,[4] the manner in which the sections constituting that history have been "created" remains strongly contested.[5] The narrative events recounted in the Tetrateuch begin with the

---

pp. 250–265; "Canon of the Old Testament," *IDBSup* [New York & Nashville: Abingdon (1975) 130–136]; "The Earliest Bible," in *Backgrounds to the Bible,* ed. M. P. O'Connor and D. N. Freedman [Winona Lake, IN: Eisenbrauns, 1987], pp. 29–37). More recently, S. Mandell and Freedman have argued that this "Primary History" was composed no later than 560 BCE and that it was known by Herodotus (*The Relationship between Herodotus' History and Primary History).* Though Freedman's theory has not, at least to date, gained any wide acceptance, the basic idea of the present canonical unity of these materials and their function as providing the only developed narrative account of "Israel" is beyond dispute. In addition to this primary history, Freedman also argues for the collection of a "prophetic corpus" as a supplement to the "primary history," including such materials as Isaiah of Jerusalem, Jeremiah, Ezekiel, Amos, Hosea, Micah, etc. A consideration of the formation of a "prophetic corpus" as a supplement to the history must be postponed to a later volume.

3 Since the pioneering work of M. Noth, the narrative account contained in the "Former Prophets" has generally been designated as the "Deuteronomistic History" (*Überlieferungs-geschichtliche Studien.* This latter term, most common among scholars today, is actually a "corrective" to Noth's "deuteronomic history" suggested by F. M. Cross and generally accepted today ("The Themes of the Book of Kings and the Structure of the Deuteronomistic History," in *Canaanite Myth and Hebrew Epic,* p. 274; originally published as "The Structure of the Deuteronomic History," *Perspectives in Jewish Learning,* Annual of the College of Jewish Studies, 3 [Chicago, 1968], pp. 9–24).

4 All this intends to state is that in the field of the academic study of the Hebrew bible, the overwhelming majority of scholars recognize that the present literary works constituting that corpus have been composed from a variety of different "sources," oral and/or written, that derive from a variety of disparate settings and dates. The degree to which these sources might be delineated and reconstructed, as well as the appropriate *Sitz im Leben* to which each is to be assigned, are most emphatically *not* matters of consensus. Additionally, the nature of the narratives themselves, i. e., their historicity or historiographic form, remains intensely debated. These issues will be addressed more fully in the following pages.

5 While the debate here commonly juxtaposes writers of the biblical narratives as "authors" or "editors," the real issue seems to concern the matter of "authorial creativity." Are these materials simply "ideational fictions," as argued by H. C. Brichto (*Toward a Grammar of Biblical Poetics: Tales of the Prophets* [New York/Oxford: Oxford University Press, 1992]), or are they reliable historical accounts of actual events (a position rarely taken by critical scholars today)? Though one might think that a position that allows for both the literary creativity of the authors and the historical intentionality of the created text, such as that suggested by M. Steinberg, would be acceptable (*The Poetics of Biblical Narrative,* pp. 23–35), such a position has not gained a large following in biblical studies.

creation of the cosmos (Gen 1:1–2:4a) and end with Israel's arrival at Abel-Shittim on the plains of Moab (Num 33:49), anticipating the entry into the land promised to them by their god. The Pentateuch, on the other hand, begins with the creation and ends with the death of Moses, but with Israel in the same location as at the end of the Tetrateuch (Deut 34:1–9). The death of Moses had been announced in Num 27:12–14 (cf. Deut 32:48–52), but is not recounted until the end of Deuteronomy. On the basis of literary analyses of the pertinent materials, it is difficult to avoid the conclusion that the account of the death of Moses once belonged to the narrative of the Tetrateuch, but has been split from its original literary setting to incorporate the book of Deuteronomy into that otherwise independent corpus.[6] The significance of this editorial redivision of the texts which came to be recognized as the "books of Moses" or Torah should not be underestimated.

If the book of Deuteronomy, and its attendant "historical narratives," was originally an independent narrative tradition that represented a particular "prophetic" viewpoint of Israelite religion and traditions that was in competition with other social and religious world views being formulated at the same time,[7] then it might be possible to suggest a new model for understanding the manner in which the Pentateuch was created. Related to this possibility is the recognition of the transformative effects of the realities of the exile and restoration, situations which necessitated a number of "survival mechanisms" if the exiles from Judah were to be able to maintain a sense of their ethnic identity in the face of great assimilative pressures.[8] If, in its "original" setting, the entirety of Deuteronomy and the deuteronomistic history, as well as selected prophetic works, might be understood as having formed a type of "pre-canonical" collection representing a particular interpretation of "Israelite" history, religion, and identity, the implications for the study of the formation and function of the Pentateuch are several.

> With the publication of the Deuteronomistic corpus in its several parts (law book, history, prophetic collection) we therefore have the following situation: (1) a document claiming immunity from later editorial intrusion containing a law and constitution that may not be altered; (2) a characterization of Moses

---

6 For an analysis of the relevant materials, see J. Blenkinsopp, *The Pentateuch*, pp. 229–231. Blenkinsopp assigns these materials to the "Priestly" narrative, a designation that will be taken up below.

7 For a discussion of these issues, see my arguments in *Narrative History and Ethnic Boundaries*, pp. 32–47.

8 For the major types of "survival mechanisms" documented for groups exiled from their native lands, see above, Chap. 1, p. 12 and n. 35.

as a prophet (Deut 18:15–18; 34:10; cf. Hos 12:13 [H, v 14]) and, corre-spondingly, a redefinition of prophecy as Mosaic; (3) a collection of Mosaic-prophetic books, the exact contents of which are unknown, ending with Jeremiah last of the line; (4) a history of the period subsequent to Moses which depicts it as one of religious infidelity followed by disaster, and there-fore a period which in no sense could be regarded as normative.[9]

If the formulation of such a collection of materials by a deuteronomistic prophetic group is placed during the period of the exile, and it is beyond dispute that the final form of the deuteronomistic history can be dated no earlier than *ca.* 560 BCE, then the Josianic dating of the book of Deuteron-omy, a linchpin of the classical documentary hypothesis for the compo-sition of the Pentateuch, might be open to question.[10] A general sketch of such a model of analysis forms the purpose of the present chapter.

The beginning point for this approach is the recognition that the deuteronomic materials may be understood as representing one particu-lar group's collection, collation, and compilation of "traditional" materials by which that particular exilic or post-exilic population attempted to define and maintain its identity—ethnic, social, and religious—in the face of as-similation by the surrounding cultural milieu in which it was resettled. At the same time, other options, based on differently selected materials, were collected and circulated, assuming their own shapes within the communities that produced them, in efforts to retain those things that formed their identi-

9 J. Blenkinsopp, *The Pentateuch,* p. 235.

10 That the book of Deuteronomy in some form closely resembling its present literary shape was a product of the Josianic reform has been accepted as a basic fact in the field of bibli-cal studies since W. M. L. de Wette first argued this position in his 1805 dissertation (*Dissertatio Critico-Exegetica qua Deuteronomium a prioribus Pentateuchi libris diversum alius cujusdam recentiorois auctoris opus esse monstratur* [Jena: Etzdorf, 1805]). Recent analyses arguing that the deuteronomistic history itself is a product of the exile, and not part of a deuteronomic move-ment associated with Josiah, have not met with widespread acceptance. The most forceful argument dating the history to the period of the exile and suggesting that the "reforms" of Josiah were at best literary creations expanding upon a possible tradition concerning the reality of such a reform is that presented by H.-D. Hoffmann, *Reform und Reformen.* The standard position taken with respect to the deuteronomistic history is that it reflects at least two layers of literary activity; the first and major edition dates to the reign of Josiah (or, according to some, Hezekiah or even Jehoshaphat) and was only retouched in selected places by a minor secondary redaction that may be dated to the period of the exile. For a summary of the variety of expressions that these redactional studies have taken, see S. L. McKenzie, *The Trouble with Kings: The Compo-sition of the Book of Kings in the Deuteronomistic History* (VTSupp 42; Leiden: E. J. Brill, 1991), pp. 1–19.

ties as Judahites. Though our information concerning the status of those who were taken into exile remains rather scant,[11] it seems certain that such competing, and possibly complementing, identity systems would find themselves striving for recognition and priority among those empowered to adopt or reject the traditions that were being recreated and reapplied.

Each of these collections may have drawn upon a number of sources and traditions, written or oral,[12] to compose their accounts, though it must be noted that no such "originals" of any putative sources are extant. Additionally, the artistic and historiographic freedom that might be invoked in the utilization of any types of sources is amply illustrated by a simple comparison of the histories of the Israelite monarchy contained in the deuteronomistic history and in Chronicles. Regardless of the underlying sources for each of these works, there can be little doubt that the social and religious situations of the communities producing these "histories" consciously recreated a past from those sources that would explain and support their present. What the present work will address, however, is not the manner of the composition of the Tetrateuch as a diachronic literary process, but rather the nature of the composition of that work as a communally functional work of religious literature. A delineation of some of the ways in which these materials might have functioned as ideological presentations of particular ethnic ideals might elucidate selected aspects of the community producing them, as well as their social, religious, and historical situations. The approach also has the advantage of avoiding the ongoing debate over the historicity of the events narrated within these materials.

At the same time, the conclusion is unavoidable that these same materials came to be regarded as historiographic and were (and are) accepted by selected groups as historically and religiously normative. The manner in which this occurred is also of interest, for at issue, in a sense, is the underlying question concerning the ways in which groups create and recreate their identities, especially across generational lines. While the vast majority of scholars accept the probability that many of the traditions reflected in the narratives contained in Genesis through Kings accurately reflect historical

---

11 For a survey of the general situations existing among the Judahites, both in exile and in Palestine, see N. P. Lemche, *Ancient Israel: A New History of Israelite Society* (Sheffield: JSOT, 1988), pp. 171–196.

12 The precise nature and number of possible existing "sources" which the authors of the present biblical narratives might have used remain a matter of dispute. On the general types of written documents common to the ancient Near East, see the discussions of J. Van Seters, *In Search of History*, pp. 209–248.

situations and are much older than the period of the exile or later, when they were placed in their present narratological forms, demonstrating this antiquity remains a very difficult matter. That the metaphor of covenant is a formative expression of the relationship between Yahweh and Israel in biblical materials, and especially in the Pentateuch, is beyond dispute, yet there are strong arguments for dating the development of that ideal to the late seventh century BCE and associating it with the deuteronomistic writer(s).[13] Similarly, when the major motifs occurring in the Pentateuchal sources are compared to similar motifs outside of that particular literary work, few if any of the Pentateuchal themes are found in texts dated to the pre-exilic period.[14]

II. Outlining a New Approach: Narrative and Ethnicity

Over the past several decades, a number of scholars have called attention to major problems associated with the dates and literary relationships commonly assigned to the various sources delineated by the proponents of the documentary hypothesis. Recent works like those of Richard Friedman,[15] Robert Coote and David Ord,[16] or, on the more popular level, Harold Bloom[17] depict the earliest written traditions of ancient Israel which are generally attributed to the Yahwistic writer as historical, archaic, and fundamental to an understanding of Israel's earliest religious, political, and historical development. Were one to depend on the analytical presentations of these works, one would remain quite confident that the Yahwistic materials constituted the earliest historical attempt to construct a history of Israel and that these tenth century BCE materials form the basis for understanding the fundamental traditions that underlie the themes of the Pentateuch and form the foundation for reconstructing the earliest religious manifestations of the united kingdom.

The apparent consensus is only that, however, for there are a number of conflicting voices regarding these "early" traditions of "ancient" Israel

13 The strongest presentation of this position is that developed by L. Perlitt, *Bundestheologie im Alten Testament* (WMANT 36; Neukirchen-Vluyn: Neukirchener Verlag, 1969).

14 For a careful cataloguing of these themes, see H. Vorländer, *Die Entstehungszeit des jehowistischen Geschichtswerkes*, and the analysis of the major results of his study by N. P. Lemche in *Early Israel*, pp. 357–385.

15 *Who Wrote the Bible?* (Englewood Cliffs, NJ: Prentice Hall, 1987).

16 *The Bible's First History* (Philadelphia: Fortress, 1989).

17 *The Book of J* (with a translation of "J" by David Rosenberg; New York: Grove Weidenfeld, 1990).

which suggest the need for a new approach to the issues related to the composition and function of the narratives contained in the Pentateuch. As a starting point, this study will incorporate the results of some of those reconsiderations of the formation of the Pentateuch and early Israelite traditions which have questioned the adequacy of the documentary hypothesis as a literary and historical explanation for the formation of the present Pentateuchal accounts of the origins of Israel. As R. Rentdorff has argued,[18] the larger blocks of tradition from which the Pentateuch is formed show little if any continuity among their differing cycles. Rather, it is through the later editorial efforts related to the deuteronomic or Priestly tradents that these stories have been connected and "unified" on a thematic level. The antiquity of such written traditions is also open to question if the arguments of H. H. Schmid are treated seriously.[19] According to Schmid, the Yahwistic materials of the Pentateuch represent a fully developed "theology of history" that could have been produced only *after* Israel's national political history had ended, i.e., during the period of the exile or later.

Schmid's late dating of the Yahwistic traditions, which would be equivalent to Rentdorff's editorial connections of the larger story cycles of the Pentateuch, finds further support in the analyses of the Pentateuchal materials by J. Van Seters. Focusing specifically upon the Abraham traditions and employing exclusively literary criteria for his analysis, Van Seters concludes that the Yahwistic narrative dates to the exilic period and was preceded by an earlier written level of the tradition which the Yahwist supplemented and expanded.[20] Just as important as the literary and exilic nature of the Yahwistic traditions are Van Seters' conclusions with respect to the Elohistic traditions of the Pentateuch. According to Van Seters, this second archaic source, commonly associated with the national history of the northern monarchy of Israel and dated to the mid-ninth century BCE, is simply a second stage in the development of the pre-Yahwistic sources. In other words, the very existence of an Elohistic stratum of the Pentateuch is called into question. Given the recognition that this Elohistic stratum does not in its present form constitute a continuous narrative, its existence as an archaic

---

[18] *Das überlieferungsgeschichtliche Problem des Pentateuch* (BZAW 147; Berlin: de Gruyter, 1977); ET, *The Problem of the Process of the Transmission of the Pentateuch.*

[19] *Der sogennante Jahwist: Beobachtungen und Fragen zur Pentateuchforschung.*

[20] *Abraham in History and Tradition; Prologue to History; The Life of Moses.* According to Van Seters, this exilic Yahwistic work was both pre-Priestly and post-deuteronomistic. As such, it was composed as an introduction to the national history that was the product of the deuteronomistic historian.

narrative source underlying the present form of the Pentateuch must be
challenged.

Such studies suggest the strong possibility, then, that the present form
of the Pentateuch with its stories of the origins of Israel as an identifiable
and distinct people among the nations is not to be dated to the period of the
united monarchies, but rather stems from the period of the exile and later.[21]
In terms of reconstructing the development of Israel's narrative traditions of
its past, this has special importance, for it strengthens the argument of the
present work that the stories of Israel's origins contained in the Tetrateuch,
i.e., Genesis through Numbers, were written during the period of the exile
at the earliest and might be understood as a complement to the "deuteronomistic history" constituting a literary entity that had no independent existence prior to that time.[22] If this is accurate, then those traditional themes
that constitute the Pentateuch[23] functioned in such a way as to provide substance and background to the variety of allusions to them already contained
in the book of Deuteronomy. While it is indeed possible that these traditions concerning the creation of the cosmos, the selection of Abraham, the
genealogy of the twelve tribes, etc., originated at various points in Israel's
history, it seems most likely that their present literary form and functions
cannot be dated prior to the exilic period at best, i.e., to *ca.* 550 BCE.[24] As I
shall argue in the following chapters, a date in the Persian period, possibly
between 520 and 400 BCE, is more probable.

Approached from this perspective, the Tetrateuchal materials in their
present form, as well as the Pentateuchal narratives, formed on the basis of
the Tetrateuch, may be understood as attempts to define the concept of the

21 For an extended critique of the traditional documentary hypothesis, see the treatment
by R. N. Whybray, *The Making of the Pentateuch.*

22 A. D. H. Mayes, *The Story of Israel between Settlement and Exile: A Redactional Study
of the Deuteronomistic History* (London: SCM, 1983), p. 141. A similar position has been taken
by M. Rose, who argues that the "Yahwistic" material was composed to form an introduction
to the deuteronomistic history that extended back to the creation (*Deuteronomist und Jahwist:
Untersuchungen zu den Berührungspunkten beider Literaturwerke* [ATANT 67; Zurich: Theologischer Verlag, 1981]).

23 According to M. Noth (*A History of Pentateuchal Traditions,* pp. 42–62), the earliest of
these themes were the deliverance from Egypt, the guidance into the land, the promises to the
patriarchs, the guidance in the wilderness, and the revelation at Sinai. These were then filled out
in narrative form as the traditions developed in the life of the community.

24 This is not to suggest that the Pentateuchal materials took on their final form at such an
early date. Recent studies strongly suggest that the editorial process associated with the composition of the Pentateuch, and probably all of the materials in the Hebrew bible, continued until at
least the latter half of the third century BCE. On this continuing editorial activity, see the arguments of G. Garbini, *History and Ideology in Ancient Israel,* p. 146.

people "Israel" on the basis of the changing cultural situations introduced by both the exile and the restoration of the Judahite community with the beginning of the Persian period. The impetuses behind the production of these narrative accounts were several. First, as alluded to above and argued in my work on the deuteronomistic history,[25] the threat of ethnic dissolution in the face of the exile gave rise to the production of one particular rendition of Israel's definition and meaning. In addition to this, however, was the necessity to supply some set of defining characteristics for the generation of Judahites who had been born and reared in exile in Babylon,[26] who had no first-hand knowledge of life in Jerusalem or Judah, or of what services at the Temple might have entailed.

The production of the materials in the Pentateuch might be approached in two differing, yet functionally complementary ways. From the perspective of a cultural materialistic analysis, these stories and the "traditions" contained therein might be viewed as superstructural responses to the unavoidable structural shifts that occurred in the society of ancient Judah by virtue of the exile and its attendant modifications of the basic Judahite society and modes of production.[27] From this perspective, four different components universal to all socio-cultural systems may be identified: the etic behavioral infrastructure, structure, and superstructure and the emic superstructure.[28] It is to the realm of the mental and emic component of culture that religions and their symbol systems belong.[29] In the case of the religion of ancient Israel in general, and of the exilic and post-exilic Judahite res-

---

[25] *Narrative History and Ethnic Boundaries,* pp. 32–47.

[26] As was observed long ago by J. Wellhausen, the centralization of worship is first demanded in the deuteronomic corpus, which he dated to the seventh century BCE, and such centralization is presumed by the Priestly writer, which he places in the exilic period (*Prolegomena to the History of Ancient Israel*, pp. 32–38). The general view of scholars has been that the ideal of centralization of worship in Jerusalem corresponded, in some sense, at some period of the history of Judah, to some concept of reality, though the only indications of such an occurrence are found only in the texts under analysis. Recent analyses of a variety of diaspora communities in Egypt and Syria suggest the possibility that Jerusalem was never given the preeminence or exclusivity claimed by the canonical materials by those "peripheral" diaspora groups that were not part of the "official" exilic participants, the latter being responsible for the production of the traditions presently contained in the canon. For these positions, see the arguments of G. Garbini (*History and Ideology*, pp. 133–50) and R. Carroll ("Israel, History of [Post-Monarchic Period]," *ABD* III, 573–576).

[27] For an in-depth presentation of this method, see M. Harris, *Cultural Materialism: The Struggle for a Science of Culture* (New York: Random House, 1979), esp. pp. 46–76.

[28] *Ibid.,* p. 54.

[29] For the differing realms to which religion and its attendant expressions belong, see M. Harris, pp. 53–54. The distinction between "etic" and "emic" as cultural descriptors was first

toration communities in particular, only the emic superstructural elements reflected in the later canonized materials remain from which scholars may reconstruct the other elements of those social units.[30]

The distinctive advantage of the cultural-materialistic analytical approach to the composition of these materials is that it understands the superstructural, or abstract, metaphoric support system of social units as dependent upon the infrastructure (or modes of production) of that unit. When the infrastructure is changed, either voluntarily or involuntarily, there will be attendant modifications to the superstructure, so as to accommodate, explicate, and support the new position. In order for a community to survive the threats to its existence that would result from the transition from being "landed" to "landless," and the concomitant modifications to the basic structures of the group, it would be essential that the symbol system by which the society defined and bounded its identity be flexible enough to accommodate the dictated changes.[31] It is generally accepted that the period of the exile and restoration represents one of the most active epochs in the formation of the identity and religion of early Judaism.[32]

With respect to the traditions contained in the Pentateuch, then, one could argue that the narratives concerning the identity of Israel constructed by these stories complement the emerging description of an "ideal Israel" that was constructed by the deuteronomistic writer(s).[33] Though that set of

made by K. L. Pike, *Language in Relation to a Unified Theory of the Structure of Human Behavior,* 2nd ed. (The Hague: Mouton, 1967). For a discussion of the different usages of these terms, see *Emics and Etics: The Insider/Outsider Debate,* ed. T. N. Headland, K. L. Pike, and M. Harris (Frontiers of Anthropology, 7; New York: Sage Publications, 1990), esp. pp. 28–83.

30 Though it is theoretically possible that archaeological remains might be utilized to reconstruct the structural aspects of the basic modes of production on which these societies were based, the imprecision of modern archaeology to correlate particular structures and units with specific individual social units makes it doubtful that more than a general description of any of the material remains of any one of the above groups will ever be possible.

31 The very flexibility and malleability of the identifying descriptor "Israel" during the first six centuries CE has been demonstrated by J. Neusner ("'Israel': Judaism and Its Social Metaphors," *JAAR* 55 [1987] 331–61). On the significance of such flexibility with respect to ethnicity, see the argument of A. P. Royce (*Ethnic Identity: Strategies of Diversity,* p. 150).

32 At what precise historical point one ceases to talk about Israelite or Judahite religion and begins to designate the religion as Judaism remains extremely unclear. Though it was once standard to refer to the period of Ezra and Nehemiah as the era of the transition from Judahite religion to Judaism, this no longer seems assured. For a discussion of some of the problems associated with the older view, see R. Carroll, "Israel, History of (Post-Monarchic Period)," pp. 573–76.

33 That the Pentateuchal materials may be understood as functioning to define and bound the people Israel as an "ethnic group" will constitute a major portion of the argument of the remainder of this book.

materials erected boundaries for the description of this ideal that tied the identity of Israel to its allegiance to the Torah, as interpreted by the deuteronomistic author(s), it presented the pronouncement of that Torah from a singular prophetic perspective. In its present literary form, Deuteronomy encompasses a single event—the farewell speech of Moses to the people Israel giving them the instructions on how, precisely, they were to obey the Torah in order to receive the promises granted to their ancestors. Though there are frequent allusions to the ancestors and the promises made to them, as well as to specific events which came to form an integral part of the Pentateuchal story as it was finally developed, Deuteronomy does not develop any traditions or narratives about these accounts. This development, in the sense of a complement to, and fulfillment of, a particular emerging conception of Israel, is completed by the Tetrateuch.

The need for some complementing materials for the ideals sketched by the deuteronomistic writer may be illustrated by recognizing the six major elements that have been identified as constituting a fully developed narrative of ethnic and national identity.[34] Though it might seem somewhat obvious, the historical mark of all ethnic groups is a *collective name*. It is this that forms the objectifiable emblem by which one person may identify him/herself with a larger entity, the distinctiveness of which is somehow directly implied, to both insider and outsider, by the designation itself.[35] In the case of the designation "Israel," as it came to be applied to the community reorganized about the Temple complex in the restoration sanctioned by the Persian authorities, it is important to note that there is an implicit claim to some type of ethnic continuity between the returning exiles from Judah who had managed to become "Israelites" during their exile from their ancestral land and those who had borne this name previously.[36] In the deuteronomistic history, the concept of Israel as a single and unified people, both as an ideal and as an historical reality, dominates the construction of that ideal throughout the deuteronomic charter.[37]

In the Tetrateuch, the origins of this ideal unified "Israel" are constructed by tracing the development of the twelve tribes, each the descen-

[34] The following "dimensions" associated with ethnic and national identities are treated in A. D. Smith, *The Ethnic Origins of Nations*, pp. 23–31.

[35] On the complexities involved in "naming," see the discussion of H. R. Isaacs, "Basic Group Identity: The Idols of the Tribe," in *Ethnicity: Theory and Experience*, ed. N. Glazer and D. P. Moynihan (Cambridge: Harvard University Press, 1975), pp. 46–52.

[36] On the variety of usages of "Israel" in the biblical materials, see G. W. Ahlström, *Who were the Israelites?* (Winona Lake, IN: Eisenbrauns, 1986), pp. 85–118, and P. R. Davies, *In Search of 'Ancient Israel'*, pp. 47–50.

[37] *Narrative History and Ethnic Boundaries*, pp. 55–85.

dant of a common individual, to provide each ethnic group with a myth of descent through which the community might develop a common bond that may be traced back into antiquity. While the "tribal" origins of Israel are generally taken as an indicator of the antiquity of the traditions, modern anthropological research with respect to the phenomenon of "retribalization" suggests that this need not be the only approach to the matter.[38] Despite whatever "tribal" traditions might be traceable to a premonarchical past, there are strong arguments that this "ideal" Israel as a unified coalition of tribes is the product of the exilic writers that has been projected to the "Mosaic" period and beyond.[39] As the ethnic entity "Israel," descended from these "tribal" ancestors, required some myth of descent, so too did the "tribal" ancestors themselves. The Tetrateuch provides these myths, tracing, by way of its genealogical structuring devices, the eponymous tribal units not only to Abram, but as far back as Adam.[40] At least in terms of the final shape of the Tetrateuch, then, the role and function of the Priestly writer(s), whose interest in and use of genealogical materials are commonly agreed upon, stand as a critical point in the production of the connected narratives constructing the mythic accounts of the origins of both the tribes and their overarching emblematic name, "Israel." That these mythic depictions of the past are placed in a "primordial" past helps to establish the

---

38 On the concept of "retribalization" as applied to ancient Israel, see the discussion of N. K. Gottwald, *The Tribes of Yahweh: A Sociology of the Religion of Liberated Israel, 1250–1050 B.C.E.* (Maryknoll, NY: Orbis, 1979), pp. 323–327. Gottwald's discussion, however, fails to note that the phenomenon need not be restricted to the earliest period of Israel's existence, but might also have occurred at later periods, e.g., during the exile in Babylon or as a response to the Persian empire's hegemony over the restoration community in Judah. That "traditions," national or ethnic, are often "created" to apply to specific situations is convincingly argued by E. Hobsbawm ("Introduction: Inventing Traditions," in *The Invention of Tradition*, pp. 1–14). Because of the creative and recreative aspects of these kinds of stories in the formation and maintenance of communal identities, it seems best to regard them as mythic in both intention and function. For a discussion of the problems associated with defining myth, especially as it has been applied to the biblical materials, see R. A. Oden, *The Bible Without Theology*, pp. 40–91.

39 This "ideal" is best represented by the deuteronomic materials and the related narratives that are contained in Joshua and Judges.

40 On the use of genealogies, especially the *tôlĕdôt* lists of Genesis, to structure the narrative and to create literary bridges between otherwise unrelated materials, see the work of T. L. Thompson, *The Origin Tradition of Ancient Israel. I. The Literary Formation of Genesis and Exodus 1–23* (Sheffield: JSOT, 1987). The role and function of genealogies in the ancient Near East, as well as the biblical materials, is presented by R. Wilson in *Genealogy and History in the Biblical World* (New Haven: Yale University Press, 1977). As has been well established, genealogies reflect social rather than biological relationships in the ancient world, and were often modified to adjust to changing situations.

claims as absolute, grounded in an ancestral past that is accepted without question.[41]

Through the stories of the patriarchs, Abram, Isaac, and Jacob, the people chosen by Yahweh as his own possession[42] are provided with a genealogical background that develops an additional element in the myths of ethnic and national identity: their claim to be the legitimate possessors of a particular land. Embedded in the traditions that develop Israel's genealogical past are also the claims to the rights of possession of the land of the ancestors. The connection of Israel's religious literature and ethnic identity with the theme of the possession of the land is so widespread that it might have a legitimate claim to being more central to the Hebrew bible than even the concept of covenant.[43] This theme forms a major part of the accounts of the promises to the patriarchs[44] and provides the basis for understanding the exilic and post-exilic presuppositions concerning the right to the land of "Canaan."[45] The stories of the patriarchs, then, construct a "golden age" during which the founders of the community, led directly by the deity, provided three motifs essential to any national or ethnic myth of origins. They located the origins of community *temporally,* describing *when* "Israel" was formed. They also located "Israel" *spatially,* describing *where* the community was created and defining the land to which it laid claim. Finally, they provided the group with a myth of *ancestry,* from which all members of the

---

[41] On the importance of such primordial claims for religious and mythological ideas that serve as foundational expressions of group identities, see M. Eliade, *The Sacred and the Profane: The Nature of Religion* (New York: Harcourt, Brace, Jovanovitch, 1959), pp. 95–99.

[42] The classical expression of Israel as Yahweh's chosen people is found in the book of Deuteronomy (7:6; 14:2; 26:18). For the deuteronomistic language and references, see M. Weinfeld, *Deuteronomy and the Deuteronomic School* (Oxford: Clarendon, 1972), pp. 327–328. Weinfeld discusses the relationship of the deuteronomic ideal of election to other biblical expressions of that concept in *Deuteronomy 1–11*, pp. 60–62.

[43] W. Janzen, "Land," *ABD* IV, 146.

[44] For an analysis of these promises of the land and the primacy of Abram in their formulation, see C. Westermann, *The Promises to the Fathers* (Philadelphia: Fortress, 1980), pp. 142–149. According to the analysis of J. Van Seters, the theme of the promise of the land is a late, exilic creation of the Yahwist, who combined two different traditions of Israel's national origins, one concentrating on the possession of the land by the exodus group, the other on an unconditional promise to earlier ancestors, now represented by the patriarchs (*Prologue to History,* pp. 215–245).

[45] N. P. Lemche has argued that the ethnic term "Canaanite" was also a development of the Persian period and served to designate hostile "ethnic" groups in the post-exilic period who were in competition with the restoration group that produced the "anti-Canaanite" material (*The Canaanites and Their Land: The Tradition of the Canaanites* [JSOTSup 110; Sheffield: JSOT Press, 1991]).

group must be descended.[46] It is through the patriarchal narratives that three of the six elements forming the identity of the people "Israel" are created. Through the accounts of their common genealogical ancestry, the descendants are identified by the collective name "Israel" that binds them both to a particular ancestor, Jacob/Israel, and to a specific territory.

For the creation of a sense of communal solidarity, another essential element in the construction of ethnic groups, two additional components are foundational. Ethnic communities are bound by shared histories and distinctive cultural characteristics. Such historical pasts and cultural continuities must be understood in terms of the manner in which they function not only to maintain communal identities, but also to create such boundaries of distinctiveness. While it is commonly assumed that there must be some historical or traditional continuity with a distinctive past from which ethnic histories and cultural characteristics are derived and the representation and application of those to groups, recent investigations illustrate that this is not necessarily accurate. In the case of distinctive cultural traits, especially those postulated as external emblems (e.g., festivals, circumcision, etc.) or those that are regarded as fundamental values (covenantal obedience, care of the widow and orphan, etc.), studies show that ethnic groups may take these from their own traditions, borrow them from others and apply them to themselves, or simply create them. Likewise, such culturally distinctive traits can be replaced by others over periods of time and changes in circumstances. What is necessary is that a sufficient number of culturally distinct emblems be established to differentiate the group from others, both from an internal and from an external perspective.[47] Such emblems, then, find themselves projected into the "traditional" past and become a part of the history and identity of the group from "primordial times."

---

46 For these characteristics of national and ethnic myths, see A. D. Smith, *The Ethnic Origins of Nations,* pp. 191–192. As Smith notes (pp. 28–29), ethnic groups do not necessarily dissolve when they lose their homelands. Rather, since ethnicity is defined and reinforced through myths, symbols, values, memories, etc., a "land of dreams" can be a more significant symbolic bond than an actual spatial territory. As an example of the way in which texts may "claim" one particular setting, while actually having been written in a much later and very different cultural milieu, see E. ben Zvi's arguments that the lists of Levitical cities and their allotment contained in Josh 21:1–45 are products of the post-monarchic period and do not reflect any earlier "historical" situation ("The List of Levitical Cities," *JSOT* 54 [1992] 77–106).

47 E. E. Roosens, *Creating Ethnicity: The Process of Ethnogenesis,* p. 12. For particular examples of the creation of "traditional" histories by various groups, see the materials in K. Whitelam, "Israel's Traditions of Origin: Reclaiming the Land," *JSOT* 44 (1989) 21–27.

The actual creation of such emblems as distinctive cultural traits and a common shared history will, if the position of the cultural materialist outlined above is taken, be understood as responses to the changing social and material situations which the group was forced to make in reaction to the shifts in the bases of its cultural and economic life. That the Judahites exiled in Babylon, as well as those resettled in Jerusalem by the Achaemenids, represent a group confronted with such a situation seems beyond dispute. What remains debated, and debatable, is the manner in which this community responded to its situation. Scholarship, since the initial formulation of the historical critical method, has agreed that one of the responses on the part of the people in exile was the compilation, in written form, of the traditions of their past which had given shape to their present. The present study will attempt to argue just the opposite. As a response to the threats of assimilation, and, concomitantly, of religious and cultural dissolution associated with the exile and restoration, the Judahite groups associated with Jerusalem compiled a past that was shaped by the needs of their present and which came to constitute the basis for a shared common past for those who would identify themselves with that group.

III. Recreating and Maintaining Ethnic Boundaries

While it may be true that the material culture of the Israelite period was not appreciably affected by the Babylonian destruction of Jerusalem and that life was not significantly changed in Palestine until the emergence of the Persian domination of the area,[48] this is not the situation described in the texts of the Hebrew bible which were produced, at least according to modern theories, by those elements of the population which had been removed from the land. In other words, the ideological presentations of the Hebrew narratives reflect the specific responses of a select group of Judahites that have, by virtue of a number of historical and political developments occurring during the period of the Second Temple, become normative for the ethnic and religious community which developed beginning with that period. That a number of Judahite groups were competing for hegemony over the land and for the right to define "Israel" as it would reshape itself as a result of the loss of the Temple and monarchy, and,

---

[48] E. Stern, *Material Culture of the Land of the Bible*, p. 229.

eventually, as it would redevelop with the restoration of the Temple and some form of hierarchical governmental realignment under the Persians, is well established.[49]

Of additional interest in this regard is the observation that ethnic groups tend to be delineated most clearly in areas that have some form of generalized political development.[50] It is clear that the Persian hegemony over the province of Judah, included in the Trans-Euphrates satrapy "Beyond the River," produced the type of environment in which emerging Judaism could begin to develop and redefine its existence as an ethnic entity distinct from those surrounding it. This development was encouraged, in part, by the Persian administration that insisted upon some form of community self-definition that was expressed by way of a standardized corpus of "traditional law" backed by the central Persian authorities and their representatives.[51] From this perspective, then, it must be noted that one of the initial forces underlying the actual creation of a canon of writings may have been a political action that was imposed upon the developing Palestinian community by a combination of Persian royal administration and a "Jewish colonial elite" that had been trained in the exile and "imported" to Judah.[52] When these factors are considered in relation to the compilation of the final traditions which now form the normative concepts of Israelite origins and religion, there are serious implications for the ways in which these external and internal material changes might have affected the development of those narrative accounts. Israel's self-definition as a people, as it would be recounted in its written "charter," the Hebrew bible, occurred during a period when the population of "Israel" was widely scattered in exile and when Judah, like "Israel," had ceased to be an independent political entity. Though the precise implications remain debated, it is clear that "religious

---

[49] For a presentation of the conflicts that can be traced in the literature of the Hebrew bible concerning the reestablishment of the cultus in Jerusalem, see P. D. Hanson, *The Dawn of Apocalyptic* (Philadelphia: Fortress, 1975), *passim*.

[50] E. E. Roosens, *Creating Ethnicity*, p. 13.

[51] J. Blenkinsopp, *The Pentateuch*, p. 239. On the Persian imperial policy and the social and political changes that occurred in Judah in the late sixth to mid-fifth centuries BCE, see K. G. Hoglund, *Achaemenid Imperial Administration in Syria-Palestine and the Missions of Ezra and Nehemiah* (SBLDS 125; Atlanta: Scholars Press, 1992), pp. 207–240. For Darius as a law "reformer," see the comments by T. C. Young, Jr., "The Consolidation of the Empire and Its Limits of Growth under Darius and Xerxes," *CAH* [2], IV, pp. 90–93. An excellent overview of the reign and achievements of Darius I is given by H. Sancisi-Weerdenburg, "Darius I and the Persian Empire," in *Civilizations of the Ancient Near East*, Vol. II, ed. J. M. Sasson (New York: Scribner's, 1995), pp. 1035–1050.

[52] N. K. Gottwald, *The Hebrew Bible*, p. 437.

traditions stiffened as politico-historical memories faded, and the authority of a text became sacred as other forms of authority were alienated."[53]

If these political and structural backgrounds concerning the life of the group and its development are accurate, even in their most general outlines, then it is clear that the compilation of Tetrateuchal and Pentateuchal materials was the result of a complex nexus of cultural developments. The necessity for consolidating those materials which became a charter for the community that was accepted by the Persian court provided a two-fold reaction: (1) the compilation of "traditions," new or otherwise, to form a unified "history" that contained and legitimated those legal traditions; and (2) an impulse to combine differing versions so as to construct a single tradition that would present the appropriate charter for supporting a diverse community. In the process, a new set of boundaries that defined the people was created and, once it had been accepted by the Persian authorities and implemented by their administrative officials, a new sense of the ideal of "Israel" as a distinct ethnic community came into being.[54]

There can be little doubt that the process itself would have been much more complex than the factors mentioned above would suggest. Since there

---

[53] S. E. McEvenue, "The Political Structure in Judah from Cyrus to Nehemiah," *CBQ* 43 (1981) 364.

[54] To reconstruct the formation of the narrative complexes of the Pentateuch in this way is to recognize the possibility of a generalizable paradigm that underlies the production of much religious literature. Rather than being exceptions, the Tetrateuch and Pentateuch seem to have been formed in some rather common, though rarely recognized ways. Their formation, as well as that of the Hebrew canon as a whole, parallels the creation and maintenance of the Mishnah, itself a product of an "Israel" that was scattered throughout the Roman empire and which had lost all sovereignty as a political entity several centuries prior to the completion of the collection. The way in which the Mishnah functions to define Judaism has been clearly presented by J. Neusner (*The Mishnah*, p. xxix):

> By "Judaism" I mean a world view and way of life formed by a group of people who regard themselves, and are properly regarded by others, as Israelites, in which the life of the group is both defined and explained within the framework of Israel's holiness. By this definition, there have been diverse forms or kinds of Judaism. But from the time of the Mishnah onward, most of these kinds have referred not only to Scripture but also to the Mishnah and its companions, the two Talmuds and cognate writings. So these diverse kinds have formed exemplifications of a single fundamental kind of Judaism. If, therefore, we wish to make sense of nearly all religious expressions of "being Jewish" and nearly all types of Judaism from the second century to the twentieth, we must begin with the Mishnah (though, obviously, we must not end there).

The same arguments might be applied equally well to the formation of the Gospel traditions and the canon of the New Testament, though such clearly lies beyond the scope of the present work.

is evidence that the Pentateuch was still open to modifications as late as the latter half of the third century BCE,[55] then it is clear that caution must be taken in postulating a precise time at which the Pentateuch was completed in its present form. If it is accepted that major portions of the Torah, and possibly sections of the deuteronomistic history, as well as *varia* associated with the remainder of the works in the Hebrew canon, could be dated to a period as late as the 4th–3rd centuries BCE, then a new model for understanding their formation is imperative. With respect to the formation of the Pentateuch, it is important to note the observation of R. Carroll:

> Conventional scholarship favors an earlier dating for Torah but mainly because it insists on viewing Ezra's lawbook as some form of the Pentateuch. There is little or no hard evidence for this claim and its only force is as a commonplace of traditional scholarship. Our ignorance of these matters is almost total, and it is part of the problem of reconstructing the history of the Second Temple period that we know next to nothing about how, when, or why these writings were produced. That they were produced is self-evident, but no *reliable* information is available which would take the matter beyond the level of scholarly hypotheses. From Ezra-Nehemiah to the Qumran scrolls we have a family resemblance of the production of scrolls imposing regulations of purity on the community and differentiating between various groups in a fundamentally sectarian way.[56]

It is precisely the issues of group identification and differentiation that provide the focus of the present attempt to construct another model for understanding the production of the Pentateuch. The Qumran texts provide one of the most important pieces of data for reconstructing the process of the production of the Pentateuch, as well as the processes underlying the formation of the other works in the Hebrew canon. It is these texts, representing fragments from every book of the canon (except Esther) and, in the case of the oldest manuscripts (e.g., 4Q Sam[b], 4Q Jer[a], 4Q Ex[b]) dating to the end of the 3rd century BCE, that provide the earliest evidence that the Pentateuch had been completed in basically the form in which we now have it.[57] Additionally, such texts as 1QS and 4QMMT[58] illustrate the ongoing

55 See above, n. 24.

56 "Israel, History of (Post-Monarchic Period)," *ABD* III, 572.

57 J. J. Collins, "Dead Sea Scrolls," *ABD* II, 89. Important to note in this regard is the fact that the biblical texts from Qumran also illustrate that the Hebrew text exhibited a great deal of diversity in form into the first century CE.

58 1QS (*serek hayyaḥad* [Manual of Discipline]) and 4QMMT (*miqṣat maʿăśê hattôrâ*, "some of the precepts of the Torah").

process of identification and definition within the larger Jewish community of the period, as well as the variable contents of the Torah. Dating the materials in the Pentateuch to the era of the Second Temple, and at some point prior to the middle third century BCE, allows for the construction of a theory that can address two of the major thematic developments evident in that body of material—temple/cultus and identity.

It is through this series of developments, which covered several generations in the process of its legitimization and institutionalization,[59] that a new "Israel" emerged and took a definitive form during the Persian period, basing its identification on the boundaries that were defined in the collected materials of the Pentateuch. This is not to suggest that the formation of the Pentateuch, or even its adaptation as scripture,[60] is to be interpreted as creating any monolithic set of boundaries for the emerging communities that would be united by the collective designation "Israel." Instead, it must be recognized that these boundaries, sometimes themselves offering competing claims,[61] provide a type of definitive base from which different groups could create the distinctions by which they defined themselves as members of this collective entity "Israel" that became the ethnic descriptor for a variety of communities.

A full consideration of the ways in which the various groups during the Second Temple period interpreted these materials lies beyond the boundaries of this study. This work, instead, will concentrate on the communities associated with the Babylonian exile and the Jerusalem restoration community, which seems to have been the one that was responsible, ultimately, for the production of the Pentateuch as it presently stands. Obviously, such a

---

59 For these processes by which reality is socially constructed, and by which identity is defined and codified, see P. L. Berger and T. Luckmann, *The Social Construction of Reality: A Treatise in the Sociology of Knowledge* (New York: Doubleday, 1966), pp. 47–128.

60 The precise point at which any portion of the Hebrew bible was adopted as "scriptural" or the exact ways in which such "scriptures" might have functioned in early Judaism remain open to debate. As M. Goshen-Gottstein notes, the matter of biblical or scriptural authority has not been an issue for Judaism since Tannaitic times (*ca.* 1st century CE). Though the written word was presumed as the source of religious authority, its application was determined by the oral interpretations of the great rabbis ("Scriptural Authority [Judaism]," *ABD* V, 1017).

61 As will be developed in the subsequent chapters of this work, there are numerous places where one set of traditions has been adjusted or corrected by the incorporation of competing sets of claims or practices. Hence, within the Pentateuch, differing ideas concerning sacrifice, festivals, etc., point to ongoing processes of self-definition that play a significant role in the formation of the materials in their final form. On this phenomenon, see J. Van Seters, "Tradition and Social Change in Ancient Israel," *Perspectives in Religious Studies* 7 (1980) 96–113.

consideration has to be somewhat hypothetical, since there exists no direct empirical evidence for either the composition of the Pentateuchal traditions or the ways in which they were applied within the community. Additionally, the probability of distinctions implied by the observations noted above concerning the etic and emic aspects of religion and social life provides a constant reminder that what the written and traditional prescriptions of a religious community are and how the religion is lived and practiced are often two very different things.

Several additional qualifiers must be added to the description of the community that was responsible for producing this literature. Given our present state of knowledge, it seems highly likely that the image of those "Judahite" descendants who "returned" from the exile in Babylon to reconstitute their traditional cultus and religion as a result of the beneficent policies of the Persian king Cyrus has been highly idealized. While there is evidence suggesting that Cyrus took a moderately benign course with respect to the reestablishment of traditional worship by groups he had subjugated, it is also probable that he was following a policy that had been successfully practiced by his Assyrian predecessors. In cities that occupied strategic positions in areas of unrest or possible international conflict, privileges and/or exempt status were often granted by the authorities.[62] If Jerusalem were to have been identified as such a strategic city, then it is possible that its reestablishment is to be understood in terms of the military and economic policies of the Achaemenids. It is clear that the Persian administrative structure of Palestine continued the basic divisions of that area that it had inherited from the Assyrian period, though it developed them more fully.[63] Approached from this perspective, then, the "return" from exile takes on a very different cast. It is possible to understand the reestablishment of Jerusalem as a strategic military and political act by the Achaemenid rulers by which they hoped to establish a base of operations in a potential frontier

---

[62] A. Kuhrt, "The Cyrus Cylinder and the Achaemenid Imperial Policy," *JSOT* 25 (1983) 93–94.

[63] E. Stern, *Material Culture of the Land of the Bible*, p. 240, and "New Evidence on the Administrative Division of Palestine in the Persian Period," *Achaemenid History IV: Center and Periphery* (Proceedings of the Groningen 1986 Achaemenid History Workshop), ed. H. Sancisi-Weerdenburg and A. Khurt (Nederlands Instituut voor het Nabije Oosten: Leiden, 1990), p. 221. The major sources available for the study of Palestine in the Persian period are presented by P. R. Ackroyd, "The Written Evidence for Palestine," *Achaemenid History IV*, pp. 207–220. An overview of this general period is given by I. Eph'al, "Syria -Palestine under Achaemenid Rule," *CAH* [2] IV, pp. 139–164. For a discussion of the problems associated with a reconstruction of the exact boundaries of Judah in this period, see Stern, pp. 245–250.

area.[64] Such an effort would fit well with the archaeological evidence that Persian troops were garrisoned in a series of permanent fortresses located in Kadesh Barnea, Beersheba, and Arad, among other locations in Judah.[65] These data suggest that the observations concerning the "returnees" made by P. R. Davies be taken very seriously:

> Hence, the 'returnees' to Yehud were not necessarily Judaean 'exiles' coming home, beneficiaries of an enlightened policy of repatriation of wronged exiles, but subjects of transportation, moved to underdeveloped or sensitive regions for reasons of imperial economic and political policy. Perhaps the ancestors of these new immigrants did come from Judaea, as the biblical literature insists, but that should not be assumed. . . . For whether originally from Judah or not, these people or their descendants would be likely to believe, or to claim that they were indigenous. Indeed, the Persians may well have tried, in order to facilitate compliance with the process, to persuade these transportees that they were being resettled in their 'homeland'. . . .[66]

In order for these newly settled groups to establish their claims to the land, as ascribed by their Persian overlord, it would be necessary to develop a symbol system that would support their claims to being the "original" inhabitants of the district. It was through the composition of a variety of mythic accounts of their ancestral past that this "Israel" developed its claims to being the genealogical descendants of the original "exiles" from the area

---

[64] A. Kuhrt, "The Cyrus Cylinder," p. 94. Kuhrt notes that the most likely candidate for trouble would have been Egypt. It is equally possible that this militarization of Judah was in response to the challenge of Greece for supremacy along the Mediterranean seaboard (see K. Hoglund, "The Achaemenid Context," in *Second Temple Studies*, ed. P. R. Davies [JSOTS 117; Sheffield: JSOT, 1991], pp. 63–64.

[65] E. Stern, *Material Culture of the Land of the Bible*, p. 240.

[66] *In Search of 'Ancient Israel'*, pp. 78–79. In a later context (p. 112), Davies states:

> The truth about the society of Yehud is this, then: it is an erstwhile Babylonian province shorn of its ruling class and governed by Babylonians, now become a Persian province and receiving a new population transplanted by the Persians with funds to build a Temple and the city of Jerusalem. This society is constituted by a fundamental contradiction: its élite is aware of its alien origin and culture, but its *raison d'être* implies indigenization: the Persians want the immigrants to accept their new land as their own. So, no doubt, do the immigrants themselves, since it is to be their land. I have raised, and set aside, the question of whether these immigrants were really descended from the Judaean deportees. The Persians probably told them that they were, they may have believed it themselves, and it may have been true. But whether or not this were the case, they would have made that claim anyway, and the claim itself is therefore no evidence.

of ancient Judah.[67] Even were this claim to be true in selected instances, it would still require some method of establishment, for these new "Judahites" were some sixty years removed from their ancestral birthrights. Some, if not all, of the returnees, then, represented second-, or even third-generation descendants from the groups removed by the Babylonians from the city and environs of Judah beginning in 597 BCE.

In order to explain the development of a body of literature that would function to define this group who had been established to advance the political and economic policies of the Achaemenid dynasty,[68] some centralized institution must be posited. The reason for this is generally overlooked, especially given the overstated views of the role and function of literacy in the ancient world.[69] In the ancient Near East, writing was the function of the scribal guilds, and these were supported by the patronage of politically empowered organizations, like the palace or the temple.[70] Such an official role for the scribes does not necessitate a completely monolithic view of the process of the composition of the materials. Given the diversity of the types of materials contained in the Hebrew bible, it seems likely that scribes from a number of differing circles or guilds (priestly, prophetic, wisdom, etc.) were responsible for the formation and transmission of the materials.[71]

67 As noted above, it is the change in the modes of production, i.e., in the basic structural patterns which define the possibilities of social organizations, that determines the mythic superstructural elements that are developed to support and to sustain the cultural patterns that were created and enforced by either political, geographic, or ecological (or a combination of all three) boundaries and realities.

68 On the structure of the Achaemenid social world, see P. Briant, "Social and Legal Institutions in Achaemenid Iran," in *Civilizations of the Ancient Near East,* Vol. I, ed. J. M. Sasson (New York: Scribner's, 1995), pp. 517–528; T. C. Young, Jr., "Persians," in the *Oxford Encyclopedia of Archaeology in the Ancient Near East,* Vol. IV, ed. E. M. Meyers (New York/Oxford: Oxford University Press, 1997), pp. 295–300; and the more extensive presentation in M. A. Dandamaev and V. G. Lukonin, *The Culture and Social Institutions of Ancient Iran* (English ed. by P. L. Kohl; Cambridge/New York: Cambridge University Press, 1989), esp. pp. 96–130.

69 See, for example, the position taken by A. Demsky, who suggests that the presence of an alphabetic writing system in Israel led to a form of widespread "passive" literacy and that during the final two centuries of the monarchy, Israel could be termed a literate society ("Writing in Ancient Israel and Early Judaism: Part One: The Biblical Period," in *Mikra* [CRINT, sec. 2; Assen/Maastrict/Philadelphia: Van Gorcum/Fortress, 1988], pp. 10–16). For a more balanced position on literacy in ancient Israel, see above, Chap. 1, n. 32, and Chap. 2, n. 52.

70 It is important to note that in the ancient world, the distinction between palace and temple is not nearly so clear as we tend to conceive of it in the modern West. Instead, the temple, along with its staff, was a direct extension of the palace and served at the pleasure of the ruling dynasty.

71 M. Fishbane, *Biblical Interpretation in Ancient Israel* (Oxford: Clarendon Press, 1985), pp. 78–84. Included in the scribal functions, as Fishbane notes, is the process of interpretation and clarification, some examples of which found their ways into the texts themselves.

No matter how one distinguishes among the possible types of scribes responsible for the production of the biblical materials, certain implications should not be overlooked. If, as is commonly accepted, these scribes constituted an intellectual, trained elite, and if, in ancient Judah, the literacy rate may be accurately estimated at approximately five percent, then the biblical materials must be understood as the product of this very restricted scribal *intelligentsia*.[72] That the materials in their final forms would present a particular, though not always consistent, ideological view would be expected. To a high degree, the scribal schools would reflect the ideological positions of their benefactors.[73]

In the case of reconstituted Judah, it may be possible to make a partial distinction between palace and temple and the patron of the scribal elements. While the Persian palace and royal household remained in the several established royal cities of Persia, they administered their realm through a variety of officials trained at their court.[74] In the case of the administration of Judah, the temple itself seems to have been the focus of the administrative personnel, making the province of Judah a "temple-community" not unlike others established by the Persian authorities.[75] The scribal guilds, along with whatever archives might have existed, would have been situated within this temple-community context, creating a highly specialized and socially privileged group that was separated from the remainder of the society of the district.[76]

The implications that this social bifurcation carries for understanding the composition of the Tetrateuch, as well as the collection and collation of other books that would form the authoritative texts of the community, must not be overlooked. They were the products of this elite, separate, temple supported, professional cadre of scribes. To conceive of the creation of the Tetrateuch as some type of popular movement is to fail to place its

---

[72] P. R. Davies, *In Search of 'Ancient Israel'*, pp. 101–105.

[73] That a group of specialized personnel should be responsible for the development of the traditions embodying the "theories" underlying the "identity" of Israel is to be expected. Because of the complexities associated with the legitimization of social world systems, the process is often performed by specialists (P. Berger and T. Luckmann, *The Social Construction of Reality*, pp. 94–95).

[74] On the Persian administration of Palestine, see H. G. M. Williamson, "Palestine, Administration of (Persian)," *ABD* V, 81–86, and above, n. 63.

[75] J. Blenkinsopp, *A History of Prophecy in Israel*, p. 227. For a more detailed discussion of the type of economy that may have accompanied this political and social form, see Blenkinsopp's discussion in "Temple and Society in Achaemenid Judah," in *Second Temple Studies*, pp. 22–53.

[76] See above, Chap. 2, n. 83.

production within the context of its own creative world. It is also to fail to understand that in the ancient Near East, the temple served as a symbol of social order that tended to authenticate and legitimate the system establishing that order.[77] In such a powerful symbolic role, the temple, and those associated with it, were in a distinctly privileged position to be able to define membership and identity within the "inner circle."

It is precisely within this temple segment of the society that the origins of the Hebrew bible are to be located.[78] Directly pertinent to this identification is the issue of ethnicity and ethnic distinctiveness as a politically expedient implement. The Achaemenid rulers, to facilitate the productivity of a region, often maintained ethnically identifiable communities, which they could tax and regulate as corporate units. To insure such distinctiveness, they would also relegate such peoples to their own specific settlements.[79] It is quite possible that the group returned by the Persians from the exile and settled in Jerusalem were intended to constitute such an ethnic unit. If so, this "exiled" group would have been given the responsibility of rebuilding the Temple to the exclusion of the indigenous population.[80] With such a group claiming descent from the "original" Judahites who had been taken into exile in control of the Temple and the revenues that it generated on behalf of the Achaemenids, issues of descent and membership would become tantamount to any concept of political empowerment.[81]

---

77 R. A. Horsley, "Empire, Temple and Community—But No Bourgeoisie! A Response to Blenkinsopp and Petersen," in *Second Temple Studies*, p. 170.

78 This is not to suggest that the variety of traditions that compose the Hebrew bible were simply created whole cloth during this period by a group of manipulative, self-serving scribal elitists at the behest of a Persian imperial mandate. Indeed, many of the traditions may be quite ancient. I am arguing, however, that the present form of the books contained in the Hebrew bible may well approximate the original forms which they took. These "originals" would have been produced by the Persian-trained post-Babylonian "Judahite" officials who were charged with maintenance of the Temple complex. The books would, most naturally, reflect the political, religious, and ethnic ideologies and beliefs of that group.

79 K. Hoglund, "The Achaemenid Context," 65–66. Hoglund also points out the "ruralization" of the population of Yehud, a decentralization of the population that is evidenced by the increased settlements in new sites during the Persian period that are in direct contrast to the settlement patterns in other areas of Palestine during this same era (pp. 57–58).

80 J. Blenkinsopp, "Temple and Society in Achaemenid Judah," 40. It is possible that this forced resettlement of Judahites in Jerusalem, with the explicit responsibilities of establishing a temple-based economy to provide revenues for the Persian crown, might be directly related to the ruralization process mentioned in the previous note.

81 Blenkinsopp (*Ibid.*, p. 45 and n. 3) argues that the members of the *qāhāl* ("assembly"), which controlled the Temple management, were, in ideal terms, the *běnê haggôlâ/běnê gālûtāʾ*

In order to appreciate the elitist nature of the ethnic mythologies created by this privileged group, one must realize that the Temple in Jerusalem, despite the common presupposition in the literature of that day (and the presuppositions of scholars today), was not the only Temple associated with early Judaism or with the descendants of Judah and Israel.[82] Likewise, the process of the reformulation of the Temple during the Achaemenid rule is not a phenomenon unique to Judah, a factor that needs to be addressed in an assessment of the historical significance of materials contained in the books of Ezra and Nehemiah. An inscription on a votive statue of one Udjahorresne, an Egyptian nobleman who was appointed by the Persian king Cambyses as a courier and a priest of the goddess Neith and whose tenure carried on into the reign of Darius I, gives the account of how Udjahorresne was commissioned to renew the cult of Neith in its dynastic sanctuary and to reorganize the institutions of the scribes and religious instruction as part of Darius' new order concerning the collection and implementation of traditional Egyptian law.[83] The parallels of Udjahorresne's mission with those of Nehemiah and Ezra are both apparent and important.[84] Notable also in this respect is the evidence from the so-called Demotic chronicle, an Egyptian papyrus from a later period, which contains an account of Darius' order that the wisest men of Egypt put the entirety of Egyptian law into writing.[85] Such matters would seem to indicate the possibilities that some of the basic outlines of the careers of Ezra and Nehemiah, most commonly associated with the completion of the Pentateuch in its final form, are to be understood against the background of Persian imperial policy rather than as accounts of pious Judahite descendants attempting to preserve their religious past.

(Ezra 1:11; 2:1=Neh 7:6; Ezra 3:8; 4:1; 6:16, 19–21; 8:35; 10:7, 8, 16). Membership in this group would be defined over against others of the region by way of genealogies and lists which would allow for the processes of inclusion and exclusion of individuals and families. There seems to be support for a position like this in the possibility that the *bêt 'ābôt* may be the product of the Persian period and the formation of such ethnic collectives as the *gôlâ* group in Judah (P. R. Davies, *In Search of 'Ancient Israel'*, pp. 79–80); this possibility was originally suggested by J. Weinberg, "Das *Bēit 'ābōt* im 6–4 Jh. v. u. z.," *VT* 23 (1973) 400–414. N. Gottwald has argued that the *bêt 'ābôt* constituted the "basic economic unit in the Israelite social system" and was thus an essential element in the premonarchic structure of Israel (*The Tribes of Yahweh*, p. 292).

[82] See above, Chap. 2, n. 62.

[83] For the text of this inscription, see M. Lichtheim, *Ancient Egyptian Literature, Vol. III: The Late Period* (Berkeley/Los Angeles: University of California Press, 1980), pp. 36–41.

[84] These parallels are presented and discussed by J. Blenkinsopp, "The Mission of Udjahorresnet and Those of Ezra and Nehemiah," *JBL* 106 (1987) 409–421.

[85] G. Widengren, "The Persian Period," p. 515.

Within this context, the composition of the Pentateuchal materials must be explained. Given the recent assaults on the integrity of the standard documentary hypothesis and the dating schema given its component parts,[86] it is apparent that any explanation will be somewhat tentative and hypothetical. Nonetheless, the social and religious situations outlined above should provide an adequate background for beginning a new paradigm for understanding the production of the materials in the Hebrew bible.[87] Critical to the development of this model is the recognition of the elite nature of the group that originally produced the document and the ways in which the Temple and cultus of Jerusalem became an "emblem of collective identity."[88] The compilation of the legal traditions of the past and the collation of the variety of "histories" of the peoples that would constitute the inner core of the restoration community, under the patronage and auspices of the Achaemenid rulers and their representatives, were undertaken by the professional scribes associated with the Persian administration. To fulfill their responsibilities to develop the ethnic and legal materials required by the Achaemenids and to secure their positions of power in the temple community created and sustained by the Persians, the scribal elements of the restoration period created the Tetrateuchal materials to supplement the narrative traditions contained in the deuteronomistic history.[89]

86 A convenient summary of the situation is contained in D. A. Knight's "The Pentateuch," in *The Hebrew Bible and Its Modern Interpreters*, ed. D. A. Knight and G. M. Tucker (Philadelphia/Chico, CA: Fortress/Scholars Press, 1985), pp. 263–296. In addition to this, one might consult the discussion in A. F. Campbell and M. A. O'Brien, *Sources of the Pentateuch*, pp. 1–20, and above, Chap. 1, n. 20.

87 A continuing issue that demands the attention of scholars, but which has gained little or no attention in the literature, is the precise process by which written sources are transformed into normative scripture. While it is simple to appeal to some ideal such as social attribution of authority, this is so abstract and vague as to be worthless.

88 Though W. Burkert originally applied this phrase to the understanding of Greek temples, it is most appropriate for the analysis of the Temple and cultus as it is developed in the literature of the restoration Judahite community (*Temple in Society*, ed. M. V. Fox [Winona Lake, IN: Eisenbrauns, 1988], p. 44).

89 T. C. Young, Jr. describes the Persian policy of governing subject groups beginning with Cyrus as follows:

> In sum, Cyrus' organizational policy may be described as one in which if you paid your taxes, offered due and appropriate homage to the Great King, remained a loyal subject of the empire, and, at least in some cases, did military service, you were allowed to follow your own customs, and to a considerable extent, pursue your own forms of government and law.

("The Early History of the Medes and the Persians and the Achaemenid Empire to the Death of Cambyses," *CAH*[2] IV, p. 43).

It must be admitted that the dating of the production of the deuterono-mistic history itself is open to debate. There exists no empirical evidence to demonstrate that it must have been created prior to the Tetrateuchal or Pentateuchal materials. There are, however, several possible indicators that this may have been the case. As is well established, there are a number of places in the Tetrateuch that cannot be explained on the basis of the sources generally associated with the documentary hypothesis. Likewise, a number of these materials have been associated with the "deuteronomistic school."[90] The possibility of deuteronomistic editing of portions of the Tetrateuchal materials suggests that a group familiar with Deuteronomy and the deutero-nomic language may have been responsible for the incorporation of the Tetrateuchal materials as a prologue to the deuteronomistic history.[91]

Additionally, the possibility must be entertained that the production of these narratives did not take place over the span of centuries, nor does the Pentateuch as we possess it represent either a combination of originally independent and parallel narrative accounts or a traditional collection of an-cient traditions that have been carefully recorded and retained over the his-tories of Israel and Judah. Within the context of the scribal guilds supported by the Achaemenid rulers and charged with the responsibilities of support-ing the Persian governors and officials established in the Jerusalem Temple community, the narrative traditions of the Pentateuch might rather have developed more or less simultaneously over a period of only several gener-ations rather than centuries.[92] With this vision of the community and its structure in mind, the role of "Ezra," the "scribe" (*sōpēr*), might be under-stood as constituting the beginning of the process of the compilation of the Pentateuch rather than representing its completion. Likewise, Nehemiah, the contemporary of Ezra,[93] represented the Achaemenid efforts to reor-

---

90 These texts, along with annotations, are conveniently grouped in A. Campbell and M. O'Brien, *Sources of the Pentateuch*, pp. 195–201.

91 It must also be admitted that these "deuteronomistic" texts could have been produced by a later editor familiar with the deuteronomic corpus who chose to imitate the deuteronomic language at certain textual junctures. As J. Van Seters has argued, a late date for the Yahwist that is post-deuteronomistic would explain why sections of the Tetrateuchal narrative appear to be acquainted with the deuteronomistic material and style without having to resort to a theory of deuteronomistic editing of the Tetrateuch (*The Life of Moses*, pp. 11–12).

92 P. R. Davies, *In Search of 'Ancient Israel'*, p. 124.

93 Despite the continued problems scholars encounter in their attempts to unravel the lit-erary jumble created by the present arrangement of the various strands of the story created in the books of Ezra and Nehemiah, it is indeed clear that in the form in which the books have been preserved in the canon, the careers of Ezra and Nehemiah are intended to overlap.

ganize and reestablish the temple community that was in turmoil during the early years of the reign of Darius I (cf. Haggai; Zechariah 1–7). If approached in this manner, the Pentateuch and deuteronomistic histories, combined to form a "primary history" that claimed indigenous status for those who produced it and which traced their claims to the land and to some type of social privilege all the way from Abram to the exile, may be understood in light of other contemporary "histories" produced in the ancient world.

Apart from the deuteronomistic history, the Pentateuch exists in a "kind of limbo,"[94] for it remains unique in the ancient world. Combined with the deuteronomistic history as a prologue, however, the Pentateuch constitutes a "primary history" that reflects a pattern of national history, tracing its origins back to the creation, that became standard in the ancient Near East and remained so long after the biblical period. As such, it might be compared to the *Babyloniaka* of Berossus or the *Aigyptiaka* of Manetho, each of which was produced during the Hellenistic period.[95] Like these "primary histories," the Pentateuch and deuteronomistic history locate the story of a particular national group within the larger context of world history. In doing so, the histories combine numerous different genres of material, from the mythic to the annalistic, to form a complete story of the nation's past.[96]

It is precisely by creating this past that the ideological accounts of this "primary history" form the bases for the maintenance of the ethnic identity of the present. This function of the Pentateuch should not be lost. It not only defines a people, but also provides a very particularistic view about reality and the shape of human existence.[97] Tradition associated with this history became accepted as the "law of Moses" and as the "law of the land." Though the exact point at which this occurred remains conjectural, it

94 R. N. Whybray, *The Making of the Pentateuch*, p. 241.

95 The *Babyloniaka* of Berossus was written for the Seleucid king Antiochus I (*ca.* 280 BCE), and extended from the creation down through the Persian period. Manetho's *Aigyptiaka*, written *ca.* 270 BCE, traced the beginnings of Egypt back to the rule of the gods and spirits, and then through the thirty known historical dynasties lasting through the Persian period (J. Blenkinsopp, *The Pentateuch*, p. 41). That these Hellenistic phenomena suggest that the Biblical historiography should be dated even later than the Persian period remains a real possibility. As R. Carroll points out, the "ideology of concealment" that projects the materials into a distant past permeates the literature of the Hebrew bible and can, if not critically addressed, lead to the assignment of materials to periods in which they were not actually created ("Israel, History of [Post-Monarchic Period]," p. 576).

96 For a discussion of Mesopotamian and Egyptian historiography and the variety of materials produced by these societies, see the summaries by J. Van Seters, *In Search of History*, pp. 55–99, 127–187.

97 D. J. A. Clines, *The Theme of the Pentateuch*, pp. 104–105.

is clear that by the mid-second century BCE, debates over the meanings of this law had become central concerns for the major elements constituting sectarian Judaism in the areas associated with Jerusalem and the Temple there. The fact that numerous sectarian documents from Qumran quote canonical materials and debate their meanings, over against competing claims of other sectarian Jewish groups, demonstrates that portions of the "primary history" had already gained some degree of authoritative status by this point in the history of the religion of Judah.

How, then, might one proceed in arguing the "who, when, where, and why" that underlie the production of this "primary history" and the "what" from which the history was produced? If the challenges to the documentary hypothesis are taken seriously, then it is possible that there were no continuous accounts of Israel's past that can be designated as "Yahwistic," "Elohistic," or "Priestly," which were later conflated by some unknown exilic tradent. Instead, it is possible that the "Priestly" materials do not represent a continuous account at all.[98] Likewise, it appears that the "Yahwistic" narratives might better be conceived of as a collection of related traditions than as a continuous source and that the "Elohistic" stratum might be absorbed into the "Yahwistic" redactional process. Of the major sources associated with the classical form of Pentateuchal criticism, this leaves only the "deuteronomic" source as a complete narrative unit with which one might begin.

As suggested above, it is with these deuteronomic materials that the present analysis will begin. Though the exact point of the production of the deuteronomic corpus must remain open to question,[99] the final history itself can be dated no earlier than 560 BCE. As a "primary history," however, the deuteronomistic work is incomplete. Through a process of compilation of a variety of archival sources available in the Temple complex in Jerusalem, scribal groups, under the auspices of Persian officials, like the governor Nehemiah or the scribe/priest Ezra, produced a prologue, in the form of the

---

[98] This position is argued by F. M. Cross in *Canaanite Myth and Hebrew Epic*, pp. 293–325. I. Engnell argued to replace the entire source hypothesis by arguing that "P" and "D" should be understood as collectors of oral traditions responsible for the compilation of the Tetrateuch and the deuteronomistic history respectively ("The Pentateuch," in *A Rigid Scrutiny: Critical Essays on the Old Testament* [Nashville: Vanderbilt University Press, 1969], pp. 50–67).

[99] See above, n. 10. Despite the continued arguments that an "old core" of Deuteronomy (chaps. 12–26) contains much archaic material, in its present form the book of Deuteronomy has been structured as a farewell speech of Moses to provide an ideological base for the presentation of the history which follows. On the dating of the book of Deuteronomy, see M. Weinfeld, *Deuteronomy 1–11*, pp. 1–17.

Tetrateuch, which completed the ethnic myth of Israel and provided a set of internal and external boundaries by which membership in the community could be defined.

The materials upon which this prologue was based were of a variety of genres, both written and oral, which would have been accessible to professionally trained scribes and upon which they could have drawn as needed to produce a final history of Israel from the creation until the loss of the nation state.[100] What the critic must come to terms with, then, is that there are, in all probability, no written sources to reconstruct, nor are there identifiable redactional layers that might be associated with various historical periods, at least not in the ways that have been done in the past. Additionally, terms like Tetrateuch, Pentateuch, and Hexateuch may have to be abandoned, at least in their traditional usages, since they are based upon the extent to which the "Yahwistic" and "Elohistic" sources could be traced.

Instead, the "primary history," beginning with the deuteronomistic corpus, presents the major literary tradition with which the scholar must begin to work.[101] Admittedly, within that corpus there are discernible shifts in style, vocabulary, genre, etc., which have been, and still may be, assigned to particular styles of presentation that may reflect particular traditional materials or sources from which the present sections were derived when the "primary history" was being composed. Because of this, the following analysis will concentrate on the ways in which these various "styles" or literary "tendencies" have been interwoven to form a composite history that constituted a complete ethnic myth. As the Achaemenid policy eventually required the codification and standardization of a corpus of "traditional" law that defined local population groups,[102] the scribes responsible for composing those materials simply detached Deuteronomy from its position as a prologue and encapsulated it into a new document that would satisfy Persian requirements. In doing so, they created a Pentateuch that became the new model for establishing the ethnic boundaries of the group and which came to be identified, at a much later period, with the Torah.

100 Given the Achaemenid suzerainty and patronage of the Temple and the accompanying scribal guilds, it is not surprising that the deuteronomistic history ends on the ambiguous note of Jehoiachin's release from prison in Babylon and his situation at the table of the king. Messianism, or even the expectation of the restoration of a monarchy, is couched in cleverly ambiguous terms, in the covenantal grant of perpetuity to the Davidic line in 2 Samuel 7.

101 In conjunction with this, I would argue that the designation "Pentateuch" is simply a scholarly term developed to attempt to explain why Judaism identified this collection with the Torah and then separated it from the remainder of the Tanak and that it is based ultimately on religious judgments rather than upon the ability to delimit particular narrative sources.

102 J. Blenkinsopp, *The Pentateuch*, p. 239.

—— ঙ 4 ড ——

THE PRIMEVAL HISTORY—ORIGINS AND RELATIONSHIPS: STABILITY AND CHAOS AS DEPENDENT UPON OBEDIENCE

I. A Sketch of the Sources

It should be noted clearly at the beginning that the following investigation of the major narratives in the Tetrateuch is not an attempt to produce a commentary on the whole of that work or to attempt a source analysis of the constituent materials. Rather, the present work will attempt to explain the composition of the Tetrateuch by utilizing the basic model of analysis that was developed and applied to the deuteronomistic history in an earlier work.[1] This model emphasized the ways in which the narratives construct a distinctive set of ethnic signifiers; those groups who adopt these accounts as parts of their own past could use these descriptors to distinguish themselves from other related ethnic groups. Hence, such narratives may construct boundaries which help to define, and redefine, the ethnic identity of specific groups. The present volume will also argue that the Tetrateuchal materials were created as a supplement to the already existing deuteronomistic history and that they form a complement to that work that, in its final form, creates a "primary history" that might be compared in scope to those of Manetho, Sanchuniathon, and Berossus.[2]

---

[1] *Narrative History and Ethnic Boundaries*, esp. pp. 1–18.

[2] Such comparisons might also be taken beyond the simple scope of each of these works. While an in-depth investigation of these "histories" lies beyond the boundaries of the present work, it is of interest to note that the works of both Manetho and Berossus were produced in response to Hellenistic rule, and both have nationalistic and ethnic aspects to them. For a discussion of some of these parallels, see J. Blenkinsopp, *The Pentateuch*, pp. 41–42.

While it seems apparent that the classical formulation of the documentary hypothesis no longer holds the consensus it once commanded, it is also clear that it is far from being discarded as a working (or workable) explanatory model for the composition of the Tetrateuch and the Pentateuch. At the same time, it is becoming more and more apparent that there presently exists little if any general consensus in the field over the precise nature or dates of the purported sources from which the Tetrateuch was composed, or the number of redactional processes through which it passed before reaching its final form. Nonetheless, to any critical reader it becomes obvious that there were "sources" underlying these materials and that the present narrative strands have incorporated a number of related, yet discernibly different, styles of presentation, which often give the impression of unevenness in the narrative flow.

To the present writer it seems that however one conceives of the literary composition of the Tetrateuch, one is faced with the issue of these "sources" which, in turn, involves some variation of a documentary hypothesis. This is not to suggest that the composition of the Tetrateuch was the result of some mechanistic redaction of already existing continuous written documents as presupposed by the classical theory. Nor is it intended to suggest that some form of either the supplementary or fragmentary hypothesis is by necessity to be presupposed.[3] Rather, it is to argue that the author(s) of these materials were dependent upon a rather large repository of ancient Near Eastern myths, legends, and folk tales, as well as native Judahite materials constituting a variety of types, which were used as "sources" from which they developed their own versions of a Judahite ethnomythography.[4]

The "sources" used by these writers should be understood using a very broad sense of the concept of "source," implying neither a set written form nor even a developed oral form. That some written materials were utilized seems beyond reasonable doubt. It does not seem overly cynical, however, to suggest that the reconstruction of any such documents is beyond possi-

---

3 A. F. Campbell & M. A. O'Brien present a brief discussion of the development and relationship among the source, fragmentary, and supplementary hypotheses, noting that despite the primacy attained by the basic source theory, appeal is still made to both of the others by modern scholars (*Sources of the Pentateuch*, pp. 2–4).

4 For the purposes of the present work, the term "ethnomythography" might better categorize the functional aspects of the original narrative productions rather than the more common designations with their particular historiographic connotations. This term implies nothing necessarily about the "historical" or "non-historical" nature of the events contained in the accounts; rather, it asserts that these narrated episodes comprise a written mythology that provides the basis for understanding the ethnic ascriptions contained in the accounts.

bility, given the nearly complete lack of empirical evidence for such reconstructions. Likewise, despite the attractiveness of the enterprise, it seems that the possibility of specifying particular ancient Near Eastern traditions upon which the author(s) depended goes far beyond the evidence that we presently possess.[5]

Nonetheless, it does not seem to be too much to suggest that the author(s) of these materials utilized forms, ideas, and genres that would have been familiar to their audience and which were drawn from the large realm of literary materials with which they would have been acquainted. At the same time, comparison of the Tetrateuchal narratives with existing parallel materials from the ancient world demonstrates that these materials have been given a thoroughly Judahite emphasis in their present form. In short, there exists little evidence at all that can be used to argue that there are direct literary dependencies between units of materials in the Tetrateuchal narrative and other contemporary literary creations. Given the present state of our knowledge of the oral and written literature of the ancient Near East and of the composition of the Tetrateuch, the most that can be asserted with some assuredness is that the author(s) of the Tetrateuchal narratives utilized forms of literature and literary styles of representation that have a variety of parallels from contemporary cultures, if by that one means the Persian and Hellenistic eras.

This should not be surprising, given what might be reasonably surmised about the author(s) of the Tetrateuch. As suggested above, the author(s) of these stories were professionally trained scribes, members of the temple staff, under the patronage of their Achaemenid masters.[6] In this role, and as a part of their training, they would have been exposed to numerous literary forms and traditions and would have had a large repertoire of materials from which to construct their accounts of "Israelite" history and identity. To satisfy the Achaemenid rulers that they constituted an ancient and legitimate ethnic entity, these scribes produced the Tetrateuch to supplement and modify the deuteronomistic account of the "history" of "Israel" in the land of Canaan to explain the reasons that this "Israel" con-

---

5 The attempt by J. Van Seters to distinguish between "eastern" and "western" tendencies in the literary genres employed by the writers of the Tetrateuch comes the closest to identifying specific extant parallels to which appeals might be made. Problematically, the categories that he proposes are extremely broad, and the specifics are often vague. For his arguments, see *Prologue to History, passim.*

6 See above, Chap. 2, n. 18.

stituted a distinct people with a legitimate and indisputable claim to that territory.[7]

While it might be claimed that these writers would have drawn upon as much "traditional" Judahite material as possible, such claims are impossible to substantiate. The precise relationship of these scribal groups to their predecessors who were trained in the now defunct royal household of the Judahite monarchy and temple staff is obscure. What does seem certain is that their training and their support came from non-Judahite sources, though it is also clear that they maintained a native tongue in which they produced their literature.[8] The most defensible position, given our present knowledge of the exilic and early Second Temple period, might be to argue that the "traditions" reflected in the Tetrateuch (and the remainder of the "primary history" for that matter) developed within the context of the exilic Judahite community from whom the post-exilic resettlers of Jerusalem claimed direct descent. To posit that these traditions have any greater antiquity within any historical Judahite society goes beyond the available evidence.[9]

With these introductory remarks completed, we may turn to the Tetrateuchal materials themselves and address how these narratives complement and modify the deuteronomistic history and provide a set of internal ethnic descriptors of and for the Judahite population. While the deuteronomistic history established a set of ethnic boundary narratives for an ideal "Israel," that same work did not provide an account of the origins and development

[7] This "history" would have had a dual audience: the Judahite restoration community and the Achaemenid royal court. The "history" was written in the language of the people of the community, i.e., Hebrew. That there was an Aramaic version, directed at the Achaemenid court, is possible, but purely conjectural. Some commentators have suggested that the practice may have been to translate a Hebrew (or any other non-Aramaic) text to Aramaic "on the spot," thus alleviating the need for an Aramaic copy (cf. R. Le Déaut, "The Targumim," in *The Cambridge History of Judaism, Vol. 2: The Hellenistic Age,* ed. W. D. Davies and L. Finkelstein [Cambridge: Cambridge University Press, 1989], p. 566).

[8] An interesting point to ponder is the relationship between language and ethnicity. While it is clear that language is a significant cultural indicator and preserver of ethnic distinctiveness, care must be taken to avoid oversimplification. Ethnicity is the result of numerous cultural influences (A. D. Smith, *The Ethnic Origins of Nations,* pp. 26–28).

[9] Along with the problem of antiquity is the problem of the presupposition that these "traditions" were in some way ubiquitous among the population of Judah throughout its history. Again, for this there is no evidence. Our knowledge of the ancient Judahite village (or "lesser") traditions is nearly nonexistent. Perhaps scattered inscriptional evidence from village sites like Kuntillet ʿAjrud, where we seem to have a type of "syncretistic" form of Yahwism, suggests that Judahite religion was much more diverse than the final official urban ("greater") tradition would suggest.

of that specially designated people that would provide for their separation from all others from archaic, if not primordial, times.[10] The reasons for this might be found in the settings and functions that may be ascribed to the production of that work. Produced in exile by Judahite descendants, the deuteronomistic history represents a direct continuity with a national/ethnic group and constructed appropriate boundaries that were intended to define and to preserve the group against the threat of assimilation to the surrounding Semitic cultures.[11] In contrast, the Tetrateuchal materials were produced by a group separated by at least a full generation, and probably two, from direct contact with the land from which their purported ancestors were taken. For their identity to be established, it would be necessary to provide specific links to the past which they could create from the variety of sources and traditions at their disposal.[12] By providing a supplementary introduction to the deuteronomistic work, they would be able to redefine their identity in terms of their new circumstances.

II. The Creation of Structures and Categories

Unlike other contemporary accounts of origins,[13] the Tetrateuchal narrative begins with a cosmology rather than a theogony. From the perspective of the ancient world within which these stories were produced, this in itself created a separate and distinct concept of the origin of the cosmos, for there is only one deity (*'ĕlōhîm*) involved in the production of the world. Most distinctive also is the choice of positioning this "Priestly" version of creation as a general preface to the work as a whole rather than integrating it into the supplementary "Yahwistic" account that follows.[14] As will be

[10] A point never to be overlooked in discussions and considerations of ethnicity and the development of ethnic boundaries is that ethnicity is *always* relational (E. E. Roosens, *Creating Ethnicity: The Process of Ethnogenesis*, p.18).

[11] For a fuller explication of this, see my *Narrative History and Ethnic Boundaries*, pp. 37–47.

[12] As will be argued below, one of the major ways in which such links with the "past" were established was through the creation and propagation of genealogies, the role of which is crucial in the accounts in Genesis. Note also the ways in which these genealogies function in connecting the work of the Chronicler, who clearly is engaged in a Second Temple rewriting of Judahite history, with the Tetrateuchal ancestors of the "distant past."

[13] Cf. Hesiod's theogony, Sanchuniathon, the Babylonian theogony, etc.

[14] As suggested above, rather than conceive of the "Priestly," "Yahwistic," or "Elohistic" sources as fully developed narrative accounts which have been utilized in whole or in part to create the present work, one might better address them as identifiable styles or genres of narrative. Such an approach does not necessitate a number of presuppositions concerning the extent

argued below in the consideration of the account of the flood, the author(s) of these materials were obviously able to interweave two different and conflicting narratives concerning the same event into a single story. But in the account of the creation, they chose to juxtapose the differing stories instead.[15] As an introduction to the story of "Israel," a carefully balanced account of the creation, organization, legitimization, and sanctification of the cosmos provides a context for the social organization that was ordained by the deity for the formation of all that emergent human society would encounter.

It is specifically the uniqueness of the way in which creation itself is presented that provides a background for the development of "Israel's" self-identity as a social unit separate from all others. As the cosmos itself was the work of one deity, so "Israel" would be the special people of that same god. Though all would be created by this god, only "Israel" would occupy the place of his chosen people. But this initial creation account, though clearly an independent unit in and of itself, in its present form is a part of a larger whole, the so-called "primeval history" that extends from Gen 1:1 through 11:26.[16] This larger narrative, commonly understood as a combination of two major sources, a "Yahwistic" story of creation supplemented by "Priestly materials,"[17] forms its own "freestanding" composition that does not necessitate the stories of the patriarchs and, hence, the genealogical and aetiological origins of the people "Israel."[18] Yet, in their present position,

---

or contents of hypothetical constructs, or the intentionality of hypothetical redactors. At the same time, we will retain the terminology to distinguish among such styles and tendencies, for it seems rather obvious to the critical reader that the present text is a sometimes uneven composite of styles and content.

15 This should not be understood as an endorsement of S. Sandmel's idea that subsequent redactors "corrected" or modified the text by adding additional stories or comments rather than actually changing or rewriting the *textus receptus* ("The Haggada within Scripture," *JBL* 80 [1961] 120). There seems to be no concrete evidence to suggest that the text had been assigned any such "special" or unchangeable qualities until long after its final production.

16 I follow here the division noted by J. Blenkinsopp, *The Pentateuch*, pp. 58–59. The *tôlĕdôt* formula for Terah, introduced in 11:27, begins the patriarchal narratives proper.

17 Whether the "Priestly" source constituted a complete narrative or, as argued by F. M. Cross, was a collection of a variety of different source materials that did not form a narratological whole (*Canaanite Myth and Hebrew Epic*, p. 310), is not of importance to the present analysis. What is significant is that contained in the accounts of the Tetrateuch are various segments within the larger whole that can be associated with a particular "Priestly" style and set of concerns that reveal some common connections among those materials.

18 On the independence of the "primeval history" from the "patriarchal stories," see the analyses of G. von Rad ("The Form-Critical Problem of the Hexateuch," in *The Problem of the Hexateuch and Other Essays* (New York: McGraw-Hill, 1966), pp. 63–67; and M. Noth, *A History of Pentateuchal Traditions*, p. 46.

they embody a particular structural unity that is directly related to the situation of the community in exile.[19] The extended nature of the genealogical aetiology formed by these stories is of note, for the name "Israel" does not occur in the narrative presentations until the renaming of the patriarch Jacob (Gen 32:29; 35:10). The emergence of the people who will bear this privileged position among all the peoples of the earth is embedded in a larger narrative of origins that traces the eponymous ancestor in an unbroken line back to the original humans created and pronounced good.[20]

It is also essential to recognize the necessity of beginning the account of "Israel's" history, in mythographic terms, with an account of the creation and population of the world by "Israel's" own personal god.[21] That it is Israel's national god, Yahweh, that is the creative power giving shape and substance to the cosmos is not explicit in the opening account, for in Genesis 1, only the generic term *'ĕlōhîm* is employed.[22] It is not until the account of the "Garden" (Gen 2:4b-3:24) that the name Yahweh is mentioned explicitly,[23] an association that connects the religious implications of the stories associated with the revelation of the name to Moses (cf. Exod 3:13–18; 6:2–4) with the accounts of the creation of the cosmos. Most importantly, the emphasis is placed upon the emergence of a particular lineage, not known until the final genealogical notice of the section (11:25), from among all the other peoples of the earth. The initial thrust of the primeval history is to place the ancestors of the group that will be revealed

[19] An important aspect of this is the recognition of the covenantal emphasis that provides a conceptual background for the primeval history that serves as an explanation for the loss of the land. As J. Van Seters notes, this is quite possibly derived from the deuteronomistic theology and, in this instance, universalizes what was originally a nationalistic ideology (*Prologue to History*, pp. 127–128).

[20] On the significance of the announcement of the "goodness" of the acts of creation, see the discussion below.

[21] In this, it should be noted, the Hebrew account of creation, despite its unique emphases in places, is perfectly in line with contemporary accounts of creation, all of which are accomplished by the authorial group's national or city god. Unlike those other accounts, the Hebrew creation account emphasizes the development and multiplication of humankind with respect to the deity, rather than simply its creation and activity.

[22] The term *'ĕlōhîm* as the divine name occurs some 33 times in Genesis 1. On the use of this term in the narrative presentations of the Hebrew bible, see the discussion of U. Cassuto, *The Documentary Hypothesis and the Composition of the Pentateuch* (Jerusalem: Magnes, 1961), pp. 27–41.

[23] The composite designation *yhwh 'ĕlōhîm*, an obvious cause of consternation to those who use divine names to separate "documents," occurs in 2:4, 5, 7, 8, 9, 15, 16, 18, 19, 21, 22; 3:1, 8 (2x), 9, 13, 14, 21, 22, 23. Elsewhere it occurs in Exod 9:30; 2 Sam 7:22, 25; 2 Kgs 19:19; Jer 10:10; Jon 4:6; Pss 72:18; 84:12; 1 Chr 17:16; 28:20; 29:1; 2 Chr 1:9; 6:41 (2x), 42; 26:18.

as Yahweh's "holy people," his own singular possession from among the peoples of the earth, as simply one group among many.[24] The development of the creation of a special people from the undifferentiated masses is essential in order to establish the basis for the formation of distinct ethnic boundaries. If, as noted above, ethnicity is anchored in relational comparisons and differentiations, then ethnicity might be understood from one perspective as a response to sameness, rather than to uniqueness. Indeed, it is precisely the "ideal" of uniqueness and differentiation that ethnic boundaries seek to establish and preserve.

For the primeval history, the emergence of "Israel," along with all humankind from the primordial common ancestors that were created by the national deity of the Hebrews, provides the basis for understanding "Israel's" eventual emergence from among the variety of nations that develop within these narratives. Before there can be a specifically defined and delineated ethnic group, there must be a variety of peoples from whom the group may be distinguished. This constitutes a major function of the stories in the primeval history. But it is not the only function, for these accounts also provide explanations concerning the nature of the world, its history, and its inhabitants that supply an explanatory basis for the development of "Israel" and its proper relationship with its patron deity. Likewise, they depict the world as being under the guiding control of this particular deity, an emphasis on universality that suggests an exilic setting at the earliest[25] and which places a certain emphasis upon the special nature of the group that would be selected by that creator deity.

In terms of both religious emphasis and ethnic ideals, the mythographic depiction of the formation of the cosmos begins in *illo tempore,* at the beginning of existentially meaningful time.[26] Unlike many of the major

24 On the nature of this designation of "Israel" as Yahweh's special possession and its implications for the formation of ethnic boundaries, see the discussion in my work, *Narrative History and Ethnic Boundaries,* pp. 57–61.

25 As is generally recognized, the trend toward a universal deity, e.g., the depiction of Yahweh in Deutero-Isaiah, etc., is a theological development that is characteristic of the post-Babylonian period and represents a departure from the national-god ideal associated with the independent monarchic states that constituted the ancient Near East prior to that time. The possible connections between the loss of land and nationhood and the democratization and universalization of the concept of the disenfranchised national deity should not be overlooked. From one perspective, the universalization of the national deity could be understood as a form of rationalization that would minimize the level of cognitive dissonance created by the loss of the state and national shrine, clear indicators of a deity's power.

26 M. Eliade's concept of myth as the history of divine activities in *illo tempore* is most appropriate to the present context (*The Sacred and the Profane,* p. 95).

creative traditions of the ancient Near East, *'ĕlōhîm* here creates without combat or conflict.[27] Instead, the cosmos is formed by way of the creative power of the spoken divine command.[28] That such emphasis would be placed upon the spoken divine word as the creative instrument is most suggestive when placed within the context of a set of mythographic materials designed to form the particular identity of a selected group. That the major focal point of the Tetrateuchal development of the nature of "Israel" will come with the revelation of the divine will in the legislative materials associated with Sinai and spoken both to and through the character of Moses finds its foundation in the very creative actions of the deity.

The how and why of the nature of the pre-creation world, described only as *tōhû wābōhû* (1:2), are not presented. Rather, the account begins with the creative activities of the deity: "When *'ĕlōhîm* began creating the heavens and the earth . . ." (1:1).[29] Creation is accomplished by the use of imperatives, followed by notices that the order was fulfilled (*yĕhî . . . wayhî;* 1:3, 6–7, 14–15; cf. 30; etc.). Description of this primordial event is kept to a minimum, noting only that *'ĕlōhîm* perceived that each of the steps in the creative process was "good" (*wayyar' 'ĕlōhîm . . . kî-ṭōb;* 1:4, 10, 12, 18, 21, 25; cf. 31). Such divine assurance of the completeness of the creative act

---

[27] Though the Hebrew traditions contain numerous references to Yahweh's conquest of a variety of chaos creatures, e.g., Rahab (*rahab;* Isa 51:9; 30:7; Pss 87:4; 89:11; Job 9:13; 26:12), Leviathan (*liwyātān;* Isa 27:1; Pss 74:14; 104:26; Job 3:8; 40:25), Behemot (*bĕhēmôt;* Job 40:15), a dragon (*tannîn;* Isa 51:9; 27:1; Jer 51:34; Ezek 29:3; 32:2; Job 7:12), and a serpent (*nāḥāš;* Amos 9:3; Isa 27:1; Job 26:13), any allusion to such combat or conflict is absent from the present context.

[28] On the variety of parallels to the creation story in Genesis 1, see the materials cited by C. Westermann (*Genesis 1–11: A Commentary* [Minneapolis: Augsburg, 1984], pp. 19–47). One of the most provocative parallels to this type of creation is provided by the text of the Shabaka Stele in which Ptah, the city-god of Memphis, is portrayed as creating by thought and speech. Interestingly, though it is common to date this story to the period of the Old Kingdom, more recent investigations of the text place its original composition to the time of the twenty-fifth (Nubian) dynasty in the late 8th-early 7th centuries BCE. For references, see M. Lichtheim, *Ancient Egyptian Literature, Volume III: The Late Period,* p. 5; for a translation of the text and critical notes, see Lichtheim, *Ancient Egyptian Literature, Volume I: The Old and Middle Kingdoms* (Berkeley: University of California Press, 1973), pp. 51–57. The simple review of the major bibliographic resources devoted to the study of the primary history would constitute a volume in itself. For extensive lists of pertinent references, see the materials presented in C. Westermann's *Genesis 1–11: A Commentary* and in G. J. Wenham, *Genesis 1–15* (Waco, TX: Word, 1987).

[29] On the debate concerning the grammatical problems associated with the translation of the opening verse, consult the commentaries.

provides an interesting commentary on the liturgically balanced structure of
the acts constituting the creation.[30]

It is the balanced division of the account into seven separate days,
six of which are occupied with the work of creation, and the final culminating day providing the sanctification of those which preceded (2:1–3),
that provides a major clue to the significance and placement of the events
of creation, which culminate with the divine formation of humankind. An
essential aspect of the entire nature of the creation, as depicted in this prologue to the ethnographic history of "Israel," is the concept of separation
and distinction. Each type of herbage producing seed is created "according
to its kind" (*lĕmînô;* 1:11–12). Such distinctions are extended to the inhabitants of the seas and the birds of the air (1:21), and finally to all the living
creatures of the earth (1:24–25). Such divisions among the plants and animals of the earth provide a background for the later introduction of the food
laws that will establish one of the critical internal social boundaries for the
separation of "Israel" from all other peoples.[31] Just as the inhabitants of the
earth are distinguished by type, so too are the structures of that universe
separated by virtue of the divine activity (*hibdîl;* 1:4, 6, 7, 14, 18).

The special status of the creation is confirmed in 1:22, when *'ĕlōhîm*
pronounces his blessing on the creatures filling the air and the waters and
gives them the command, "Be fruitful and multiply" (*pĕrû ûrĕbû*). All that
remains for the completion of the act of creation is to form the animals that
will inhabit the earth, and this is accomplished on the sixth day (1:24–28).
After the clearly demarcated action of creating the non-human inhabitants of
the earth, the perspective of the narrative shifts drastically, transporting the
reader/hearer[32] into the heavenly council to witness the decision to create
humankind[33] in a particular manner and to provide it with a specific function
vis-à-vis the other creatures inhabiting the heavens, waters, and earth. This

30 For an outline of the structure of Genesis 1, see J. Blenkinsopp, *The Pentateuch,* p. 61.

31 Cf. the lists of clean and unclean animals in Leviticus 11 and Deuteronomy 14. H. Eilberg-Schwartz argues that the structural connections of Leviticus 11 with the form of Genesis 1
reflect the priestly efforts to mirror the divine nature of creation in the food laws and to reflect
the same basic differentiations made in that cosmogony. Likewise, he suggests that Leviticus 11
represents a reworking of the materials of Deuteronomy 14, an important point to note in understanding the relationship of the Tetrateuchal materials to the deuteronomistic history (*The
Savage in Judaism: An Anthropology of Israelite Religion and Ancient Judaism* [Blooming-
ton/Indianapolis: Indiana University Press, 1990], pp. 218–221, 255–257).

32 On the aural/oral aspects of ancient literature, see above, Chap. 1, n. 32, and Chap. 2,
n. 52.

33 For an examination of the role of the divine council in the ancient Near East and the
ways in which it has been accommodated to the exclusive nature of Israelite religion, see my

formal literary shift of perspectives emphasizes the separate and special nature of the creatures to be created. Using the formal plural imperative characteristic of addresses to the council, ʾĕlōhîm enjoins the members to create "humankind" (ʾādām) in "our image, after our likeness" (bĕṣalmēnû kidmûtēnû; 1:26; cf. 5:1).[34] The association of the form of ʾādām with the divine further differentiates humanity from the rest of the animal population of the earth. In addition to such a formal manner of distinction, ʾādām is provided with a specific purpose that separates it from the remainder of creation. ʾādām is created in the image of ʾĕlōhîm "so that he may have dominion" (wĕyirdû; 1:26)[35] over the creatures inhabiting all three created spheres.

Both the form and the special function of ʾādām separate humankind from the other aspects of creation and provide the basis for commonality and separation according to distinctive categories, two factors that are essential to the formation of ethnicity. That humankind is given the preeminent position among the variety of animals created separates it from all other created life.[36] With the completion of the decision on the form and function of ʾādām, the narrative returns to its previous descriptive form and

---

work, *The Assembly of the Gods: The Divine Council in Canaanite and Early Hebrew Literature* (HSM 24; Chico, CA: Scholars Press, 1980). As a corrective to the arguments in that work, I would note that the Canaanite evidence serves to establish the rather ubiquitous nature of the concept of a council of the gods shared by the cultures of the Levant rather than as any direct historical or cultural predecessor of the Hebrew traditions which record developments of that motif separated by nearly a millennium from the Canaanite documents. Likewise, I would also argue that much of the so-called "early" Hebrew literature might better be regarded as exilic or post-exilic in origin. Otherwise, I would argue that the basic descriptions of the motif of the council and the ways in which it functions in the Hebrew bible remain quite functional and defensible.

[34] The participatory aspect of the selected deities in the creation of humans is common in the Babylonian accounts of the creation of humanity. See, for example, the sections of *Enuma Elish* and *Atra-Hasis* that deal with the creation of humankind. Likewise, that human form would mirror divine form, both male and female, should occasion no real surprise. While the scholarly consensus continues to be that Israelite tradition was aniconic in nature from a very early period, there is no evidence apart from the biblical injunctions against images to suggest any such historical actuality. It might be argued that the development of such a strong aniconic tradition occurred during a period when the images associated with the worship of Yahweh had been destroyed, most especially after the period of the Babylonian exile, after the plundering and destruction of the Temple. In this way, the development of an "imageless" religion might be explained on the basis of a reflective response to an historical situation.

[35] It is critical to note that the second clause here expresses a purpose or result that is dependent upon the conditions noted in the previous clause. For this translation, involving the sequence of cohortative + unconverted imperfect/jussive, see T. O. Lambdin, *Introduction to Biblical Hebrew* (New York: Charles Scribner's Sons, 1971), §107, p. 119.

[36] It is notable that this is a distinctive break from the Babylonian idea of the creation of humans for the purpose of doing the work of the gods.

notes the fulfillment of the act: both male and female (*zākār ûněqêbâ*) complete the categories of ʾ*ādām* created by ʾ*ělōhîm* (1:27). In a manner parallel to the completion of the creation of the non-land animals, ʾ*ělōhîm* pronounces his blessing upon humanity and repeats the command to multiply and fill the earth (1:28; cf. 1:22).[37] Here, however, the command to dominate is added to the command to multiply, in contrast to the command given to the other animals. ʾ*ādām* is then granted the right to eat from all the vegetation bearing seed, a prerogative extended to the entirety of creation (1:29–30). With the order of creation completed, ʾ*ělōhîm* saw that "all he had made was very good" (*kol-ʾăšer ʾāśâ wěhinnēh-ṭôb měʾōd;* 1:31), an observation that concludes the sixth and final day of creation.

Yet this divinely formed model of the cosmos was not complete, for the divine actions on the seventh day liturgically reinterpret the whole. It was on this day that "ʾ*ělōhîm* rested (*wayyišbōt*) from all his labor which he had performed" (2:2), an action that led to his blessing on that particular day and to its sanctification (2:3). The act of creating the cosmos is interpreted in religious terms with this setting apart of the seventh day, an event which provided a calendrical and ritual structure for the community that would emerge as "Israel." Though explicit mention of the "Sabbath" does not occur in the Pentateuchal materials until Exod 16:23, it seems clear that the use of the verb *šābat* in vv. 2–3 intends to designate the rest prescribed for the *šabbāt* celebration.[38] The seventh day is established as a day of rest on analogy with the actions of the deity. Additionally, this distinction of one particular day establishes a cyclical pattern by which time might be kept based on sabbath celebrations. Hence, cosmic time ceases to be profane time and is ritually transformed into sacred temporality by this special day. In terms of ethnic signification, sabbath observance and Jewishness became identified. Mythographically, this identity may be traced back to the very formation of the cosmos as a portion of the divine plan.

III. The Creation of Individuals and Community

With the full creation now sanctified and the world into which "Israel" would move established in a stable, organized manner, the author(s) of the

---

37 This same command recurs in Gen 8:17 and 9:7 and connects those accounts of "new" creative acts with the original act of divine creation.

38 For the regulations concerning the sabbath, see Exod 20:8–11; Deut 5:12–15. The origins of this practice remain completely obscure. Given the propensity of religious and ethnic literature to retroject identifying practices into the distant past, it is impossible to establish a time of origin for this particularly "Israelite" custom.

story move from the cosmic level of description to the more individual, shifting by way of one of the five *tôlĕdôt* notices that structure the primeval history.[39] "These are the generations of the heaven and the earth when they were created"[40] both summarizes the preceding actions and introduces the materials that follow. The reference to "creating" (*bārā'*) might be taken as a reference back to the divine actions of Gen 1:1a or might be applied to the narrative that follows, though those stories do not refer to "heaven and earth" but only to the events associated with the "garden" (2:8). The very ambiguity of the referent of this initial *tôlĕdôt* serves as an appropriate bridge between these accounts of creation that differ in both style and content. By placing the notice here, rather than at the very beginning of the account, the author(s) bring the two stories into a conceptual proximity that allows them to "fold over" the narrative in a type of retelling of a portion of the initial incident.[41]

The placement of this first *tôlĕdôt* list is critical, for it fulfills a dual function in the development of the nature of the earth and its relationship to *'ĕlōhîm,* now combined with the personal name of "Israel's" patron deity, Yahweh, to form the conflated and somewhat problematic designation, "Yahweh God."[42] But it is exactly this conflation that provides the basis for the transition not only between the "Priestly" and the "Yahwistic" accounts, but also between the universal-cosmic creative event and the particular-personal stories that follow. The creation of the structures of the universe

---

39 J. Blenkinsopp, *The Pentateuch,* pp. 58–59. The other four series occur in 5:1, 6:9, 10:1, and 11:10.

40 *'ēlleh tôlĕdôt haššāmayim wĕhā'āreṣ bĕhibārĕ'ām;* 2:4a.

41 This common biblical practice of duplicating accounts, with internal and stylistic inconsistencies, has been designated as "expansive-resumptive" by H. C. Brichto (*Toward a Grammar of Biblical Poetics,* pp. 13–14).

42 For references to the occurrence of this phrase, see above, n. 23. With the exception of Exod 9:30, the combination is confined in the Pentateuchal materials to Genesis 2–3. It is generally interpreted as a "bridging" device to link the "Priestly" designation of the deity, *'ĕlōhîm,* to the "Yahwistic" narrative that is reconstructed so as to employ only the designation Yahweh for the divine. Clearly, these occurrences present problems to the classical documentary hypothesis, proponents of which must attempt to explain these instances by appealing to a number of conflating redactions through which the text passed. Problematic to such an explanation, however, is the fact that in the Yahwistic materials, it occurs only in these two chapters. The situation is further confused by the evidence from the versions, since there seems to be little if any consistency in the translation of this composite name. In the LXX, for example, *yhwh 'ĕlōhîm* is translated by *ho theos* in 2:4b, 5, 7, 8, 9, 19, 21; 3:22, but by *kyrios ho theos* in 2:15, 16, 18, 22; 3:1, 8 (2x), 9, 12, 14, 21, 23. Whatever name might have been used in the purported documents reconstructed to underlie this section, it has been completely obscured by the authorial processes which were responsible for the present text.

has been completed (*šāmayim*/*mayim*/*ʾereṣ*) and the creation itself separated into its distinctive generic categories. With the transition provided by both the *tôlĕdôt* notation and the conflated designation for the deity, the story shifts to concentrate on the personal creation of individuals, people who will be given names and will begin the genealogical clues by which "Israel" will be able to trace its lineage to both its god and its land.[43]

An additional bridge between the creation stories is provided by the emphasis on "world" (*ʾereṣ*) and "cultivatable land" (*ʾădāmâ*). Throughout the initial account, reference is consistently to *ʾereṣ*, with the singular exception of 1:25, which refers to *ʾĕlōhîm*'s creation of the creeping things of the *ʾădāmâ*. This shift from *ʾereṣ* to *ʾădāmâ* is hardly incidental, given that in 1:26, the reference to this same aspect of the creation is connected with *ʾereṣ*. The bridge formed by this interplay is concluded with the notice in 2:5 concerning the status of creation: Yahweh God had not caused any rain to fall, so there was no herbage on the earth (*hāʾāreṣ*), nor was there a man to till the cultivatable soil (*wĕʾādām ʾayin laʿăbōd ʾet-hāʾădāmâ*). When this story is understood as an expansion on the previous story, the reader/hearer is taken back to the third day of the creation, when *ʾĕlōhîm* created herbage on the earth. Further, it builds upon the knowledge of the creation of *ʾādām* and gives an explicit reference to the way in which he will be expected to dominate and subdue the earth (1:26, 28). From this perspective, *ʾādām* will fulfill its divinely ordained function by tilling the soil, the very substance from which he was formed (*yāṣar;* 2:8).[44]

The living human is placed by Yahweh God in the garden in Eden (*gan-bĕʿēden;* 2:8) which he had planted and in which he had caused trees for food to grow (2:9).[45] The location of this paradisial garden is of utmost

---

43 As is generally recognized, ethnicity is commonly connected with a particular land, even if such connections are fictitious. In ethnic groups they tend to be historicized and placed at the "beginnings" of existential time.

44 The phonetic similarities between *ʾādām* and *ʾădāmâ*, while etymologically suggestive, should be understood as word plays and not as any direct etymological connection between these terms. That *ʾādām* becomes a "living soul" (*nepeš ḥayyâ*) by virtue of receiving the "breath of life" (*nišmat ḥayyîm*) from the deity could also be taken as an internarrative expansion on the ideal of *ʾādām* having been created in the image of the divine (1:26–27). This same idea of likeness and imagery is conveyed by the use of the verb *yāṣar,* which, when used of making pottery, has the explicit connotation of shape and likeness.

45 J. Blenkinsopp notes that the Eden story is not referred to in any pre-exilic text. It is not until the Neo-Babylonian period that mention is made of this myth (Ezek 28:13; 31:9, 16, 18; 36:35; Isa 51:3; Joel 2:3; *The Pentateuch*, pp. 64–65). As with the majority of place names, the etymology of *ʿēden* remains conjectural.

interest, for it is explicitly noted that it is "in the east" (*miqqedem*).[46] The garden itself is located at the confluence of four rivers, two of which are clearly identifiable—the Tigris and the Euphrates.[47] Clearly, ʾ*ādām* is settled in the garden located in the vicinity of Mesopotamia. Such a location provides not only for the later patriarchal migrations from Ur of the Chaldeans, but also for the location of the exilic groups, or those claiming descent from such groups, who were responsible for the final form of the story. ʾ*ādām* is placed in the garden in order "to till it and to watch over it" (*lĕʿobdāh ûlĕšomrāh;* 2:15), which reiterates and expands the responsibilities already associated with ʾ*ādām* (cf. 2:5; 1:26, 28).

There are two special trees in the garden which ʾ*ādām* will be required to "watch over": "the tree of life . . . and the tree of the knowledge of good and evil" (ʿ*ēṣ haḥayyîm . . . wĕʿēṣ haddaʿat ṭôb wārāʿ;* 2:9).[48] In the first direct command given to ʾ*ādām*, the fruit of the "tree of the knowledge of good and evil" is directly forbidden as food: to eat of that tree would result in death (2:17).[49] The parameters of existence are here narrowed. What is and is not allowable as food is redefined (cf. 1:29). Despite the fact that there is no direct prohibition against eating from the "tree of life," the prospects of death and mortality are introduced into the story.

[46] It is also possible to translate *miqqedem* as "from of old/antiquity," though in light of the geographical notice occurring in 2:10–14, it is clear that the reference is spatial and not temporal. While it is clear that 2:10–14 appears to interrupt the narrative flow of the story, there is little convincing reason to regard it as a secondary intrusion into the text.

[47] The connection of the land of the living with the distant rivers is explicit in the description of the dwelling place of Utnapishtim after the flood, for he is settled by the gods "in the distance, at the mouth of the rivers" (*ina rūqi ina pî nārāti,* Gilgamesh XI.194–198). It is difficult not to associate this paradisial location with the dwelling place of the god El in Canaanite mythology, "at the sources of the rivers, in the midst of the double-deep" (*mbk mhrm qrb ʾapq thmtm;* CTA 2.III(?).4; 3.V.14–15; 4.IV.21–22; 6.I.32–34; 17.VI.47–48).

[48] On the grammatical problems associated with the construction of *haddaʿat,* consult the commentaries. I understand *daʿat* here as a Qal infinitive construct. As with the description of the location of the garden, it is common to see the reference to the tree of life as secondary, since it plays no role in the story until 3:22. Such an interpretation is not convincing, however. While it is clear that the association of these trees in the common mythology of the ancient Near East is without parallel, this attests only to the creativeness of the author(s) of this section and to their ability to combine differing mythological motifs to create a distinctive story of their own.

[49] The phrase *môt tāmût,* "you shall surely die," is unambiguous. That the death penalty is not carried out as expected when the man and woman directly break this command (3:1–24) points to what I have referred to elsewhere as the "divine paradox" that forms an essential theme in the narrative portions of the Pentateuch and the deuteronomistic history (cf. *Narrative History and Ethnic Boundaries,* pp. 223–227).

In yet another narrative digression, the author(s) further individual-
ize the account, noting that 'ādām was alone, a situation which Yahweh God
did not perceive as good (2:18). Such a simple expansion on the story provides for a transition from the general "humankind" to the individual
"person" and also shifts the emphasis on the nature of the creation onto a
specific familial form of social organization. In the quest to remedy the first
aspect of the creation that has been noted as "not good" (lō'-ṭôb), Yahweh
God decides to make a "suitable companion"[50] for 'ādām, and, as a result,
creates the animal world "from the ground" (min-hā'ădāmâ; 2:19).[51] In an
exercise of his dominion over the creation, 'ādām gives names to the creatures, but does not find a suitable companion among them (2:20).[52]

In his second effort to correct the "flaw" in the creative process,
Yahweh God places 'ādām in a deep sleep and fashions "woman" ('iššâ)
from his ribs.[53] Unlike the animals, she is created from a part of 'ādām; like
those other creatures, however, she is brought to the man to be named
(2:22; cf. 2:19–20). In designating her 'iššâ, "woman, wife," 'ādām plays
upon the phonetic similarities of this name with the designation of its origins from 'îš, "man, husband" (2:23). The dual meanings of the terms are
clear in the connections made immediately with the epilogic statement concerning marriage, a saying which transforms the account of the creation
of man and woman into an establishment of the institution of marriage as
the basic form of male-female relationship created from the beginning and
given divine sanction. This concluding statement to the episode completes

50 The literal translation of 'ēzer kĕnegdô would be "a helper as his counterpart," or the
like. An essential aspect implied by the phrase is the equality of status of the creature to occupy
this position as well as the oppositeness of this being. At the base of the phrase is the idea of
complementarity. In this connection, it is notable that the only aspect of yhwh 'ĕlōhîm's creation
that is not pronounced good is 'ādām in an isolated state.

51 It is interesting to note that the effort to create a suitable helper for 'ādām forms the creatures from the same substance from which 'ādām had been created (2:19), but without the
"breath of life" breathed by Yahweh God (2:7).

52 It is commonly recognized that the MT's reading lĕ'ādām should be repointed to read
lā'ādām. Likewise, the generic "human" should be read in 3:17 and 21. It is not until 4:25, anticipating the genealogical notice in 5:1–5, that 'ādām is to be taken as a proper name.

53 As J. Van Seters has noted, there is no known ancient Near Eastern parallel to the creation of the first couple (*Prologue to History,* p. 116). If there is any source or tradition upon
which the author(s) of this account have relied, it has not yet been discovered. Rather than posit
possible sources, it seems best with this account, as with the others, to recognize the rather large
possible repertoire of materials from which these professional scribes might have drawn and the
myriad possible combinations of motifs that they might have created in constructing their own
myth of the creation of humankind.

a transition in emphasis in the initial two chapters of the primeval history. The account has moved from the level of the cosmic, to the individual, and now to the shape of the community. Likewise, the emphasis on the fate of the ground, *'ădāmâ*, has shifted from its initial insterility to one of sterility. A parallel transformation will occur with this first human pair.

This transformation begins with the opening line of the next story, which records the failure of the first couple to obey the divine command. It begins with the observation that "the man and his wife were both naked (*'ărûmmîm*), but they were not ashamed" (*wĕlō' yitbōšāšû;* 2:25).[54] This connection of shame with nakedness makes a statement about the nature of the creation and the place of the humans within it. Being naked, the first couple was on the same status level as the other animals created by Yahweh God.[55] Indeed, a central point in the story of humankind's disobedience to the divine command is the development of distinctions between the human realm and that of the other animals created by Yahweh God. To this point, all are the same. The earlier command to dominate the other creatures and the function of tilling the soil, while giving humans a special role, do not differentiate them from the other animals.

This situation is changed with the introduction of the snake, the craftiest (*'ārûm*) of all the creatures produced by Yahweh God.[56] The snake, in the manner of standard fable, is endowed not only with an intellectual capacity, but also with the ability to speak. As it begins to quiz the woman concerning God's permission to eat "from every tree in the garden" (*mikkol 'ēṣ haggān;* 3:1), it becomes apparent that there is little if anything beyond the names assigned to the creatures to distinguish among them.[57] The

---

[54] It is critical to note that the connection of nakedness and shame is not related to issues of sexuality. The couple does not become sexually active until 4:1.

[55] R. Oden argues that the clothing of the couple in 3:21 by Yahweh God represents the divine's way of symbolically distinguishing between the divine and human realms (*The Bible Without Theology,* pp. 98–105). It is important to note, as Oden alludes, that clothing *also* distinguishes humans from the rest of the animal world. That clothing and civilization go together in the ancient Near East is illustrated by the change in status that clothing represents with the acculturation of Enkidu by the harlot in the epic of Gilgamesh.

[56] The choice of the serpent (*nāḥāš*) as the animal that "tempts" the human couple has, as would be expected, evoked numerous explanations. I suggest that the snake was chosen because of the legendary nature of the craftiness of the snake that allowed the word play between "naked" and "crafty." The connection of the snake with evil or with Satan reflects theological developments that were not original implications of the text.

[57] A number of issues concerning the role and significance of the snake might be addressed. Whether the snake is engaged in any type of "temptation" of the woman is clearly open to question. As the scene is written, none of the language of "tempting," "seducing," etc.,

woman's reply confirms the snake's query, but she extends the answer to include the injunction in 2:17 that restricted the eating from the "tree of the knowledge of good and evil." The woman's answer introduces a note of ambiguity into the dialogue, for in responding to the snake, she provides the location of the forbidden "tree": according to the woman, *'ĕlōhîm* had forbidden them to eat the fruit "of the tree which is in the midst of the garden" (*hā'ēṣ 'ăšer bĕtôk-haggān*), or even to touch it, "lest you will die" (*pentĕmūtûn;* 3:3).

This ambiguity is created by the fact that, as the narrative stands, there are *two* forbidden trees "in the midst of the garden": the "tree of life" and the "tree of the knowledge of good and evil" (2:9). The prohibition against eating, as well as the subsequent death penalty, however, named only the latter (2:17). Similarly, it is only the "tree of life" that has been explicitly described as located "in the midst of the garden" (2:9). The designation of the forbidden tree as simply "the tree" or "the tree in the midst of the garden" (3:3, 6, 11,12, 17), rather than as "the tree of the knowledge of good and evil," introduces an additional note of ambiguity into the account. What tree is being discussed? What are the issues being developed? How will the resolution contribute to an understanding of nature or of the world?[58]

The snake's retort displays a direct challenge to the divine: "You certainly shall not die!" (*lō'-môt tĕmūtûn;* 3:4). Now the snake provides an explanation for God's having forbidden them to eat from this tree. "God knows" (*yōdēa' 'ĕlōhîm*) that on the day they eat, their eyes will be open and they will become "like god, knowing good and evil" (*kē'lōhîm yōdĕ'ê ṭôb wārā';* 3:5).[59] No specialized theological issues are embedded in this challenge. The snake's statement is really quite clear; what separates the created realm from the creator's is the ability to discern between good and evil. Armed with this assurance, the woman recognizes that the tree is good and that it might provide the ability of discernment (3:6), an exercise of human

---

is present. Rather, the snake simply appears and questions the woman concerning God's instructions given to them concerning the food from the various trees in the garden. How the snake and the woman know of the command is also an interesting issue, since the command in 2:16–17 is given explicitly to *hā'ādām*.

58 It is possible to alleviate a portion of the ambiguity by understanding *'ēṣ* as a collective in this context and having the participants in the story refer to both trees. If this path is taken, it reduces some of the problems with the narrative and helps to explain the reappearance of the "tree of life" in 3:22. On the use of *'ēṣ* as a collective, see the lexica.

59 The motif of becoming "like the gods" is found especially in the Adapa story, where Adapa nearly obtains immortality, but fails to eat the food offered by Anu.

judgment that might be taken as an indication that humans already had a degree of reasoning power that did not necessitate the eating of the fruit of the forbidden tree.

Yielding to their own discretions, and in direct violation of the one and only command given to them by Yahweh God, the couple ate the fruit. As the snake had told them, their eyes were opened (3:7). Yet they did *not* become "like god." Instead, they knew that they were naked (*wayyēdě'û kî 'ērummîm hēm;* cf. 2:25). In place of discerning between "good and evil" that was anticipated as the result of eating the fruit, they knew only that their status had changed. No longer was nakedness their proper state. No longer were they part of the animal world. They had, like Enkidu, become "like god."[60] As a result of their actions, they now took steps to separate themselves from the world to which they had formerly belonged—they made themselves girdles from leaves. Presumably, given the information provided by the story, the ability to discern good and evil brought with it the self-recognition of shame (cf. 2:25). What remains unanswered is the response of the divine to the direct breach of his command.

According to 2:17 and the speech of Yahweh God, the man and woman were now condemned to die. According to the snake, this would not happen. Interestingly, it is the snake who is right. They do not die, but they do forfeit the possibility of remaining in the garden and having access to the benefits that such a status would accord them. One of the most important of such benefits was the presence of Yahweh God in the garden and the personal relationship that existed between the divine and human realms. This relationship would be redefined as a result of the act of disobedience. Upon hearing Yahweh God walking in the garden, the couple hid themselves "in the midst of the trees of the garden" (*bětôk 'ēṣ haggān;* 3:8), i.e., in exactly the same place as the location of the tree from which they had been forbidden to eat. In response to God's call, the man answers that he was afraid and had hidden "because I was naked" (*kî 'ērōm 'ānōkî;* 3:10; cf. 3:7; 2:25), displaying a degree of knowledge that he had not previously possessed. When questioned by Yahweh God about the source of his knowledge, the man immediately attempted to place the blame on the woman, who then accused the snake of tricking her (3:11–13). With this, all the guilty parties are named before Yahweh God, who then pronounces a three-fold curse upon

---

60 *kīma ili;* Gilg. I. iv. 34. Interestingly, Enkidu's learning the ways of the human world resulted in his rejection by the animal kingdom with which he was initially identified.

the rebellious group.[61] The snake is directly cursed for its role in the episode and is separated not only from humans, but from the the rest of the animal kingdom (3:14–15). Because of her disobedience, the woman will be destined to give birth in pain and be dominated by her husband.[62] The disobedience of the man led to a curse placed upon the soil (3:17–19) that would lead to man's having to till the land in order to get it to produce food. The idyllic life of 'ādām in the garden will now become one characterized by toil/labor ('iṣṣābôn; 3:16, 17; cf. 5:29) until he should return to the ground ('ǎdāmâ) from which he was taken (cf. 2:7).

The consequences of the first couple's actions are clear. They cannot remain in the garden, for there remains the "tree of life." Before the couple is expelled from the garden, two items remain to be addressed. All of the other creatures had been named by 'ādām except the woman, who had only received the designation 'iššâ (2:19–20, 23). As an example of the manner in which 'ādām will be able to rule over 'iššâ (cf. 3:16), he now names her ḥawwâ, explaining that "she became the mother of all that lives" (hīw' hāyětâ 'ēm kol-ḥāy; 3:20).[63] The reference to "living" forms a two-fold connection, for it points both to the procreative powers of the woman (4:1–2)

---

61 While the poetic form of the curses in 3:14–20 invites speculation concerning its independent existence or an extensive oral prehistory, there is no evidence to suggest that the section was not composed for the present context and that its contents are derived directly from the story being created by the author(s).

62 The meaning of 3:16 (cf. also 4:7) is debated. The MT is commonly translated: "your desire is for your man, and he will rule over you" (wě'el-'îšēk těšûqātēk wěhû' yimšol-bāk). A. J. Bledstein suggests that těšûqâ may also be translated "desirable," yielding a meaning that it is the woman who is desirable to the man, but that the man will have the ability to dominate her, thus maintaining the equality of the genders that forms an element in the first part of the story ("Was Eve Cursed? [or Did a Woman Write Genesis?]," *BibRev* 9 [1993] 44).

63 The etymology of the name ḥawwâ is obscure. It commonly is connected to the root ḥwh, "to live," but the connection between the two remains debated. The LXX renders the name zōē, "life" in this instance. Whether there is any etymological or mythological connection between the name ḥawwâ and the early Aramaic ḥewyā', "serpent," though intriguing, remains conjectural. The title "mother of all living" is an appropriate title for a goddess, especially one associated with birth, e.g., Mami, or with fertility, e.g., Asherah, etc. Any such reconstructions involving an identification of "Eve" and the snake, or "Eve" and a creator goddess would have to yield to the recognition that the author(s) of the present tale have completely reworked any original story to form a new one. While it is common to regard this verse as a secondary addition to the text, it is possible to understand it as an essential and, hence, "original" part of the whole. From one perspective, it gives immediate fulfillment to the punishment of the woman, for man is given the power to name her, thereby categorizing her, especially with the application of the epithet to her name. At the same time, it prepares the way for the birth of offspring and the formation and continuation of a lineage that forms the connective structures of the entire history.

and to the problem of the "tree of life" (*ʿēṣ haḥayyîm*). Now Yahweh God makes clothing for them from skin and dresses them (3:21), thus distinguishing the human couple not only from the remainder of the animal world, but also from the realm of the divine. To complete this division, it is necessary to expel the couple from the divinely created and maintained garden.

In a speech reminiscent of the divine address in 1:26, Yahweh God confirms to his heavenly court that humankind has become like one of them, knowing good and evil. To keep them from eating the fruit of the "tree of life," and "living forever" (*ḥay lěʿōlām;* 3:22), Yahweh God sent him out of the garden "to till the ground" (*laʿăbōd ʾet-hāʾădāmâ;* 3:23; cf. 2:5) from which he was taken. While there can be no doubt as to the severity of humankind's failure to obey the simple command of Yahweh God to refrain from eating from the trees in the midst of the garden, it is notable that humankind's function in creation, "to till the soil," could only be realized *outside* the garden. Because of the disobedience, however, the task would be fulfilled now only at the cost of great effort (3:17–19). The armed cherubim guarding the way to the "tree of life" insured that immortality would not be obtained by *ʾādām*, nor would humankind be readmitted to the garden.

The "Yahwistic" edition of the story of creation expands greatly upon the more formalized "Priestly" account and individualizes the nature of the creative actions of God, personalizing both the creative process and the human creatures that were part of that creation. It also goes beyond the "Priestly" story, expanding the narrative of the creation of humans and animals to account for the separation of the human and animal realms, as well as that of the divine and human arenas. The basic categories of life have been established, as well as the basic nature of humankind. A significant part of that nature is defined by the disobedience of the couple to the command by Yahweh God, which led to the loss of paradise, i.e., to exile.[64] Hence, these stories concerning creation also stand to explain the fate of the

---

[64] N. Lohfink connects the structure of this story with that of the deuteronomic covenantal theology, noting the following elements: (1) Yahweh founded Israel outside of Canaan; (2) Yahweh brought Israel into the land; (3) Yahweh gave Israel the law as the obligations of the covenant; (4) if Israel fulfilled those obligations, it would prosper; (5) if Israel failed, it would be sent into exile ("Die Erzählung vom Sündenfall," in *Das Siegeslied am Schilfmeer* [1965], pp. 91–92; cited by J. Van Seters, *Prologue to History,* p. 127). If this is correct, then it is clear that the creation account, at least those sections associated with the "Yahwist," displays an interpretive knowledge of basic parts of the deuteronomistic materials.

later nation "Israel": to fail to obey Yahweh God's commands may bring death or exile.

IV. The Development of Cultures

With the first humans now exiled to the world at large, the author(s) continue the account of the development of the social world.[65] This episode, however, shifts perspectives from the actions of the original pair to those of the offspring of that pair, located now in the larger arena of the created world. The account of the two brothers, Cain and Abel, offspring of the pair expelled from the garden for their disobedience to the divine command, shares a parallel structure with the story of their parents' failures: wrongdoing is followed by punishment and expulsion and "mitigation of the penalty."[66] In functional terms, the story presents a foundation for the divine judgment that will be given in 6:5 that humankind was capable of devising only evil, not good, in its heart.

The episode begins with the notice that the man "knew" (*yāda'*) Eve, his wife, and she bore him two sons: Cain, a tiller of soil (*'ōbēd 'ădāmâ;* 4:2; cf. 2:5; 3:23), and Abel, a shepherd (*rō'ēh ṣō'n*).[67] Not only does this beginning introduce new characters into the narrative, but it also segments the genealogical line that is being developed. This segmentation is significant, for it allows for the development of equivalent, and sometimes competing, lines from which ancestors might be derived. Such genealogical

---

65 The story of Cain and Abel does *not* represent a new myth. Rather, it is a direct continuation of the story of creation that will not be complete until the establishment of culture in general.

66 J. Blenkinsopp, *The Pentateuch*, p. 69; see also J. Van Seters, *Prologue to History*, p. 139.

67 It is interesting to notice that there is an etiology given for the name Cain, but none for Abel. Of Cain (*qayin*) it is said by Eve, "I have created a man with Yahweh" (*qānîtî 'îš 'et-yhwh;* 4:1b). J. Van Seters attempts to connect this with the account of the creation attributed to Marduk, in which the following line occurs: "the goddess Aruru created the seed of mankind together with him (Marduk)" (*ᵈaruru zēr amēlūti ittišu itbanû; Prologue to History*, pp. 123–124). While the two sayings might be literarily and semantically equivalent, it is difficult to see how they are to be related in the present context. In contrast, Abel (*hebel*) receives no etymological explanation in the text. Though the name is commonly traced to Akk. *aplu*, "son, heir," rather than to the Hebrew root *hbl*, "to be or act emptily," hence the noun *hebel*, "emptiness, vanity," a strong case can be made for the latter, based upon the function of this character in the story. Abel, I would argue, is not a figure drawn from any ancient mythic tradition, but rather an authorial creation to meet the needs of the narrative. The word occurs only here as a proper name in the Hebrew bible.

shifts also allow the narrator to develop and supplement selected genea-logical lines to expand and comment on particular groups or characteristics of groups.[68] From Eve, "mother of all living," spring the ancestors of agri-culture and pastoralism, establishing the foundations for the support and development of culture at large. Within this context, the narrative reempha-sizes the separation of the human and divine realms, for the two brothers bring offerings to Yahweh. Without narrative explanation, it is noted simply that Yahweh "looked favorably" ($\check{s}\bar{a}^c\hat{a}$) upon Abel's gift (4:3–4), an act that angers Cain. These events provide the basis for understanding the address by Yahweh in 4:7 that provides an important connector with the narrative's development of the fate and future of humankind. In response to Cain's anger, Yahweh replies: "If you do well, is there not a lifting up? And if you do not do well, then sin is crouching at the door. Its desire is for you, but you must master it."[69] It is this announcement to Cain that de-velops the divine perspective concerning human freedom. With the knowl-edge of good and evil, humans have the capacity for either. If they do well, then they can expect exaltation;[70] if they do evil, then they can expect punishment. The covenantal ideals of obedience and proper behavior are now applied to humans outside of the garden, as they had been to those inside.

With no explanation, Cain makes the incorrect choice of actions and kills his brother. Violence and death are thus introduced into the narrative.[71] When Yahweh questions Cain about his brother, Cain chooses to lie, further distancing the human and divine realms and their relationship.[72] Alongside

---

[68] On the role and function of genealogies in the ancient Near East, see the treatment by R. Wilson, *Genealogy and History in the Biblical World,* pp. 56–136.

[69] This verse is textually problematic, and its translation is somewhat conjectural. There are obvious parallels between this statement and the concluding portion of the punishment of the woman in 3:16, though the precise meaning of the parallel remains elusive.

[70] As E. A. Speiser has noted, the "lifting up" or "exaltation" ($\acute{s}\check{e}^{\,\flat}\bar{e}t$) stands in direct con-trast to the "fallen countenance" that characterized Cain's anger (4:6; *Genesis* [AB 1; Garden City, NY: Doubleday, 1964], p. 33).

[71] It is interesting to speculate on whether the killing of Abel might be understood as Cain's usurpation of the divine prerogative of life and death. To this point in the narrative, Yahweh has had the power to threaten death (2:17), but no one has been put to death. There is one allusion to killing, however, contained in 3:21, which notes that Yahweh clothed the first couple with tunics of "skin" ($^c\hat{o}r$), an act that presumably would have required the death of the animals involved.

[72] An interesting parallel is created here with the earlier misdeed in the garden. In re-sponse to each, Yahweh begins his query by asking where someone is. In the garden he asks the whereabouts of the man ($^{\flat}ayyekk\hat{a};$ 3:9); of Cain he asks where ($^{\flat}\hat{e};$ 4:9) his brother is.

violence and death, however, are also introduced guidelines for human relationships. Inadvertently, Cain proclaims that he is to be the one to look
out for his brother (4:9). Just as the actions of ʾādām had affected his
relationship to the ground (ʾădāmâ; 3:17–19), so too would the deeds of
Cain. Cain, like the serpent before him, is directly cursed.[73] The agricultur-
alist who could have represented the genealogical continuation of humans
as workers of the cultivatable ground is condemned to be separated from
that task and instead become a "homeless wanderer" (nāʿ wānād; 4:12). As
Cain recognizes, separation from Yahweh and community makes one liable
to death at the hands of strangers (4:14). Yahweh, however, was not willing
to abandon Cain completely, despite the severity of his misdeed. Instead,
he placed a "sign" (ʾôt) upon him to distinguish him, and pledged seven-
fold vengeance on anyone who should kill Cain. Then he drove him "east
of Eden" to dwell in a "land of wandering" (4:15–16). For those exiled to
the east, located in Babylon or Persia, distinguished from others by their
particular religious "signs," such a story could only provide a type of support for a group fearing death and assimilation at the hands of strangers.
Yahweh would take a perfected form of vengeance on any who would kill
his specially designated people.

Despite this punishment of Cain, it would still be he, as a "tiller of the
soil" and as the eldest son of ʾādām, who would provide the critical genealogical link in the continuation of the story. It is precisely the genealogical references in 4:17–26 and 5:1–32 which provide the connective
tissue holding the various "traditional" stories together and supply a critical
interpretive clue to understanding the nature of the composition of the variety of styles in the primeval history. The Cainite and Sethite genealogies in 4:17–26 are commonly associated with the "Yahwistic" writer,
and the Adamic genealogy of 5:1–32 (commonly excluding v. 29), with the
"Priestly" author.[74] What is most instructive about this genealogical section
of the narrative is that the two sections seem to reflect, at least minimally,
knowlege of a common source. Five of the names contained in the two lineages are identical, and four appear to be variants of each other. At the same
time, they are not presented in the same order, nor do they contain the same
narrative expansions. The "Priestly" version is more stylized than the "Yah-

---

73 Note here the formal similarity between the curses delivered on both: ʾārûr ʾattâ
min- . . . ("you are cursed from . . ."; 4:11; 3:14). The result of the curse is that each is separated
from the community to which it had once belonged.

74 On the retention of the terms "Yahwistic" and "Priestly," see above, n. 14.

wistic,"[75] though it does contain its own internal commentaries on selected members.

Any theory that attempts to explain the composition of the primeval history (and the Pentateuch as a whole, ultimately) must be able to account for the existence of two varying, and somewhat internally contradictory genealogies in such clear literary proximity to each other. The answer to the problem is to be found in the narrative function of each of the genealogical depictions of the development of humankind. The "Yahwistic" version, tracing the lineage from Cain to Lamech, and then segmenting with Lamech's sons and daughter[76] by his two wives, emphasizes the continued development of violence in the world, coming to a crescendo in the song of Lamech (4:23–24) and his avowal to be avenged seventy-seven times in contrast to Cain's seven-fold vengeance. This spread of violence is related via the genealogy to the spread of culture, for it is Cain's son Enoch who builds the first city and names it after himself (4:17),[77] and it is the seventh member of the lineage, Lamech, whose offspring are the founders of various forms of culture.[78] The implications of the lineage passing through Cain, however, suggest that the curse placed on Cain is extended to his descendants. Hence, from this perspective, the cosmos continues to develop in a way inimical to the divine plan. But not all humankind need be traced through this one particular branch represented by the line of Cain. After the establishment of civilization, a contrasting parallel line is presented in 4:25 with the line of Seth, the third son born to ʾādām and his wife (cf. 4:1). Seth fathered a son Enosh, during whose life humans "began to invoke the name of Yahweh" (*hûḥal liqrōʾ bĕšēm yhwh;* 4:26b). In contrast to the proliferation of violence that characterized the line established through Cain, the

---

[75] On the form of the genealogy in chap. 5, see R. Wilson, *Genealogy and History in the Biblical World,* pp. 159–160. It is common to connect the "Priestly" account in 5:1–32 directly to 2:4a and to assert the earlier existence of a full genealogical account.

[76] The mention of a daughter by name is unusual in the genealogies of Genesis, though the generic notice of the birth of daughters to individuals is standard in Gen 5:1–32. I would suggest that these emphases placed upon the daughters, especially the implications of the name of the sister of Tubal-Cain, "pleasant, pleasing" (*naʿămâ*), are to be understood in the context of the story concerning the dissolution of order in the cosmos contained in 6:1–4. See the treatment below.

[77] Reading here *kišmô* for the *kĕšēm bĕnô* of the MT.

[78] As R. Wilson notes, the seven antediluvian ancestors who were responsible for the development of culture in the "Yahwistic" genealogy reflect a number of conceptual parallels with the *apkallu* traditions of Mesopotamia and possibly Phoenicia (*Genealogy and History in the Biblical World,* pp. 149–154).

line of Seth and Enosh offered the possibility of a different future through the worship of Yahweh, the god who had created the original ancestor of all.

It is precisely the function of the parallel "Priestly" account to emphasize the possibility of this alternate course for humans. This is suggested by several aspects of the ten-generation lineage presented in 5:1–32.[79] This genealogy is linked directly to the creation of humankind contained in Gen 1:26–27 and is headed by the reference to "the book of the generations of Adam" (*sēper tôlĕdôt ʾādām;* 5:1), representing the second major portion of the genealogical divisions of the history. As with the introductory section of the "history," which contained two contrasting stories of creation, the *tôlĕdôt* reference does not introduce accounts, but rather forms a bridge between them, implying to the hearer/reader that *each* account represents a version of the generations of humankind. A second bridge between these two genealogies is formed by tracing the lineage of Adam, now clearly used as a proper name, through Seth and then Enosh, reflecting the tradition contained in 4:25–26 and omitting any reference to Cain or Abel.

As with the Cainite genealogy in 4:17–24, the seventh member of the lineage is singled out for special narrative development. In 5:21–23, this seventh person is Enoch (cf. 4:18). The special nature of Enoch is emphasized by the enigmatic reference that "Enoch walked with God and he was no more because God took him" (*wayyithallēk ḥănôk ʾet-ʾĕlōhîm wĕʾênennû kî lāqaḥ ʾotô ʾĕlōhîm;* 5:24; cf. 22). The formulaic reference to the death of the ancestor ("and he died," *wayyāmōt*) is missing in this notice. Whatever might have been the original meaning implied by this phrase, it seems safe to suggest that it carries some kind of notice of the possibility of divine approval. This is certainly the case when the reference to "walking with *ʾĕlōhîm*" is applied to Noah (6:9), whose connection with righteousness is developed in the ensuing narrative. In this genealogical segment, it is possible to "walk with god" rather than to disobey his commands. With the birth and naming of Noah, the genealogy segments, as did the Cainite narrative, projecting the account into its next episode.[80]

---

79 It is common to note in this context that the account of Berossus contains ten names before and after the flood, thus presenting a mythological parallel for the genealogies presented in 5:1–32 and 11:10–26.

80 Lamech's naming of Noah, and the etiology provided for that name, breaks the formulaic regularity of the narrative and reflects back to the cursing of the *ʾădāmâ* in 3:17–19 and 4:17. The special nature of Noah is reflected in the idea that he will somehow offset, or at least provide some relief from, the curse which Yahweh had placed upon the ground (5:29).

V. The Flood and its Aftermath: Starting Over

Though the author(s) might have represented the possibility of human-kind's choice of righteousness over evil, the development of the narrative illustrates that the latter would dominate, leading to a complete dissolution of the creation in the account of the flood. The tone for this is set in the be-ginning of a new account, the introduction to the story of the destruction and recreation of the earth, found in 6:1–8.[81] As the third of the *tôlĕdôt* sec-tions of the primeval history (6:1–9:29), the story of the generations of the flood represents the climax of that section of the Pentateuch, both the-matically and chronologically. Despite the mythological character of these, they contain a very deliberate and calculated chronology, artificial though it may be. According to the chronology of the MT, the flood occurs in the year 1656 AM, which means that over a full third of the history of the world, from the perspective of the rededication of the Temple in 164 BCE, has been compressed into the initial six chapters of the biblical story.[82] The chronological strands of the genealogy in Genesis 5 are continued in the story of the deluge and locate these events within primordial time.

The account of the intermingling of "the sons of god/divine beings" (*bĕnê hā'ĕlōhîm*) with "the daughters of humankind" (*bĕnôt hā'ādām*) is generally interpreted as a fragment of an older story that has been abbre-viated to provide an introduction to the "Yahwistic" version of the flood story. It is difficult, however, to determine any absolute criteria by which one might separate 6:1–4 from 6:5–8, which recounts Yahweh's response to the situation that had developed in the earthly realm. Indeed, the entire sec-tion recounting the story of the flood presents an extensive challenge to the critic because of its clearly composite nature. Despite the fact that a number of differing flood traditions appear to have been combined in this instance to form one narrative, the independent existence of such narratives remains extremely speculative.[83] What is presented in the final text is the story of a

---

81 There is no reason to disassociate 6:1–4, the story of the commingling of the "sons of god" and the "daughters of man," from 6:5–8, God's decisions concerning the nature of hu-mankind and its destruction, though they are generally interpreted as having originally been separate.

82 As is well known, the MT, LXX, and Samaritan Pentateuchs differ drastically in terms of chronology employed. For a discussion of these matters, see J. Blenkinsopp, *The Pentateuch*, pp. 47–49, and the literature cited therein.

83 The numerous parallels among the biblical accounts and those contained in the Sumero-Akkadian stories of the flood and their versions are too many and too popular to

universal flood which brings about the complete dissolution of the order of the cosmos, i.e., a return to chaos.

When the divine and human beings interbreed, the division between these two realms that was an essential dividing line within the accounts of the creation is erased, throwing the creation into disorder. The basic nature of this division between human and divine is reflected in Yahweh's response, obscure though it is, contained in 6:3. Humans will not live forever: because they are flesh, their lifespan will be limited to one hundred and twenty years.[84] Though the connection with limitations placed upon human life and the actions of the *bĕnê hāʾĕlōhîm* is not clear, it is obvious that the author projected some type of connection. This is to be found in 6:4, where the offspring of such unions are noted. The *bĕnê hāʾĕlōhîm* and *bĕnôt hāʾādām* produced the warriors of old, who were renowned (*ʾanšê haššēm*).[85] Whatever the claims to fame of such "semi-divine" beings might

---

recount. It is abundantly clear that there existed a variety of sources for a story about a flood from which the author(s) of the biblical narrative could have created their own. At the same time, it appears quite evident that there are unavoidable contradictions in the biblical story, which leads to the probability that at least two different and competing accounts of a flood have been combined. The mastery with which this conflation has occurred is often overlooked. An excellent discussion of the differing ways of reading the composite story of the flood, fore-grounding either the unity or the duality of the present text, is presented by A. F. Campbell and M. O'Brien, *Sources of the Pentateuch*, pp. 213–219. According to the standard division of the sources, only the "Priestly" version yields a reasonably complete narrative of the flood. More recently, J. Van Seters has attempted a reevaluation of the source division and has concluded that it is the "Yahwistic" version that is complete and that the "Priestly" account contains only minor embellishments and supplements to the main narrative (*Prologue to History*, pp. 160–164). That such an argument could be seriously mounted should caution one against depending too greatly on reconstructed sources as the basis of analysis unless the case can be made from evidence outside the text being analyzed.

84 The textual problems here are numerous, but it seems clear that a meaning along these general lines is intended. J. Van Seters suggests that *bĕšaggam* be interpreted as *bĕ + še = baʾăšer + gam* (="because also") and that the references to the age limit and to the Nephilim are secondary to the "original" text (*Prologue to History*, pp. 150–151). If the reference to an "ideal" age limit is posited as secondary to the text, it might be understood as the result of the inclusion of Deuteronomy as the final section of the Tetrateuch, thus forming the Pentateuch, since of all the heroes' ages given in the Pentateuchal materials, only that of Moses totals one hundred and twenty years. It might, on the other hand, be anticipating this reference (Deut 34:7), and thus be quite original to the present context.

85 6:4a connects the Nephilim (*nĕpîlîm*) with these warriors. It seems clear that this reference is an intrusion into the text. The only other references to the Nephilim are found in Num 13:33 (2x) and in the commonly emended text in Ezek 32:27. It is tempting to find an intentional play on words between the phrase "men of renown" (*ʾanšê haššēm*) and the name Shem (*šēm;* 5:32; 6:10), who will become the ancestral line from which Abram will spring (11:10–26).

have been, their human elements would limit them to a non-divine lifespan. The fruit of the "tree of life" would not leave the garden.

This section represents a clear dissolution of order reflected in the roles and functions of the actors in the narrative. The role of the *běnê hā'ělōhîm*, the members of Yahweh's council (1:26; 3:22; cf. 11:7), has been completely subordinate until this point. Here, however, whether as a rebellion or simply as an act, the "sons of god" take the initiative[86] and act within the human realm. This clearly blurs the distinctions between human and divine spheres that had been established with the clothing of the humans and their expulsion from the garden. Their actions challenge the very function for which the woman was created in the garden, i.e., as a suitable companion for *'ādām*, not for *běnê hā'ělōhîm*. Further, the mating of the *běnê hā'ělōhîm* with the *běnôt hā'ādām* to produce a class of "warriors" introduces a class of individuals not previously a part of creation. These actions represent the onset of chaos.

Since it was the divine who had ordered the cosmos by virtue of the creative word, so too would its dissolution be spoken by him. Yahweh recognizes that humankind was incapable of conceiving of anything except evil (*ra'*) in his heart (6:5). Despite the ability to discern good (*ṭôb*), humankind concocted only the opposite. In response, Yahweh "repents" (*wayyinnāḥem*) for creating *'ādām* (6:6) and proclaims his decision to blot out humankind "from upon the face of the ground" (*mē'al pěnê hā'ădāmâ;* 6:7; cf. 7:4). No longer is humankind cursed from the ground (cf. 3:17–19; 4:11–12); now its complete destruction has been proclaimed.

But the ways of the divine remain mysterious and unpredictable, especially in those instances where it seems that there is no reason for such unpredictability. Earlier, death had been promised to the couple on the day on which they would eat from the "tree of the knowledge of good and evil," but that had not happened. Now Yahweh proclaimed that he would destroy all creatures from upon the earth, but that also would not occur, by virtue of another decision by Yahweh. In a simple and straightforward sentence, the

---

[86] On the efforts to reconstruct a myth of a heavenly rebellion and the ousting of the rebel gods from heaven, see P. D. Hanson, "Rebellion in Heaven, Azazel, and Euhemeristic Heroes in 1 Enoch 6–11," *JBL* 96 (1977) 195–233. Whatever mythological background might be reconstructed for understanding some possible original, it is clear that a heavenly rebellion *per se* is not what is intended by the present text. As R. S. Hendel has noted, whatever the original mythological background of Gen 6:1–4 might have been, it has now been integrated fully into the primeval history ("Of Demigods and the Deluge: Toward an Interpretation of Genesis 6:1–4," *JBL* 106 [1987] 25–26).

author(s) note: "Now Noah found favor with Yahweh" (6:8). The last major figure named in the Adamic line (5:30–32) is singled out from the rest of the creation and represents the hope for a new beginning from the deluge that would return the earth to chaos.

The *tôlĕdôt* formula concerning Noah occurs in 6:9, connecting the introduction of the story (6:1–8) with the accounts of the flood and its resolution that are described in 6:10–9:17.[87] The materials in 6:9–12, often assigned to the "Priestly" source on the basis of vocabulary and repetition with the preceding, expand upon the introduction of 6:1–8 and offer an explanation of why Noah was favored and how the earth had become corrupt. Noah is described in a two-fold manner: he was a "righteous man" (*'îš ṣaddîq*), "perfect among his generation" (*tāmîm hāyâ bĕdōrōtâw;* 6:9).[88] He clearly stood in a special relationship with the deity, as had Enoch, for he too was described as "walking (habitually) with God" (cf. 5:22, 24). In contrast to common humankind that was apparently able to devise only evil (6:5), Noah represented the real possibility of acting in the proper relationship with the deity. Yet the righteousness of one could not offset the sinfulness of the general creation.[89] Whether the righteousness and perfection of Noah were passed to his three sons (6:10; cf. 5:32) is not stated. Indeed, nothing is made of them at this point except their names and lineage.

The earth becomes corrupt, filled with violence, and this corruption is due to the actions of "all flesh" (*kol-bāśār;* 6:12). Yahweh's sudden announcement to Noah that he is going to destroy all living creatures from upon the earth[90] gives the clear impression that there has been an ongoing relationship between Yahweh and Noah, something that is implied by the description of Noah in 6:9. Despite the repeated emphasis on the corruptness of flesh and the divine decision to destroy it, the destruction will

---

87 Compare the functions of the notices in 2:4a and 5:1. The short story containing the planting of the first vineyard and the cursing of Canaan contained in 9:18–28 is not a part of the *tôlĕdôt* of Noah, but stands as an introduction to the following *tôlĕdôt* formula which connects it with the "Table of Nations" in Gen 10:1–32.

88 Each of these designations carries cultic implications. "Righteousness" is commonly associated with a life lived in conjunction with covenantal demands, while "perfection" carries the cultic implication of being "free of defect." On the possibilities of such perfection in the human realm, cf. Gen 17:1; Deut 18:13; Josh 24:14.

89 This very issue will emerge again, in a more extended form, in Genesis 18 and the debate between Yahweh and Abraham over the fate of Sodom and Gomorrah.

90 Read here *mē'et-hā'āreṣ* (6:13b); the *m* has been mistakenly separated and read as a pronominal suffix with the preceding verb.

not be as complete as it might initially appear. Instead, Noah is given instructions to build an ark and prepare to take his family and representatives of all living creatures aboard it so that a new creation might emerge from the chaos to be created by the deluge.[91] This result is anticipated by the announcement to Noah by Yahweh that "I will make my covenant with you" (*wahăqīmōtî 'et-běrîtî 'ittāk;* 6:18; cf. 9:9, 11, 15, 16). The humans that will emerge from the ark and who will be the only ones to survive the cosmic deluge will be the direct descendants of this one righteous individual with whom Yahweh has established his covenant. To emphasize Noah's righteousness, it is noted that he did all that Yahweh commanded him (6:22; 7:5).

Yahweh had remembered (*zākar*) Noah and those with him on the ark (8:1; cf. 9:15, 16, 19:29; Exod 2:24; 6:5; Lev 26:42, 45), and the earth had dried completely by the first day of the first month of the 601st year of Noah's life, i.e., on New Year's day (8:13; cf. 7:11).[92] Noah and his family are then commanded to leave the ark and to bring out all the animals so that they might multiply upon the face of the earth (8:17; cf. 1:22, 28). In response to Yahweh's saving Noah and his family, Noah, the righteous man, builds an altar (*mizbēaḥ*) to Yahweh and offers holocaust offerings (*'ōlôt*) upon it.[93] Yahweh's response to the pleasing smoke of the sacrifice forms an inclusio with 6:5: he promises that he will not again curse the ground (*hā'ădāmâ*) because of humankind. This represents a change in Yahweh's perspective, for he persists in his recognition that "the inclination of the human heart is evil from its youth" (*yēṣer lēb hā'ādām ra' minnĕ'ûrāw;* 8:21; cf. 3:17). Nonetheless, he promises never again to destroy all living creatures.

This decree represents an important insight into the nature of the divine. As noted in 6:6, the deity has the ability to change its mind, to repent, and do something different than it had planned or announced earlier.

---

[91] For the numerous parallels with other flood stories and listings of the inconsistencies within the biblical account, see C. Westermann, *Genesis 1–11*, pp. 395–406. It might be argued that the numerous inconsistencies and contradictions that characterize the biblical account of the flood emphasize the dissolution of order in the creation and its return to *tōhû wābōhû* (1:2).

[92] It is commonly recognized that there are several levels of chronology present in the final form of the story. How the reference to New Year's day is to be related to the following verse that notes that the earth was dried up on the twenty-seventh day of the second month remains debated.

[93] Cf. 12:7, 8; 13:18; 22:9; 26:25; 33:20; 35:1, 3, 7. Elsewhere in Genesis, the *'ōlâ* offering is mentioned only in 22:2, 3, 6, 7, 8, 13 in connection with the binding of Isaac. Whether this story is meant to imply that it is legitimate for the righteous to build altars and to offer sacrifices without benefit of a priesthood is not clear.

Now, for whatever reasons convincing to deities, Yahweh had decided that the cause for his destruction of all life (with some rather blatant exceptions) would not again constitute a legitimate reason for acting in such a manner. The formal liturgical confirmation of this is presented in 9:1–17, which draws upon elements of the creation account in 1:1–2:4a, and helps confirm that the emergence of Noah, his family, and the creatures from the ark represents a new creation that is under divine control, just as the old one had been. But as the divine mind had changed, so too would the balance of nature be changed in this new creation. Instead of being limited to eating the produce of the ground, humans were now given the right to eat all that lived. The only restriction would be to refrain from eating blood (9:3–4), providing the first of the ritual prescriptions differentiating between acceptable and unacceptable foods. The failure to adhere to this prohibition would lead to God's requiring the blood of the offender, i.e., the death penalty (9:5–6). No exceptions are noted. This seems to reflect another shift in the divine perspective. While Yahweh had protected Cain, despite his having shed the blood of his brother (4:15), henceforth he would require the death of the offender.

A new order was established. Now Yahweh offered a universal covenant (*bĕrît*) with Noah and all that came forth from the ark (9:8–9). Never again would Yahweh destroy the earth with a flood, and the rainbow would serve as the sign of this promise. No obligations were attached to the covenant, yet humankind was under the directive to avoid the proliferation of violence that had led to the destruction of the old order. The creation would endure, but the question that remains unanswered is how humankind would respond to the new order in this new world. The events narrated in the next segment of the narrative begin to form an answer to this question.

VI. The Spread of Civilization

The three sons of Noah are named yet again in the introduction to the next episode of the primeval history (9:18; cf. 5:32; 6:10; 7:13). The segmented genealogy which begins the narrative helps to establish the nature of the new creation. All humankind will now be descended from one of the three sons of Noah, a situation allowing for the type of differentiation of groups from which ethnicity may be constructed. Notably, Ham is introduced in this genealogical instance as "the father of Canaan" (*'ăbî kĕnā'an;* 9:18b, 22a), a reference that provides a basis for understanding the story which follows.[94] It would be from these three sons that all the earth would be dispersed (*nāpaṣ*), a choice of terms that connects the account here with the initial episode of the next section, the story of the "tower of Babel" and the scattering (*pûṣ;* 11:4, 8, 9) of the populations of the world (11:1–9).

In this somewhat obscure account, the aged Noah, called a "man of the soil" (*ʾîš hāʾ ădāmâ;* 9:20; cf. 2:5; 3:23; 4:2, 12), reflecting the fact that man's task on the earth had not changed, plants and harvests the first vineyard. While the meanings of the events narrated in the ensuing story are rather opaque, it is clear that Ham, the father of Canaan, has committed some grave offense against his father's honor.[95] As a result, Noah places a curse on Canaan, the son of Ham, proclaiming that Canaan would be a servant to his brothers. In reading the story, which provides the justification for the cursing of Canaan, it is difficult to miss the *ad hoc* nature of the explanation. The entire episode serves to establish a hierarchical relationship among the offspring of the three sons of Noah from whom the nations of the earth would develop. The mention of Canaan is critical to the unfolding of the genealogical lists that will provide the ethnic labels by which competing groups will be distinguished from the ancestors of "Israel" and to provide a dichotomous relationship that will allow "Israel" to separate itself from all others. As the biblical narratives develop the boundaries of "Israelite" ethnic identity, "Canaan" will serve to designate all that is *not* to be associated with "Israel."[96] "Israel's" "later" claims to subdue and dominate the Canaanites and their "relatives"[97] find their justifications in the structure of this newly developing creation.

This episode is connected to the "Table of Nations" (10:1–32) by the fourth *tôlĕdôt* formula used to structure the primeval history. This *tôlĕdôt* list provides linear genealogies for each of the sons of Noah, giving the

---

[94] The author(s) provide no background for the sudden introduction of Ham as the father of Canaan. The reference seems awkward, as does the appearance of Ham in the story which follows. While it is often suggested that in the "original" form of the story, Canaan, not Ham, was one of the sons of Noah, and that such an "original" initially had only one, or perhaps two sons involved, such reconstructions remain conjectural.

[95] Numerous efforts have been made to interpret what might have been intended by the reference to Ham's seeing the "nakedness of his father" (*ʿerwat ʾābîw;* 9:22). While it is commonly given sexual connotations, it must be admitted that the present meaning of the reference is completely obscure.

[96] On the purely rhetorical and symbolic use of the term "Canaanite" in the Hebrew materials, see N. P. Lemche, *The Canaanites and their Land.*

[97] These are listed in the offspring of Canaan in 10:15–19.

names of the sons born to them after the flood (*'aḥar hammābûl;* 10:1).
Interestingly, the genealogies are given in the reverse order of the standard notices of Noah's sons, i.e., Shem, Ham, and Japhet (5:32; 6:10; 7:13;
9:18; 10:1). Since it will be through the line of Shem that Abram (11:26),
and hence "Israel" will emerge, Shem's line is presented last to connect the
stories of Abram with the emergence of the populations of the earth. The
sons of Japhet are recorded in 10:2–5, followed by the sons of Ham
(10:6–20) and of his son, Canaan (10:15–19),[98] and finally by the sons of
Shem (10:21–32).[99] The genealogical table ends with a summary notice
concerning the sons of Noah that forms an inclusio with the notice in 10:1
and brings this *tôlĕdôt* to an end.

With this, the various national groupings of the earth receive their ancestral gentilics, and the basis for genealogical divisions is provided.[100]
From the common background of the ancestry of one righteous man, Noah,
the earth is now populated by related, but distinctive peoples. The final
tôlĕdôt of the primeval history constitutes another example of the resump-
tive-expansive technique of the author(s) of these materials. This section
will provide for the dispersion of humankind over the world, i.e., for the
connection of different groups with different lands and languages, two of
the primary ingredients for distinguishing among ethnic entities. Despite
the references in the Table of Nations to individual national languages (e.g.,
10:5, 20, 31), 11:1 notes that all the earth had one language (*śāpâ 'eḥāt*) and,
upon their journey from the east (*miqqedem;* 11:2; cf. 2:8; 10:30), found a
valley in Shinar (Babylon), where they settled. There they decided to build
a city with a tower, whose top would reach to the heavens.[101] The reason for
such an action is explicitly given: "so that we might make a name for our-

---

98 Among the offspring of Canaan are mentioned the Jebusites, Amorites, Girgashites,
and Hivites, names commonly associated with the inhabitants of Canaan within the deuteronomistic narratives.

99 Verse 21 notes that Shem is "the ancestor of all of the sons of Eber" (*hû' 'ăbî kol-bĕnê-
'ēber*), the eponym that provides the basis for the gentilic, *'ibrî,* "Hebrew."

100 While the majority of the Table of Nations is generally assigned to the "Priestly"
source, it is commonly held that it also contains a number of references to be attributed to the
"Yahwistic" writer. What is clear is that the Table is a composite construction which is designed
to fulfill a particular purpose within this narrative. What sources, if any, might have provided a
background for its construction, like so many others, remain completely conjectural.

101 The connection of the tower with the ziggurat Etemenanki in Babylon is generally
maintained and quite possibly accurate. At any rate, it is clear that the story refers to a tower-like
structure that would allow humanity to bridge the gap between the divine and human worlds.

selves" (*wĕnaʿăśeh-lānû šēm*) "lest we be scattered upon the face of all the earth" (*pen-nāpûṣ ʿal-pĕnê kol-hāʾāreṣ;* 11:4). The reference to "making a name" reflects in two different directions. It recalls the "warriors of old" who had descended from the intermingling of the "sons of god" and the "daughters of humans" (6:4) that had constituted a part of the dissolution of order that had led to the deluge, and it represents an attempt to "break" the genealogical lines associated with Shem (*šēm*) that have already been established. Likewise, the desire to keep from being scattered across the earth constitutes a human attempt to thwart the development of humankind that had already been recounted (9:19; 10:5, 32).

Yahweh's response to these acts is predictable. He goes down to "see" what is happening and realizes that if they are successful in their efforts, humans will be capable of anything (11:5–6).[102] Paralleling his actions prior to the initial creation of humankind, Yahweh addresses his heavenly council, invoking them to participate in his plan to alter their proposed course of action (11:6–7; cf. 1:26). Despite human efforts to bridge the distinctive gaps between the human and divine realms, the divine would not allow this to happen (cf. 3:22–24). As a result, and in accord with the notices already given in the genealogies, humankind was scattered upon the earth and was provided with different languages and lands.

The fifth and final *tôlĕdôt* formula, announcing the genealogy of Shem, connects this account to the repetition of the Shemite line, which extends the lineage from Shem through Terah, where, as with the previous genealogies of Adam and Noah, the genealogy segments (11:10–26).[103] With the introduction of Terah, the primeval history comes to a close. The way is paved to begin the description of the particular ancestors of "Israel" and to provide a background for understanding what made them and their descendants so special in a world filled with differing national and ethnic groups. From a variety of traditions and materials, the author(s) of Genesis 1–11

---

[102] This realization that humans will be able to accomplish whatever they devise should not be divorced from the divine realization that humans, despite the potential for developing the good, tend to concoct only evil (cf. 6:5; 8:21).

[103] This genealogy is clearly artificial and is designed to connect the account of the scattering of the nations with the lineage of Shem and the introduction of Abram. While it is common to note the parallels of this section with the line of Adam, and note the ante- and post-diluvian ancestors, it should be noted that the MT and Sam of Gen 11:10–26 list only nine ancestors. The LXX expands it to ten, thus creating a symmetrical balance not displayed by the other versions.

have constructed an account of the structures of creation, the primacy of Yahweh as creator, and the importance of the line of Shem, one of the three ancestors of all of the postdiluvian creation. From among such related groups would be developed explanatory boundaries that would separate them as special, provide a particular lineage, and connect them to a particular land, by which they would identify and define themselves.

——— ஐ 5 ௧ ———

THE PATRIARCHAL STORIES: MYTHS OF MIGRATION AND THE PROMISE OF THE LAND—THE CHARACTER OF A PEOPLE

I. Promises of Land and Progeny

The ideological triumph of the biblical story is to convince that what is new is actually old. It has been successful to the point of establishing a virtually unchallenged premise of biblical scholarship.[1]

When one turns to the stories of the patriarchal ancestors of "Israel" recounted in Genesis 12–50,[2] the problems associated with the analysis of the texts and their composition become much more complicated than those accompanying the "primeval history." In general terms, the character of Genesis changes with the introduction of the patriarchs, for it is commonly perceived that these figures usher the narrative into the area of human history and out of the arena of mythological speculation.[3] The major problem that

[1] P. R. Davies, *In Search of 'Ancient Israel'*, p. 114.

[2] While it is common to assign the patriarchal narratives to Genesis 12–35 and to understand the materials associated with Genesis 37–50, which deal with the stories of Jacob's sons in general and Joseph in particular, as an originally independent composition with a source and redactional history peculiar to itself, it is not at all clear that it ever circulated separately from the surrounding materials. For that reason, I include consideration of these materials alongside the stories associated with the patriarchs and will argue that the Joseph stories are an essential and original part of the composition of the "primary history." For a discussion of some of the major compositional problems commonly associated with the Joseph stories, see A. F. Campbell and M. A. O'Brien, *Sources of the Pentateuch*, pp. 223–237.

[3] Since the publication of the works by T. L. Thompson (*The Historicity of the Patriarchal Narratives: The Quest for the Historical Abraham* [BZAW 133; Berlin/New York: W. de Gruyter, 1974]) and J. Van Seters (*Abraham in History and Tradition*), scholars have recognized the problems associated with any attempt to reconstruct a history of a "patriarchal" period. None-

the critic encounters in analyzing the composition and function of these materials lies in the highly fragmentary nature of the stories that are recounted
about the ancestors to which "Israel" traces its origins. Despite efforts to
reconstruct oral and/or written cycles of stories associated with individual
patriarchal figures that were later combined by an editor to form this narrative section of Genesis, scholars rarely emphasize that the stories that we
do have do not constitute any whole or connected literary account of any of
the patriarchs. Rather, each reconstructable cycle contains selected vignettes
which give the appearance of some type of chronological and narrative
progress only by virtue of their present redactional arrangement. Even if one
posits that there were selected written traditions from which the author(s) of
the patriarchal stories chose their narratives, one is left to explain the variety
of conflicting and conflating accounts that the author(s) chose to include.[4]

   The major failure of the efforts to reconstruct the strata of traditions
that compose the final, and, I might insist, *only* version of the Pentateuchal
narrative that exists,[5] is the inability of critics to locate individual redactional layers within any known historical and socio-cultural situation that
would provide a reasonable explanation for the creation and use of those
materials. An example of the type of explanation used to justify various redactional efforts might be instructive. The "Yahwistic" source is most com-

---

theless, the prevalent attitude in the field is that these stories recount on some level the activities
of real people, despite our complete inability to place these stories into any documentable historical situation. It should be emphasized that the shift in perspective that most scholars adopt
when they begin an analysis of the stories associated with the patriarchs is based on presuppositions regarding the content, and not the form, of the narrative accounts.

   4 Author(s) have the ability to create literary quandaries both by intent and by accident.
For the present analysis, I will work on the presupposition that the writers of these materials
were aware that there were a number of inconsistencies and redundancies in their narrative and
that these were understood as contributing something to the function and meaning of the story
as written. Further, most of the conflicts and inconsistencies among the accounts present problems *only* if one presupposes a knowledge of the *whole* of the narrative. It is possible that the
narrative was originally used in small sections and not read/heard as a continuous whole.

   5 While there exist a number of chronological and textual variations among the major
manuscript traditions represented by the Sam, LXX, Vulgate, and MT, there do not exist any
major variations in the Pentateuchal materials concerning the basic content and arrangement of
episodes or omission of characters, etc. In other words, all extant material evidence indicates
that the present form of the text of the Pentateuch is the only form of that narrative that exists.
For understanding the history of the creation and composition of the text, it seems more reasonable to begin here and try to explain how such a text might have been created and what functions
it might have been intended to serve than to explain it on the basis of the redaction of a number
of recreated "traditions" whose origins, transmission, meaning, form, and function exist only
within the realm of theoretical constructs.

monly dated as the earliest of the Pentateuchal narratives. According to the general consensus, "J" composed its narrative of Israelite origins sometime during the "golden age" of King Solomon, and it served as a propaganda document creating a "national history" supporting the Davidic line and the succession of Solomon to the throne.[6] While this has obviously been found to be an appealing type of answer, it suffers several fatal flaws, not least of which is the continued controversy concerning the dating and identification of the extent of such a "Yahwistic" source.[7]

Given the recent efforts to reconstruct the history of ancient Palestine, including Israel and Judah as national states,[8] it has become more and more obvious that there is little if any historical correspondence between the Palestine that can be reconstructed from the archaeological settlement patterns and attendant data and the depiction of "Israel" that is the product of the biblical materials. As P. R. Davies has argued, scholars must make clear distinctions among three different "historical" entities: "historical" Israel, "biblical" Israel, and "ancient" Israel.[9] The failure to distinguish among these three very separate categories of materials can only cloud the rather murky understandings of the process of composition further. One of the clearest aspects of this, as applied to the "J" document, concerns the time of its composition, i.e., in the time of the "united monarchy." Problematically, the "united monarchy" exists *only* as a construct found *within* the ideologically conditioned presentation of the Hebrew narratives. There is little historical evidence to suggest that a unification of the national states of Israel and Judah ever occurred, that such might have been possible as early as the tenth century BCE, or that it was orchestrated by David and maintained by his son Solomon.

---

6 See, for example, N. K. Gottwald, *The Hebrew Bible: A Socio-Literary Introduction*, p. 137. Cf. above, Chap. 1, pp. 6–8.

7 For an overview of the confusion dominating the discussions concerning the "Yahwist," see A. de Pury's article, "Yahwist ('J') Source," in *ADB* VI, 1012–1020, and the accompanying bibliography.

8 See most recently the extensive work of T. L. Thompson, *Early History of the Israelite People*. Specific examples of the types of problems that underlie the attempts at reconstructing the history of this period are noted by N. P. Lemche, "Is it Still Possible to Write a History of Ancient Israel?" *SJOT* (1994) 165–190.

9 *In Search of 'Ancient Israel'*, pp. 11–20. For Davies, the first of these refers to the population and culture of highland Palestine during the Iron Age and is reconstructed on the basis of archaeological and comparative sociological and geographical data. The second refers to the "Israel" that is created within the narratives of the Hebrew bible. The third is a scholarly construct, based upon the careful correlation of the "historical" and "biblical" pictures.

Once these data are given serious attention, the entire setting and function of a "J" source as a pro-Davidic national epic dissolve. The "Yahwist"
becomes a scholarly construct that has no setting in any discernible historical or cultural situation. The same arguments might be directed against the
reconstructions which assign the "Elohist" to the ninth century BCE and
see in it the efforts to construct a "competing" national epic for the newly
divided monarchy of the North. Clearly, the biblical account and the historical accounts require differing solutions. Such a view as this need not be
seen as in any way cynical. It is, rather, simply to recognize that a great deal
of the history of the criticism of the Hebrew bible has been performed by
scholars who had and/or have, intentionally or not, applied a particular
theological set of premises that have become a part of the accepted wisdom of the field.[10] From the perspective of the academic study of religions,
it should occasion no surprise whatsoever that the actual history of a group
and their recapitulation of their past, understood as an ethnomythography,
bear little resemblance to one another. Given the textual evidence that is
available to the modern scholar, any attempt to explain the composition of
the Tetrateuch or the Pentateuch must *begin* with the recognition of an observation made by T. L. Thompson: ". . . *all of the narrative material in the
pentateuch is unquestionably contemporaneous with the final redaction*"
(italics in the original).[11] Since this final redaction is the only edition that
we possess, it seems reasonable to begin the investigation by attempting
to locate it within a particular historical and social context and to explain
some of the ways in which it functioned to identify and define the people
who created it and who adopted it as an account of their past.

With this beginning premise, we might turn to the issue of the patriarchs and note that these stories are connected by several interrelating
motifs. The narrative development of these motifs into a larger complex
provides a background for understanding the references to the patriarchs
and the promises made to them in Deuteronomy, where they play a highly
significant role, yet are simply presumed and never developed.[12] The background for these promises, and the "proper" responses to them, are pro-

10 On this issue, see the provocative observations of R. A. Oden, Jr., *The Bible Without
Theology*, pp. 1–29.

11 *The Origin Tradition of Ancient Israel*, p. 62.

12 T. Römer has argued that the actual names of the patriarchs, i.e., Abraham, Isaac, and
Jacob, have been added to the references to the "fathers" in the book of Deuteronomy by the
final redactor of the Pentateuch and that prior to that redaction, the references were simply
to some otherwise unnamed traditional ancestors with whom the promise of the land had been
connected (*Israels Väter: Untersuchungen zur Väterthematik im Deuteronomium und in der*

vided by the stories concerning the "ancestors" that are developed in Genesis. Of importance to note is that these promises concerning the gift of the land most especially are *not* fulfilled in the narrative accounts until the stories of Joshua.[13]

It is clear, however, that the author(s) of these materials intended the stories of the patriarchs to be understood as a continuation of the accounts providing for the primeval history, for they have adopted an analogous *tôlĕdôt* structure as a frame for these narratives[14] which continues the genealogical lines of descent established in the preceding materials. In addition to the priority given to genealogies throughout these stories, the motif of the promise of the land is linked directly to the issue of descent from Abram. Land, identity, and the wandering quest for the fulfillment of the promises tie together the stories of the ancestors of "Israel" and their search for the fruition of Yahweh's promises.[15]

---

deuteronomistischen Tradition [Orbis Biblicus et Orientalis 99; Göttingen: Vandenhoeck & Ruprecht, 1990]). This position has been critiqued extensively by N. Lohfink, who argues that the initial reference to the patriarchs in Deut 1:8 explicitly identifies the ancestors and establishes their identity for the remainder of the book (*Die Väter Israels in Deuteronomium: mit einer Stellungnahme von Thomas Römer* [Orbis Biblicus et Orientalis 111; Freiburg, Switzerland: Universitätsverlag/Göttingen: Vandenhoeck & Ruprecht, 1991]). A review of these two positions is offered by S. L. McKenzie in *JBL* 112 (1993) 128–130. J. Van Seters, taking a position closely related to that of Römer, argues that the references to the "fathers" in Deuteronomy referred originally to the generation associated with the exodus and that the connection of the promise of the land to the patriarchs represents a conflation of two traditions by an exilic Yahwist (*Prologue to History*, pp. 227–245).

13 For this reason, the narrative sources underlying the Pentateuch are often extended into Joshua and portions of Judges. If one begins with the presupposition that the accounts in the Tetrateuch are chronologically earlier and are independent of the deuteronomistic literature, then this is a position for which some strong (though not necessarily convincing) arguments might be adduced. If the opposite starting point is chosen, then it is not necessary to presuppose or reconstruct any such continuous narrative sources concerning the fulfillment of the promise of the land underlying these accounts.

14 J. Blenkinsopp outlines this *tôlĕdôt* structure as follows (*The Pentateuch*, p. 99):

1. 11:27–25:11 Terah (Abraham)
2. 25:12–18   Ishmael
3. 25:19–35:29 Isaac (Jacob)
4. 36:1–37:1   Esau-Edom
5. 37:2–50:26 Jacob (Joseph and his brothers)

As with the primeval history, the third *tôlĕdôt* formula introduces the central event in the story.

15 Despite the common presupposition that such materials could only have been collected and redacted over a lengthy period of time, it is just as likely that such editorial activity could have taken place over a very brief period. Indeed, N. Whybray has suggested that only one author and/or edition of the Pentateuch needs to be posited (*The Making of the Pentateuch,*

D. J. A. Clines points out in his analysis of the Pentateuch:

> And more than most stories, more even than most epics, the Pentateuch
> refuses to leave the goal unspecified or to allow it to be only gradually un-
> veiled; in the Pentateuch the goal is explicit from the beginning in the prom-
> ises that call for fulfilment. Especially if Genesis 12 is read as a recapitulation
> and redefinition of the primal intentions of God for man (land, descendants, a
> divine-human relationship), the Pentateuch gives its hand away at its very be-
> ginning—not, indeed to foreshorten the enormous distance between Gene-
> sis 1 and Deuteronomy 34 or to dissipate the sense of movement, but pre-
> cisely to signify that the reality it portrays, of relentless movement toward a
> goal, is the major significance this vast segment of human history holds.[16]

The selection of the line of Abram and his descendants as the ones to receive Yahweh's blessings and gifts emphasizes at every point one of the
most basic questions that concerns *homo religiosus*—the nature of the relationship between the human and the divine realms. The nature of "Israel's"
identity as an ethnic group, distinct and separated from all others, is defined
in part by the ways in which the "primary history" as a whole resolves the
issues associated with the nature of the divine/human relationship.

The genealogy of Terah is repeated in 11:27 and provides the introductory bridge to the stories concerning Abram contained in 11:27–25:11.
The movement of Terah's family from Ur of the Chaldeans (11:28)[17]
to Haran, in order to go "to the land of Canaan" (*lāleket ʾarṣāh kĕnaʿan;*
11:31), introduces the journey motif that will dominate the remainder of the
Pentateuchal narrative. It also provides the goal of these wanderings by
mentioning the precise destination for the first time. To preview the complexity that may be involved in the narrative fulfillment of the promises, the
genealogy introduces Abram's wife, Sarai, and notes that she was barren
(11:30). With this background provided for the introduction of the explicit
promises, the story turns to Yahweh's address to Abram.

There is no introduction or explanation of the prior relationship between Abram and Yahweh: Yahweh speaks and Abram obeys. Abram's
obedience to Yahweh's commands will become paradigmatic as both a
model of and a model for proper behavior with respect to the divine com-

---

pp. 232–233). In a similar vein, P. R. Davies has argued that a single dedicated scribe during a
lifetime of work could easily have produced a final "deuteronomistic" version of the Pentateuch
(*In Search of 'Ancient Israel'*, pp. 96–97).

16 *The Theme of the Pentateuch* (JSOTSup 10; Sheffield: JSOT, 1978), p. 106.

17 On this problematic designation, at least for those theories that argue for a second millennium provenance for these stories, see the commentaries.

mand.[18] He is directed to go to the land which Yahweh would show him and where Yahweh would present him with an unconditional grant[19] that would provide the basis for the identification of his descendants with that particular land and lineage. Abram would become a "great nation" (*gōy gādôl*), his name would be great and it would become a blessing (12:2). The promise is put into universal terms, noting that "in you all the families of the earth will be blessed" (*wĕnibrĕkû bĕkā kol mišpĕḥōt hāʾădāmâ;* v. 3b; cf. 28:14; 18:18).[20] The importance of this aspect of blessing should not be overlooked, for it will be through the name and lineage of Abram that all the inhabitants of the earth will be brought back into the relationship originally established at creation (1:28). Further, Yahweh pledges always to side with the family of Abram (12:3a), providing the potential for a privileged status for all who would come into contact with this group.

In response, Abram, with his nephew Lot, journeys to the "land of Canaan" and Abram settles in Shechem.[21] Abram's status as a foreigner, one who has come from outside the land of Canaan, is made clear by the reference to the fact that "then the Canaanite was in the land" (*hakkĕnaʿănî ʾāz bāʾāreṣ;* 12:6b). It is while he is a sojourner in a foreign land, a landless wanderer not unlike Cain, that Abram is granted the promise of the land to which he has come at Yahweh's command. The promise comes by way of a direct revelation of Yahweh to Abram[22] and tells him, "I will give this land to your offspring" (*lĕzarăkā ʾettēn ʾet-hāʾāreṣ hazzōʾt;* 12:7). There is no ambiguity concerning the nature of the promise: the land that is "presently"

---

18 On this dual aspect of models, see C. Geertz, "Religion as a Cultural System," in *The Interpretation of Cultures* (New York: Basic Books, 1973), pp. 93–94.

19 On the conceptual distinctions between a royal "grant" and a "suzerainty-type covenant," see M. Weinfeld, "The Covenant of Grant in the Old Testament and in the Ancient Near East," *JAOS* 90 (1970) 184–203.

20 While it remains a matter of debate whether the Niphal of *brk* should be rendered as a passive or as a reflexive, the meaning seems obvious.

21 While it is often argued that the Lot stories represent a secondary collection or cycle that was originally independent of the Abram accounts, it is not possible to remove the references to Lot or the stories associated with him from the stories without destroying what narrative continuity exists in the present text. For that reason, the references to Lot must be understood as an integral part of the present narrative structure of the Abram stories. Likewise, the chronological references in 12:4b-5, which connect this story with the previous chronological notices contained in the preceding genealogies, are assigned to the "Priestly" writer, though it seems possible that the author(s) of the passage have simply chosen to use this particular style to provide chronological references within these accounts.

22 *wayyērāʾ yhwh ʾel-ʾabrām;* 12:7; cf. 17:1; 18:1; 26:2, 24; 35:9.

inhabited by the Canaanites will be given to those who can trace their lineage to Abram.[23]

Most significant, from the perspective of the author(s) of this text and its promise, is that the land is pledged *not* to the generation of the narrative present, but rather to those who would be its descendants. The promise constitutes a part of a created "collective memory" that would bind and bound the "offspring" of this original ancestor. But the very nature of the divine promise is put into an interesting perspective itself, for it has already been noted that Sarai, the wife of Abram, was both barren and childless (11:30). In order for the divine to fulfill its pledge, this situation would require a remedy. It is this issue, a "rightful heir," that provides a focus for the remaining stories concerning Abram. An essential point that will be developed within the stories of Abram and his offspring is the variety of genealogical branches that will be developed as relatives of the Abramic family, but as "outsiders" to the promise of the land. The variety of the segmented genealogical orders that the narratives present will define, in ethnically explicit ways, who has and who does not have a "legitimate" claim to the land of Canaan.

In response to this revelation, Abram builds an altar to Yahweh (12:7), a deed which confirms Abram's recognition of Yahweh's act and promise (cf. Noah, 8:20). After traveling from Shechem to the hill country east of Bethel, Abram builds another altar and "called upon the name of Yahweh" (*wayyiqrā⁾ bĕšēm yhwh;* 12:8; cf. 13:4; 26:25; 4:26). Abram's recognition of the divine leadership of Yahweh and his dedication to the fulfillment of Yahweh's demands, expressed in the erection of altars and the worship of the deity, express the reestablishment of a relationship between the human and the divine that returns humankind, at least in this one instance, to the status it was intended to have at the creation. Now the land lay before Abram and his family. The fulfillment of the promises of the deity remained to be recounted.

II. Promises Threatened and Fulfilled

Such fulfillment, at least through Abram's wife Sarai, is thrown into jeopardy with the endangerment of the matriarch recounted in the story of

23 If N. Lemche is correct in his analysis of the rhetorical use of the term Canaanite in the Hebrew bible, then this promise must be understood as part of the Persian period claims to a right to possess the land that was already inhabited by a variety of competing ethnic groups (*The Canaanites and their Land,* pp. 156–173).

Abram's descent into Egypt and the ruse to fool the Pharaoh (12:10–20).[24] Whatever interpretations might be derived from the text, as it presently stands, it serves two functions. It shows how Abram, in passing his wife off as his sister, was able to increase his wealth greatly, all at the expense of the Egyptians. Such a despoiling of the Egyptian royalty may anticipate the later promise to Moses and "Israel" that they would not leave Egypt empty-handed (Exod 3:21–22; 12:35–36). Though Pharaoh had taken Sarai as his wife, thus endangering the purity of the line of Abram,[25] Yahweh intervened, afflicting the Egyptians with "great plagues" (*nĕgāʿîm gĕdōlîm;* 12:17). As a result, the Pharaoh sends them out with great wealth. The reflexes with the story of the Egyptian bondage and exodus are too clear to be over-looked. Egypt will not be able to hold the descendants of Abram any more than they were able to hold him. Instead, Egypt would become a source of wealth for them as it had for Abram.

Returning now to the region of the Negeb,[26] Abram and Lot find themselves in conflict. Because of the property accumulated by each, they are unable to dwell together in the land, especially since both "the Canaanite and Perizzite were also dwelling there" (13:6–7).[27] When Abram directs

---

[24] This episode continues to be a linchpin in the discussions of the composition of patriarchal stories because of the close parallels found in 20:1–18 and 26:1–11. Despite efforts to assign them to different sources or to see them as oral variants on a particular type of folk tale, there seems to be little evidence to suggest that they existed apart from the present setting. J. Van Seters' literary analysis of these stories suggests that both 20:1–18 and 26:1–11 are literarily dependent upon the account in 12:10–20 (*Abraham in History and Tradition,* pp. 167–183). The explanation for Abram's directing his wife to lie about her relationship to him remains unclear. It can no longer be maintained that this reflects some sort of relationship with the *aḫātūti* contracts from Nuzi.

[25] The issue of purity, in the sense of the maintenance of proper marital alliances, plays a crucial role in the development of the patriarchal genealogies. Because of the involvement of the divine as a guiding force in the narrative, simple birth rank is no guarantee of genealogical priority. Hence, the definitions of legitimate and illegitimate heirs and lineages may be declared by the divine in such a way as to define and bound the descent groups being described.

[26] The geographical references are used frequently to tie otherwise independent units of tradition together. 13:1 returns to the Negeb, the area where Abram was wandering prior to the famine which sent them into Egypt (12:9).

[27] As is often the nature of storytelling, exaggeration demands that the audience, whatever its position, accept certain statements that are, when placed in real terms, preposterous. The idea that Abram and Lot were so wealthy that the land of Canaan was unable to provide ample room for their flocks, thus leading to conflicts between the two groups, requires that the reader suspend any disbelief and become a type of "ideal authorial audience," if the story is to engage the reader or hearer in a serious manner. On the variety of audiences that might be postulated for a work, see P. Rabinowitz, "Truth in Fiction: A Reexamination of Audiences," *Critical Inquiry* 4 (1977) 125–130, 134–135.

Lot to separate from him and to choose the land on which he would live
(vv. 8–9), Lot chooses the area to the south of the Jordan, a district compared to the "garden of Yahweh" (*kĕgan-yhwh;* v. 10), all of which was
well-watered. Yet this very choice provides a foreshadowing of the events
to be developed in chaps. 18–19, for v. 10 notes explicitly that all of this
was *before* Yahweh destroyed Sodom and Gomorrah (19:24–25), places
filled with evil men (13:13).

This story of the separation of Lot from Abram is far from secondary to
the presentation of the history of the patriarchs, for it provides the background for an extension of the promise of the land to be given to Abram.
After they part, and it is noted that Abram dwelled "in the land of Canaan"
(*bĕʾereṣ kĕnāʿan;* 13:12), Yahweh directs Abram to look in all directions and
promises to give the land that he sees (cf. 12:1b) to him and his offspring
"forever" (*ʿad-ʿôlām;* vv. 14–15).[28] The connections between the land and
those who would trace their lineage to Abram are now able to reach across
the ages. The promise that he would become a "great nation" is reiterated
by the promise that his offspring would be as innumerable as the "dust of
the earth" (13:16; cf. 12:2). In response to Yahweh's renewed and expanded
promise, Abram journeys to the oaks of Mamre near Hebron and builds an
altar (vv. 17–18; cf. 12:7), again showing his obedience by way of the
proper responses to Yahweh's words.

The narrative development of the fulfillment of the promises to Abram
is indirectly postponed with the account of the attack of the four kings of
the East against the five city-states of the southern plain, an attack that leads
to the abduction of Lot, nephew of Abram. Genesis 14 has created tremen-
dous problems for the classical documentary hypothesis, not only because
of the literary peculiarities of the chapter, but also because the events described defy any identifiable historical possibilities.[29] In its present form
14:1–24 serves not as a comment on any political or historical realities from
the time of Abram, but rather as a statement on the status of the fulfillment

---

28 The unconditional and eternal natures of the promise make it analogous to the deuteronomistic grant of kingship to the Davidic line (2 Samuel 7). This emphasis on the eternality
of the grant allows for numerous ideological shifts that might be made to maintain the idea of
the promise in light of changing and conflicting historical situations which the group holding to
such a belief might endure.

29 Despite numerous ingenious efforts to identify Amraphel (*ʾamrāpel*), Ariok (*ʾaryôk*),
Chedorlaomer (*kĕdorlāʿōmer*), and Tidal (*tidʿāl*) with kings of Babylon, Assyria (?), Elam, and
Hatti (?) respectively, all such identifications seem to be historically improbable. C. Wester-
mann summarizes the matter: "A punitive expedition of a coalition of four empires, Elam,
Babylon, Hatti, and a fourth, against five city kings is historically improbable, if not inconceiv-

of the promises of land and prosperity which had been made to him. No clearer indication of Abram's fame or power (cf. 12:2) could be given than in the story of his mustering of his retainers and his rescue of Lot (14:12–16). In conjunction with his two allies and his 318 personal retainers (14:14), Abram set out against the four kings of the East and recaptured Lot and all of the property which they had seized in their attack on the cities. Upon his return, he was greeted by the king of Sodom, one of those cities that had been defeated (14:17).

But here the narrative flow is further interrupted by the episode concerning Melchizedek and Abram (14:18–20), an account which, I argue, has been placed in this position for very specific cultic and etiological purposes. Melchizedek, "king of Shalem" (*melek šālēm*)[30] and "priest of El Elyon" (*kōhēn lᵉʾēl ʿelyôn;* 14:18), appeared from nowhere, bringing food and wine to Abram. Melchizedek, like the four kings of the East, or the five kings of the cities of the plain, belonged to the days of the heroic past when the ancestors were blessed by Yahweh and in which the present generations might base their claims to possession of the land. With no introductory remarks, Melchizedek pronounces a blessing upon Abram by El Elyon, "creator of heaven and earth" (*qōnēh šāmayīm wāʾāreṣ;* 14:19). The significance of this blessing is made clear by Abram's response: he gives a "tithe of everything" (*maʿăśēr mikkol*) to Melchizedek, priest of El Elyon, thus recognizing the rights and prerogatives of this priest over even the chosen one of Yahweh.[31] Further, Abram makes the explicit identification of Yahweh with El Elyon when he raises his hand in pledge and disassociates himself from any connection with the king of Sodom (14:22).[32]

---

able" (*Genesis 12–36* [Minneapolis: Augsburg, 1985], p. 194). It is interesting to note, however, that the earliest time that these "empires" could ever be understood as working as "allies" would be during the Persian period, when each of these older kingdoms had been conquered and incorporated into the empire. With respect to the five kings of the cities of the plain, their names are not attested apart from the present text. Likewise, these five cities are mentioned together only in Genesis 14. Sodom, Gomorrah, Admah, and Zeboiim are mentioned together in Deut 29:22 and Gen 10:19, while Hos 11:8 mentions Admah and Zeboiim together.

[30] *šālēm* is traditionally identified with Jerusalem (cf. Ps 76:3). There is little reason to doubt that the author(s) of the present text intended that the reader/hearer make this identification.

[31] On the role of the tithe, see Gen 28:18–22; Deut 12:6–19; 14:22–27; 26:12–15; Num 18:20–32; Lev 27:30–33; Neh 10:37–38; 12:44; 13:5. In later Jewish tradition, the tithe is noted as including all food, anything cultivated, and anything which grows from the earth (*m. Maʿaś. Š.* I.1).

[32] This overlapping of references is clearly intended to bridge the otherwise awkward transition back to the story concerning the king of Sodom that began in v. 17.

By way of this brief episode, the stories of Abram are connected to the initial account of the creation of the heavens and earth by *ʾĕlōhîm,* who had, in turn, been identified with Yahweh, and who was now to be equated with *ʾēl ʿelyôn,* the god of Jerusalem. As subtle as it might be, the continuing identification of Yahweh, the personal god of "Israel," with the variety of epithets associated with differing local deities[33] universalizes the conception of Yahweh and magnifies the importance of Jerusalem, the city in which his Temple was built.[34] Abram's acceptance of the position of Melchizedek as priest of this deity and his tithing from all his conquered possessions provide the model for the support of the Jerusalem priesthood that would become a serious issue in the days of the reestablishment of the temple cultus. In addition to these critical cultic aspects contained in this story, there is also a clear exoneration of the divine word. Abram has become a person of great wealth and power, one who has been blessed by Yahweh, the creator of the cosmos. Likewise, to be able to conquer the mighty kings of the East surely qualified one as a "great nation," even if no nation were yet directly associated with the patriarch.[35]

All that is lacking for the ground to be prepared for the eternal gift of the land to Abram and his offspring is the notice of the birth of a legitimate heir. The issues introduced are two-fold: legitimacy and genealogy. Since Sarai was barren, the reader/hearer must be suspicious of the manner by which Abram might obtain children. The double accounts of the covenant between Yahweh and Abram, framing as they do the birth of Ishmael, bring precisely these matters into focus and offer a resolution. In 15:1–21, Abram receives clarification and reassurance of the parameters of the promise.

---

33 For a discussion of the major epithets of deities that were associated with Yahweh in the Hebrew tradition, see M. Smith, *The Early History of God: Yahweh and the Other Deities in Ancient Israel* (San Francisco: Harper & Row, 1990), pp. 1–40. Caution should be exercised, however, in the arguments concerning the antiquity of many of the epithets and the "periods" of Israelite history to which they are assigned. Many, if not all, can be traced, in one form or another, to the Babylonian or Persian periods and could have been adopted during those times.

34 This process would be just as important for the period of the "Second" Temple as it would have been for the Solomonic shrine. Indeed, care must be taken when evaluating the descriptions of the importance of the Solomonic shrine in light of the emphasis placed on it by the materials justifying the position of the "Second" Temple as an effort to "restore" the "traditional" religion and culture of the area (cf. T. L. Thompson, *Early History of the Israelite People,* pp. 417–419).

35 It is interesting in this regard to note that Abram is called "the Hebrew" (*hāʿibrî;* 14:13), which constitutes the first time that this epithet is used in the stories of "Israel's" past. The history of the development of this ethnic label and its relationship to social status groups, e.g., the *ḥapiru* of the Amarna age, remains debated.

When Abram claims that a certain member of his household, Eliezer of Damascus, is his only heir, Yahweh responds that Abram's biological offspring would be the one who would constitute the line of inheritance.[36] These offspring would be, as promised earlier, innumerable (15:5; cf. 13:16). Abram's response to the promise is again paradigmatic: "he trusted Yahweh and he [Yahweh] considered it to him [Abram] as righteousness" (15:6; cf. 6:9).

This evaluation of Abram leads to a shift in style and an announcement by Yahweh in which he reveals his identity to Abram yet again. In terms of the development of the documentary hypothesis, this repetition of a revelation and promise to Abram serves as an indicator that another source, the "Elohistic," has been incorporated into the more dominant "Yahwistic" narrative at this point by the final editors.[37] But this repetition need not be understood as representing some second or third source of materials. It might just as easily be interpreted as an attempt by the author(s) of this section to reconfirm the previous promises in two ways: first, the non-biological heir would *not* represent the line of inheritance; second, the fulfillment of the promise would *not* be immediate.[38] To a large degree, the covenantal promise introduced in 15:7–21 anticipates not only portions of the tradition not developed until the accounts in Exodus, but also a familiarity with the deuteronomistic materials.[39]

---

36 15:2b is obscure in its present form. The meaning of *ben-mešeq*, which occurs only here, is conjectural, and the phrase *hû' dammeśeq*, "it is Damascus," appears to be a gloss on the previous problematic phrase. On the difficulties of this section and bibliography for attempted solutions, see C. Westermann, *Genesis 12–36*, pp. 219–220. Whatever the status of Eliezer, it is clear that he is regarded as a non-biological descendant of Abram who, for whatever reasons, had, from the presentation in the narrative, the legal right of inheritance. It is interesting to ponder whether the rejection of this person from Damascus might have any implications for defining the new "restoration" community that might have found competition from other cities in its district.

37 See above, Chap. 1, pp. 6–7, esp. n. 24.

38 The concept of divine promise-delay-fulfillment, characteristic of the ideological constructions of the deuteronomistic history, is used throughout the Tetrateuch as a connecting theme that allows the author(s) great leeway in constructing a variety of twists and detours in the plot, yet at the same time maintains the integrity of the divine promise.

39 R. Rendtorff has argued that the traditions in Exodus-Numbers represent a different set of traditions than do those presently attested by the patriarchal stories and that they did not belong together in their original stages of formulation (*The Problem of the Process of Transmission in the Pentateuch*, pp. 84–89). Two points about such a position must be noted: (1) this does not need to imply that two complete oral or written traditions were simultaneously in existence; (2) the linking of the patriarchal promises and the exodus traditions is provided by the basic narrative structure of Deuteronomy, which might be understood as the final thematic

In language reminiscent of the covenantal style of address associated with Sinai/Horeb, Yahweh identifies himself as "Yahweh who led you from Ur of the Chaldeans to give you this land to inherit" (15:7; cf. 11:28, 31; Exod 20:2; Deut 5:6). When Abram requests confirmation of the promise given in vv. 1, 4–5, Yahweh responds by instructing him to make preparations for a ritual performance that provides the context for a new revelation to the patriarch.[40] In this vision, Abram learns that his descendants would dwell in a land not their own and would be oppressed for four hundred years. Then they could come forth with great property (cf. 12:10–20; Exod 3:21–22; 12:35–36). Abram himself would live a long life and go to his grave in peace. Only in the "fourth generation" (*dôr rĕbî'î*) would his descendants return here, since "the iniquity of the Amorites" (*'ăwōn hā'ĕmōrî*) was not yet complete (15:13–16). The attribution of this to a differing source is not unexpected, since, as it stands, this dream-revelation reflects a knowledge of the events to be developed in Exodus-Numbers.[41] But it plays an important role in the development of the narrative, for it provides assurance that despite the seeming impossibility of the promise being fulfilled, the divine has provided for precisely that. Lengthy exile could not offset the primordial promises to the patriarchs.

By virtue of the presentation of these actions, the revelation itself becomes a part of the covenant, for the concluding notice concerning the ritual states that "on that day, Yahweh made a covenant (*bĕrît*) with Abram:

---

statement that provided the impetus for the combination of original independent traditions concerning Israel's origins.

40 15:9–10; 17. In the form in which this ritual is presented, it might be understood as a type of incubation rite by which the participant prepared himself for the reception of the divine word/vision. This is confirmed by the fact that the revelation is given to Abram after he falls into a "deep sleep" (*tardēmâ;* 15:12; cf. 2:21). Because there is evidence of a similar ritual involving the cutting in two of animals at Mari, it is common to assign an early date to this account. Such cannot be defended, however, since the closest biblical parallel to this type of ritual comes from Jer 34:18–19, which at its earliest dates to the Babylonian period.

41 This revelation contains a number of interesting possibilities. The four-hundred-year period of oppression contrasts with the four hundred and thirty years noted in Exod 12:40. (In the LXX, this includes Abram's wanderings.) The reference to the fourth generation being the one to return to the land is problematic, since it would require figuring one hundred years per generation, a figure which seems extremely high. An interesting possibility is one suggested by J. Skinner that counts the generations from Levi, Kohath, Amram, and Aaron/Moses (Exod 16:16–19) as a possible basis for this reference (*Genesis* [ICC; Edinburgh: T. & T. Clark, 1910], p. 282). The punishment of the nations, here represented by the Amorites, for their abominations before Yahweh is a theme common to the deuteronomistic writer (cf. 1 Kgs 14:24; 2 Kgs 21:2; etc.).

'to your offspring I will give this land, from the river of Egypt to the great river, the river Euphrates'" (15:18).[42] Appended to the promise is a list of ten peoples who would be dispossessed by the gift of the land to Abram's descendants. An essential point about this covenantal promise that is commonly overlooked is that though the promise is made to Abram, the gift is directed to his offspring. That is, the recipients of the promise are those of the *present* generation who can trace their lineage to this figure to whom was given this solemn promise by "Israel's" god.

The tension of the unfulfilled promise of a biological heir provides the narrative thread upon which a number of other issues concerning the separateness and special nature of the people who are to be descendants of this lineage will be introduced. The manner of inheritance and the nature of genealogical purity are introduced in the account of the birth of Ishmael to Abram and Hagar, the Egyptian handmaiden of Sarai. It is important to notice that Hagar's Egyptian lineage is emphasized (16:3), introducing a genealogical implication that has already been rejected once in the story (12:10–20).[43] The issue in the present story is status—whether or not this son, borne by an Egyptian mother, would be the legitimate biological heir promised in 15:4. On the surface, the issue is resolved when Sarai, with Abram's permission, drives the pregnant Hagar away (16:4–6).

The issue is obscured, however, with the introduction of another actor into the story, the "messenger of Yahweh" (*maPak yhwh;* 16:7), who finds Hagar in the wilderness and promises that her offspring will be multiplied beyond counting, a promise analogous to the one given to Abram in 15:5.[44]

---

[42] This description of the land is significant, for while these are noted as Israel's ideal borders elsewhere, there is no period in the biblical account when Israel and/or Judah ever claimed to control such a vast empire. It is interesting to ponder whether these idealistic descriptions might reflect the general extent of a later geographical division that developed in the Persian period. As J. M. Miller and J. Hayes have pointed out, Herodotus (*Histories,* III, 91) notes that Palestine fell into the fifth Persian satrapy, called Abar Nahara ("Beyond the River"), and included the eastern Mediterranean seaboard (including Cyprus) (*A History of Ancient Israel and Judah* [Philadelphia: Westminster, 1986], p. 454).

[43] There are numerous parallels in the ancient Near East concerning attempts by barren wives to provide their husbands with male heirs. For a survey and evaluation of these practices, see T. L. Thompson, *The Historicity of the Patriarchal Narratives,* pp. 252–269.

[44] This sudden introduction of the *maPak yhwh* presupposes that the reader/hearer is acquainted with the figure and its role in Israelite religion and culture. The exact nature of this figure is debated: is the *maPak* a divine or a human figure? For a discussion of the nature of this figure, see C. Westermann, *Genesis 12–36,* pp. 242–244. Whatever answer is given, it seems clear that the *maPāk* is to be understood as one of the legitimate forms of divine communication with the human realm and represents an additional dimension for bridging the divine/human

Despite the etiology of Ishmael's name and the comment on the way in which he will relate to his brothers (16:11–12), there is nothing in this story to indicate that he is *not* to be considered the rightful heir to Abram. The first indication of this does not occur until the middle of the next section of the story (17:16), a fact that makes the assignment of chapter 17 to an independent source somewhat difficult.

From the outset it must be noted that the "Priestly" story of the covenant contained in 17:1–27 is repetitious. It is also clear that it functions in a different manner than the previous stories, for it carries with it a cultic requirement that becomes the emblem of membership in the community of "Israel." In its present form, this chapter presupposes the birth and blessing of Ishmael and provides a literary preview of the offspring who *will* constitute the legitimate heir for Abram and "Israel." If an independent "Priestly" version of the covenant did exist, it has been reworked in such a way as to incorporate it into the present narrative development by the final author(s) of this piece. Chronologically, this section connects with the previous one by noting that thirteen years had passed since the birth of Ishmael by recounting that Abram was now 99 years old (17:1; cf. 16:16).[45] Again Yahweh appears to Abram, introduces himself as "El Shadday,"[46] and implores Abram to "walk continually before me and be perfect" (*hithallēk lĕpānay wehyê tāmîm;* 17:1), references which recall Enoch (5:22, 24) and Noah (6:9).

This account of the covenant, however, involves much more than a simple repetition of the previous promises. In this account, the status of Abram is changed, as is signified by the change in his name to Abraham (17:4–5).[47] Rather than becoming a "great nation" (*gôy gādôl;* 12:2), Abra-

---

separation that was established earlier in the narrative. On the connections of this figure with Yahweh's heavenly court and with the phenomenon of prophecy, see my work, *The Assembly of the Gods*, pp. 209–226.

45 To interpolate from the reference in 16:3 that Sarai had given Hagar to Abram to bear him a son after he had been in the land for ten years, one could calculate that Abram had been in Canaan some twenty-four years at the beginning of Genesis 17.

46 The epithet *'ēl šadday* is commonly associated with the "Priestly" writer, especially in light of Exod 6:2–3, where the name is connected with Yahweh. It should not be overlooked that this explicit identification is made in 17:1. In terms of the development of the epithets attributable to Yahweh, this one, just like that given by Hagar in 16:13–14, represents the absorption of a variety of divine designations under one universalized deity.

47 The Hebrew traditions know of two forms of the patriarch's name: Abram and Abraham. The former occurs only in Gen 11:26–17:5, Neh 9:7, and 1 Chr 1:27. It is possible that Abram (*'abrām*) is a short form of *'ăbîrām,* though this longer form is never applied to the patriarch (compare *'abnēr/'ăbînēr*). Abram/Abiram would mean "the/my father is exalted." The

ham would become the ancestor of "numerous nations," a shift in emphasis that universalizes the import of the promises to Abraham and that focuses directly upon the issue of the legitimate heir to the promises of the land. Yahweh would establish his covenant with Abraham and his offspring as an "eternal covenant" (*běrît 'ôlām;* 17:7, 13; cf. 13:15; 9:16). The covenant grant is stated explicitly: "all the land of Canaan for an eternal possession" (*kol-'ereṣ kěna'an la'ăḥuzzat 'ôlām;* 17:8). Circumcision would be the "sign of the covenant" (*'ôt běrît;* v.11) between Yahweh and Abraham and his descendants. All males would participate in the benefits of this grant, i.e., participation in this ritual would define those who would be recognized as offspring of Abraham (17:10–14).[48]

At the age of ninety-nine Abraham was circumcised, and, in response to Yahweh's command, he circumcised all the males in his household (17: 23–27). Framed by the account of covenant and the fulfillment of its obligation is Yahweh's announcement of the blessing of Sarai, which changes not only the status of Sarai by changing her name, but also the status of Ishmael, by noting that he would not be the heir to the promise.[49] Rather, Sarah would be given a son whose name would be Isaac (*yiṣḥāq*)[50] and with whom Yahweh would establish his eternal covenant (17:19). The promises given to Abraham would be fulfilled in the descendants who could trace their lineage through Isaac, a critical distinction to understand in the

---

etymology and translation of Abraham (*'abrāhām*) are less certain. A folk etymology for the name is given in Gen 17:4–5, relating the name to the notice that Abram would become the "father of a multitude of nations" (*'ab-hāmôn gôyîm*). The form *'abrāhām* is best understood as an Aramaic expansion of *'abrām* which has the same basic meaning and form (L. Hicks, "Abraham," *IDB* I, 15).

[48] The absolute binding nature of this command is made clear by the note in 17:14b regarding any male *not* circumcised: "his life shall be cut off from his people. He has broken my covenant" (*wěnikrětâ hannepeš hahîw' mē'ammeyhā 'et-běrîtî hēpar*). The Hebrew bible contains some 19 cases of this *kārēt* penalty, which is to be understood as a divinely enforced punishment for deliberate sins against the divine. For a discussion of this, see J. Milgrom, *Leviticus 1–16*, pp. 457–460.

[49] The name change from Sarai to Sarah (*śāray > śārâ*) parallels the changing of Abram to Abraham. Notably, no etymology is given for Sarah to parallel that of Abraham (v. 5), though the reference to kings (v. 16) connects with the promise given to Abraham (v. 6).

[50] The text does not develop the theme of Abraham's laughter over the announcement that Sarah would have a son as an explicit etymology for the name Isaac (17:17). The reference, along with that to the laughter of Sarah in 18:12–15, provides for an understanding of the name in its context. The name *yiṣḥāq* is probably a shortened form of an original theophoric name (cf. *yišmā'ē'l*, "may god hear"). If this is correct, then the full form of the name would mean "May God laugh" (L. Hicks, "Isaac," *IDB* II, 728).

formation of national and ethnic identity. Though others might be able
to make genealogical claims to be offspring of Abraham, the promise, by
divine designation, would be maintained with those descended through this
lineage alone. Upon other Abrahamic lineages might be blessings of prosperity (17:20), but such would not constitute the major beneficiaries of the
promise. The line of descent through Isaac provides a basis for eliminating
competing claims to the right to the land, an important element in the formation and maintenance of identity for those "restoring" Jerusalem and
claiming exclusive rights of inheritance.

This "Priestly" ritualized covenantal account is not independent of the
surrounding narrative materials, however, for the promise to Sarah provides
a direct link to the following stories concerning the fate of Lot and the
righteous. In 17:21b it is noted that the child promised to Sarah would be
born "at this time next year," a motif that is also reflected in 18:10–14.
A similar doublet is created with the motif of laughter in response to the
announcement (17:17; 18:12–15). In its present context, the covenant of
circumcision is directly dependent upon the preceding account of the birth
of Ishmael and the ensuing accounts of the renewed announcement to Sarah
and Abraham, which also introduce the accounts concerning Lot and
Sodom and Gomorrah.

The stories about Sodom and Gomorrah intertwine a number of themes
to form a very complex account in which a critical theological issue receives its answer by way of a story. Yahweh appears as one of three "men"
(*'ănāšîm;* 18:1–2, 16) who are welcomed by Abraham in a scene that is the
epitome of hospitality.[51] Against this background, the announcement of the
upcoming pregnancy of Sarah is repeated, containing appropriately a reference to laughter, to connect it with the previous story (18:9–15; 17:15–19).
The issue of the divine promise of offspring to Abraham and Sarah introduces a major theological question for the community at large.

Embedded in the account of the destruction of Sodom and Gomorrah
is the larger issue of the efficacy of righteousness. The stories of Sodom
and Gomorrah provide the vehicle for an answer by Yahweh to Abraham's
pointed question concerning the justice of the divine: "Will you really
sweep away the righteous with the wicked?" (*ha'ap tispeh ṣaddîq 'im-rāšā';*

---

51 On the theme of hospitality as a symbol of community and unity, see S. Niditch, "The
'Sodomite' Theme in Judges 19–20: Family, Community, and Social Disintegration," *CBQ* 44
(1982) 365–75. While it is common to understand the account in Judges 19 as a reflection of the
story in Genesis 19, it is just as possible that the story of Lot is built upon the story of the outrage
at Gibeah.

18:23b). The ensuing dialogue (18:24–33) offers only a partial answer to that question, for Yahweh concedes that for the sake of ten righteous men he would spare a wicked city (v. 32). The issue does not stop with ten, however, for implied throughout the entire discussion is the ultimate question that Abraham is asking: "Can *one* righteous person offset the sinfulness of many?"[52] This is a most appropriate question to be asked by the single individual who had been accounted as righteous (*ṣĕdāqâ;* 15:6) because of the trust he had placed in Yahweh.

The answer to the question is only implied by the contrast of the inhospitality of the people of Sodom with the hospitality of Lot (19:1–9). Lot's hospitality toward Yahweh's two messengers is parallel to that of Abraham, a fact that explains why he and his family are saved from the destruction of the city (19:10–22). One of the most important elements in the account of the destruction of these two cities (19:23–29) is the witness to the divine wrath taken out on those who did evil. From the spot where he had debated with Yahweh, Abraham looked out upon the smoke arising from the plain where Sodom and Gomorrah had been (19:27–28). Part of his query to the divine was answered by the sight before him. There had not been ten righteous men for whose sake Yahweh would spare the city. But what about one? Interestingly, 19:29 notes that God had "remembered" (*wayyizkōr*) Abraham, and delivered Lot from the destruction.[53] The reader/hearer is left to ponder the answer to the implied question: perhaps the righteousness of one like Abraham can provide escape from destruction for others.

But Lot provides more than simply an indirect answer to this important question. His survival of the disaster that befell the cities of the plain allows for an etiological account of the birth of Moab and Ammon in a manner that displays clear enmity between those peoples and the descendants of Abraham (19:30–38). The story is geographically significant because it provides an explanation for the reason that Abraham does not take possession of the land chosen by Lot: these areas went to Lot's offspring. The land that was to be inherited legitimately by Isaac was still in the process of being defined.[54]

---

52 There is little to support the assertion of C. Westermann that ten represents a natural limit and hence an end to the discussion (*Genesis 12–36,* p. 292).

53 On the theme of Yahweh's "remembering" covenants with particular individuals, see Gen 8:1; 9:15, 16; Exod 2:24; 6:5.

54 From Abraham's perspective, the fate of Lot remained unknown. Lot is not mentioned again in the narrative after the birth of Moab and Ammon. This genealogical tie is reflected in Deut 2:9, 19.

After the brief delay in the progress of the story represented by the endangerment of the lineage by outside contamination, this time by Abimelek of Gerar (20:1–18),[55] the promise to Abraham and Sarah is fulfilled with the account of the birth of Isaac (21:1–4). Intertwined with the account of the birth of the legitimate heir is a second account of the blessing of Ishmael.[56] The notice of the fulfillment of the blessing promised to Ishmael (21:18; 16:10–12) has important geographic and genealogical implications. Ishmael, promised to be the ancestor of a great nation, is now assigned an area in which he will dwell, the wilderness of Paran (*midbar pārʾān;* 21:21). This area, like that belonging to Ammon and Moab, will not be part of the inheritance of Isaac. The manner by which disputes over territory might be settled is illustrated in the episode concerning Abimelek of Gerar and a conflict concerning a well. Abraham and Abimelek are able to resolve their differences by way of a covenant (21:27), the first to be made between human partners in the biblical account.[57] The etiology of the name Beer-Sheba (v. 31) provides a claim to this important area that later will figure prominently in the narrative. In response to the resolution of the matter, Abraham invokes the name of Yahweh, "god of eternity" (*ʾēl ʿôlām;* 21:33), further identifying his personal god with the epithets implying universality, especially when uttered in a "foreign" land (v. 32).[58]

---

55 See the comments on 12:10–20, above. In its present form, the account of Abimelek's encounter with Abraham and Sarah is more than a simple expansion on the parallel account in chap. 12. Part of the issue addressed here reflects directly upon the questions raised in Abraham's dialogue with Yahweh concerning the efficacy of righteousness. When Yahweh reveals to Abimelek that he has sinned and is about to be killed (20:3), Abimelek protests with a question that is pregnant with meaning in the context of an exiled community: "Lord, will you also slay a righteous nation?" (*ʾădōnāy hăgôy gam-ṣaddîq tahărōg;* 20:4). While most commentators treat *hăgôy* as a dittography and read *hăgam* in its place (cf. *BHS*), there is no textual support for the emendation. Indeed, the question in its present form reemphasizes the seriousness of an answer to the question posed by Abraham, for in the case of Abimelek, he was completely innocent of any intentional wrongdoing (20:5–6).

56 21:8–21 is commonly assigned to the "Elohist" because of the way in which it parallels the story in 16:4–15. The fact that it is the *malʾak ʾĕlōhîm* that answers Hagar (21:17) as it had in 16:7–12 suggests that this account is composed as an intentional supplement to that one and not that it had any independent existence as a part of a parallel document. 21:22–34 is also assigned to the "Elohist," but there is no independent evidence for such a division of sources.

57 The issue of water rights and the introduction of Abimelek at this point lays the background for the same issues which will arise in 26:1–35 between Abimelek and Isaac.

58 An observation that might be pertinent in the present context is the apparent lack of a consistent narrative development within the materials concerning the patriarchs. That the stories seem extremely episodic and somewhat disjointed is generally attributed to the work of the editors/redactors who selected episodes from the various source documents at their disposal to weave the present tapestry that yields an image that is often hard to define. Worth pondering, if

In response to Abraham's invocation, God decides to *test* Abraham's obedience. Critical in understanding this section and its relation to the formation of identity and ethnicity is the manner in which it defines the human/divine relationship. Despite Abraham's life of obedience and Yahweh's promises to him, it does not place him beyond the realm of testing or having to demonstrate his continued loyalty to Yahweh and, hence, membership in the select group. The price of belonging can be great. Yahweh's orders to Abraham are quite unambiguous: he is to take his only son Isaac and offer him as a burnt offering at the place that Yahweh would designate (22:2). How this may be understood within the context of Yahweh's mandate that Abraham walk before him continually and be perfect (17:1b) develops with the continuation of the story.

Abraham followed the order of Yahweh perfectly, making all the preparations and binding Isaac for the sacrifice (22:3–10), only to be stopped by the injunction of the *malʾak yhwh*.[59] Despite the fact that the reader or hearer is left to ponder what might have happened had the *malʾak yhwh* not intervened, it is clear from his announcement that Abraham has passed the test. "Now I know that you fear god" (*kî ʿattâ yādaʿtî kî yĕrēʾ ʾĕlōhîm ʾattâ*) is the proclamation from heaven (22:12). The proper response to the commands of the deity seems to be clearly defined: Abraham had to be willing to sacrifice the promise made to him in order to secure it for his offspring. These acts, along with the etiology of the place name (v. 14), provide the background for the presentation of a prophetic oracle that reconfirms the entirety of the promises made beginning in the initial call of Abraham in 12:2–3.[60] Offspring, prosperity, and blessing are all reassured

---

only to reject, is the possibility that there were no documents that contained a continuous story of the patriarchs, but only independent episodes (oral, written, invented) that have been paratactically joined in the present shape. It is further possible that the materials were *never* intended to be read as a whole, but only as short didactic episodes from which the readers might expound a meaning for the hearers.

59 On this figure, see 16:7–12; 19:1, 15; 21:17; 22:15; 28:12; 31:11; 32:2. This chapter is traditionally assigned to the "Elohist," though the occurrence of the name Yahweh in vv. 11, 14, 15, and 16 makes it clear that it has been "recast" into its present form. It is just as likely that this represents a free composition on the part of the author(s) attempting to make a comment on the nature and necessity of obedience, rather than an independently existing episode.

60 While it is clear that 22:15–18 is in a different style that interrupts the narrative flow of this unit, this does not mean that these verses represent a secondary addition to the text. Instead, this prophetic announcement, presented by the *malʾak yhwh*, forms a type of inclusio with this portion of the story of the patriarchs. The major focus of the stories will shift away from the fulfillment of the promises to Abraham and concentrate on the ways in which they are continued in Isaac, the legitimate heir.

precisely because Abraham obeyed the word of his god (22:16–18; cf. 15:6).
The reassurance here is given in terms of a prophetic oracle, identified by
the phrase "saying/oracle of Yahweh" (*ně'um-yhwh*), that sets it apart from
the surrounding narrative and emphasizes the divine nature of the saying.[61]
This oracle provides the opportunity for the *mal'ak yhwh* to repeat Yahweh's
sworn oath that he would fulfill his promises to Abraham and to his offspring.[62]

An important bridge is provided in the narrative with the introduction
in 22:20–24 of the descendants of Nahor, Abraham's brother who was last
mentioned in 11:29. Of the various offspring noted, two will be most important in the upcoming stories: Qemuel, father of Aram (*'ăbî 'ărām;* v. 21;
cf. 10:22), and Bethuel, father of Rebekah (v. 22). Now the eponym of the
land of Aram, the home of Rebekah, who will become the wife of Isaac
(chap. 24), is related to Abraham and his descendants (cf. Deut 26:5) and
will form an important element in the development of the proper marriage
alliances that will identify the descendants of the promise. Such anachronistic references to Aram, like those to Philistia (21:34), Ammon (19:38),
Moab (19:37), or the ten population groups to be dispossessed by Abraham
and his offspring (15:19–21), suggest not only a time of composition when
such groups could be understood as ethnic entities, but also a time when
"Israel" was not the sole inhabitant of the land. Such diversity of population
groups could only bring with it multiple claims to hegemony over the land.

The account of the agreement between Abimelek and Abraham over
the well at Beer Sheba reveals one way in which the descendants might be
able to claim certain territories. The story of the acquisition of a burial cave
by Abraham illustrates another. This account of Abraham's purchase of the
cave at Machpelah from the Hittite, Ephron, son of Zoar, for which he paid
full price, is the only account, apart from the story of the land purchased by
Jacob from the Shechemites (33:19–20; but cf. 48:22), in which a portion

---

61 The phrase *ně'um yhwh* occurs only here in Genesis. Though the phrase is not restricted
to the prophetic books, it occurs only rarely in narrative contexts. Indeed, the phrase occurs only
one other time in the Pentateuch, in Num 14:28, where it is also employed in the context of a
divine oath.

62 This is the first time in the accounts in Genesis where Yahweh is depicted as taking an
oath. Whether it is too much to suggest that this is to imply some type of legally binding guarantee to the recipients of the oath is open to question. It does present a background for its
common appearance in the deuteronomic materials (e.g., Deut 1:8, 35, etc.). Such a legal background is clearly implied in other oaths that are emphasized in the patriarchal materials, e.g.,
21:23–24, 31; 24:7, 9; etc.

of Canaan is legally purchased by the ancestors of "Israel."[63] Notable about this chapter is the manner in which the details of the negotiations are worked out (23:11–16), illustrating that such land purchases should be done in full accord with the accepted legal practices of the day.[64]

III. The Heirs: Marriage and Migration

With his wife and the ancestral matriarch buried in the family cave in the midst of the land that would be given to their descendants, the only issue left to be resolved in the account of the life of Abraham concerns the marriage of the legitimate heir, Isaac. Such an account is of primary importance, for it provides a prototypical example of marriage for those who claim inheritance in this "family." As the text makes clear, the appropriate form of marriage is endogamous. As the genealogies define the family, certain lineage groups are included and, obviously, certain ones excluded.[65] The separation of Abraham's lineage from the "indigenous" population is clearly presented in the oath he exacts from his major-domo: "You shall not take a wife for my son from the daughters of the Canaanites (*mibbĕnôt hakkĕna'anî*) in whose midst I am dwelling" (24:3, 37). The qualifier supplied here is as important as the choice of gentilics, for the oath excludes all those presently understood as inhabiting the land.[66]

Instead, his servant is commissioned to procure a wife for Isaac from Abraham's homeland (*môledet;* v. 4), a pointed reminder that Abraham had

---

63 J. Blenkinsopp, *The Pentateuch*, p. 102.

64 For the argument that the legal practices reflected in chap. 23 have numerous parallels with Neo-Babylonian and Persian customs, see J. Van Seters, *Abraham in History and Tradition*, pp. 98–100. The reference to the Hittites being in control of the area of Hebron should not be used as a basis for reconstructing any demographic profile of the historical period, whatever that might be, but rather as a rhetorical device used to demonstrate the proper ways by which the ancestors and their descendants might "reclaim" their land. The assignment of 23:1–20 to the "Priestly" writer is based on the presupposition that this text originally continued the account in 21:2–5.

65 The issue of the appropriate form of marriage in ancient "Israel" remains a matter of debate since the Hebrew bible reflects both exogamous and endogamous marriage styles, often during the same "periods." It is clear, however, that during the formative period of the restoration efforts associated with Ezra and Nehemiah, endogamy became the officially accepted marriage relationship. On the variety of marriages reflected in the patriarchal materials, see R. Oden, "Jacob as Father, Husband, and Nephew: Kinship Studies and the Patriarchal Narratives," *JBL* 102 (1983) 189–205.

66 Notably, Deut 7:1–3 specifies that "Israel" is to avoid intermarriage with any of the seven population groups (*šib'â gōyîm*) that were to be disinherited by them.

migrated to this land of promise from elsewhere. Further, under no circumstances was Isaac to be allowed to return there to dwell (vv. 6, 8). Abraham's migration was a one-way affair, at least for this generation, and had been completed in accord with the command of "Yahweh, god of the heavens," who had promised this land, the land in which he now dwelt, to his offspring (vv. 7, 40). As the narrative recounts the procurement of Rebekah, daughter of Bethuel, son of Nahor, brother of Abraham, it further specifies this "native" land. It is none other than Aram Naharayim (*'ăram nahărayim;* 24:10; cf. 22:21), the district in which lay "the city of Nahor" (*'îr nāḥôr*).[67] The text could hardly be more explicit in identifying the location of the kinspeople of Abraham from whom a wife was to be taken. They were those people from Mesopotamia whose lineage was the same as that of Abraham. Marriage alliances were to be determined through proper genealogical lines.

The cultural as well as genealogical aspects of the relationship are also emphasized in the narrative, for Laban, the brother of Rebekah, who acts as her major spokesperson,[68] and the servant of Abraham both invoke the same deity, "Yahweh, god of Abraham" (24:12, 27, 42, 48). Yahwism did not originate with Abraham, nor with his call to go to the land of Canaan. Yahwism had its origins in the land of Abraham's birth, Aram Naharayim, the land from which those repatriated Judahite "returnees" would migrate, just as had their ancestor Abraham, father of Isaac. It was to this offspring that Abraham gave all he had before dying at "a good old age" (*běśêbâ ṭôbâ;* 25:8; cf. 15:15) and being buried in the family burial cave with his wife Sarah.[69] By the time of his death, Abraham had fulfilled the promise of his new name: he had become the father of many nations (cf. 17:4–5). Yet, despite the blessings heaped upon him and his family, his legitimate heir, as distinct from his other descendants, still had no permanent land. The fulfillment of the promises was to be understood in terms of process, not as a

67 While this is often identified with the city of Haran (C. Westermann, *Genesis 12–36,* p. 185), it seems more likely that it is referring simply to a general area. This is clearly the way it was taken by the LXX, which translates Aram Naharayim as Mesopotamia.

68 Rather than being an explicit statement on any type of familial arrangement, the prominence of Laban, rather than Bethuel, in these stories serves to introduce this figure who will play a critical role in the parallel accounts of the marriage of Jacob.

69 To emphasize the legitimacy of Isaac over all others, the text points out that Abraham also had six other sons by Keturah (25:1–4). One of these was Midian, an eponym that will figure prominently in the revelation of Yahweh to Moses in Exodus 3. These, the narrative emphasizes, were not to be the heirs of Yahweh's promises.

single event that was irreversible.[70] This observation provides an important interpretational key to understanding the Pentateuch, since the promise of the gift of the land is *not* fulfilled in that particular corpus. As D. J. A. Clines has emphasized, the continued accounts of the partial fulfillment of the promises to the ancestors imply also the partial non-fulfillment of those same promises.[71]

The stories associated with Jacob and contained under the rubric of the third *tôlĕdôt* formula, the *tôlĕdôt* of Isaac (25:19–35:29), are linked both chronologically and genealogically to the stories that have preceded.[72] The issue of Rebekah's barrenness is quickly removed (25:21; contrast Sarah, 11:30), and the birth of Isaac's two sons is immediately recounted. Unlike the numerous stories told about Abraham, those associated with Isaac (24:1–67; 25:19–27:45) serve only to provide the background for the narration of the continuation of the promise and the insistence on endogamous marriage with properly designated kinspeople. Embedded in this transition from the original ancestor (Abraham) to the ethnic eponym (Jacob/Israel) are the stories recounting the manner in which the divine could continue to designate the legitimate heir to the promises given to Abraham and passed on to Isaac. To complicate the matter of inheritance, the author(s) narrate the birth of twins to Rebekah, the elder of whom, Esau, was not to be the chosen inheritor of the blessings promised to Abraham. Instead, the two children were to become two peoples, and "the older will serve the younger" (*rab ya'ăbōd ṣā'îr;* 25:23). Such a scenario carries important implications for a disenfranchised people who had no national identity and whose very ethnic identity was in danger of assimilation to the surrounding culture.

---

[70] As shall become clear in the presentation of the remaining stories of the promises to the ancestors, I do not agree with those scholars who consider the grant or promise to Abraham to be without condition. Rather, I understand the promise to involve a dialectic at its very base: Yahweh will remain faithful to his promise, but always has the power to revoke it if Abraham or his descendants fail to follow Yahweh's commands. This basic tension and inconsistency is endemic to the narrative presentation of the ways in which the human and divine realms interact in the biblical materials. As I have argued elsewhere, this "divine paradox" forms an important ideological position in the deuteronomistic history (*Narrative History and Ethnic Boundaries*, pp. 223–227).

[71] *The Theme of the Pentateuch*, p. 29.

[72] It should not be overlooked that this chronological connection, generally associated with the "Priestly" writer, also allows the section to stand apart from those previous stories while providing an interpretive background for understanding their relationship to those other accounts.

Yahweh's pronouncement concerning the children (vv. 23–24) also sets the tone for the relationship between "Israel" and Edom that will be developed in the remaining narratives concerning Esau and in related Hebrew materials.[73] Two such different sons brought predictably contrasting responses from their parents: Isaac preferred the hunter, Esau, while Rebekah was partial to the "gentle man" ('*îš tām*; 25:27), Jacob.[74] The enmity between the two is first reflected in the narrative that addresses the "right of the first-born," an important concept with respect to inheritance.[75] The way has already been prepared for the abrogation of the right of the first-born to inherit the promises given to the father. Just as Ishmael would not be the legitimate heir of Abraham, so Esau/Edom would not possess the patriarchal promises passed through his father Isaac.

The narrative emphasizes this fact twice, to draw attention to the divinely legitimated role of Jacob. In the first instance, Esau sells his inheritance rights to Jacob for a bowl of porridge (25:29–34), thus forfeiting his birthright (v. 34). Clearly, the simple right of primogeniture does not automatically qualify one as "worthy" to possess the promise. Instead, some degree of ingenuity might also be an attribute that could be helpful to those attempting to gain recognition for their claims to land. In the second episode (27:1–45), Jacob, with the help and instructions of his mother Rebekah, deliberately tricks his father Isaac into giving him the blessing that was presumably intended for Esau.

This second account builds upon the theme of the first one, but is not independent of the previous narrative recounting the encounter of Isaac and

---

[73] The descriptions of the appearance of the children are used as etiologies for their names (25:25–26). Esau was so called because of his ruddy appearance, hairy like a garment. Jacob, on the other hand, was so named because "his hand was holding the heel of Esau" when they were born. Later in the story, a second etiology will be given for Esau, noting that he also bore the name Edom, derived from the red ('*ādōm*) pottage for which he sold his birthright. Outside of the narratives in Genesis, the continued enmity between "Israel" and Edom is reflected in texts such as Obadiah, Ezekiel 35, Mal 1:2–4, etc.

[74] It is tempting in this context to see in the reference to Jacob as '*îš tām* a reflection of Noah and Abraham, to whom the adjective *tām* is applied (6:9; 17:1).

[75] As is commonly recognized, the standard practice of inheritance in the ancient Near East was based upon the principle of primogeniture. According to Deut 21:15–17, the eldest son is to receive double the portion of the inheritance of the father than what is received by the other sons. This custom is often negated in the biblical stories, e.g., the loss of inheritance by Reuben (Gen 49:4; 1 Chr 5:1) or by Esau (25:29–34; 27:27–29, 39–40). In the latter case, it is far from clear that the legal traditions of the ancient world would have upheld the claim of Jacob over against Esau. It must be remembered that the purpose of the story here is etiological and didactic, not legal.

Rebekah with Abimelek of Gerar, called now a Philistine king (26:1).[76] The central message of the first portion of this narrative revolves around Yahweh's promise to fulfill his oath to Abraham (vv. 3–4), gifts that would be given to Isaac, "because Abraham obeyed my voice and observed my commandments, my ordinances, and my instructions" (*ʿēqeb ʾăšer-šāmaʿ ʾabrāhām běqōlî wayyišmōr mišmartî miṣwôtay ḥuqqôtay wětôrōtay;* 26:5).[77] Clearly those promises are not unconditional. Yahweh's fulfillment of his promises may be directly related to the issue of obedience to his command. Or, by his grace, it may not be. It is this tension that created the constant paradox with which the biblical writers struggled and about which their religious world revolved. It should not be overlooked that the promise that would be continued through Isaac was given to him while he was in a foreign land.

Both prosperity and blessing are emphasized in the account of Isaac's sojourn in Gerar, demonstrating that Yahweh's blessing brought great wealth to Isaac (26:12), an important issue related to the matter of inheritance in the next chapter. Esau's loss of inheritance, in practical terms, went far beyond the simple loss of the promises to the land and of becoming a source of blessing to the nations. Also enveloped in the account of Isaac's "exile" in Gerar[78] is a story concerning conflicts with the people of Abimelek over water rights, an account that builds clearly upon the previous stories concerning Abraham (cf. 21:22–34). These conflicts, like those between Abraham and Abimelek, are resolved by a covenant (26:28–31; cf. 21:27), resulting not only in a treaty of peace, but also rights to the water, an absolute necessity for survival in an often hostile environment.[79] Isaac, at

---

[76] On the parallels of 26:1–11 with 12:10–20 and 20:1–18, see above, n. 24.

[77] The terminology here is highly reminiscent of Deuteronomy and the deuteronomistic writers. For examples, see M. Weinfeld, *Deuteronomy and the Deuteronomic School,* pp. 336–337.

[78] It should be noted that each of the three patriarchs, Abraham, Isaac, and Jacob, for reasons of either famine (Abraham and Isaac) or internal familial threats (Jacob) is forced to go to lands outside of the "promised land," and there each greatly increases his wealth at the expense of the indigenous rulers of the land. The symbolic value of these stories for groups finding themselves in "exile" should not be underestimated.

[79] It seems quite clear that 26:12–33 represents an account parallel to that found in 21:22–34. The former is normally ascribed to the "Yahwist," while the latter is attributed to the "Elohist." Beyond the fact that the two stories share a number of stylistic parallels, there is little concrete evidence suggesting that they were not composed by the same person. The reasons for assigning these parallel and repetitious stories, with contradictory accounts, like the double etiology for Beer Sheba (26:32–33; 21:29–31), seem less apparent if one does not assume that the stories were intended to be read alongside one another.

each and every point, seems to be a reflection of Abraham and a perfect vehicle for the continuation of the promise.[80]

As though to reinforce the spurning of his birthright, Esau is reintroduced with references to his choice of wives. In contrast to the "proper" marriage of his father, and the parallel of his brother, Esau chooses Hittite women as his partners, i.e., exogamous unions. Such intentional rejection of proper relations has parallels in the following narrative recounting the manner in which Jacob, at the urging and with the direction of Rebekah, deceived his father into giving him the blessing intended for the first-born (27:1–45). The blessing he receives establishes his ideal social standing: "peoples will serve you and nations will bow down to you" (*ya'abdûkā 'ammîm wĕyištahăwû* [Q] *lĕkā lĕ'ummîm;* 27:29), a blessing that clearly reflects the idea of a reversal of the present social order when incorporated by "descendants" who were themselves subjects to a foreign power.[81]

Despite the manner in which Jacob had duped his aged father into blessing him, the blessing is reconfirmed by Isaac himself, who summoned him to bless him and to forbid him to take a Canaanite wife (28:1).[82] He was to go to Padan Aram (28:2; cf. 25:20; 48:7), to the house of Bethuel, his mother's father, and to take one of the daughters of Laban, his mother's brother, as a wife.[83] Jacob obeyed his father and went, having now the assurance that he would receive not only the blessing of his father Isaac, but also the "blessing of Abraham" (*birkat 'abrāhām;* 28:4). Emerging within

80 One is tempted to question whether the entirety of the accounts of Isaac is not derived, in literary terms, either from those concerning Abraham and Jacob or from the background literary motifs and forms upon which those were built. It seems highly questionable that there ever existed any independent cycle of stories, either oral or written, concerning Isaac.

81 When Esau discovers the "theft" of his blessing, an act which, in all probability, would have carried no legal weight in the ancient world, he asks his father for another blessing. While Isaac clearly can revoke his blessing on Jacob and give it to Esau, he doesn't. Instead, Esau, who has already proven himself unworthy of the rights of the first-born, not only by selling his birthright, but also by marrying women from among the people of the land, receives a lesser blessing that confirms his subjugation to Jacob. Notably, the blessing on Esau recognizes that eventually Esau/Edom would break away from Jacob/"Israel" (27:39–40; cf. 2 Kgs 8:20, 22).

82 27:46–28:9, which begins by noting Rebekah's fear that Jacob, like Esau, would take a Hittite wife (cf. 26:34), is often attributed to the "Priestly" writer. It may be understood just as easily as a reconfirmation of both the blessing and reaffirmation of endogamous marriage as the ideal form for "Israel" to follow. The references to God as *'ēl šadday* (28:3–4; cf. 17:1) are not sufficient reasons for finding a separate source or document here.

83 As has been noted in numerous studies of kinship relations in the Hebrew bible, the avuncular marriage relationship represents a type of ideal for many cultures. Contrast the obedience of Jacob in following this type of marriage alliance with the actions of Esau, who chose to take an Ishmaelite wife (28:8–9) in addition to his Hittite women.

the story are sure indicators that genealogy and marriage are developing as boundaries that separate insiders, who possess the promise/blessing of Yahweh, from the outsiders who, though related, cannot trace their lineage back through the legitimate line.

It is at Beth-el that Jacob receives the formal announcement from Yahweh that the promise to the ancestors would pass through his line. In a dream which supplies an etiology for Beth-el (28:12–15,19), Yahweh appears to him and announces: "I am Yahweh, the god of Abraham your ancestor and the god of Isaac" (*'ănî yhwh 'ĕlōhê 'abrāhām 'ābîkā wē'lōhê yiṣḥāq;* 28:13). No matter what epithets might be applied to the personal deity of the ancestors in selected episodes of the narrative, such announcements as these make it clear that Yahweh is the god to whom they are to be understood as applying.[84] In response Jacob vows that if Yahweh will protect him on his journey and return him to his father's house, "then Yahweh will be my god" (*wĕhāyâ yhwh lî lē'lōhîm;* v. 21). Such an apodosis to the conditional provides an interesting insight into the working of the authorial process here, for in the character of Jacob, the one who will bear the eponym "Israel" and represent the only genealogical line for the people who will trace their origins to him, the issue of divine direction is confused with the concept of human control. Known to both hearer and reader is the fact that Yahweh is already the god of Jacob, whether Jacob admits it or not. The promise passed along to Jacob further assures that Yahweh will watch over him and his way, but not necessarily without obligations. Such is reflected in the reference to giving Yahweh a tenth of his wealth and to making Beth-el a place of worship (v. 22) in response to Yahweh's help. At the same time, the placement of the vow here allows the author(s) to delay its fulfillment, a narrative device that is common by this point, and to present the intervening stories dealing with Jacob's marriage, children, and wealth.

In accord with his father's wishes, Jacob goes east to Aram, where he arrives at the house of Laban in the area of Haran (29:1–14) and there marries the daughters of his mother's brother (29:15–30).[85] With these unions,

---

[84] Despite the continuing emphasis upon the use of specific names as indicative of particular sources and documents, there is more than enough overlap in the use of divine names to make this criterion questionable at best. For an assessment of the criterion of different divine names as indicators of particular sources, see R. N. Whybray, *The Making of the Pentateuch*, pp. 63–72.

[85] The parallels between chapters 29 and 25 are well known. All that is necessary to account for them is the recognition that they represent variations on standard type-scenes and do not necessarily presuppose each other nor any lengthy pre-history, either oral or written.

Jacob is able to surpass Abraham in his quest for heirs, for in 29:31–30:24
(cf. 35:22b-26) are recounted the births of eleven sons and one daughter to
Jacob's two wives and their two hand-maids.

Leah	*Zilpah*	*Rachel*	*Bilhah*
Reuben	Gad	Joseph	Dan
Simeon	Asher		Naphtali
Levi			
Judah			
Issachar			
Zebulun			
Dinah (d)			

Of the variety of tribal eponyms that would constitute the descendants of
"Israel," the first eleven were born in Aram/Mesopotamia, the homeland
of their forefathers.[86] The land of Palestine, which would become the focal
point of contention, both in the stories of the "primary history" and in the
"restoration" of Jerusalem in the Persian period, belonged to them by right
of the promise to their ancestors. These claims to the land thus become a
part of the primordial past made accessible in the present by the stories recounting them.

Through his own cunning, and with Yahweh's blessing, Jacob accumulated wealth comparable to that of Abraham and Isaac (30:25–43), a
fact that leads to his return to the land of his birth. Indeed, it is the result
of Yahweh's command (31:3, 11–13) that Jacob gathered his family and
possessions and began the journey home. His success had been the result
of the fact that "the god of my father, the god of Abraham and the 'fear'[87]
of Isaac" (*'ĕlōhê 'ābî 'ĕlōhê 'abrāhām ûpaḥad yiṣḥāq;* 31:42; cf. 28:13) had
been with him. It was this god who would stand as guarantor of the treaty
that Jacob and Laban made (31:53) that defined further the lands that Aram
and Jacob would claim as their own. Jacob's offering of sacrifices con-

---

86 The complexity of the issue of the social status of each of the sons is not addressed directly in these stories but is a major issue in the development of the "histories" of each of the
"tribal" groups in the deuteronomistic history. There the preeminent role is given to Judah.
Whether the tribal groupings here reflect any type of historical tribal alliances, or even real
tribes at all, is not an issue for the present argument. What is important is the recognition that
lineage traced back to "Israel" must still be understood in terms of hierarchical relationships.

87 On the problems associated with the phrase *paḥad yiṣḥāq,* see E. Puech, "Fear of
Isaac," *ABD* II, 779–780.

cludes both the treaty and Jacob's sojourn in a foreign land. Always under the protection of Yahweh, the god of the ancestors whose power was not restricted to any geographic borders, Jacob had prospered, even though he had been driven out of his homeland by his own brother. Even while in exile he had maintained the purity of his descent, marrying only within the appropriate family lines and, as a result, bearing sons and a daughter who would further define "Israel."

Now, however, to conclude the symbolic migrations of "Israel," the narrative must return him to the land he and his offspring are to inherit. Jacob's return to the land is narrated in detail, with special attention given to the magnanimous fashion by which he hoped to win the favor of his brother Esau.[88] Having implored God for favor from the wrath of his brother and reminded God of his promise to make his offspring too numerous to count (32:10–14),[89] Jacob had his fated encounter with the "man" (ʾîš) at the river Jabbok (32:25–30). Against the background of a feared encounter with Esau, Jacob instead struggled with a mysterious being who renamed him "Israel," announcing: "you have struggled with god and with men and have prevailed" (śārîtā ʿim-ʾĕlōhîm wĕʿim-ʾănāšîm wattûkāl; 32:29b).[90] This aspect of "Israel's" nature was part of the character of its ancestor Jacob. It also forms an important aspect of the culture that associated itself with this patriarch, for it would "regain" its lost prominence specifically by "prevailing" in its encounters with others, both human and divine.

In addition to the renaming of Jacob, the story provides the etiological basis for the establishment of a specific cultural boundary by which "Israel" will separate itself from other groups. As a part of the development of the food taboos that were developed as distinctive characteristics associated with the ethnicity of "Israel," the story of the encounter of Jacob and the

---

88 Far from being a fragment of any kind of extensive myth, the brief notice of the encounter of Jacob with the "angels" (malăkê ʾĕlōhîm; 32:2–3) and the etiology of Mahanayim ("two camps") is a literary creation that bridges the account of the less than friendly parting between Laban and Jacob and the feared encounter with Esau. Further, the dual mahănāyim plays upon Jacob's division of his household into "two camps" (šĕnê mahănôt; 32:8).

89 Cf. 28:13–14. The potential conflict between Jacob and Esau is heightened by the earlier reference in 27:41b to Esau's resolve to kill his brother.

90 As with the previous encounter with extra-human characters, this piece may be understood as a literary construction that provides an etiology for the name "Israel" and which connects an important aspect of "Israelite" identity with the naming of this eponymous ancestor. While it might draw upon mythic representations of river demons, etc., there is no need to posit any folkloristic tradition behind this episode.

"man" results in an injury to the sinew of Jacob's hip (the sciatic nerve) that provides the reason that this sinew is not eaten by "Israelites" (Gen 32:34; cf. *m. Ḥul* 7).[91] When and where such a practice might have developed remains unclear, but in its present context, it occurs as a basic identifying factor associated with those who would call themselves "Israelite" and trace their descent through Jacob/Israel.

The meeting between Jacob and Esau is resolved with no major conflict and results in Jacob's buying a parcel of land from the sons of Hamor, the father of Shechem (33:19).[92] This final notice is important, for it introduces two of the actors, Hivites (34:2), who will figure into the following narrative that further defines membership in the community of "Israel."[93] Jacob's daughter, Dinah (30:21), was dishonored by Shechem, son of Hamor, who thus incurred the wrath of Jacob's sons, who proclaimed that he had "committed an outrage in Israel" (*kî nĕbālâ ʿāśâ bĕyiśrāʾēl;* 34:7) by lying with the daughter of Jacob.[94] This very announcement by Jacob's sons performs an important transition in the text since it transforms the personal name "Israel" into a geographic designation. While clearly anachronistic, it nonetheless makes the important distinction between what was allowable among the indigenous population of Canaan and what was permissible

91 This food taboo is not mentioned elsewhere in the Hebrew bible. The issue of food taboos and their origins remains a matter of debate. For an overview of some of the major issues, see P. J. Budd, "Holiness and Cult," in *The World of Ancient Israel: Sociological, Anthropological and Political Perspectives,* ed. R. E. Clements (Cambridge: Cambridge University Press, 1989), pp. 282–290, and the literature cited therein.

92 As noted earlier, this is the only text apart from Genesis 23 that mentions a patriarchal purchase of land in Canaan.

93 C. Westermann (*Genesis 12–36*, pp. 535–537) notes correctly that the narrative in Genesis 34 presupposes the prohibitions of marriage with the indigenous population found in Deut 7:3 (cf. Josh 23:12–13). He argues that the redactor of these materials has, with Deuteronomy 7 in mind, combined two originally independent stories to create the present one. The evidence for two independent narratives is derived completely from the present text. It is clear, however, that the present story does reflect a knowledge of the deuteronomic prohibition. That the author(s) would place this story here, immediately following the naming of Jacob "Israel" and the introduction of a food taboo, is hardly coincidental.

94 On the connotations of *nĕbālâ* and its use in the deuteronomistic corpus, especially in connection with sexual misdeeds, see Deut 22:21; Josh 7:15; Jgs 19:23, 24; 20:6; 2 Sam 13:12; cf. Jer 29:23. C. Westermann (*Genesis 12–36*, pp. 538–539) correctly notes the dependence of 34:7 on 2 Sam 13:12. It is commonly assumed that Shechem raped Dinah, thus provoking the response of Jacob's sons. This view has been challenged by L. Bechtel, who sees in this story a conflict of perspectives *vis-à-vis* relationships with outsiders ("What if Dinah is not Raped? [Genesis 34]," *JSOT* 62 [1994] 19–36).

within "Israel,"[95] and traces the origins of this practice back to the origins of the very name "Israel."

As an intentional ploy to show the inferiority of the descendants of Hamor, the sons of Jacob misled them into believing that the two ethnic groups could intermarry if the Shechemites were to circumcise every male; then, and only then, could "we become one people" (*wĕhāyînû lĕʿam ʾeḥad;* 34:13–15). That the "Israelites" were being intentionally deceitful (v. 13) suggests that they were completely aware that such exogamous practice, at least with the indigenous population, was explicitly forbidden (cf. Deut 7:3; Josh 23:12–13). Instead of giving Shechem their sister, Simeon and Levi entered the city and killed all of the males while they were still suffering the effects of their circumcision, took Dinah, and plundered the city (34:24–27). In a pointedly symbolic fashion, the acts of the "Israelites" here expressed Yahweh's judgment (*dînâ*) upon the intermingling of "Israel" and "Canaan." Though Jacob may have feared reprisal from the "inhabitants of the land" (*yōšĕbê hāʾāreṣ;* 34:30), the "terror of God" (*ḥittat ʾĕlōhîm;* 35:5) fell upon the cities surrounding them and they did not pursue them as they journeyed to Beth-el as commanded (35:1–5).

Before they departed, Jacob commanded his household to purify themselves and to "put away foreign gods" (*hāsîrû ʾet-ʾĕlōhê hannēkār;* 35:2; cf. Deut 31:16; Josh 24:23; Jgs 10:16; 1 Sam 7:3). In anticipation of the arrival at Beth-el and the erection of an altar there (vv. 6–7), Jacob further defined the distinctive nature of "Israel" as a "holy people" chosen by their god. At Beth-el, God under the epithet of *ʾēl šadday* appeared to reconfirm the change of Jacob's name to "Israel"[96] and to bless him with the announcement that kings would come forth from him (35:11; cf. 17:6, 16) and with the renewal of the promise of the land (v. 12).

The account of the *tôlĕdōt* of Isaac, concentrating on the life of his son Jacob, concludes with the account of the birth of Jacob's twelfth son, Benjamin, to Rachel, a brief renumeration of his offspring (35:22b-26; cf. 29:31–30:24), and finally with the notice of the death and burial of Isaac (35:27–29). In the lengthy (but highly uneven and episodic) account of

---

95 The rhetorical aspects of this type of ethnic ascription to competing groups should be understood as a standard practice in the formation of ethnic boundaries and not as a description of actual historical practices.

96 Notably, the authority of the "man" who announced the name change in 32:29 is confirmed with the notice that *ʾēl šadday* sanctioned the change and blessed Jacob/Israel under this new guise.

the life of Jacob, the eponym "Israel" was created. Now the lineal descent line was determined and had branched into a segmented genealogical array. The ancestral eponym had engendered twelve more eponyms who would become important organizational elements in the development of the character of "Israel" through the stories narrated about it.[97]

IV. Establishing Ethnic Boundaries

It is these stories about Abraham, Isaac, and Jacob that, when placed alongside the accounts in the "primeval history," provide narrative expansions that form the basis of the developing mythologies of ethnic origins. Of the eight categories of myths that provide the supporting bases for defining and reinforcing ethnic individuality, the stories of Genesis provide for four: stories of origins in time; accounts of origins in space; specifications of ancestry; and myths of migration.[98] "Israel" had now become both a distinctive people with an exclusive divine claim to a particular land and an individual who could trace "his" claim back to the "original" ancestor, Abram. The myths of origins and migration created a specific lineage that would stand over against any "indigenous" claims to the right to the lands promised to Abram and his offspring. But the patriarchal stories do not end here, for there is one final *tôlĕdôt* formula that occurs to introduce the generations of Jacob and which focuses upon the vicissitudes of his offspring centering upon the activities of Joseph. Few texts in the Tetrateuch represent the problems of modern critical analysis of the history of the composition of the materials as well as the stories associated with the family of Jacob contained in Gen 37:1–50:26. While the classical source critical approach views the basic stories as a combination of "Yahwistic" and "Elohistic" materials, with very light "Priestly" editing,[99] literary critics have emphasized the ways in which the Joseph stories originally constituted an independent "novella" which has been supplemented by a number of ele-

97 The fourth of the *tôlĕdôt* sections is contained in 36:1–37:1 and provides the story of the descendants of Esau/Edom through his Canaanite wives (36:2). It fulfills the promise of 25:23 that Jacob and Esau would become "two nations" (J. Blenkinsopp, *The Pentateuch*, pp. 106–107) and recounts how Edom came to possess the regions associated with Mt. Seir. Most notable here is the clear anachronism contained in 36:31–39, the list of Edomite kings who ruled before there was a king in Israel.

98 On these categories of ethnic myths, see A. D. Smith, *The Ethnic Origins of Nations*, p. 192.

99 For a presentation of the various divisions of these materials since the time of J. Wellhausen, see C. Westermann, *Genesis 37–50* (Minneapolis: Augsburg, 1986), pp. 18–22.

ments to create a composite narrative that is presently connected with the preceding patriarchal stories.[100]

There exists no textual evidence for the independent existence of either an account of the patriarchs without the inclusion of the stories of Joseph or an independent account of the Joseph story itself. In short, the only evidence for the existence of either set of materials is from the present form of the Tetrateuch in which they are included and which defines the forms in which they are presented.[101] While it is clearly possible to "deconstruct" the narrative of Genesis 37–50 into several "independent" stories, e.g., the story of Joseph the royal courtier, the novella of Joseph and his brothers, the account of Judah and Tamar, and then use these "reconstructions" to argue for a process of composition,[102] there is simply no evidence to support the theory that the existing text was composed in this manner.

This is not to dispute the possibility that such "reconstructions" of both "original" texts and redactional processes might be accurate. It is only to remind the reader that the evidence for the reconstruction is all internal to the argument itself and is supported only by its own presuppositions. Further, these reconstructed processes of composition do not reveal anything about the potential functions of the texts as documents that were used in the life of the communities that produced them. So, while such investigations might provide some interesting theories about the theoretical manners by which texts might have been written, they tell very little about how the text might have functioned in the creation and maintenance of the identity of a group, which is the directing focus of the present study. Thus, I shall attempt to address how these materials might have functioned within the context of the Persian-era community attempting to recreate the story of its origins and to locate its claims to the possession of the land in the accounts of its primordial origins in space and time, its ancestry, and via its migrations.

---

[100] This view is represented by G. W. Coats, *Genesis, With an Introduction to Narrative Literature* (FOTL 1; Grand Rapids, MI: Eerdmans, 1983), pp. 259–315.

[101] The observations that the literary digressions from the story found in chaps. 39–41, Joseph in the foreign court, have literary parallels with the Egyptian "Tale of two Brothers" and "Tale of Sinuhe" indicate only that the author(s) of these materials might have been familiar with a number of "stock" genres of their day. Certainly the account of the prosperity of the foreigner at the court of the foreign king contained in the Joseph materials has its closest biblical parallels in the narratives contained in Daniel 1–6, which clearly date to the late Babylonian period at the earliest.

[102] See, for example, the attempt of J. Van Seters to reconstruct an "original" ending to the Jacob account (*Prologue to History*, pp. 317–318).

It is precisely this last mythological element, migration, that provides the necessary link in the overarching narrative between the stories of the ancestors and those concerning their immediate descendants who would find themselves in need of liberation from bondage, another important motif in the development of ethnic myths.[103] As contained in the present form of the text, the stories about Joseph provide the narrative vehicle that transports Jacob/"Israel" and his twelve sons into a foreign land, Egypt, from which their god, Yahweh, would deliver them from bondage and designate them as his special possession, defined by both lineage and obedience to the divine word, the two major boundaries for the community that have been developed throughout the stories of the creation and the ancestors.[104]

The *tôlĕdôt* of Jacob begins with the story of the way in which Joseph, his favorite son, was sold into slavery in Egypt by his jealous brothers (37:1–36). The concentration on the internal intrigue and intricacies of the "tribal," and hence, genealogical relationships, could play an interesting role among a group that perceived itself as having been unjustly sent into exile/slavery in a foreign land. The subsequent story, the account of Judah and Tamar (38:1–30), displays quite clearly the episodic nature of the composition.[105] Judah, here being used as a "negative" example of appropriate behavior for a son of Jacob, is portrayed as marrying a Canaanite woman (38:1–2) and having three sons, the eldest of whom married Tamar (v. 6). After the death of Tamar's husband, Er, the story serves as an exposition on the importance of the levirite marriage (cf. Deut 25:5–10), an institution which, whether ever actually instituted or not, carried important implications for the closely knit nature of a community that was in constant danger of assimilation. The importance of fulfilling the institution could not be more clear than in the notice of the fate of Onan, who failed to act properly with respect to his deceased brother's wife: Yahweh "killed him also"

---

103 For examples of myths of migration and exodus that appear to have been created by cultures out of socio-political motives to establish an ethnic solidarity rather than from any "historical" memory, see K. Whitelam, "Israel's Traditions of Origin: Reclaiming the Land," *JSOT* 44 (1989) 24–28.

104 The necessity of obedience has not constituted a major focus so far in the narrative. It will become a central focus in the accounts associated with Sinai. In Deuteronomy, obedience to Torah is the defining characteristic of the community from its inception.

105 Critics are generally agreed that this story interrupts the narrative flow of the Joseph story and that it represents a completely independent composition that has been secondarily inserted into the present context. This may be so; still, it is there as a part of the whole, and those who would like to argue that Genesis represents an attempt at a unified composition need to explain why this obvious intrusion is here.

(*wayyāmet gam-ʾōtô;* v. 10b). While the reason for the placement of the story here is not at all clear, it is possible that it provided a commentary on the appropriate response to a brother lost, i.e., Joseph.

On the completion of the story of Judah and Tamar, the narrative returns to follow the fate of Joseph, sold to the Egyptian master, Potiphar (39:1; cf. 37:36). Though falsely accused and imprisoned (39:7–23), Joseph nonetheless was able to rise to prominence in the foreign court, becoming second only to the person of Pharaoh (40:1–41:57). Significantly, the union of Joseph with the daughter of an Egyptian priest (41:45) resulted in the birth of Manasseh and Ephraim (41:50–52).[106] The significance of this for those in exile should not be overlooked. In the context of the end of the story of Jacob's life, Jacob would bless Ephraim and Manasseh, proclaiming Ephraim to be the greater of the two (48:9–20), making them the legitimately recognized heirs to the inheritance of their father. Indeed, as Jacob recounts the revelation at Bethel (cf. 35:6, 9–12), he reiterates the promise of the land as an "eternal possession" (*ʾăḥuzzat ʿôlām;* 48:4; cf. 17:8). Even those born in exile whose genealogy might be open to question may still share in the possibility of having an inheritance in the land.

The purpose of the narration of the Joseph stories and the lengthy digression from the fulfillment of the promises is to be found within the context of the accounts of the encounters of Joseph with his brothers in Egypt and his reunion with his father (42:1–46:30). Joseph's fate and fortune were hardly left to chance. Instead, Joseph himself is able to announce the divine reason behind all that has happened to him when he tells his brothers: "God sent me before you to establish for you a remnant (*lāśûm lākem šĕʾērît*) in the land and to keep you alive (*ûlĕhaḥăyôt lākem*) by a great deliverance" (45:7; cf. 50:20). Through his own exile and servitude, he would be exalted and become a vehicle by which his brothers, the descendants of Jacob/"Israel" would be preserved and given life. They would be the remnant of "Israel."

It is while in Egypt that the "70 sons of Jacob" (46:8–27; cf. Exod 1:1–5) prosper as God had promised: "So Israel[107] dwelt in Egypt, in the

---

106 It is interesting to note that Joseph, who would not return from Egypt, was given an Egyptian name, *ṣapnat paʿnēaḥ* (the transcription of the Egyptian ḏd-p3–nṯr-jw.f-ʿnḫ, "the god speaks and he [the one who bears the name] lives"), and married an Egyptian wife, to whom were born Manasseh and Ephraim (G. Oller, "Zaphenath-Paneah," *ABD* IV, 1040).

107 In this instance "Israel" designates a people, i.e., an ethnically identifiable group quite separate from the Egyptians. In this same vein, they are assigned their own land, Goshen (45:10; 47:27). They are further distinguished by virtue of the ethnic designation as "Hebrew," *ʿibrî,*

land of Goshen. They acquired property in it and they were fruitful and multiplied greatly" (47:27). "Israel," the final of the three "individual" ancestors
to whom Yahweh had given his promises, had now become a "great nation"
(*gôy gādôl;* 46:3) as promised. As a vehicle of blessing, "Jacob blessed
Pharaoh" (*waybārek yaʿăqōb ʾet-parʿōh;* 47:7b, 10a). But God had no plans
to leave this nation in Egypt. He had already revealed in his appearance to
Jacob that he would bring them out of that land (46:4; cf. 50:24; 15:13–16).
Their migration and history would not be complete until they returned to
the land that had been promised to their ancestors. The exile in Egypt would
be simply a time of growth and prosperity from which a mighty nation,
"Israel," the descendants of one man, would culminate in the liberation of
the nation and the inauguration of the golden age in the land promised to
them in *illo tempore.*

When one attempts to discover the plot line that connects the highly
disparate narratives contained in Genesis 12–50, one finds that there is very
little movement. The collected traditions concerning Abraham, Isaac, and
Jacob are connected by the themes of the promise of the land, the promise
of a nation, and the promise that they would become the vehicle of blessing
to the other nations of the earth.[108] It is not the result of any literary artistry
or redactional sophistry that these three themes provide the major common
links among the otherwise episodic traditions concerning the partriarchs. If
these separate stories were intended to be understood as just that, despite
the overarching chronology that has been supplied to the whole, then the
problems of repetitions, doublets, inconsistencies, and gaps disappear. If the
patriarchal stories were understood as didactic accounts that might be used
to illustrate and "flesh out" the references to the "fathers" and Yahweh's
promises to them, already made in Deuteronomy, then the necessity of
positing some lengthy period of oral and/or written transmission disappears.
The present collection might be understood as the result of a continuing

---

applied to Joseph (39:14, 17; 41:12) and to a land (40:15). In 43:32 it was noted that for Egyptians to eat with "Hebrews" constituted an abomination (*tôʿēbâ*). Additionally, their occupations
as shepherds and cattle breeders set them apart from the Egyptians for the same reasons. Rather
than to search for some evidence that these latter two practices of separation reflect some historical or social reality, it is more likely that each of them refers to a type of self-separation
imposed on the "Hebrew" group by the author(s) of the account.

108 As emphasized above, the promises of the possession of the land to be given to the
offspring of the patriarchs that create this sense of connectedness mean that the story of the Pentateuch is one of the failure of the fulfillment of the promise (cf. 12:7; 13:15; 15:18; 17:8; 24:7;
26:3, 4; 28:4, 13; 35:12; 48:4).

growth of materials within the scribal schools that functioned as stories which created a shared, common "history" and ethnicity to the people who participated in their recital. This fact is reiterated in the continued promises that were to be extended to "your seed after you" (*zarăkā ʾaḥăreykā;* 17:7, 8, 9, 10; 35:12; 48:4).

—— ဇာ **6** ၡ ——

THE EXODUS STORIES:
MYTHS OF BONDAGE AND LIBERATION:
THE BACKGROUND OF COVENANT

I. Exile and Identity: Reincorporating the Past

When one moves from the narratives of Genesis, especially those addressing the patriarchs (12:1–35:29), to the stories of Israel's liberation from
Egypt, even with the inclusion of the transitional story of Jacob/Joseph
(37:1–50:26), one is immediately struck by the lack of reference to the one
theme that unites the patriarchal stories—the three-fold promise to the patriarchs.[1] In Exodus, reference to the oath sworn to the ancestors occurs
in only two narratives, both of which are highly deuteronomistic in form
and are dependent upon the narratives in Deuteronomy for their content.[2]
The first references are contained in 13:5, 11, in the midst of the legislation
of the celebration of the Passover. The second set of references occurs in
32:13 and 33:1, i.e., in stories associated with Israel's apostasy *vis-à-vis* the
incident of the golden calf. Apart from these two places, the narratives of
Exodus seem to have no connection to, or direct dependence upon, the patriarchal stories of Genesis.

Additionally, those texts that do mention the patriarchs and/or refer to
Yahweh's promise to them have the appearance of being editorial glosses.

---

1 Despite the common conclusion that different elements of the promises belong to differ-
ent redactional layers of the patriarchal stories, it remains clear that this same redactional
activity cannot be posited in the formation of the narratives that are presented in the book of
Exodus. These arguments are clearly stated by R. Rentdorff ("The 'Yahwist' as Theologian?
The Dilemma of Pentateuchal Criticism," *JSOT* 3 [1977] 2–9; *The Problem of the Process of
Transmission in the Pentateuch*, pp. 177–206).

2 For supporting arguments, see the discussion below.

Exodus begins with a clear editorial reference to the list of people who went into Egypt with Jacob that is given in Gen 46:8–27. In 19:3, the Israelites are referred to as "the house of Jacob" (*bêt ya'ăqōb*). Otherwise, the name Jacob does not appear in Exodus apart from the stylized lists noted below. A similar situation is encountered with references to Joseph, which occur only in 1:5, 6, and 8, and which form an editorial bridge with the concluding narrative of Genesis. References to Abraham and Isaac are confined to the standardized references contained in 2:24; 3:6, 15, 16; 4:5; 6:3, 8; 32:13; and 33:1. A brief consideration of these passages is instructive with respect to the editorial or authorial processes underlying the books of Genesis and Exodus. In 2:24b, in the notice concerning the death of the "new king" and the continued enslavement of the people,[3] the author notes that God "remembered his covenant with Abraham, with Isaac, and with Jacob" (*wayyizkōr 'ĕlōhîm 'et-bĕrîtô 'et-'abrāhām 'et-yiṣḥāq wĕ'et-ya'ăqōb*).[4] In the revelation of the divine name to Moses, Yahweh identifies himself as follows: "I am the god of your father, the god of Abraham, the god of Isaac, and the god of Jacob" (*'ānōkî 'ĕlōhê 'ābîkā 'ĕlōhê 'abrāhām 'ĕlōhê yiṣḥāq wĕ'lōhê ya'ăqōb;* 3:6; cf. 3:15, 16). These references, just like those in 6:3, where Yahweh tells Moses that "I appeared to Abraham, to Isaac, and to Jacob as El Shaddai, but by my name Yahweh I was not known to them" (*wā'ērā' 'el-'abrāhām 'el-yiṣḥāq wĕ'el-ya'ăqōb bĕ'ēl šadday ûšmî yhwh lō' nôda'tî lāhem*),[5] link the upcoming stories of Exodus with the accounts of the patriarchs in Genesis. Each of these references to the patriarchs, while ostensibly belonging to one of the commonly identified sources, stands in its present position as a general editorial link within the narrative complex of Exodus, and it is, without further criteria for identification, impossible to

---

3 On the way the author(s) have structured the introduction around the emergence and death of the "new king over Egypt" and have used this to introduce the major themes of the first portion of the book, see below.

4 The theme of Yahweh's "remembering" (*zākar*), which is an indication of forthcoming divine action, also occurs in Gen 8:1; 9:15, 16; 19:29; 30:22; Exod 6:5 (cf. 32:13); Lev 26:42 (2x), 45. While these passages, along with Exod 2:24b, are commonly associated with the "Priestly" writer, the evidence for such is sparse. As R. Rendtorff has noted, the non-specific nature of these references might suggest a reference back to a general idea rather than to a specific literary rendition of a promise, though it is possible that the author has Gen 17:7–8 in mind. In any event, these references are, for Rendtorff, late editorial connectors (*The Problem of the Process of Transmission in the Pentateuch*, pp. 86, 168, 192).

5 J. Blenkinsopp argues that 3:6, 15, 16; 4:5 are to be assigned to the "D" version of the call of Moses, while those in 6:3, 8 represent a "P" alternative to this account (*The Pentateuch*, pp. 150–153).

assign to any particular strand of narrative. It seems best, in the situation, to look for a more suitable method of analysis for the composition of Exodus.[6]

In short, the narratives in Exodus make few if any references to the stories of Genesis and do not seem to be dependent upon the major themes developed there. Nor should they be expected to. As I have argued throughout, the idea of reading these accounts as though they were intended as a literary or narrative whole is a modern, or at least, post-biblical idea.[7] Instead, the narratives composing the Pentateuch were written or redacted[8] as didactic narratives and instructional units that could be used as wholes or in part for illustrating the major aspects of Israelite identity and ethnicity that were the concern at the moment.[9] As such, they functioned within the context of the provenance of the cult, at least at the initial stage, and that is the one with which the present discussion is concerned. Promulgated by the priests of the reconstructed temple complex, with the backing of the Achaemenid dynasty to recreate and consolidate the ethnicity of the people of the province of Jehud, the stories selected for inclusion in these expan-

---

6 The patriarchs are also referred to in 32:13, in the context of Yahweh's threat to destroy his rebellious people and give the patriarchal promise of a great nation to Moses and his descendants (32:10). This is avoided by Moses' intercession, which implores Yahweh to "remember" (*zĕkōr*) Abraham, Isaac, and Jacob. In 33:1, Moses is instructed to lead the people to the land promised to the fathers. As will be argued in the next chapter, the narrative accounts in chapters 32–33 are most likely derived from the deuteronomic materials and might be suggestive of a process of composition quite different from that suggested by the documentary hypothesis.

7 While there is much to commend the arguments of B. Peckham (*History and Prophecy, passim*) with respect to the manner in which the variety of traditions contained in the completed *TANAK* may be understood as ongoing critiques of previous positions that attempt to incorporate and maintain those materials and ideals of the past and to reformulate them in a new and appropriated form, I am not convinced by his presentation that this may be taken as an adequate manner to explain the actual composition of the text itself. Too much depends upon reconstructions of redactional and compositional units that cannot be demonstrated as ever having existed independently from their present position in the final canonical arrangement.

8 While it is dangerous to posit the existence of any particular stories or accounts prior to their composition as part of the Pentateuch, given the complete lack of textual evidence for the independent existence of any of the variety of those materials, it must be admitted that a variety of these could have been circulated among the scribal schools in either written or oral form before they were recast as part of a longer Pentateuchal narrative.

9 The practices of Torah reading that are reflected in Josephus and in the Mishnah suggest that such was common, but not that there was any attempt to read the entire Torah over a specified period or even to recite the materials of the Torah in their canonical order. The establishment of a set pattern of complete readings is not attested until the Talmudic period (*b. Meg* 29b).

sions on the previously known themes of Deuteronomy reflected, and re-
fracted, the experiences of the group which produced and proclaimed them.
This occurs, of course, within the context of religious and historical metaphors, by which this particular group proclaims its basic identity as the
legitimate inheritors of the traditions of the exiles of the now defunct
monarchic state of Judah.[10]

One of the major metaphors that is developed in the deuteronomic
corpus and which becomes a defining characteristic of developing early
Judaism is that of "exile."[11] What makes this metaphor so important is that
it carries with it an implied complement—restoration. As it is utilized in
the materials that constitute the Hebrew bible, emphasis is constantly
placed upon the latter. Most significantly, in the Jerusalem "restoration"
community reorganized in the Persian period, those who were "restored"
coincide, ideologically, with those who were "exiled." Hence, as we shall
argue below, the very "fact" of exile became a defining characteristic of
the emerging group itself, at least in the literature produced by the community in Jerusalem and Judah. Despite the possible historical referents that
may coincide with both the bondage in Egypt, understood as it came to be
as a type of exile, and the exile in Babylon, each must be examined in the
light of the resulting liberation or restoration group that developed and
which sustained these traditions themselves. Further, if our reconstructions
of the development of the written traditions are approximately correct, then
each of these sets of traditions can be understood only against the background of the ideologies constructed by the Persian restoration community in Jerusalem. As the dynamics of the rhetoric were developed and
found their way into the realm of the "historical," the "exiles" who returned
from Babylon and Persia became the "true" remnant of the population of
Judah.[12]

---

10 This type of historiography which refers back to a "canonical" past to substantiate
present nationalistic claims has been coined "creative" historiography by D. Mendels and is
characteristic of Near Eastern historiography in contrast to the Greek traditions associated with
Thucydides (*The Rise and Fall of Jewish Nationalism* [New York: Doubleday, 1992], pp. 35–45).

11 This is not to suggest that the concept of exile in the development of Judaism was
merely metaphorical. That selected inhabitants of Samaria/Israel and later Jerusalem/Judah
were exiled from their land by the Assyrians and Babylonians respectively is a documented
matter. What I am arguing, however, is that these historical events have been given a very powerful formative role in the ideological literature that was developed to create and sustain the
Jerusalem community in the Persian period and following.

12 On the tendentious nature of this claim, see P. R. Davies, *In Search of 'Ancient Israel'*,
pp. 84–89.

The implications of the power of this claim are notable, for it was these returning "Judahite" exiles who possessed the political backing of the Persians who "restored" the "pre-exilic" cultus in Jerusalem, thus reestablishing "older traditional" practices, while at the same time conforming to the standard "temple economy" utilized by the Persians to administer their realm. It was through this process that a legitimizing myth of liberation and restoration was created. As "Israel" had originally acquired its promised land upon its escape from Egypt,[13] so too would "Judah" regain its land upon its return from Babylon. The "restoration" of the "earlier" cultus, and, concomitantly, the definition and maintenance of the official Temple and its supporting society, fell to the control of those who were "returned" to the land by the Persians and who had their support in their efforts. This very rhetoric of "restoration" and "preservation" is consistent with that of temple and cultic "restorers and restorations" common to the ancient Near East.[14]

None of the above comments is intended to impugn the historicity or the accuracy of any of the traditions utilized in the compilation of these materials. Rather, they reinforce the approach and analytical method of the present study. The religious and cultural implications of the compilation of these traditions into a standardized form are the central focus of the investigation. From the perspective of the "restoration" community that was responsible for reestablishing the primacy of Jerusalem in the Persian province of Jehud, a collection of narratives recounting what would become the "shared traditions" of the communities of Judaism that were to develop functioned as the "written" statement of the boundaries of the ethnic and religious group who would be identified as Jews, i.e., descendants of the province and people of Jehud. For this group, and for the scribal guilds responsible for the recording of these accounts, as well as their cultic promulgation, a major bonding metaphor was that they were the direct descendants of a people who had been "restored" to their ancestral land after an extended period of "exile."

Yet the "exile" in Babylon from which the group claimed to have been restored constituted only the most recent experience of separation from their divinely guaranteed homeland. Essential to their basic identity as "Is-

---

13 This vision of a great "second exodus" that culminates in a "new thing," i.e., the creation of a new community in Jerusalem, constitutes a dominant theme in the presentations of Deutero-Isaiah, a prophetic collection that was clearly recast in part by that prophet's supporters who were responsible for Trito-Isaiah during the early Persian era.

14 For the development of this theme, see T. L. Thompson, *Early History of the Israelite People*, pp. 415–418.

raelites" was their commonly shared "experience" of an exodus from forced bondage in Egypt, an element of their ethnic history that became a central cultic and confessional component. Because of the centrality of the idea of the divinely led escape from Egyptian bondage to the concept of being "Israelite," it should occasion little surprise that the recital of these events received a major emphasis within the cultus, both as a public and a private, familial ritual. While it is no longer fashionable to understand the account of the exodus as a cultic legend which historicized the events narrated therein,[15] one cannot escape the conclusion that the narrative of Exodus 1–15 has its religious culmination in the establishment of the celebration of the Passover festival. As will be developed in the discussion below, the ritual recreation of the "past" liberation from Egypt provides an essential bonding element in the concept of "Israelite" ethnicity.

This is not to suggest that the accounts in the book of Exodus show no connections to the preceding materials. Clearly, the events narrated in Exodus presuppose the connection of the people in Egypt to the descendants of the patriarchs of Genesis. Further, and just as importantly, the Exodus materials concentrate on developing the relationship between Yahweh, the god who had called the patriarchal figures and had offered them the promises of land and progeny, and their descendants. In Exodus 1–24 three essential elements in the establishment of this "relationship" between "Israel" and Yahweh are developed that begin to shape the boundaries of Israel's self-identity. The presentation of the figure of Moses constitutes the first element in this process. It will be through Moses that the divine will and commands will be mediated; Moses will provide the leadership model through which Israel will learn of what it is to become (Exod 1:1–4:31). In the conflict with the Pharaoh (5:1–15:21), Yahweh demonstrates his incomparable power and majesty, humbling the forces of Egypt and liberating his people. With the establishment of the festival of Passover, the method is provided for the ritual recreation of the experience of liberation from Egypt for "future" generations.[16] In the commemoration of this freedom from

---

15 For the classic statement of this view, see J. Pedersen, "Pessahfest und Pessahlegende," *ZAW* 52 (1934) 161–175.

16 From the perspective of those who were responsible for the final composition of these materials, whatever the antiquity of the variety of practices contained in the narratives might have been, it was their "present" that constituted the "future" generations to which the texts refer. The religious drama created by the ritual reactualization of the exodus becomes the means by which the participants are able to internalize the "past" being reenacted. This is not to discount the possible historicity of some actual exodus. It is, however, to argue that the function of the text is to create a communal identity, not to recount events through any historiographic method or manner.

bondage, Yahweh claims this people as his own. It is in the third part of this section that Yahweh places explicit claims *upon* his people (15:22–24:18). Having delivered them from Egypt, Yahweh furthers his relationship with Israel by offering them the obligations of the covenant, revealed at Mt. Sinai and mediated through Moses. It would be the acceptance of this covenant that would provide the formal ethnic boundary markers for Israel, for, as will be argued in the next chapter, the people's covenantal obligations, expressed through their ritualized life and service to Yahweh, form their very ethnicity.

II. The Figure of Moses: Exile and Return— A Prophetic Paradigm

The necessity for the development of such an identity is provided in the opening stories of the book of Exodus. It is possible to approach these accounts from two different perspectives. On one hand, they are directly linked to the stories in Genesis, which ended with the notice of the death of Joseph (50:26). Exod 1:1–5 opens the account with a reiteration of the list of the seventy people who went into Egypt with Jacob (Gen 46:8–27).[17] The manner in which this account begins is most interesting: "These are the names of the Israelites. . . ." (*wĕʾēlleh šĕmôt bĕnê yiśrāʾēl. . . .* ; 1:1a). This designation for the group in Egypt as *bĕnê yiśrāʾēl* utilizes an ethnic designator that points in two directions: it may be understood as a reference back to the accounts of the change of Jacob's name to Israel (Gen 32:28–29; 35:10), or it might be taken as an identification of the latter "restoration" community's attempt to identify itself with the people who were in Egypt.

Additionally, the mention of Joseph in 1:6–8 might be taken as a reflection of the stories of Genesis, recounting the manner by which Israel came to find itself in Egypt. Yet these two instances, among others, suggest only the possibility of references to some generally known body of traditions or stories, and do not necessitate the positing of continuous written

---

[17] It is commonly noted that the LXX gives the total of the people going into Egypt as 75, both here and in Exod 1:5 and Gen 46:27, due to its inclusion of five additional descendants of Joseph. This same tradition is reflected in 4QGen-Exod[a]. It should be noted that the manuscript partially published by F. M. Cross as 4QExod[a] (*The Ancient Library of Qumran*, rev. ed. [New York: Doubleday, 1961], pp. 184–186) is now named 4QExod[b]. For the text of 4QGen-Exod[a], see E. Ulrich, *et al.*, *Qumran Cave 4: VII: Genesis to Numbers*, pp. 7–30. 4QExod[b] is presented on pp. 79–95. Such variations as these demonstrate that even by the third century BCE, the final form of the texts that were beginning to be regarded as scripturally authoritative had not been fixed. See above, Chap. 2, n. 44.

sources underlying the narratives in the Tetrateuch.[18] Taken from this perspective, it might be argued that the initial stories of Exodus, like the individual narratives of Genesis, do not necessitate an intimate literary knowledge of the preceding materials. More significant, however, is the recognition that even an intimate connection of these accounts with those that preceded need indicate only that the author(s) of the present materials were acquainted with the narratives of Genesis and built upon that knowledge. It is a very different matter to argue that they were working with preexisting sources that represented a whole approximating the Tetrateuch prior to the composition of any particular individual set of stories. It could even be suggested that the lists of descendants going into Egypt might be understood as expansions upon the notice in Deut 10:22 concerning the descent of seventy offspring of Jacob into Egypt, rather than seeing the reference in Deuteronomy as a reflection of earlier stories. Regardless of how such matters may be resolved, what is more important to the present discussion is the manner in which the writer(s) of these materials have constructed their introduction to both the people constituting "Israel" and their circumstances as exiles in a foreign land. These matters are addressed clearly in the opening six verses of the book.

Just as issues of location and ancestry are central to the story, so too is the matter of prosperity. One element of the promise to the patriarchs was that of numerous offspring,[19] and this theme is introduced at the beginning of the account of the sojourn in Egypt. It is not surprising that this element of the promise would be placed at the forefront of the story, since a common concern of groups in exile is the establishment of some mechanisms by which they may hope to maintain their identity in the face of the threat of assimilation into the surrounding foreign cultures. Clearly one such solution to the problem of minority status would be to reproduce as quickly as possible. This is precisely the mode of survival implied by the story, which places great stress upon the fact that "the Israelites were extremely fruitful and increased very greatly so that the land [of Egypt] was filled with them (*ûbĕnê yiśrāʾēl pārû wayyišrĕṣû wayyirbû wayyaʿaṣmû bimʾōd mĕʾōd wattimālēʾ hāʾāreṣ ʾōtām;* 1:7).

While there is no direct reference to the patriarchal promises, the allusion seems clear. The Israelites had become strong enough to be perceived as a threat by their "host" country. It is notable that prior to the reference to

---

18 See, on this position, the comments of J. Blenkinsopp, *The Pentateuch,* pp. 150–151.
19 For references, see D. J. A. Clines, *The Theme of the Pentateuch,* pp. 32–33.

their strength and prolific ability to multiply, there is no hint that the sojourn in Egypt had been anything less than voluntary. The narrative quickly reverses that impression.[20] When a "new king" (*melek-ḥādāš;* 1:8) arose in Egypt, representing a generation different from the one under whom Joseph had prospered, a new tone is introduced into the account.

With the introduction of this figure, who, interestingly, is never named,[21] the situation in which the "Israelites" find themselves suddenly changes. Now the king of Egypt expresses the fear that because of its great strength, "Israel" might join with its enemies and battle against it. Such a development would lead to the realization of another hitherto unexpressed fear, that Israel would "go up from the land" (*wĕʿālâ min-hāʾāreṣ;* 1:10). The literary technique that is employed in this instance should not be overlooked, for it is critical to an understanding of the manner in which the story is told and the functions it fulfilled. The "king of Egypt," representing the forces opposed to Israel and its freedom and survival, is displayed as incompetent in all his decisions throughout the story. At no point does this "outsider" appear able to fathom the importance of the events unfolding around him or to perceive that his opponent is none other than the creator of the universe. The author(s) of the story, quite adeptly, do not hide such information from the reader/hearer of the account. Egypt and its new king fear the physical might of Israel and the political and military implications that it implied in the ancient (and modern) world. What Egypt, in all its "wisdom," should have been in awe of was the god of this people.

This is precisely the point of the story of the two midwives, Shiprah and Puah. In order to decrease their strength, the Pharaoh subjected the "Israelites" to forced labor on his royal storage cities, Pithom and Ramesses.[22]

---

[20] Embedded in the presentation of what is commonly considered the "first" account of a covenant with Abram (Genesis 15) is a clear reference to the fact that this "stay" in Egypt was anything but voluntary. Gen 15:13–16 is a clear "prediction" of the exodus, revealed to Abram in a vision. Likewise, Gen 46:3 contains a direct reference to the fact that while Israel is in Egypt, it will become a great nation. Interestingly, the former is commonly associated with the Elohistic narrative, while the latter is generally assigned to the Yahwistic account.

[21] It seems very unusual that the Pharaohs responsible for the oppression of the people would remain nameless. Such a technique might be extremely understandable in a situation like that of the late sixth century BCE when Egypt was in rebellion against the Persian empire. Pseudonymity, not only for authors, but also for major actors in stories, could prove to be a plus. Additionally, the decision not to name particular historical personages adds to the adaptability and flexibility of the metaphorical aspects of the account.

[22] The extent to which Egypt utilized slaves for state building projects is not clearly documented. At the same time, it is not really important whether Egypt actually engaged in such a practice or not; what is critical is that the author(s) attributed such activity to the Egyptians and

Most unexpectedly, Israel continued to grow stronger. The more the Egyptians oppressed them, the greater they became, the recognition of which led only to further oppression (1:11–14). To bring this unexpected growth to an end, the Pharaoh enters into direct communication with the two Hebrew midwives.[23] The very unlikelihood of such a scenario is commonly overlooked. Additionally, commentators generally fail to understand the anticipatory aspects of the story of the midwives. Their devotion to the god of Israel, expressed quite appropriately as their "fear," the standard ancient Near Eastern designation for reverence and respect for the deity, provides a model to which later actions might be compared.

Because the midwives held their ancestral god in such respect, they chose not to follow the command of Pharaoh to kill all of the newborn Israelite males (1:17).[24] The scene challenges the reader/hearer to suspend all disbelief in the development of the story when the midwives explain their actions by noting how much more vigorous the Hebrew women were in giving birth than the Egyptians (1:19). That the Pharaoh would apparently accept such an explanation as justification for disobeying a direct royal order stretches the imagination to the limit. Yet, at precisely the point where one might expect the Egyptian ruler to order the punishment of these two rebellious slaves, the account returns the focus to the real force determining the direction of the story—the divine realm. "God dealt favorably with the midwives" (*wayyêṭeb 'ĕlōhîm lamyallĕdōt;* 1:20);[25] it will be the divine realm that determines the outcome of actions in the stories of the exodus. Such is essential to providing the background within which the Hebrews enslaved in Egypt will establish their identity.

---

the audience accepted it as factual. The explicit mention of these two cities, the construction of which is dated to the nineteenth dynasty, is generally used to "date" the events in this account.

23 That the Hebrew population had only two midwives (1:15) to serve a population of some 600,000 men on foot, not counting women, children, and elderly (12:37), is commonly taken as an indication that the events narrated have been conflated quite dramatically. For discussions, see the commentaries.

24 In addition to the unlikely conference between the king of Egypt and the two midwives belonging to an enslaved population, it should not be overlooked that the decision to kill the newborn males as a method of population control makes little sense. The further incongruity of the decision may be seen when one remembers that the Pharaoh is also in the process of eliminating the future of his corvée labor force.

25 As a result of their reverence for the deity and the deity's favorable response to them, the midwives are rewarded with "houses" (*bāttîm;* 1:21). This could refer either to physical "houses" or to "families." This particular theme is not developed further. In light of the references to the continuing increase in population, it is tempting to understand this in terms of "offspring."

In response to the continuing increase in the strength of the Hebrews, Pharaoh gave the fatal order "to all his people" (*lĕkol-'ammô*) that every new-born Hebrew male was to be thrown into the Nile (1:22). This command, aimed at the annihilation of the slaves, provides the transition to the story of the birth of the one who would lead them out of their state-imposed bondage—Moses.[26] Clearly, anyone who would have the ability to lead the Israelites out of their bondage in Egypt would have to be a charismatic figure, endowed by the deity with special attributes. The Egyptian decision to kill the first-born males of the Israelites is not only a threat to the entire future of the people "Israel," but also a direct encroachment on the claims of Israel's god.[27] Immediately after this public announcement, the narrative shifts to private activities. Born to an unnamed Levite and his wife was a son.[28] Though the story of the birth of the son is independent of the previous materials, it builds directly upon the knowledge of the Egyptian decree. Because of the dangerous situation, the parents attempt to hide their son from the Egyptians, but are forced to devise a special plan to save his life (2:1–6).

With an eye always turned to the ironic, especially when it casts the Egyptian overlords in a negative light, the story emphasizes that it was none other than Pharaoh's own daughter who saved the child, despite the fact that she recognized that he was "one of the Hebrews' children" (*miyyaldê hā'ibrîm;* 2:6). The fact that she was able to make such a recognition should

---

[26] The figure of Moses dominates the stories from Exodus 2 through Deuteronomy 34. Since it is precisely the stories contained in those materials that constitute the collective "history" of Israel's emergence as a people and which contain the basic descriptions of the relationship of Israel with its god, Yahweh, it should occasion little or no surprise that Moses becomes the paradigm of the divine-human mediator. For an extensive treatment of the variety of images associated with Moses in the Hebrew traditions, see G. W. Coats, *Moses: Heroic Man, Man of God* (JSOTSup 57; Sheffield: JSOT, 1988). The parallels between the stories of the birth of Moses and the birth of Sargon of Akkad are well known. For the text of the latter, see *ANET*, p. 119.

[27] The possession of the first-born constitutes a subtheme throughout the Exodus materials that explains the conflict between the commands of Yahweh, expressed through Moses and Aaron, and the actions of Pharaoh in response to those commands. For Israel, the first-born male, both human and non-human, was understood as belonging to Yahweh (Exod 13:1–2, 14–15; 34:19–20; Deut 15:19–20; etc.). The first-born of the animals and produce were to be offered to Yahweh, while the first-born of the people were to be redeemed (Num 3:45–48; 18:15–18).

[28] Amram, Moses' father, and Jokebed, his mother, are not named until Exod 6:18–20; Num 26:58–59. Building upon the theme of the first-born, the story allows the reader/hearer to infer that Moses is also a first-born child. It will be revealed later in the story that he had older siblings, Aaron and Miriam (Exod 2:7; 6:20; 7:7; Num 26:59).

not be overlooked. In order for Israel to formulate distinctive ethnic boundaries, it was necessary that a clear distinction be maintained between those things that were Hebrew/Israelite[29] and those that were Egyptian, i.e., non-Israelite. No indication is given as to how this distinction might have been made, only that it was possible for the daughter of Pharaoh, with a simple glance, to ascertain that the child was Hebrew. In order to raise the child, the Pharaoh's daughter inadvertently reunites him with his mother, who acts as his wet-nurse (2:7–10). As would be expected, the child prospers and grows up and is like a son to the daughter of Pharaoh, who, in turn, reveals the identity of the child in etiological terms, by naming him Moses, "he draws out [of the water]" (*mōšeh*), deriving the name from the explanation, "because I drew him out of the water" (*kî min-hammayim mēšîtîhû;* 2:10).[30] Little did the daughter of Pharaoh know that Moses would be the one who would draw Yahweh's people out of the land of Egypt, fulfilling the fears expressed by the king in 1:10. Slowly, the fate of those who would oppress Israel is being determined by an unseen force.

The direct involvement of the divine will not be made explicit until the account of the theophany in Exodus 3.[31] As a prelude to this revelation, Moses' own exile is described, presenting yet another metaphoric ideal for self-description by those identifying themselves as Hebrews/Israelites. The story moves directly to the next critical period in Moses' life—his forced exile from Egypt (2:11–25). In the context that is developed by narrators, exile takes on another nuance, for Moses is forced into exile away from his true "brothers," and not simply from what he had considered his native "land." This dual aspect of "exile" provides for a highly flexible metaphor that could be applied across many strata of society and numerous historical

29 Despite the numerous historical problems that may be associated with this simple equation, it should be noted that for the author(s) of the Exodus account, this identification is absolute.

30 While it is possible that the name "Moses" is to be derived historically from the Egyptian root *mśy*, "born," which is well documented in such theophoric names as Ramesses and Tuthmoses, the emphasis of the present story is upon the Hebrew folk etymology provided in 2:10 (S. Hermann, *A History of Israel in Old Testament Times* [Philadelphia: Fortress, 1975], p. 66). The ironic happenings are emphasized further when the daughter of the Egyptian king not only provides the new-born hero of the story with a name that foretells his destiny, but also explains that name in the language of the people her father had enslaved. The probability that the Egyptian royal household spoke the dialect of the Hebrew slaves seems quite small.

31 L. Eslinger has noted that this emphasis on divine control makes all the events in the narrative subordinate to Yahweh's power and goal, which are clearly stated in Exod 10:2 ("Freedom or Knowledge? Perspective and Purpose in the Exodus Narrative [Exodus 1–15]," *JSOT* 52 [1991] 43–60).

situations. The reason for his exile from Egypt is put in explicit kinship terms (2:11–14). When he witnessed an Egyptian beating "a Hebrew man from his kinspeople" (*ʾîš-ʿibrî mēʾeḥāw;* 2:11), he killed the Egyptian and hid his body. Interestingly, when he attempted to mediate a dispute between "two Hebrew men" (*šěnê-ʾănāšîm ʿibrîm;* 2:13), he met with rejection. This emphasis upon Moses' sympathy for his people in the face of their constant rejection of him will emerge as a part of the story of the deliverance of Israel and its developing relationship with its god.

As a result of his efforts to save his people from their Egyptian over-lord, Moses was forced to flee from the threat of Pharaoh's punishment (2:15). He journeyed to the land of Midian (*ʾereṣ-midyān;* 2:15), and there found a new home in the tents of his relatives, the Midianites.[32] The kinship relationship here is important for, when Moses marries Zipporah, the daughter of the "priest of Midian," he has not married outside acceptable genealogical patterns.[33] Even in exile, Moses could be a model for establishing proper communal relationships. Despite his kinship with the Midianites, Moses was nevertheless exiled from his "true" people, a fact brought to the forefront in the etiology provided for his son, Gershom (*gēršōm*): "I was a sojourner in a foreign land" (*gēr hāyîtî bě̄ʾereṣ nokrīyâ;* 2:22). The concept of exile is, from the very beginning of their story, an integral part of the identity of "Israel."[34]

The transition to the commission to Moses to return from his exile and to lead Israel out of its enslavement and "back" to its land is provided by

[32] According to the genealogy developed in Gen 25:1–6 (//1 Chr 1:32–35), Midian was one of the sons of Keturah, Abraham's second wife, who bore him six sons. The importance of this genealogical relationship should not be overlooked, since Moses will marry Zipporah, the daughter of Jethro, the priest of Midian. The problems associated with the differing names given to this priest of Midian have been long recognized. The medieval commentator Rashi, commenting on Exod 4:18, where the MT calls him Jether (*yeter*), noted that Moses' father-in-law had seven names. On the attempt to explain the variations in the name of the Midianite leader, based upon traditional source analysis, see W. F. Albright, "Jethro, Hobab, and Reuel," *CBQ* 25 (1963) 1–11.

[33] According to Num 12:1, Moses married a Cushite woman (*hāʾiššâ hakkušît*), i.e., an Ethiopian. It is possible that this, along with the differing names of his father-in-law, represents a variant tradition. R. de Vaux has noted that in Hab 3:7, Cushan (*kûšān*), a tribal name, parallels Midian and hence might represent the same group (*The Early History of Israel* [Philadelphia: Westminster, 1978], pp. 330–331).

[34] This etiology is representative of an idea that is repeated throughout the Pentateuch (cf. Exod 18:3; 22:20; 23:9; Lev 19:34; Deut 10:19; 23:8). Likewise, it represents an important reflex of the promise to Abram found in Gen 15:13–14. The phrase "remember that you were slaves in the land of Egypt" is also characteristic of Deuteronomy (for references, see M. Weinfeld, *Deuteronomy and the Deuteronomic School*, p. 327).

the reference to the death of the Egyptian king who had originally imposed the labor upon them (2:23). As the narrative shifts between the notices of death and birth, the perspective is changed from the human to the divine level. As had happened earlier (1:12–14), the Israelites groaned from their labor. This time, however, a new response is noted: "When God heard their groan, God remembered his covenant (*wayyizkōr 'ĕlōhîm 'et-bĕrîtô*) with Abraham, with Isaac, and with Jacob" (2:24; cf. 6:5). The recollection of the covenant (cf. Gen 17:7–8, 19) moves the activity of the divine into the forefront of the narrative and connects the events that will occur here with both the promises to the ancestors and the covenantal proceedings that would occur on Sinai. This transition supplies the background for the commissioning of Moses and his return to his people. Through Moses Yahweh would reveal his identity to Israel.[35]

Bearing the appropriate metaphorical role of the "shepherd," Moses "came to the mountain of God at Horeb" (*wayyābō' 'el-har hā'ĕlōhîm ḥōrēbāh;* 3:1b).[36] The theophanic mountain of Israel's patron deity now becomes the locus of all the actions that will occur until the people journey forth from Sinai in Num 10:11–12. It is here that Yahweh reveals himself to his messenger Moses, and here that he creates his chosen people by way of a covenant and its requirements for purity.[37] The hierophany in 3:2–22 establishes the direction of the following narrative, for in these verses Yahweh reveals himself to Moses as the god of his ancestors (*'ānōkî 'ĕlōhê 'ābîkā;* 3:6) whose presence renders the revelatory space sacred (*'admat-qōdeš hû';* 3:5).[38] Hence, by virtue of this appearance to Moses, Yahweh not only iden-

35 Reading 2:25b with the LXX: "and he made himself known to them [the Israelites]" (*wayyiwwāda' 'ălêhem*).

36 The designation Horeb for the mountain of revelation is generally assigned to the Elohistic and deuteronomic materials; the name Sinai belongs to the Yahwistic and Priestly materials. It is clear in the final forms of the traditions that the two are regarded as synonymous.

37 The various "Priestly" materials constituting the narrative composition stretching from Exodus 25 to Leviticus 27 regarding the regulation of the cultus are normally separated from the remainder of the narrative and are treated as though they are not an essential part of the development of the stories. As an example, it might be noted that J. Blenkinsopp, in his treatment of the formation of the Pentateuch, addresses these materials in some nine pages (*The Pentateuch,* pp. 217–225). As I will argue in the next chapter, these cultic regulations cannot be separated from the remainder of the story without distorting the concept of the special identity of this people that is a major purpose and function of the text.

38 Source critical analysis of 3:1–15 assigns the majority of the text to the Elohistic narrative (1, 4b, 6, 9–15). The remainder is commonly assigned to the Yahwist. Whether such clear distinctions can be made on the basis of the evidence remains debated. Many commentators maintain that despite the presence of sources, the present text represents a literary unity. For a

tifies himself as Moses' ancestral god, but also transforms this mountain into a sacred locale.[39]

The purpose for the hierophany is revealed in 3:6–22. Yahweh informs Moses that he has seen the oppression of his people and that he has come down to deliver them from Egypt and to direct them to the land they were destined to possess (3:7–8).[40] Clearly, Yahweh will control the events to follow. The human intermediator of these divine actions will be Moses. Yahweh will send him to Egypt, and he will lead out "my people, the Israelites" (*'ammî běnê-yiśrā'ēl;* 3:10). The identification of the people as "my people" is important, for one of the most significant aspects of the entire concept of Israelite ethnicity is the direct relationship between the people and their god. In reply to Moses' query concerning his qualifications for the task, Yahweh answers, "I will be with you" (*'ehyeh 'immāk;* v. 12). Throughout the entire account, Yahweh's presence and power will determine the shape and destiny of the actors in the drama, for Yahweh's actions and words establish the relationships that are deemed significant. The entire character of the escape from Egypt is shaped by the auxiliary command given in 3:12b: "When you have led the people out of Egypt, you shall worship God on this mountain" (*'al hāhār hazzeh*). The general itinerary and character of the relationship with the people to be delivered from Egypt are given further shape.

In response to Moses' query concerning his name, Yahweh reveals his identity.[41] This self-revelation, however, establishes much more than Yahweh's relationship with the patriarchs and with their descendants. In the following commission to Moses (3:18–22), Yahweh provides an outline of

---

discussion of the various positions, see B. S. Childs, *The Book of Exodus* (OTL; Philadelphia: Westminster, 1974), pp. 51–71.

[39] As such, Sinai/Horeb is established as one of the two major divine mountains in Hebrew tradition. Alongside Sinai/Horeb, Zion will be established as the abode of the deity and the source of his instructions (e.g., Isa 2:3). As J. Levenson has demonstrated, these two religious foci constitute complementing and sometimes competing centers in Hebrew tradition (*Sinai and Zion* [Minneapolis: Winston Press, 1985]).

[40] In their present form, these verses are decidedly deuteronomistic. As R. Boling has noted, the Hebrew bible has some 21 such stereotyped lists of nations in which the order and number of names fluctuate (*Joshua* [AB 6; New York: Doubleday, 1982], p. 165).

[41] The problems associated with the revelation of the divine name are generally recognized. It is clear that 3:13–17 has undergone a series of redactional changes and that 3:15–17 is either deuteronomistic in character, suggesting either a deuteronomistic revision of selected portions of the Tetrateuch or, more probably, a familiarity with the deuteronomistic materials by the redactors of this section. For a discussion of the problems associated with the revelation of the divine name, see B. S. Childs, *The Book of Exodus*, pp. 60–70.

the events that will follow. With the elders of Israel, Moses is to go to
Pharaoh and announce that "Yahweh, god of the Hebrews" (*yhwh ʾĕlōhê
hāʿibrīyîm*),[42] has appeared to them and requires Pharaoh to let the people
go into the wilderness to sacrifice to Yahweh, their god (3:18). The identification between "Hebrew" and "Israelite"[43] is firmly established. It would
be they who would be the "people" of Yahweh and whose identity would be
defined through their service to him.

In the following verses, Yahweh details what will occur (3:19–22). Because he is Yahweh, he is already aware that only after he has struck Egypt
with the power of his wonders will Egypt consent to his order and send out
his people (3:19–20). While on one hand this is a clear assertion of Yahweh's incomparable power over the human realm, on another it confirms a
critical aspect of Yahweh's relationship with Israel. Israel was brought out
of its bondage under the Egyptians solely by virtue of Yahweh's power to
recreate the existing social order.[44] The complete reversal of the present situation is emphasized through Yahweh's notice that not only would Israel go
out from Egypt, but the Egyptians would also look upon them with favor
and their Egyptian neighbors would give them great wealth, simply upon
request. In this way, Israel would "plunder" Egypt (3:21–22; cf. 12:35–36).

This entire section containing the revelation of Yahweh's name, the
commission of Moses, and the announcement of the divine plan demonstrates the foundational religious view that characterizes Israel's understanding of its god (3:5–22). For Israel, Yahweh alone is God and responds
to his people's cries. Yahweh remembers and upholds his covenant and acts
from his holy mount (Sinai/Horeb/Zion) to deliver his people and to settle
them in the land of promise, where he will always be with them. Each of
these factors constitutes an important element in Israel's identification of
itself as a distinct ethnic community created and maintained through its religion. In the accounts of the exodus, what is being presented is the nature

42 More commonly the phrase occurs as *yhwh ʾĕlōhê hāʿibrîm*. This designation of Yahweh occurs only in the context of addresses to the Pharaoh (cf. 3:18; 5:3; 7:16; 9:1, 13; 10:3) and
does not occur outside the book of Exodus.

43 For a discussion of the problems associated with the relationship of these terms, see
N. P. Lemche, "'Hebrew' as a National Name for Israel," *Studia Theologica* 33 (1979) 1–23.

44 The most obvious of all survival strategies that could be developed by a people in exile
and oppressed by foreign power would be a complete reversal of the power structure. In the case
of minority groups, however, such events are most unlikely to occur. Hence, expectations for
such may be projected into the divine realm. An exiled group looking to its "past" for hope
might find it in the memory of divine actions that could be understood in paradigmatic terms.

of Yahweh and his actions on behalf of his people. The narratives associated with Sinai/Horeb and beyond will develop another aspect of this identity—Israel's response to the actions of its god. The development of the nature of the relationship between Yahweh and Israel constitutes a unifying element in the stories of the Tetrateuch.

The character of Moses, commissioned in prophetic terms, now faces a significant, yet predictable problem. How is he to gain support for his mission? How is he to demonstrate the legitimacy of his message and his role as leader over the people?[45] Yahweh responds by providing him with three signs that were to be performed, if necessary, in order that the Israelites might believe that Yahweh had sent him (4:2–9). When Moses complains that he is not a "man of words" (*ʾîš děbārîm*; v. 10), Yahweh responds by promising to be with his mouth (v. 12). When Moses requests that Yahweh send someone else, Yahweh angrily rejoins by stating that Moses' brother Aaron, "a skilled speaker" (*dabbēr yědabbēr hûʾ;* v. 14), is already on his way to meet Moses. Just as Yahweh had promised to be with Moses' mouth, so too would he be with Aaron's (4:14–15).

This series of interchanges between Moses and Yahweh is significant, for it reveals how totally the events are under the control of God. Yahweh is able to anticipate and address every contingency in immediate terms. In describing the relationship that would exist between Moses and Aaron, Yahweh also provides a definition of the relationship that exists between himself and his prophets: "He will be your mouth and you will be his god" (*wěhāyâ hûʾ yihyeh-lěkā lěpeh wěʾattâ tihyeh-lô lēʾlōhîm;* 4:16). The underlying conception of the role of Moses is clearly related to the definition of the prophet that is found in Deut 18:18–22. What the prophet speaks is what Yahweh directs him or her to say. As Moses would instruct Aaron, so Yahweh would instruct Moses. The stage, then, is set for the performance of the deeds which have been announced. Yahweh would deliver his people from Egypt, using Moses and Aaron as his spokespeople. Moses had been commissioned and empowered. He had even received an entourage in the person of his own "prophetic spokesperson." All that remains to be re-counted is the description of the fulfillment of these proclamations.

The transition to this next section is provided by Moses' return to Egypt. Yahweh informs him that those who were seeking his life are dead

---

[45] The manner by which an intermediary might gain social recognition and acceptance varies greatly among cultures. For a presentation of some of the ways in which this might be achieved, see R. Wilson, *Prophecy and Society in Ancient Israel* (Philadelphia: Fortress, 1980), pp. 51–62.

(4:19; cf. 2:15) and reminds him of the events to come (v. 21; cf. 3:20). In doing so, Yahweh provides a nuance to the identity of Israel that supplies an important clue to understanding how Yahweh will demonstrate his power. In classical prophetic form, Moses is to announce the following to Pharaoh: "Thus says Yahweh: Israel is my son, my first-born" (*kōh 'āmar yhwh běnî běkōrî yiśrā'ēl;* v. 22).[46] Pharaoh's refusal (3:20; 4:21), however, would not occur without a complete knowledge of the consequences, for the prophetic conveyance of the divine message concludes with the announcement that if Pharaoh should refuse to send out the people, "then I shall kill your son, your first born" (*hinnēh 'ānōkî hōrēg 'et-binĕkā běkōrĕkā;* v. 23; cf. 12:29–30).

Both the immediacy of the threat and the guarantee of its fulfillment are suggested by the enigmatic account of Yahweh's attempt to kill Moses as he sets out on his journey for Egypt (4:24–26).[47] Despite the ambiguity of the pronominal references in the section, several points are clear. The central issue is circumcision. Until this ritual requirement is fulfilled (cf. Gen 17:10–14), Moses will not be allowed to complete his journey. The threat of the death of the first-born of Egypt (4:23) anticipates the actuality of Yahweh's act (12:29–30), which provides the impetus for the exodus and the etiology for the celebration of the Passover festival. As will be argued in the next section, the celebration of this ritual provides the means by which individuals could internalize this "past" and share in the common history of the people Israel. Before one could participate in that event, however, one must have been circumcised (Exod 12:43–51). This variety of themes is further connected by the role of the first-born and the concept of service to Yahweh. Associated with the Passover legislation and the narrative of the exodus is the presentation of the regulations for the dedication of the first-born to Yahweh (13:1–16). In symbolic terms, one might be tempted to understand Yahweh's attack on Moses as his attack against the "uncircumcised," i.e., those who could *never* belong to his people. Zipporah's actions remove this "obstacle" and enable Moses to complete the initial part of his mission, to return to Egypt. After Moses meets up with Aaron at "the moun-

---

46 For a discussion of the role of the prophet as a messenger, see C. Westermann, *Basic Forms of Prophetic Speech* (Louisville: Westminster/John Knox, 1991 [German original, 1960]), pp. 98–114, or J. F. Ross, "The Prophet as Yahweh's Messenger," in *Israel's Prophetic Heritage,* ed. B. Anderson and W. Harrelson (New York: Harper & Row, 1962), pp. 98–107.

47 The problems associated with this passage and the attempts at their resolution are too numerous to address here. For a good overview of this section, see J. I. Durham, *Exodus* (WBC 3; Waco, TX: Word, 1987), pp. 56–59, and the literature cited therein.

tain of God" (*běhar hā'ĕlōhîm;* 4:27), the narrative moves directly to Egypt, where Moses and Aaron do all that Yahweh had commanded and "the people believed" (*wayya'ămēn hā'ām;* v. 31). The questions of recognition and authority among the Israelites were answered for the moment. Moses and Aaron were now ready to lead the people out to serve Yahweh their god. Convincing Pharaoh, however, would be Yahweh's task.

III. The Exodus: Yahweh's Power Ritually Recounted

The narrative moves immediately to its development of the outline of upcoming events that was presented in 3:18–23. Moses and Aaron, standing in the presence of the Pharaoh,[48] announce in prophetic terms the divine command: "Thus says Yahweh, the God of Israel: Send out my people that they might hold a feast for me in the wilderness" (*kōh-'āmar yhwh 'ĕlōhê yiśrā'ēl šallaḥ 'et-'ammî wĕyahoggû lî bammidbār;* 5:1). Pharaoh's reply, which is completely predictable if the narrative was read as a whole, provides the key to understanding the magnitude of the divine acts which will follow. "Who is Yahweh that I should obey him? . . . I do not know Yahweh. . . ." (*mî yhwh 'ăšer 'ešma' lĕqōlô . . . lō' yādatî 'et-yhwh. . . . ;* 5:2). Pharaoh thus chose to disobey Yahweh and keep his people from serving him as he had commanded. In other words, because of his lack of knowledge of Yahweh, the Egyptian king felt free to ignore the announcement of Yahweh's chosen prophet. By virtue of his announcement, Pharaoh also provides an explanation for the series of plagues with which he will be afflicted; through these acts of Yahweh, Pharaoh will come to know Yahweh (7:17; 8:6, 18; 9:14, 29). It is this same proclamation that anticipates the fulfillment of the threat announced to Moses (and to the reader/hearer) in 4:22–23. Pharaoh's failure to send out the first-born of Yahweh could only result in the death of the first-born of all Egypt.

If one removes the action from the specific historical context in which it is presented and understands these narratives in the context of an exiled people looking for hope of some form of restoration and return to their land, then Egypt and the Pharaoh may be understood in metaphoric terms as any land and ruler that would try to enslave the people of Yahweh and

---

[48] As was the case with the Hebrew midwives, the idea of two Hebrew slaves, one of whom had been sought by the crown for a capital offense, having an audience with the Pharaoh stretches the imagination to the limits. In this narrative, it gives testimony to the significance that is to be accorded to the people of Yahweh and is evidence of his overwhelming power.

hinder them from their service to him. The might which Yahweh would exercise against Egypt would stand as assurance to his people that he would hear their cry and would uphold his covenantal promises to their ancestors to secure them in their promised land. From Israel's perspective, the failure to serve Yahweh as he had directed is contained in the response of Moses and Aaron to Pharaoh. If they, the Hebrews, were not allowed to offer sacrifices to "Yahweh, our god//the god of the Hebrews" (*'ĕlōhênû*// *'ĕlōhê hā'ibrîm*), then he might afflict them with pestilence or the sword (5:3). The irony of the request cannot be missed. Israel, who knows Yahweh, knows the potential consequences of disobedience; Pharaoh, who lacks such knowledge, will learn them.

This initial meeting of Moses and Aaron with Pharaoh presents the foreshadowing of another theme that will be developed in the story— Israel's failure to obey Moses and Yahweh. The pattern of increasing oppression of the Hebrews established in the initial portions of the story is here repeated (1:12, 20): Pharaoh responds to Yahweh's command by increasing the people's work load (5:6–9). Naturally, these events lead to the rejection of Moses and Aaron by Israel's own overseers (5:21). When Moses inquires of Yahweh concerning the increased "evil" to which the people are being subjected (5:22–23), he receives an answer that reiterates the predictions that have already been given. Since Pharaoh has refused to obey, "Now you will see what I am going to do to Pharaoh" (*'attâ tir'eh 'ăšer 'e'ĕšeh lĕpar'ōh;* 6:1). All of the oppression has served simply as a prelude to the upcoming demonstration of Yahweh's power.

This first audience of Moses and Aaron with Pharaoh, during which they fail to obtain the release of Israel, constitutes a transition to Yahweh's reaffirmation of his commitment to free his people from their oppression. This confirmation is conveyed through a second account of the call and commission of Moses and Aaron (6:2–7:7), a section which is universally attributed to the "Priestly" writer.[49] The distinction of sources here is important, for it calls into question the role and function of the stories being presented. If the standard observation is valid that the repetition of the call adds nothing to the story and is, therefore, redundant, then one might wonder why it has been placed here. Further, if 6:2–7:7 constitutes an independent call narrative that formed part of a separate "Priestly" version of the story, why was it not combined with the earlier "JE" account in 3:1–4:17, thus alleviating the repetition? After all, such composites are well attested in

---

49 M. Noth, *Exodus* (OTL; Philadelphia: Westminster, 1962), pp. 58–59.

the Pentateuch (cf. Gen 6:1–9:17; Exod 13:17–14:31). What must be addressed is the redactional decision to "repeat" the call and commission of Moses at length at this point. Two factors need to be reemphasized with respect to the Pentateuchal sources. In the first instance, the accounts were probably not simple imaginary creations. There were no doubt a number of different sources that provided a basis for the composition of the Pentateuchal materials. Additionally, given even an optimistic overview of the actual sources which we possess, and here I do not mean those that we may reconstruct, we must admit that we have very little empirically verifiable evidence for such sources. As A. Campbell and M. O'Brien note: "We know remarkably little about the conditions under which texts were produced, how they were distributed and who read them, or how and where they were preserved and made available."[50]

If, however, we appeal to the practice of Torah reading that was standardized in the synagogues of the early centuries of the common era, we might find a different avenue of approach to the problem. There, selected portions of the Pentateuch were read according to a regular scheme.[51] Such a practice may reflect more than simple practical concerns. It is possible that the Torah as a whole might have been compiled with some such cultic implications in mind.[52] If such a possibility is admitted, then one might view the "repetitions" in a different manner. The call of Moses in 6:1–7:7 repeats the call in 3:1–4:17, literarily speaking, only if they are read together. If they are read as liturgical pieces, i.e., if the Pentateuchal narratives are not conceived as a unified literary whole, then the repetition is of a completely different sort. The divisions of the narrative and the accompanying doublets and repetitions might be more didactic than literary, more functional than redactional.

Beginning with this possibility for reading the ongoing story of Israel's deliverance from Egypt, we may return to the "Priestly" account of the call of Moses. Whether due to a different source or tradition, the author(s) of the Exodus materials present this version of the account with a different emphasis than they had in the former. This account builds directly upon the announcement in 6:1 that Moses would see what Yahweh was going to do

---

[50] *Sources of the Pentateuch,* p. 204.

[51] See above, Chap. 2, n. 101. For a chart of the Sabbath readings, see L. Jacobs, "Torah, Reading of," *EncJud* 15:1249–1252.

[52] While there is clear evidence that portions of the Torah were read as part of the synagogue services during the first century CE (Josephus, *Ag. Ap.* 2 § 175; *Ant.* 16 § 43; Acts 13:15; etc.), it is doubtful that this included a systematic reading of the entire Pentateuch.

to Pharaoh and Egypt and stands as an introduction to the accounts of the plagues (7:8–13:16). Yahweh reveals his name to Moses (6:2), noting that he had been known to the patriarchs as "El Shadday" (*'ēl šadday;* 6:3).[53] Because he had heard Israel's groaning (*na'ăqâ;* 6:5; cf. 2:24) and because of his covenant with their ancestors to give them the land of Canaan (6:4), he would lead them out of Egypt and give them that land. Indeed, this would be the very act that would confirm the identity of this people Israel and form the basis for their relationship with Yahweh. "I will take you for my people (*lî lě'am*) and I will be your god (*lākem lē'lōhîm*). You will know (*wîda'tem*) that I am Yahweh your god (*'ĕlōhêkem*) who brought you out from under the burdens of Egypt" (6:7). This display of power that would lead to the gift of the land would be the means by which both Israel and Egypt (cf. 5:2) would become aware of Yahweh's identity and incomparability.

In covenantal terms, this action will become the "historical prologue" that establishes Yahweh's claim on his people Israel and on the world. Yahweh's act of deliverance will take the people to the land. There they will serve him in accordance with his directions. As a people, Israel is defined by this relationship, inextricably connected to both their deity and their land. As in the former account of the call, Moses protests that he is not an accomplished speaker and that Pharaoh will not listen to him.[54] To confirm the authority and identity of Moses, the passage presents a brief genealogy that, though it interrupts the flow of the story, provides a description of the priestly legitimacy of Yahweh's spokesperson.

This priestly emphasis is important for understanding the relationship in which Moses is to stand with both Pharaoh and Aaron. Whereas 4:16 described Moses' relationship to Aaron, 7:1 extends the comparison to include Pharaoh. "I will make you as god to Pharaoh (*nětattîkā 'ĕlōhîm lĕpar'ōh*) and Aaron, your brother, will be your prophet" (*nĕbî'ekā;* 7:1). Whatever

---

53 It is important from the standpoint of the final composition of the Pentateuchal materials to note that this epithet for Yahweh is associated most particularly with the Priestly source. Likewise, its use outside the Pentateuch suggests that this epithet for Yahweh may be exilic in origin. See, for example, J. Van Seters, "The Religion of the Patriarchs," *Bib* 61 (1980) 226–227. A contrasting argument for the antiquity of the epithet is presented by F. M. Cross, *Canaanite Myth and Hebrew Epic,* pp. 52–60.

54 Cf. 4:10–16. Here Moses says that he is "uncircumcised of lips" (*'ăral sĕpātāyim;* 6:12, 30), a metaphorical way of saying that his mouth will not perform in the manner that Yahweh intended. For this usage of "uncircumcised" in the Hebrew materials, see H. Eilberg-Schwartz, *The Savage in Judaism,* p. 149.

power the king of Egypt might have had, it would not extend over Moses or his prophetic spokesman, Aaron. Despite Moses' power *vis-à-vis* Pharaoh, Yahweh would, nonetheless, "harden the heart of Pharaoh" in order that Yahweh might increase his signs and wonders (7:3; cf. 3:19–22). In this way would Pharaoh and all his people come to know Yahweh (7:5; cf. 5:2). Metaphorically, not only the Egyptians, but also any oppressor of Israel would know Yahweh by the manner in which he would deliver his special people from bondage.

This restatement of Yahweh's purpose leads directly to the encounters with the Pharaoh which constitute the first nine of the ten plagues that are recounted (7:8–11:10). In the present form of the narrative, the plague accounts are highly repetitive, arranged in three sets of three,[55] emphasizing at each turn the absolute powerlessness of Pharaoh and the Egyptians before the might of Yahweh. It is clear that the traditions of Yahweh's scourging of Egypt were recounted in a variety of forms.[56] Here, however, their function is clear: they provide the introduction to the final plague, the death of the first-born, and the etiological basis for the commemoration of the Passover festival. In providing this background material, they reemphasize the importance of the physical demonstration of Yahweh's power. Israel and the world must come "to know" that it was Yahweh, and Yahweh alone, who was able to perform these deeds. By expanding the traditions concerning the "signs and wonders" that Yahweh had performed in Egypt (Deut 4:34; 6:22; 7:19; 26:8; 29:2; 34:11; Pss 78:43; 105:27; 135:9; Neh 9:10; etc.),[57] the author(s) provide the "evidence" that should lead to such knowledge. Repeatedly directed to Pharaoh is this explanation for the plague to come:

---

[55] For an analysis of the symmetrical structure of the plague accounts, see N. Sarna, *Exploring Exodus: The Heritage of Biblical Israel* (New York: Shocken, 1986), pp. 68–78.

[56] It is commonly recognized that Pss 78:43–57 and 105:28–36, each of which refers directly to traditions concerning the plagues in Egypt, contain different sequences from those contained in the exodus traditions. The exact relationship between these poetic accounts and the narrative version of Exodus is unclear. For a detailed investigation of the variants, see the chart presented by J. L. Mihelic and G. E. Wright, "Plagues in Exodus," *IDB* 3: 823. A description of the classical source divisions and the characteristics of each source is contained in B. S. Childs, *The Book of Exodus*, pp. 131–139.

[57] J. Van Seters argues that Deuteronomy reflects no knowledge of the plague traditions and that it was the Yahwist who first introduced the plague theme into the Exodus narrative sometime after the composition of Deuteronomy. Hence, the J writer was acquainted with the traditions of Deuteronomy and was supplementing, and, hence, modifying, those traditions for a new application ("The Plagues of Egypt: Ancient Tradition or Literary Invention?" *ZAW* 98 [1986] 35–36; *The Life of Moses*, pp. 77–112).

"In this you will know that I am Yahweh" (*bĕzōʾt tēdaʿ kî ʾănî yhwh;* 7:17; cf. 8:6, 18; 9:14, 29).[58] Connected to this demonstration of power is the recognition of the obligation to service that is to define Israel, for also repeated to Pharaoh is the command: "Send out my people that they may serve me" (*šallaḥ ʾet-ʿammî wĕyaʿabdūnî;* 7:16, 26; 8:16; 9:1, 13; 10:3; cf. 4:23; 5:1; 10:7). The special distinction to be made between Israel and Egypt emerges in the context of the fourth plague, that Yahweh would separate his people from the Egyptians so that they would not be affected by the various forms of pestilence (8:18; 9:4; 11:7).

The effect of the plagues is the destruction of Egypt (10:7) that finds its full expression in the announcement to Israel that its fortunes were about to be reversed and that it would despoil Egypt entirely (11:2–3; cf. 3:21–22; 12:35–36). Before this could occur, however, one additional plague was announced (11:4–8). As already announced to Moses (4:22–23), the culminating event would be the destruction of the first-born of Egypt. Predictably, Pharaoh refused to send the people out, and, just as predictably, he subjected his land to another demonstration of Yahweh's power. It is important to note in this context that the triadic arrangement of the plagues and their paratactic presentation suggest the possibility that they could be used in a variety of ways. Any particular triad might be used to introduce the final affliction, as could any combination. It need not be assumed that, in a cultic context, all nine were necessarily presented in preparation for the account of the final event leading up to the expulsion of Israel from Egypt.

The cultic nature of the "events" recounted becomes apparent in 12: 1–13:16, for this section presents not only the account of the plague itself (12:29–34) and the actual departure from Egypt (12:35–42), but also the cultic prescriptions for the ritual reactualization of those events, commemorated in the festival of Passover/Unleavened Bread and in the dedication of the first-born to Yahweh.[59] Israel's life in service to Yahweh begins as a preparation for the departure from Egypt. The celebration of this ritual and the participation in the sacred time which it creates signify a new begin-

---

58 J. Blenkinsopp notes that this theme is also central in the prophetic oracles of Ezekiel that are directed against Egypt (Ezek 29:9, 16, 21; 30:19, 26; 32:15) (*The Pentateuch,* p. 140).

59 That the feasts of Passover and *maṣṣôt* were originally separate festivals seems to be clear from the manner in which the biblical materials present them. Likewise, it is not at all apparent how the dedication of the first-born might have been originally related to these celebrations. It is clear, however, that for the author(s) of the traditions in Exodus, these two festivals were celebrated together and provided the background for understanding the command to dedicate the first-born to Yahweh. For a discussion of the various reconstructions of the history of these traditions, see B. S. Childs, *The Book of Exodus,* pp. 183–195.

ning, for this reenactment will occur in the first month of the year (12:1). The Passover celebration is described in 12:2–11 as a familial, household ritual in which every adult member of Israel was to participate. In contrast to this family-based description of the Passover celebration is the pilgrimage celebration described in Deut 16:1–8. In the latter instance, the sacrifice of the Passover offering is restricted to Jerusalem, i.e., "in the place which Yahweh will choose to make his name dwell" (*bammāqôm 'ăšer-yibḥar yhwh lĕšakkēn šĕmô šām*; 16:2; cf. 16:6), and explicitly denied in the outlying cities (16:5–6). For the deuteronomic tradition, the familial, individual celebration is represented as a communal, pilgrimage sacrifice to be offered only at the central shrine.[60] The foundational account of the origins of the festival, however, locates the observance of the ritual in the home. The complementary nature of these two positions will become important in the consolidation of the people in the "restoration" community.[61]

In the context of the exodus traditions, however, they bind the community together by defining those who would leave Egypt as those who had participated in the celebration of this "eternal ordinance" (*ḥuqqat 'ôlām*; 12:14, 17) commemorating not only Yahweh's destruction of the first-born of the Egyptians, but also his judgment against all the gods of Egypt (12:12). The communal nature of the performance of this ritual and its role in defining membership in the community is revealed in the injunction against whoever fails to follow the cultic prescriptions and who eats from something that contains leaven: "Anyone eating something leavened, that person will be cut off from the congregation of Israel, whether he is a sojourner or a native of the land (*kol-'ōkēl maḥmeṣet wĕnikrĕtâ hannepeš hahîw' mē'ădat yiśrā'ēl baggēr ubĕ'ezraḥ hā'āreṣ*; 12:19; cf. 12:15).[62] To be

[60] A full account of this supplementation of the deuteronomic ideal will be presented in Chap. 9, when we address the reasons for combining the deuteronomistic history and its foundational book, Deuteronomy, with the Tetrateuchal narrative.

[61] According to M. Haran, the tension created here is only an "optical illusion" that results from the attempts of the exodus traditions to provide an etiology for the celebration of the Passover, thus disassociating it from its original cultic, pilgrimage setting, and placing it in Egypt (*Temples and Temple-Service in Ancient Israel: An Inquiry into the Character of Cult Phenomena and the Historical Setting of the Priestly School* [Oxford: Clarendon, 1978], pp. 347–348).

[62] Though there are a number of differing interpretations of what, precisely, being "cut off" from the congregation might imply, it seems clear that some later Jewish communities, e.g., the sectarians who produced the Qumran documents, viewed the punishment as excommunication from the community (1QS 8.22–24). For a discussion of the variety of views and a presentation of the types of sins for which this punishment was invoked, see J. Milgrom, *Leviticus 1–16*, pp. 457–460.

understood in this same context is the description of those who may participate legitimately in eating the Passover/Unleavened Bread (12:43–51). It may be performed by "all the congregation of Israel" (12:47). No foreigner may take part. The servants of the Israelites may, but, like the sojourner, only if they have been circumcised (12:44, 48). No one who is uncircumcised (*'ārēl;* 12:48) may participate. One regulation (*tôrâ 'aḥat*) will be observed by all. Membership in the community of Israel, defined by participation in this ritual reactualization of the events of the final plague and the exodus from Egypt, is restricted to those who can show their inclusion in the covenant concluded with Abraham (Gen 17:9–14).

The transgenerational aspect of the ritual recreation of these events is further demonstrated by the instructions given by Moses concerning the blood of the sacrifices (12:21–24). These commands are to be regarded as "a precept to you and to your sons forever" (*lĕḥoq-lĕkā ûlĕbañêkā 'ad-'ôlām;* 12:24). When the people would enter the land that Yahweh was to give them, they were to celebrate this ritual in accordance with these rules.[63] The account of the plague itself is recounted in 12:29–34, immediately following the notice that Israel did as Yahweh had commanded (12:28). As the narrative is arranged, the proper performance of the ritual brought about the narrative actualization of the events commemorated by the rite. With the death of the first-born of Egypt, the display of Yahweh's power that had been announced in 4:22–23 was fulfilled. It was time for Pharaoh to send out Yahweh's first-born, which he does with the command: "Go and serve Yahweh as you said" (*lĕkû 'ibdû 'et-yhwh kĕdabberkem;* 12:31). The god that was so unknown to Pharaoh in 5:2, whom he thought he could ignore, had now made his power and identity plain to all Egypt. Nothing could make this more apparent than Pharaoh's request that Moses and Aaron place a blessing on him also (12:32)—a drastic departure from his position that threatened Moses with death if they should ever again meet (10:28).

After despoiling the Egyptians as foretold (12:35–36; cf. 3:21–22), Israel left Egypt, along with a "great mixed multitude" (*'ēreb rab;* v. 38),[64] thus ending a 430-year sojourn in Egypt (12:40), a lengthy exile from the

---

63 According to Josh 5:2–12, Israel celebrated the Passover immediately upon crossing over the Jordan into the land of Canaan in a ritual recreation of the exodus event. For an analysis of the manner in which the deuteronomistic historian has crafted this account to fulfill the commands of Deuteronomy, see my analysis in *Narrative History and Ethnic Boundaries*, pp. 107–119.

64 J. Levenson argues, based upon the usage in Neh 13:3 (cf. Ezra 9:2 and Lev 24:10), that the phrase *'ēreb rab* should be translated "'a large number of people of mixed blood'" (*The

land of their ancestors.[65] With Egypt completely humbled before the power and might of Yahweh and with Israel possessing the wealth of the Egyptians, the account moves to the explanation of the sanctification of the first-born to Yahweh (13:1–16). As with the celebration of the ritual of the Passover, Israel was to observe this upon its entry into the land of Canaan (13:3–4), for, as Israel is to explain to its children, it is a sign and memorial of what Yahweh had done in Egypt (vv. 8–10). In terms of cultic and community identity, the dedication of the first-born to Yahweh creates a society that understands itself as separated from others and sanctified (*qdš*) to the service of the deity through the act of redemption (*pādâ*). While emphasizing the incomparable power of Yahweh in remembering his covenant with the ancestors and humbling the power of Egypt, the narrative also anchors the cultic prescriptions of Passover, Unleavened Bread, and the dedication of the first-born to the common historical memory of the exodus from Egypt. Through the yearly performance of these rituals, Israel would continually recreate this past and ritually internalize this identification of itself with its god who created and sustained it.

Though it is common to understand the plagues against the Egyptians as culminating with the death of the first-born, there remains in the narrative one additional demonstration of Yahweh's power in delivering his people—the event at the sea (13:17–14:31). Here Yahweh demonstrates his power over Pharaoh and his entire army, destroying both in the final act in the drama that has been built in stages. The mystery of the power of the divine to stage such a defeat is conveyed by the conflated manner in which the story of deliverance at the sea is presented.[66] Essential to understanding the presentation of the events is the assurance that Yahweh was continually present with his people, leading them as a "pillar of cloud" (*'ammûd 'ānān*)

Hebrew Bible, the Old Testament, and Historical Criticism, p. 180). If this is accurate, then participation in the Passover celebration becomes even more important in defining and bounding the community.

65 The number 430 presents numerous problems, especially since it differs from the length of the Egyptian sojourn given in other places (cf. Gen 15:16, four generations; Gen 15:13, 400 years). Both the Sam and the LXX calculate the 430 years as the time in which the ancestors of Israel were in Canaan and Egypt. Likewise, the number of the young men (600,000) leaving Egypt (12:37; cf. Num 1:46; 26:51) is also problematic when one calculates what the total number of the people would have been.

66 It is commonly recognized that the present text is a composite of a Yahwistic, an Elohistic, and a Priestly account, followed, in 15:1–21, by an independent poem celebrating Yahweh's defeat of the Egyptians. For the source analysis, see B. S. Childs, *The Book of Exodus,* pp. 218–224.

by day and a "pillar of fire" (*'ammûd 'ēš*) by night (13:21–22). The victories won, just like the afflictions already directed against Egypt, would be the result of Yahweh's activities, not those of humans. This final act would demonstrate to both Israel (14:31) and Egypt (14:4, 18), once and for all, that it was Yahweh who had done these things. As a result, even Pharaoh and his people would give honor to Yahweh (14:4, 17, 18).

But neither Yahweh's presence and power nor his love and devotion for his people alleviate the "realities" of existence. The journey to the land promised to Israel would involve many hardships. The return from exile, despite Yahweh's direction, would not be simple. This is clearly stated in the notice that Yahweh changed the route of travel because he feared that the people might change their minds when they saw battle (13:17–18).[67] To test this fear, Yahweh sends them on a new route and hardens the heart of Pharaoh in order to cause a confrontation (cf. 4:21; 9:12; 10:20, 27; 11:10; 14:4, 8, 17; Josh 11:20). Predictably, Pharaoh decides to pursue Israel and selects the choicest of his chariotry for the attack. Also predictably, the people panic upon seeing the Egyptian army and note that it would have been better to remain in Egypt and serve them (14:10–13). Clearly, Israel has not yet come to understand that its identity is to be found in service to Yahweh and Yahweh alone. What was about to occur, however, would change this. Moses announces to the frightened Israelites: "Take your stand and see the deliverance of Yahweh that he will perform on your behalf today" (*hityaṣbû ûrĕ'û 'et-yĕšû'at yhwh 'ăšer-ya'ăśeh lākem hayyôm;* 14:13).

To prepare the people for the final chapter in the devastation of Egypt, Yahweh gives directions to Moses concerning Israel's crossing "through the midst of the sea on dry ground" (*bĕtôk hayyām bayyabbāšâ;* 14:16).[68] The presence of Yahweh, now presented as his "messenger" (14:19–20; cf. 23:21–22), separated the two camps, keeping the Egyptian army at bay. Implied by this separation is the central concept of the separateness of Israel, a distinction implied precisely by the presence and power of Yahweh and his

---

67 The narratives concerning the route by which the Israelites went up from Egypt, like the account of the event at the sea, seem to combine several different sources and suggest more than one route. For an attempt at reconstructing the itinerary, see R. de Vaux, *The Early History of Israel*, pp. 376–381.

68 The "dry ground" tradition of crossing through the sea represents what is generally considered to be the "latest" of the accounts concerning this event. The histories of the different prose and poetic traditions are discussed by F. M. Cross, *Canaanite Myth and Hebrew Epic*, pp. 133–137.

heavenly entourage.[69] As Egypt pursued Israel through the sea, Yahweh destroyed them (14:21–29). The warfare, like the victory, belonged to Yahweh alone. Despite all of the events that had preceded, the event at the sea would become the central focus of Israel's confessions of the history of its relationship with Yahweh, for "on that day, Yahweh delivered Israel from the power of Egypt" (*wayyôšaʿ yhwh bayyôm hahûʾ ʾet-yiśrāʾēl miyyad miṣrāyim;* 14:30). When Israel witnessed this, as Moses had directed (14:13), they responded in the appropriate manner: "The people feared Yahweh and believed in him and in Moses, his servant" (*wayyîrĕʾû hāʿām ʾet-yhwh wayyaʾămînû bĕyhwh ûbĕmōšeh ʿabdô;* 41:31). Yahweh had fulfilled his promises to deliver his people from the bondage of Israel. In response, Israel believed and stood in proper reverence of Yahweh, celebrating his victory in song and rejoicing.[70]

IV. Yahweh's Claims and Israel's Responses: The Formation of Ethnic Distinctiveness

The "Song of the Sea" (15:1–18) contains more than a simple poetic commemoration of Yahweh's great deed, for it connects that activity with Yahweh's guidance of his people "to your holy abode" (*ʾel-nĕwēh qodšekā;* 15:13), where they were planted "on the mount of your heritage" (*bĕhar naḥălātĕkā;* v. 17). The journey out of Egypt was only the first stage in the establishment of the relationship between Israel and Yahweh. The second stage would begin with the pilgrimage to his "holy mount," which had formed a part of the original commission to Moses (3:12). There Israel would receive the instructions for the way in which it was to serve Yahweh.

---

69 For my analysis of the various roles and functions of the "messenger of Yahweh" (*malʾak yhwh*) as a member of the divine council, see *The Assembly of the Gods,* pp. 209–226.

70 Exod 15:1–21; for a reconstruction of the "Song of the Sea" and its relationship with the other traditions commemorating the exodus, see F. M. Cross, *Canaanite Myth and Hebrew Epic,* pp. 121–144. G. J. Brooke notes that a fragment of this chapter from Qumran (4Q365) suggests that according to some traditions Miriam might have had her own "Song of the Sea" that differed from the present one. It has now been lost or replaced by the poem in 15:1–19 ("Power to the Powerless: A Long Lost Song of Miriam," *BARev* 20/3 [1994] 62–65). According to E. Tov, 4Q365, designated 4QReworked Pentateuch^c, provides at least seven additional lines of text immediately before the text of Exod 15:22–26. These lines constitute the largest preserved expansion in 4QRP (fragments 4Q364–367). It is possible that this represents an exegetical tradition that recreated the Song of Miriam based on the contents of the Song of Moses. For the text, see J. Vander Kam, E. Tov, *et al., Qumran Cave 4: VIII: Parabiblical Texts, Part I* (Oxford: Clarendon, 1994), pp. 269–271.

It would be in this service of the deity that Israel would receive its distinctive identity, which would make it an ethnic and religious entity separate from all others. But it would also be within this context that the developing covenantal relationship would be called into question, for while it is clear that Yahweh had chosen Israel, the beginnings of the murmurings in the wilderness make it unclear whether Israel would choose Yahweh.[71] This uncertainty is developed in the introductory accounts of the journey through the wilderness contained in 15:22–18:27 and continued in Num 10:29–36:13. While it is commonly recognized that the account of the covenantal formulation at Sinai and the attendant priestly instructions contained in Exod 19:1–Num 10:28 interrupt the account of the journey, in the present form of the narrative they preserve an integral part of the story of the development of Israel's identity through its service to Yahweh. This identity is based upon much more than simple blind obedience to a divinely offered covenant; it is based on the realization that all relationships shift and modify themselves, succeed and fail, and depend continually upon the reintegration of differences following crises. The relationship of Israel with its god, like human relationships, constitutes a form of social drama that is responsive, in part, to the conceptions of the deity and his nature.[72]

No time is lost in establishing the problematic nature of Israel's responsiveness to Yahweh and his designated leader, Moses. After only a three-day journey, the people began murmuring against Moses because of the bitterness of the water at Marah (15:22–24). Responding to this crisis, Yahweh instructed Moses in the sweetening of the waters (15:25a). Rather than record a response on the part of the people to this miraculous act, the author(s) instead note that Yahweh there established a "statute and ordinance (*ḥōq ûmišpāṭîm*) and there he tested him [Israel]" (*wĕšām nissāhû;* 15:25b). The test is quite simply stated: if the people obeyed Yahweh and if they acted in the proper way and if they heeded "his commandments" (*miṣwōtâw*) and observed "all of his ordinances" (*kol-ḥuqqâw*), then he

71 D. J. A. Clines, *The Theme of the Pentateuch*, p. 48. For a general discussion of the murmuring traditions, see G. W. Coats, *Rebellion in the Wilderness* (Nashville: Abingdon, 1968).

72 On narrative as a form of "social drama," see V. Turner, "Social Dramas and Stories about Them," in *On Narrative*, ed. W. J. T. Mitchell (Chicago: University of Chicago Press, 1981), pp. 142–163. Religious narratives often reflect the paradoxical nature of the divine/human relationship that manifests itself in the seemingly contradictory aspects of life. This "divine paradox" is an essential aspect of the narrative presentation of the deuteronomistic historian and his presentation of the implications of the covenantal relationship between Yahweh and Israel (see my *Narrative History and Ethnic Boundaries*, pp. 223–227, 231–235).

would not afflict them with the "sickness" (*hammaḥălâ*) which he had placed upon Egypt (v. 26). In anticipation of the covenantal relationship that provides Israel's defining characteristics, Yahweh provided the basis for a test. Failure to obey Yahweh's instructions would lead to the covenantal curses, in this instance, the same afflictions which he had placed upon Egypt.

Since the people's murmurings at Marah provided the background for their being tested, it seems only fitting that the next narrative event, the story of the manna and quail (16:1–36), would also be connected with the themes of murmuring (v. 2) and testing (v. 4). The testing would be to determine "whether he [Israel] will follow my instruction or not" (*hăyēlēk bĕtôrātî 'im-lō'*). Israel is now depicted as a cultic community, "the assembly of all Israel" (*kol-ʿădat bĕnê-yiśrāʾēl*; v. 1) and "all the congregation" (*kol-haqqāhāl*; v. 3). By providing them with food in the wilderness, Yahweh would again demonstrate his power as Israel's god. The cultic aspects of the account are emphasized by the introduction of special provisions for gathering, cooking, and storing the food for the Sabbath (vv. 5, 22–30). Apart from the theme of the murmuring against Moses and Aaron, the entire account of the manner in which Yahweh provided for his people may be understood as a test to determine whether the people would obey Yahweh's instructions concerning the Sabbath observance as outlined by Moses (vv. 22–26). In this the people failed, since some chose to search for food on the day that was set apart for Yahweh (v. 23), prompting Yahweh to ask: "How long will you refuse to listen to my commands and my instructions?" (*ʿad-ʾānâ mēʾantem lišmōr miṣwōtay wĕtôrōtāy;* 16:28).

The answer to this question will be given in a variety of forms throughout the remainder of the Pentateuchal story, which would cover some forty years. In a clearly anachronistic statement, the author(s) note that the people ate manna for forty years.[73] This reference clearly demonstrates a connection with the tradition reflected in Josh 5:12 that the manna ceased once the people had crossed into the land of Canaan and had performed the proper cultic actions. It also anticipates the judgment on Israel's rebelliousness which is recounted in Num 14:33–34 and is reflected in a variety of Israel's traditions (Num 32:13; Deut 1:3; 2:7; 8:2; 29:4; Josh 5:6; Am 2:10; 5:25;

---

[73] This is not the only anachronism in this section; 16:34 notes that as an act of commemoration and as a witness to future generations, Aaron placed a jar of manna "before the Testimony" (*lipnê hāʿēdūt*), i.e., before the Ark containing the Testimony of the covenant (cf. Exod 25:16; 31:18; 34:29; 40:20; etc.).

Neh 9:21; etc.). By implication, it also provides an answer to the question asked by Yahweh in 16:28. Israel would refuse to follow Yahweh's word for at least forty years. In response to this disobedience, Yahweh would not allow them to leave the desert and enter the land.

Clearly, Israel had yet to understand Yahweh's power and purpose for them and their proper response to his actions. This is underlined in the account of the murmuring against Moses at Rephidim (17:1–7). Again they complain against Moses, who interprets their actions as testing Yahweh (17:2), arguing that he had brought them into the wilderness to kill them (17:3), demonstrating again (cf. 14:11–12; 16:3) their failure to comprehend the creative and life-giving aspects of the exodus from Egypt. In response to the people's failure to perceive the power of Yahweh's presence in their midst, Yahweh provides them with water at the "rock at Horeb" (*haṣṣûr bĕḥōrēb;* v. 6). The people do not recognize that they have already reached the mountain that had constituted the immediate goal of their journey.[74] The failure of the people is underlined by the double etiology provided for the place where they had tested Yahweh, Massah, "testing," and Meribah, "place of strife." There they had asked the impertinent question: "Is Yahweh in our midst or not?" (*hăyēš yhwh bĕqirbēnû ʾim-ʾāyin;* 17:7b). The following account of the defeat of the Amalekites occurs at this same site (17:8–16). Amalek's defeat and Yahweh's pledge to destroy them completely (17:14–16) reinforce Yahweh's presence not only in the midst of his people, but also at his holy mountain.

While he is encamped at "the mount of God" (*har-hāʾĕlōhîm;* 18:5; cf. 3:1), Moses' father-in-law comes to him, bringing his wife, Zipporah, and his two sons, Gershom and Eliezar, both of whose names are directly related to the sojourn and exodus from Egypt (18:3–4). Here Jethro serves as a paradigm, demonstrating the proper response to Yahweh's actions. When Moses recounts the mighty acts of Yahweh, Jethro, the Midianite priest (18:1; 3:1), blesses Yahweh, confesses him to be "greater than all gods" (*gādôl yhwh mikkol-hāʾĕlōhîm*), and offers sacrifices to him (vv. 10–12).[75] The evidence of Yahweh's power and presence, understood by Jethro, who

---

74 While it is commonly maintained that the people do not reach Sinai until Exod 19:1, it is clear that the author(s) identify this action as occurring at that locale (cf. 3:1). The failure to perceive this is the result of reading the texts in a strictly linear fashion and ignoring the possibility that the materials constitute a collection of vignettes rather than a strict linear story-line.

75 Jethro's actions have led many scholars, who accept the basic historicity of these narratives, to find the origins of Yahwism in Midian. For a discussion of this possibility and a presentation of the evidence, see R. de Vaux, *The Early History of Israel,* pp. 330–338.

had not witnessed the demonstrations of such, should have been all the more apparent to those who had seen them.[76]

But Jethro's visit served another function, for, in his "reorganization" of the judicial system (18:13–27), he highlighted the role of Moses as the mediator between Yahweh and the people. The people would come to Moses "to inquire of God" (*lidrōš ʾĕlōhîm;* v. 15), anticipating the function played by Moses as the mediator at the oracle tent, the "Tent of Meeting" (*ʾōhel môʿēd;* 33:7–11).[77] As Yahweh's chosen mediator, Moses would make known the "ordinances of God and his instructions" (*ʾet-ḥuqqê hāʾĕlōhîm wĕʾet-tôrōtaw;* v. 16; cf. 18:20). This description of Moses' function, now that Israel had left Egypt, establishes his role in the events that will follow at Sinai. Likewise, the reorganization of a judicial system that would establish Moses as advisor (vv. 24–26), but which would delegate responsibility (vv. 22–23), would provide the people with a system of governance that had not been made explicit previously. It would provide a mechanism for the administration of the legal prescriptions given in the "book of the covenant" (20:22–23:33), a miscellaneous collection of legal materials that were understood as illustrative of the juridical procedures operative in Israel from its "origins." Despite such reorganization plans, Moses alone would "make known to them the way in which they should go and the things they should do" (*wĕhôdaʿtā lāhem ʾet-hadderek yēlĕkû bāh wĕʾet-hammaʿăśeh ʾăšer yaʿăśûn;* 18:20b).[78] With the people organized under the organizational principles suggested by Jethro and instituted by Moses, Israel was prepared for the next stage in its developing relationship with its god.

At the third new moon after leaving Egypt, Israel was encamped at the "wilderness of Sinai" (*midbar sînāy;* 19:1). Since they had already been at the "mount of God" (*har-hāʾĕlōhîm;* 18:5), i.e., Horeb (*haṣṣûr bĕḥōrēb*), since 17:6, the preparations for the theophany recounted in 19:1–25 present another episode concerning Israel's activities at the sacred mountain. Encamped now "before the mountain" (*neged hāhār;* 19:2), they underwent

---

[76] An interesting parallel might be found with the response of Rahab to the reports of Yahweh's actions in Josh 2:9–11. On the significance of this confession in the deuteronomistic narrative, see R. Polzin, *Moses and the Deuteronomist*, pp. 85–91.

[77] For the *ʾōhel môʿēd* as the place of encounter between Yahweh and Moses, see R. J. Clifford, "The Tent of El and the Israelite Tent of Meeting," *CBQ* 33 (1971) 221–227.

[78] The way in which this resembles the role of the prophet described in 1 Sam 9:6 should not be overlooked. Moses, as the paradigm of prophecy in Israel, is presumed by the deuteronomistic corpus (cf. Deut 18:18–22).

final preparations to meet their god and finalize the basic nature of their relationship. The key to this encounter is provided by the announcement of Yahweh in 19:4–6a. Moses is directed to announce a two-fold proclamation to the people. The first part was a simple declaration that they had witnessed what Yahweh had done to the Egyptians and how he had brought them to him with great demonstrations of his power and presence (19:4). The second provided the outline for the nature of the relationship that was about to be established and which had been alluded to in earlier passages (16:4, 28). Though there had been certain obligations placed upon the patriarchs, e.g., to follow Yahweh, to perform the ritual of circumcision, the promises of the land and progeny had a certain unconditional aspect to them. With the arrival at Sinai and the introduction of a new phase to the relationship, this was about to change.

Yahweh had acted on behalf of his chosen people to deliver them from Egypt. Now, he placed conditions on the continuation of the relationship. "Now, if you will surely obey me and keep my covenant (*'et-bĕrîtî*), then you will be my special possession (*wihyîtem lî sĕgullâ*) among all the peoples, for all the earth is mine, and you will be a kingdom of priests to me (*tihyû-lî mamleket kōhănîm*) and a holy nation" (*wĕgôy qādōš;* 19:5–6a). Three distinctive elements concerning "Israel's" self-identification emerge from this passage. Their way of life was to be regulated by the covenantal relationship established by Yahweh. A form of legal tradition would determine who they were, and this tradition, like all in the ancient Near East, would have its idealized origins in the divine realm. Second, they would become a very special national unity, for they would become Yahweh's "kingdom of priests," a designation that clearly implies that they had been selected to serve Yahweh, who was master of all the earth, in a way that set them apart from all other nations. They were to be priests. Third, as priests, their concerns would naturally be different from the concerns of other groups, for they would, by extension, be a "holy nation." They would be unique among all other religious and ethnic groups by virtue of their special position in the worship of Yahweh.

Yet it is this very position of privilege that provides the basis for the tension that naturally characterizes the relationship. Israel's privileged status would be dependent upon its obedience to its deity. In covenantal terms, when they were successful in following the divine will, they would be maintained. But, and this is an equally important aspect of such idealized relationships, what would happen when they failed? Would their god still protect them and remain in their midst? It is this matter that remains to be worked out in the narrative and to be answered in terms that are understandable, in some functional manner, for the development of an ethnically and religiously distinctive group.

The question of Israel's willingness to accept the responsibilities attendant to the formation of such a special position and relationship with the deity is resolved with the people's response to Moses' announcement of Yahweh's dictum: "All that Yahweh has said, we will do" (*kōl ᵓăšer-dibber yhwh naᶜăśeh;* 19:8). With this affirmation, Israel accepted the obligations associated with the covenantal relationship offered them by Yahweh which obligated the people to follow the directions given by their god. The narrative builds now to the formal ratification of this covenantal ideal that will accompany the theophany through which the specifics of the covenant will be given to Moses, the divinely selected mediator.[79] The ways in which the covenantal instructions and stipulations are presented and accepted provide a prelude to the explication of the specific boundary-formulating precepts that establish the exclusivity of the identity of Israel.

In anticipation of the theophany, the people sanctified themselves and prepared for the third day when Yahweh would descend upon "mount Sinai" (*har-sînāy;* vv. 10–11). From there he would speak with Moses from a thick cloud so that the people would be able to hear (v. 9). Such an hierophany would render the mountain itself sacred, so that anyone who touched it during this period of revelation was to be put to death (v. 12). Only Moses would be allowed to approach the presence of Yahweh on the holy mount on Yahweh's command (v. 20).[80] The description of the theophany is in-

---

[79] Since the pioneering work on covenant done by G. Mendenhall ("Covenant Forms in Israelite Tradition" *BA* 17 [1954] 50–76), the major parts of the ancient Near Eastern suzerainty-type treaties have been identified and are generally understood as providing the background for the covenant at Sinai. Research since Mendenhall's article has shown that there is little evidence to suggest that the Hebrew covenant form is borrowed from the classical Hittite suzerainty treaty of the late second millennium BCE. Instead, the Sinai covenant should be understood within the context of the general international treaty forms that dominated the ancient Near East throughout the biblical period. As D. J. McCarthy noted in his study of the various treaty forms, ". . . we find in the treaties a common basic structure with the overlord proclaiming a set of stipulations and the underling obliged to accept them under divine sanction. This surely reflects a ratification ceremony involving the announcement of the terms and the vassal's taking oath before the gods to observe them. This double moment is basic" (*Treaty and Covenant: A Study in Form in the Ancient Oriental Documents and in the Old Testament,* rev. ed. [AnBib 21a; Rome: Biblical Institute Press, 1978], p. 140).

[80] The reference in 19:22 to the priests (*kōhănîm*) also being required to sanctify themselves for the theophanic appearance of Yahweh is, like the judicial realignment described in 18:13–27, clearly anachronistic. In the present structure of the story, however, the presence of

terrupted with the announcement of the "Ten Commandments" (20:1–17//
Deut 5:6–21; cf. Exod 34:28; Deut 4:13; 10:4).[81] This announcement of
Yahweh's commands to Israel is a prelude to the formal ratification of the
covenant recounted in 24:1–18. In their present form, the commands constitute a part of the larger sets of instructions that are given to Israel and,
from a synchronic perspective, must not be separated from the rest of the
covenantal stipulations. At the same time, these commands do present an
interesting formulation of the basic instructions of the deity and provide an
outline and structure for the community at large. Interestingly, the narrative
presentation of the divine instructions in Deuteronomy also begins with the
presentation of the Decalogue.[82] The commandments, as presented, presume
the exodus events, for the suzerain offering the treaty, Yahweh, identifies
himself explicitly in those terms (20:2). In response to this "historical" prologue by which Yahweh claims the allegiance of his people, he makes clear
what the "ground rules" for the covenant are. He pledges to act faithfully
('ōśeh ḥesed) with those who "love" him and who observe his commandments (v. 6) and to punish those who "hate" him to the third/fourth generation (v. 5).[83] Likewise, he alone is to be worshipped by Israel in an image-

---

the priesthood might be required by the accounts of the sacrifices that would be given in 24:5–7.
Rashi, recognizing the problem caused by the reference to the priesthood, notes that *kōhănîm* in
this instance must refer to the first-born sons, since the line of Aaron had not yet been consecrated for the priesthood.

81 It is clear that it "interrupts" the narrative action to provide a divine announcement of
a portion of the stipulations that will come to constitute one element of the Torah. As I have
argued throughout, however, such narrative interruptions need not be understood as secondary redactional arrangements that have been placed in a pre-existing text. Though this is the
common historical critical approach, it is not necessarily the only possible one. It might be
better to understand this literary arrangement as a part of the original intention of the author(s)
of the text, who may have been interested in constructing a shorter, didactic piece, like the one
contained in 19:1–20:23, for a single reading that, in this instance, could be understood as representative of the whole. Interestingly, synagogue practice selects 18:1–20:23 for a single
sabbath reading.

82 If it is legitimate to understand Deuteronomy as providing a type of "social manifesto"
of Israelite ethnic and religious identity, as I have argued elsewhere (*Narrative History and
Ethnic Boundaries*, pp. 55–85), then this positioning of the Decalogue might be understood
as one of the many ways in which the Tetrateuchal author(s) attempted to parallel the contents and structures of Deuteronomy and to complement the narratives contained in it. On the
deuteronomic character of the language of the Decalogue, see J. Blenkinsopp, *The Pentateuch*,
pp. 207–209.

83 The covenantal implications of the verb "to love," and, obversely, "to hate," are well
known. See, for example, the observations of W. L. Moran, "The ANE Background of the Love
of God in Deuteronomy," *CBQ* 24 (1963) 77–87.

less type of cult (vv. 3–4) that is centered upon the remembrance of the Sabbath by way of refraining from any type of work on that day.

These stipulations provide the basis by which the community is to dedicate itself to Yahweh. In 20:12–17, certain restrictions are placed upon the group as a whole, describing in the most general of terms some of the ways in which relationships internal to the community are to be conducted. While the present form of the Decalogue may reflect a long history of development quite apart from the narrative materials associated with Sinai, it is critical to note that the Decalogue introduces the diverse materials associated with the theophany at the holy mountain.[84] The initial report of the theophany begun in 19:1–25 is concluded in 20:18–21, with the people requesting that Moses be their spokesperson (20:19) from the fear that any direct encounter with the deity would lead to their death. With respect for the sacred space created by the hierophany, the people stayed at a distance while Moses approached the cloud symbolizing the presence of Yahweh (20:21; cf. 19:9).

In a new address to Moses, Yahweh presented selected legal and cultic prescriptions that have come to be known as the "Book of the Covenant" (20:22–23:33). This loosely connected collection of "judgments" (*mišpāṭîm;* 21:1), which Moses was to present to the people, again interrupts the narrative flow. As a clearly independent collection which would seem to have its own redactional history apart from the narrative frame into which it has been placed, these "judgments" provide examples of the legal system that was to structure the society when it settled in the land.[85] Given the nature of the materials included in these rulings, it is clear that they presume an agricultural, settled society—one that would be *envisioned* from Sinai, but that did not yet exist. The importance of the inclusion of these materials, like so many of the instructions to follow, is found precisely in this act of envisioning the community and its life. In other words, it constitutes an idealized vision of Israel's future, the future it would have when it entered the covenant and the land. The collected laws themselves are all centered around the demand for the exclusive worship of Yahweh (20: 23–26; 23:13), the primary condition of the covenant which was based upon Yahweh's deliverance of his people.[86]

---

[84] On the distinctive nature of the Decalogue, see B. S. Childs, *The Book of Exodus,* pp. 393–397.

[85] For an outline of the contents and arrangement of these materials, see B. S. Childs, *The Book of Exodus,* p. 460.

[86] The list of festivals in 23:14–17 requires that, three times a year, all the males will appear before Yahweh at the festivals of *maṣṣôt, qāṣîr,* and *'āsîp.* A comparison of this list with

As additional evidence of the reliability of this vision for Israel, Yahweh promised to send his "messenger" before the people, both to watch over them and to bring them to the place that he had established (23:20). This announcement begins a type of epilogue (23:20–33) to the "Book of the Covenant" and reflects a highly deuteronomic style that suggests that the author(s) of this section were cognizant of the deuteronomistic traditions. Yahweh's protection and deliverance are directly dependent upon Israel's obedience to his commands (v. 22). The reward for such obedience would be the gift of the land (v. 23). Once all the cultic paraphernalia of the foreign gods there had been destroyed, there would be no sickness, miscarriage, or barrenness in the land (vv. 24–26). Obedience could recreate paradise, in a covenantal sense. Reflecting the mixed traditions of the taking of the land found in Joshua and Judges, 23:30–31 notes that the inhabitants would be driven out slowly so that Israel would eventually possess its idealized territory (23:31; cf. Gen 15:18; Deut 1:7; Josh 1:4; 1 Kgs 5:1; etc.). The original inhabitants would all be expelled so that they would not constitute a snare for Israel nor cause it to sin.

In response to the people's affirmation to do what Yahweh commands (19:8), Yahweh promises his presence, guidance, and deliverance, promises that would establish Israel in its ideal form. All that remains to be presented in the narrative account, then, is the manner by which Israel will formally accept its obligations and become a voluntary partner in this exclusive divine-human relationship. This is recounted in 24:1–11. Yahweh summons Moses, Aaron, Nadab, Abihu, and the seventy elders to come up to him and worship at a distance (24:1). In anticipation of the covenantal ceremony to follow, Moses announces to the people who did not go up the mountain "all the words and all the judgments" which Yahweh has spoken, and the people answer that they will do all that Yahweh has commanded (24:3; cf. 19:8). The opening and closing scenes frame the account of the theophany at Sinai with the confession of all Israel that it accepts the obligations of the covenant placed upon it by its god. After writing down all the words of Yahweh, Moses builds an altar and erects twelve pillars at the base of the mountain (v. 4). There sacrifices are offered to Yahweh and blood is sprinkled on the altar (vv. 5–6). Next, Moses reads the "Book of the Covenant" (*sēper habbĕrît*) to the people, who again affirm, "All which Yahweh has spoken, we will do and we will obey (*kōl ʾăšer-dibber yhwh naʿăśeh*

the festival lists in Exod 34:18–23, Deut 16:1–8, and Lev 23:1–44 illustrates the fluidity present in the festival traditions.

wĕnišmăʿ; v. 7; cf. 24:3; 19:8). With the sprinkling of the "blood of the covenant" (*dam-habbĕrît*) upon the people, the covenantal ceremony is complete
(v. 8). Israel is now covenantally bound, both by oath and by blood, to
Yahweh for its identity and its existence. A people have been created and
basic boundaries established. To be elaborated, however, remain the precise
processes by which Israel is to become the "kingdom of priests" and the
"holy nation" that is their idealized form. These details will constitute the
basis of the next chapter.

With this ceremony concluded, Moses and the assembly delegated in
v. 1 go up the mountain (v. 9).[87] There they see the god of Israel and they
eat and drink (vv. 10–11). It is notable that the covenantal affirmation ceremony in vv. 2–8 is followed, or perhaps commemorated, by a meal, just as
the event of the Passover had been (12:1–28). The account now is drawn to
a close by Yahweh's summons to Moses to come up the mountain to receive
"the stone tablets and the Torah and commandments which I have written to
instruct them [Israel]" (*lūḥōt hāʾeben wĕhattôrâ wĕhammiṣwâ ʾăšer kātabtî
lĕhôrōtām;* 24:12). In obedience, Moses ascends the "mountain of God"
(v. 13) and enters into the theophanic cloud to receive the Torah that will
consolidate the boundaries and identity of Israel. There he will remain for
forty days and forty nights, not descending the mountain until 31:18.

---

[87] As with so many portions of this narrative, 24:1–11 is commonly viewed as a composite text, containing either Yahwistic and Elohistic materials or, according to others, materials
from another source. Like this entire section, however, the narrative might be read in a non-
linear manner. The action is interrupted with divine addresses and human responses, and all of
the actions are thus incorporated under the larger umbrella of the theophany at Sinai.

7

THE CULTIC ENCAMPMENT AND THE PURITY OF THE PEOPLE: IDENTITY, SACRALITY, AND THE DIVINE PARADOX

I. Tabernacle and Cultus: The (Re)Construction of Sacred Space

Ethnicity is a cultural construct that is formed by establishing boundaries which consolidate the group as a distinctive entity and separate it from other surrounding and competing communities. When the process of ethnic formation is successful, the group becomes able to perpetuate itself biologically. But supporting the formation of such a discernible group is a set of shared cultural values and history by which the members identify themselves and are identified by others.[1] According to Israel's account of its past, the group that left Egypt, though identified as "Israel" and defined by its genealogical descent from Jacob, had yet to develop the boundaries that would distinguish it as a people. The events occurring at Sinai, however, provided the initial defining properties for this group, designated as Yahweh's "first-born" (Exod 4:22). This would be the first generation of "Israel" that would be defined by its dedication to the covenant and its stipulations that would provide the basis for the divine-human relationship that supplies the key to understanding the formative aspects of the narratives recounting these "events."[2]

---

[1] F. Barth, "Introduction," *Ethnic Groups and Boundaries*, pp. 10–14.

[2] One of the most significant points in the formation of boundaries and identity occurs with the transition of generations, i.e., when the initial community passes on the developing structures to the next generation. On the nature of this process by which traditions are legitimated and objectified, see P. Berger and T. Luckmann, *The Social Construction of Reality: A Treatise in the Sociology of Knowledge*, p. 93.

If the community of "Israel" were to become self-sustaining beyond the initial generation that entered into this covenantal relationship, then it must develop some method by which its "history" and its covenantal obligations might be continued. To become a "kingdom of priests" (*mamleket kōhănîm;* Exod 19:6) would require a cultus, for in the ancient world, religion, cultus, and identity were inseparable. The absolute centrality of the cultus and the symbol which provided its focal point, the Temple and its rituals, must be understood as inseparable from the concept of the Torah provided at Sinai. While it may be possible to distinguish particular literary threads and traditions that may be understood so that the story of Israel might be recounted *without* the inclusion of Sinai, it must be emphasized that that is a modern historical critical reconstruction and *not* the way in which the religious community of "Israel" defined itself in terms of the covenant and understood its destiny.[3] Despite the probability that the Pentateuchal materials, especially those associated with Sinai, have come from a variety of different sources and reflect differing histories of transmission and redaction, the only form in which they exist and in which they were actually used by an identifiable group is their present canonical shape. What can be argued with a high degree of confidence, additionally, is that this form of the Tetrateuchal and Pentateuchal materials was the result of the temple scribal guilds working during the Persian and Hellenistic periods. Whatever history might be reconstructed on the basis of the traditions contained in this document must begin by addressing the problems of origins and functions within the temple cultus. To reconstruct a history of Israel apart from this cultus is to recreate an Israel that is not identifiable with the one that the Pentateuchal author(s) attempted to describe or define.

In addition to these observations, it is critical to note precisely which temple cultus is to be made the focus of investigation. It is generally assumed that the Temple, along with its attendant cult, that was the focus of the Persian period community was a direct continuation of the Temple and cultus established under Solomon. That the cultus continued essentially unchanged until the Persian era seems historically improbable.[4] Instead, it

---

3 G. von Rad argued that the traditions associated with the exodus and settlement in Canaan and those connected to the events at Sinai were originally independent of each other. The Sinai traditions were, for von Rad, the later of the two and were a secondary insertion into the Tetrateuchal narrative ("The Form-Critical Problem of the Hexateuch," pp. 13–20). On the theological presuppositions that have supported this tendency, see J. D. Levenson, *The Hebrew Bible, the Old Testament, and Historical Criticism,* pp. 10–15.

4 Until recently, it has been assumed that the idea of "exile" and "restoration" that dominates the biblical materials associated with the exilic period refers to actual historical events.

must be recognized that the Temple that was reorganized under Persian royal hegemony provided the focal point for a particular economic and sociopolitical organization that provided a specific symbol of ethnic identity for those associated with it.[5] Likewise, the temple staff that would have returned from "exile" would have been separated from the temple personnel that went into "exile" by at least a generation, if not more. While that personnel might have claimed direct continuity with the earlier Jerusalem Temple, the lengthy break must be recognized. Whatever training they may have received could not have avoided Babylonian and/or Persian influence. Likewise, whatever power they might have had was that which was granted by their Achaemenid suzerains.

Just as critical as the recognition of intense foreign influence, in religious, political, and social terms, is the dramatic shift in the nature of the Temple that was reconstructed and reorganized under Persian hegemony. What was once a dynastic shrine that stood as a symbol of national independence and identity was now a provincial shrine, restored by a foreign government upon which it was completely dependent for its existence. Whatever ethnic identity might have been associated with the national state of Judah was now transformed into a new ethnic and religious community.[6] The religious claims that this "Israel," "restored" from "exile" to its "former" position now bearing legitimate and absolute claim to the land "promised" by its sovereign deity, found their locus not in the variety of popular claims and traditions that might have existed at that time, but rather in the center and symbol of the Temple in Jerusalem. The old Judahite dynastic shrine that was destroyed by the Babylonians was restored as the unifying and defining characteristic of the people "Israel."

The point of the creation of this group, along with its identifying ethnic boundaries, is located in the ritual recreations of the "events" recounted in the "shared histories" produced by this "restoration" temple guild. What can hardly be overemphasized is that the claims made within the literature that constitutes the Pentateuch are *religious* claims about a particular version of

---

With the recognition that the very concepts themselves are highly ideologically charged, it can no longer simply be assumed that those who "returned" to "restore" the cultus in Jerusalem were direct descendants of those who had been taken into "exile." For a fuller statement of this position, see P. R. Davies, *In Search of 'Ancient Israel'*, pp. 75–84, and T. L. Thompson, *Early History of the Israelite People*, pp. 415–423.

5 For a discussion of the role and function of the Temple during the Achaemenid period, see J. Blenkinsopp, "Temple and Society in Achaemenid Judah," pp. 22–53.

6 On the interplay between ethnicity and national identity, see A. D. Smith, *The Ethnic Origins of Nations*, pp. 129–152.

a reconstructed past. Though modern historical critical investigations have recognized that there is a religious aspect to these materials, the major focus of study has been on their historicity, or, with the emphasis of literary critical studies, on their literary nature. In all of this, something of the primary functions and purposes of the literature has been lost. That the literature of the Hebrew bible should evoke a response that understands it as historically real occasions no surprise. One might argue that this is one of the things that religious literature attempts to do. In broader terms, a definition of religion like that offered by C. Geertz might be helpful to this discussion. Geertz defines religion as:

> *(1) a system of symbols which acts to (2) establish powerful, pervasive, and long-lasting moods and motivations in men by (3) formulating conceptions of a general order of existence and (4) clothing these conceptions with such an aura of factuality that (5) the moods and motivations seem uniquely realistic.*[7]

What is produced by the Pentateuchal literature is a particular symbol system that defines "Israel," in very specific terms, as a special ethnic and religious group. While the materials contained in that literature may reflect traditional Israelite and Judahite stories, in their present form they have been cast to reconstruct a particular past that creates a type of "dynamic stability" for reformulating the central identifying metaphor, i.e., "Israel." Through the location of this identity in the ancient past, a history of continuity can be created even where it may not have existed previously. For the Jerusalem community established under Achaemenid rule, the Temple and its ritual cultus both created and sustained the identity of "Israel" through both the literature it produced and propagated and the rituals, both public and private, that it repeated to transmit that created past to new generations.

With this understanding of the centrality of the cult and Temple for the promulgation of the Pentateuchal materials and the identity of the people, we might return to the materials of Exodus and Leviticus. With the covenantal relationship between Yahweh and Israel confirmed by public acclamation, sacrifice, and ceremonial meal, Israel identified itself through its obligations to the service of Yahweh.[8] But such service, by which Israel would be defined, would extend beyond Mt. Sinai. Hence, it was necessary for Yahweh to make provision for his continued presence in the midst of the

---

7 "Religion as a Cultural System," p. 90 [italics in the original].
8 Cf. Exod 3:12; 4:23; 5:17; 7:16, 26; 8:16; 9:1, 13; 10:3, 7, 8, 11, 24; etc.

people. The issue of the requirements of this divine presence is the major ideal embodied in the elaborate instructions given to Moses for the construction of the cultic paraphernalia in 25:1–31:17 and fulfilled in 35:1–39:31.[9] The central focus of the cultic implements that are to be constructed is the Tabernacle, which will serve as the locus of Yahweh's presence among the people once they depart from Sinai (40:34–35). The climax of these efforts is presented in Exod 40:1–38 with the erection of the Tabernacle and all the accompanying cultic materials according to Yahweh's command.[10]

The fact that the command to perform these acts, all given to Moses while he was on Mt. Sinai, is not immediately followed by the notice of their fulfillment is essential to understanding why 25:1–40:38 is to be treated as a whole. The materials separating 25:1–31:17 from 35:1–40:38 clearly represent traditions that have no direct, apparent connection to the materials dealing with the construction of the Tabernacle, etc. Their presence in the middle of this otherwise straightforward presentation of the divine instructions to Moses and the obedient fulfillment of those commands, however, indicates the skillful ability of the author(s) of these stories to create a new story by combining originally distinct, unrelated stories. The dutiful obedience of Israel to Moses' commands takes on a renewed importance because of the account of the golden calf (32:1–35). This story immediately follows the conclusion of the instructions to Moses concerning the proper form of service to Yahweh and threatens Yahweh's presence among the people (33:1–23). The narrative drama that is played out redresses the crisis created and leads to a reintegration of the people by way of a renewal of the covenant (34:1–35). When the passage is understood in this way, a clear pattern emerges: command—disobedience—crisis/redress—renewal. This pattern, as will be argued below, constructs the basis for the ongoing relationship between the divine and human realms.

---

9 These two sections are universally ascribed to the Priestly source, though it is often noted that the section recording the fulfillment of the commands reflects a different and somewhat more logical arrangement. While 35:1–39:31 represents a nearly verbatim repetition of 25:1–31:17, the repetition is essential to the presentation, as I shall argue below. On the various ways in which these two sections have been analyzed, see B. S. Childs, *The Book of Exodus*, pp. 529–532.

10 The traditions concerning the Tabernacle (*miškān*) and the Tent of Meeting (*ʾōhel mōʿēd*) represent a possible conflation of traditions. It is often noted that the Tent of Meeting does not seem to have been associated with the Ark of the Covenant, but has secondarily been identified with the Priestly Tabernacle, thus uniting two originally different types of portable shrines. For a discussion of these materials, see R. de Vaux, *Ancient Israel: Vol 2: Religious Institutions* (New York: McGraw-Hill, 1965), pp. 294–297.

While he was on the mountain for forty days and forty nights (24:18), Moses was shown the "pattern" for the Tabernacle and all the implements that were to accompany it in the service (25:9, 40; 26:30; 27:8). The earthly Tabernacle, which would be the place of the presence of Yahweh with his people, would be, in mythic terms, of heavenly design. All of this is presented as a divine speech to Moses, and the directions presume the ability of the wilderness group to obtain all the materials and to manufacture all the necessary implements.[11] With respect to this lengthy series of commands, Israel will prove to be completely faithful to Yahweh's orders (39:42). It is precisely this issue that makes the account of the order for, and construction of, the Tabernacle and cultic implements the perfect vehicle for the account of the manufacture and worship of the golden calf.

Two major points emerge from the command to construct the Tabernacle and Israel's completion of the command: by its obedience to Yahweh's commands, Israel is able to provide a place for the presence of Yahweh among his people. This constitutes one side of the "divine paradox" that is developed as the central focus of the story, for, by way of a simple ideal of absolute justice and response, a "guarantee" for this religious relationship is constructed.[12] It seems entirely appropriate for the author(s) describing the nature of the relationship between Israel and Yahweh to divide the account of the making of the Tabernacle and Israel's act of obedience with the account of its apostasy and the near dissolution of the covenant. This act would provide the basis for the development of the other side of the relationship—the absolute necessity of Yahweh's love and mercy. It is critical also to note that the account of the golden calf and its aftermath is framed by the notice concerning the observance of the Sabbath (31:12–17; 35:1–3). As 31:13 notes, the Sabbath was a sign (*'ôt*) between Yahweh and Israel throughout their generations that was to remind them that it was Yahweh who sanctified them. Quite clearly, the one thing that distinguished

---

11 While it remains debated whether there actually existed some tent-shrine that was a focal point of the cultus during the "wilderness period" or whether the account is a projection of some ideal form of temple pattern back to that "period," one thing is clear. The accounts concerning the construction of the Tabernacle and its implements constitute an ideal vision of a heavenly pattern for an earthly creation. In critical terms, it must be emphasized that the purpose of the account is religious and not historical. For an attempt at a reconstruction of the Tabernacle, see R. Friedman, "Tabernacle," *ABD* VI, 295–299.

12 For the arguments that at the level of deep structure, religious and moral reasoning frequently creates an unresolvable tension between the belief in the reality of moral retribution and the necessity for the suspension of that belief, see R. M. Green, *Religion and Moral Reason: A New Method for Comparative Study* (New York: Oxford University Press, 1988), pp. 3–23.

Israel from all other nations was this relationship with Yahweh, a relationship that was initiated and sustained by him. Israel's role was one of service to the deity as prescribed by his commands. These were conveyed at Sinai through the covenantal mediator, Moses, who, after forty days and nights on the mountain, was given "the two tablets of the testimony, stone tablets written by the finger of God" (*šĕnê lūḥōt hāʿēdūt lūḥōt ʾeben kĕtūbîm bĕʾeṣbaʿ ʾĕlōhîm;* 31:18).

Yet, as Yahweh provided details of the relationship to Moses in a form that could be preserved and followed by the people, the people ruptured the alliance at its most basic level. They failed to follow the most foundational directives of the covenantal agreement by having Aaron make a god or gods (*ʾĕlōhîm;* 32:1, 4) for them, since they did not know what had happened to Moses.[13] Interestingly, Aaron responds by fashioning an image of a calf for them, an *ʿēgel massēkâ,* about which he proclaims: "This is your god, O Israel, who brought you up from the land of Egypt" (*ʾelleh ʾĕlōhêkā yiśrāʾēl ʾăšer heʿĕlûkā mēʾereṣ miṣrāyim;* 32:4).[14] He also calls a "feast for Yahweh" (*ḥag lĕyhwh;* v. 5), an act that suggests that from his perspective

---

[13] The story of the golden calf in Exodus 32 is commonly understood as a polemic against the cultic iconography in Israel that was established by Jeroboam I after the division of the monarchy (cf. 1 Kgs 12:26–33). Such a view is exemplified by F. M. Cross, *Canaanite Myth and Hebrew Epic,* pp. 198–199. On the numerous points of contact between these two narratives, see M. Aberbach and L. Smolar, "Aaron, Jeroboam, and the Golden Calves," *JBL* 86 (1967) 129–140. W. I. Toews argues, however, that Exodus 32 does not contain a polemic against Jeroboam, but rather one against the iconographic practices of the Israelite state, of which the account of Jeroboam represents but one particular case (*Monarchy and Religious Institution in Israel under Jeroboam I* [SBLMS 47; Atlanta: Scholars Press, 1993], pp. 124–125).

[14] It is grammatically proper to read the subject of this verse as plural, i.e., "these are your gods," as is commonly done. The narrative portion of the story itself, which always refers here to a single image (*ʿēgel massēkâ*), however, suggests that it should be rendered by the singular. As B. S. Childs points out, the issue is exegetical, not grammatical, and depends upon the relationship of this story to that in 1 Kings (*The Book of Exodus,* p. 556). The origins of this narrative remain debated. It seems clear that the particular language and style of Exodus 32, which is shared with Deut 9:8–29 and 1 Kgs 12:26–33, mark this narrative as distinctly deuteronomistic. Whether it is the work of the deuteronomic school, or of a writer or writers who were acquainted with the deuteronomic and deuteronomistic materials, is difficult, if not impossible, to ascertain. Assertions like those of W. I. Toews, that the parallel passages in Deut 9:12–14 and 25–29 are literarily dependent upon Exod 32:7–14, need to be demonstrated (*Monarchy and Religious Institution in Israel under Jeroboam I,* p. 126). An equally convincing case might be made for exactly the reverse dependency. J. Blenkinsopp, for example, suggests that the entire "calf" complex, Exodus 32–34, might be best understood as a deuteronomic composition (*The Pentateuch,* pp. 192–194). A third alternative is suggested by J. Van Seters, who argues that the calf episode reflects the Yahwist's expansions on the older deuteronomistic story (*The Life of Moses,* pp. 290–318).

in the story, at least, there was no problem with such an association. For the writer(s) of this section, however, it is clear that this action represents total apostasy, for it violates the injunction against images (20:4–5) and identifies this "molten calf image" as the god who had led them up from Egypt, the action that had consistently provided the basis for the covenantal relationship.[15]

From the standpoint of the concept of absolute justice, Yahweh's response to the actions of the people is both predictable and appropriate. From the divine perspective, the manufacture, worship, festival, and sacrifices dedicated to the "molten calf image," as well as its identification with Yahweh's saving actions, constituted irrefutable evidence that Israel had "quickly turned from the way" (*sārû mahēr min-hadderek;* 32:8). Because this "stiff-necked" people had rejected him, he would consume them and transfer the promises that had been given to the patriarchs over to Moses, for Yahweh proclaims to him, "I will make of you a great nation" (*wĕ³eʿĕśeh ³ôtĕkā lĕgôy gādōl;* v. 10). If Yahweh were to fulfill this threat, Israel's story would come to an end. Moses' response, however, provides another side of the prophetic/priestly office which he represents: he immediately intercedes with Yahweh on Israel's behalf.[16] Moses asks Yahweh to repent of the evil he has planned, imploring him to remember Abraham, Isaac, and Israel, his "servant" (vv. 12–13). Yahweh responds by repenting (v. 14). The merciful aspect of the divine has overridden the absolute justice side of Yahweh's character. Israel, it appears, would be spared and the promises to the patriarchs maintained.

15 Cf. Exod 3:17; 6:6, 7; 7:5; 12:51; 13:3, 9, 14, 16; 16:6; 18:1; 20:2; etc. As might be expected, there is little agreement over the origins of Israel's aniconic tradition. R. Hendel offers a review of some of the major positions and then argues that the tradition had its origins in both a rejection of Canaanite symbolism and Israel's antimonarchic biases ("The Social Origins of the Aniconic Tradition in Early Israel," *CBQ* 50 [1988] 365–82). For an attempt to provide a comparative study of aniconism in the ancient Near East, see T. N. D. Mettinger, *No Graven Image? Israelite Aniconism and Its Ancient Near Eastern Context* (ConBOT 42; Stockholm: Almqvist & Wiksell, 1995). Such arguments, however, begin by accepting both the reality of the prohibited practice and its antiquity. I suggest that a more adequate approach to understanding the origins of this practice would be to look to a period when Israel, or Judah, was actually engaged in a form of imageless worship, such as during the exile, and to investigate the ways in which the material change of culture might have affected the supporting mythological superstructure. The exposure of the "exiles" to the religion of Achaemenid Persia might also be considered a contributing factor in the development of this tradition.

16 The priestly role will not be turned over to Aaron until the final consecration and dedication of the priesthood in Lev 8:1–36. Prior to that narrative event, Moses fulfills the role of priest.

But Israel would not be reinstated without being punished, for to enter the covenantal relationship with Yahweh involved responsibilities that would be enforced. Moses now left the divine presence and, carrying the "two tablets of the testimony" (*šĕnê lūḥōt hāʿēdût;* 32:15; cf. 31:18; 32:16), descended from the mountain. These tablets constituted the visible symbol of both the divine instructions and the covenantal agreement. When Moses viewed the "molten calf image," the visible evidence of Israel's "turning from the way," he smashed the tablets, symbolizing the breaking of the covenant and the condemnation of Israel for its apostasy. The way for the restoration of the people was prepared by the ritual destruction of the calf image.[17] When Moses confronted Aaron, accusing him of causing the people to sin, Aaron replied quite innocently that it was the people who were "intent on evil" (*bĕrāʿ hûʾ;* v. 22).[18]

It is clear, then, that Israel has acted against the commands of Yahweh and must accept responsibility for that action. The manner in which the punishment is instituted presents an interesting scenario. Moses summons all those "who belong to Yahweh" (*mî lĕyhwh*) to come to him, and "all the Levites" (*kol-bĕnê lēvî*) respond (32:26). They then pass through the camp, killing some 3,000 people, brothers, friends, and neighbors, as instructed by Moses (vv. 27–28). This punishment of Israel at the hands of the Levites, those who rallied to Moses' commands, served as a type of ordination, a "rite of passage" of sorts, to the priesthood. To complete the process of restoration, Moses reascends the mountain to atone for the people's sin before Yahweh (vv. 30–31) and requests that if Yahweh is not willing to forgive Israel's sin, then "blot me out of your book you have written" (*mĕḥēnî*

---

[17] On the significance of this ritual, see S. E. Loewenstamm, "The Making and Destruction of the Golden Calf," *Bib* 48 (1967) 481–490, and L. G. Perdue, "The Making and Destruction of the Golden Calf—a Rejoinder," *Bib* 56 (1975) 237–46.

[18] Aaron's role in this entire episode is difficult to interpret, given that he will ultimately be ordained as Yahweh's priest, and his sons will continue that position. F. M. Cross suggests that there is an anti-Aaronic polemic involved here, originating quite possibly from competing Mushite circles. In an earlier form of the narrative, Aaron's role would have been more extensive (*Canaanite Myth and Hebrew Epic*, pp. 198–199). While it is clear that Aaron is depicted in a negative light here, what is not clear are the motivations of the final redactor(s)/author(s) for including him in the text. It is worth noting that these events occur prior to his ordination as priest and do not disqualify him from being Yahweh's priest. Rather than to explain Aaron's statement about the calf image simply emerging from the fire (32:24) as some type of effort to excuse his actions, it might be better to understand the statement within the context of the ancient Near Eastern ritual associated with cultic images whereby the human involvement in the production of the statues is ritually denied. For the Mesopotamian ritual of disassociation, see T. Jacobsen, "The Graven Image," in *Ancient Israelite Religion*, pp. 15–32.

nā' missiprĕkā 'ăšer kātābtā; v. 32). But Moses, as intermediator, is not responsible for the sins of the people, especially since he has fulfilled Yahweh's commands. Yahweh refuses to forgive the people as a whole, and likewise refuses to blot Moses from his "book."[19] Instead, those who sinned against him would be removed from this people. Moses had prepared the people for punishment; now Yahweh would complete the deed. Exod 32:35 notes simply that Yahweh sent a plague on the people because of what they had done with respect to the calf.

Yet even with the punishment of those who had sinned, the issue of restoration remains. Directly related to this is the matter of Yahweh's presence with his people. As the preceding narrative has illustrated, the divine-human relationship allows for the possibility of the divine either annulling the relationship or allowing it to continue. In this case, Yahweh chose to punish the evildoers and to allow his people and his promises to them to continue. Yet, because this people had proven themselves to be such a "stiff-necked people" (*'am-qĕšēh-'ōrep;* 33:3; cf. 32:9), Yahweh would not maintain his presence in their midst, lest he consume them (33:3, 5). Instead, he would send a "messenger" (*mal'āk;* v. 2; cf. 23:20) to lead them to the land of promise. This failure at Sinai had direct consequences for the relationship between Yahweh and the people. As soon as the people heard Yahweh's decision, however, they went into mourning and did not put on their "ornaments" (v. 4). Despite the obscure nature of this reference, as well as the redundancy of the divine command to remove their "ornaments" (v. 5), it is clear that the people recognized the implications of their failures and the seriousness of their situation.

The resolution to the problem is found in the placement and function of the Tabernacle/Tent of Meeting (33:7–11). It is widely recognized that the description of the Tent of Meeting in 33:7–11 interrupts the story of Yahweh's decision and Moses' intercession and probably represents a different tradition concerning an ancient tent shrine. Whatever origins might be reconstructed for this particular piece, in its present form it should be understood as a part of the divine decision concerning Yahweh's response to the people (33:5). Moses erects the *'ōhel mô'ēd* "at a distance outside of the camp" (*miḥûṣ lammaḥăneh harḥēq min-hammaḥăneh*) so that "all those who sought Yahweh" (*kol-mĕbaqqēš yhwh;* 33:7) could come to the Tent. Yahweh had decided not to withdraw completely from his people. Instead, a pillar of cloud (vv. 9–10; cf. 13:21; 14:19, 24; 16:10; 19:9; etc.) descend-

---

19 Cf. Ps 69:29; Isa 4:3; Ezek 13:9; Dan 12:1; etc.

ing upon the Tent would attest to Yahweh's personal presence, if only to communicate directly with Moses, his selected servant (v. 11).[20]

To attempt to assure the continuation of the presence of Yahweh, Moses asks that Yahweh make known to him his ways (33:13). The importance of Yahweh's presence is emphasized in Moses' intercession, for he requests that Yahweh not lead them up from this place unless his presence goes with them (v. 15). As Moses points out, it is Yahweh's presence that distinguishes Israel "from all the people who are on the face of the earth" (*mikkol-hā'ām 'ăšer 'al-pĕnê hā'ădāmâ;* v. 16). Without Yahweh, quite simply, Israel would lose its unique identity and become one with all the other nations. Yahweh agrees to do what Moses has asked: his presence shall go before his people (33:17; cf. vv. 14–15). Moses has successfully interceded for Israel and, for the narrative moment, has been able to close the gap in the divine-human relationship that had been created by the golden calf incident. When Moses requests that he be allowed to see Yahweh's "glory" (*kābôd;* 33:18), Yahweh takes the opportunity to reveal an important side of the divine nature. Yahweh announces to Moses that he will cause all of his "goodness" (*ṭûb*) to pass before him, and "I will be gracious to whom I will be gracious and I will be merciful to whom I am merciful" (*wĕḥannōtî 'et-ăšer 'āḥōn wĕriḥamtî 'et-'ăšer 'ăraḥēm;* 33:19). This statement represents an important element in Israel's understanding of the divine nature, for it presents a different side to the zealous deity who punishes the sons for the offenses of their fathers (20:5). While a sense of absolute justice, an "eye for an eye," may characterize one side of the divine (21:24–25), this is balanced by the merciful nature of Yahweh. In the present instance, one is left to ponder which of the divine attributes was dominant in the decision to continue in the presence of this less than obedient people. Though allowed only to see Yahweh's back (33:20–23), Moses had been assured through a direct theophany that Yahweh would continue with his people.

---

[20] It is notable that the tradition here concerning the Tent of Meeting makes no mention of the Ark of the Covenant, which was an essential element associated with the Tabernacle (25:10–22; 37:1–9). Likewise, the divine presence associated with the Tent here seems to be transitory, as opposed to the idea of the permanent "tabernacling" of the divine presence in Israel's midst. On the relationship of the Ark to the Tent of Meeting, see R. de Vaux, "Ark of the Covenant and Tent of Reunion," in *The Bible and the Ancient Near East* (New York: Doubleday, 1971), pp. 136–151. While 33:7–11 is commonly associated with the Yahwistic source, M. Noth regards it as an insertion from a special source, arguing that the Tent of Meeting first appears in the Yahwistic narrative in Numbers 11, which is literarily primary to both Numbers 12 and Exod 33:7–11 (*A History of Pentateuchal Traditions,* pp. 128–129, 244–245).

These events prepare the way for the final restoration of the people in their relationship with Yahweh through the establishment of a new covenant. With this, the "social drama" initiated by the crisis that endangered the continued existence of the community was resolved, and the people were reintegrated into the proper relationship with their god. The account of the renewal is linked directly to the story of the apostasy by noting that Moses prepared two tablets like the first ones which he had broken upon seeing the golden calf image (34:1; cf. 32:19). After ascending the mountain with the tablets in hand, Moses encounters the divine again in the cloud. In response to Yahweh's passing before him, Moses proclaims Yahweh's attributes in a manner that combines the concepts noted in 20:5 and 33:19 and which summarizes the human-divine relationship and its highly paradoxical nature. Yahweh is "compassionate and gracious" (*raḥûm wĕḥannûn*), "great in steadfast love and truth" (*rab-ḥesed weʾĕmet;* 34:6), "extending steadfast love to thousands" (*nōṣēr ḥesed lāʾălāpîm*), and "forgiving iniquity, transgression, and sin" (*nōśēʾ ʿāwōn wāpešaʿ wĕḥaṭṭaʾâ;* 34:7). At the same time, Yahweh "does not exempt from punishment" (*wĕnaqqēh lōʾ yinaqqeh*), and he "visits the iniquity of the fathers upon the sons and grandsons until the third and fourth generation" (*pōqēd ʿāwōn ʾābôt ʿal-bānîm wĕʿal-bĕnê bānîm ʿal-šillēšîm wĕʿal-ribbēʿîm;* 34:7). In the restoration of Israel to its previous status, this tension must be recognized. While Yahweh was gracious, loving, and responsive to the needs of his people, he also required obedience and enforced justice. Just how, and to what degree, each of the above characteristics would influence individual situations would remain to be seen in the continuation of the relationship.

Moses invokes Yahweh to go in their midst despite their "stiff-necked" nature, to pardon their iniquity, and to take the people as his own possession (34:9). In 34:10–28, Yahweh makes a new covenant with Israel, noting that he will drive out the inhabitants of the land before them, warning them to make no covenants with them, and demanding that they destroy the cultic implements of the people in the land (34:11–13; cf. 23:20–26). Exclusive service to Yahweh and Yahweh alone must be the identifying characteristic of this people. At Yahweh's command Moses wrote down "the words of the covenant, the ten commandments" (*dibrê habbĕrît ʿăśeret haddĕbārîm;* 34:27–28), which constituted the content of the covenant Yahweh had made with Israel (34:27, 10).[21]

---

21 Rather than attribute 34:11–26 to the Yahwistic writer, as is commonly done by source critics, J. Blenkinsopp argues that these verses are part of a continuous narrative running from

The reestablishment of the covenant and the restoration of the community constitute the proper situation for a new manner of theophany that would reflect the way in which Yahweh and Israel would interrelate when Israel followed the divine prescripts. The power of the presence of Yahweh to transform human reality is emphasized by the story concerning the transfiguration of Moses' appearance, if not his very being (34:29–35). As a result of his direct encounter with Yahweh in the Tent, the "skin of his face was radiant" (v. 29).[22] So visible was this awe-inspiring transformation of Moses' visage that all the people, including Aaron, were afraid to approach him (v. 30). Yet, in classical terms, this manifestation of the power and presence of the sacred also drew the people toward Moses when he summoned them and commanded their obedience to Yahweh's word (34:31–32).[23] In this manner, the entire congregation of Israel was informed of "all which Yahweh had spoken to him on mount Sinai" (*kol-ʾăšer dibber yhwh ʾittô bĕhar sînāy;* v. 32). Notable also is that the story gives the impression that this transformation had some permanent effects on Moses, for when he was not in Yahweh's presence in the Tent, he would cover his face with a "veil" (*masweh;* 34:33–35) both as a symbol of his transformed state and as a type of protection for the people.

This story concerning the effects of the contact between the human and the divine is important, for it immediately precedes the account of Israel's complete obedience to the divine will and, by extension, the potential transformation of the people in a manner similar to Moses', if Yahweh were to go in their midst. Exod 35:1–40:38 represents a type of new beginning for the restored covenant community. In contrast to the rebellion that characterized Israel's response to the first effort at establishing the covenant, the people respond to the renewal of the relationship in the properly prescribed

---

Exodus 32 through 34 and that the language and style are more consistent with that of the deuteronomic school than with the Yahwistic narrative (*The Pentateuch,* pp. 192–194). For discussions of the relationship of this "cultic Decalogue" to the parallel "Decalogues" contained in Exodus 20 and Deuteronomy 5, consult the commentaries.

22 For an analysis of the meaning of this difficult section and an overview of the variety of attempts made at understanding it, see M. Haran, "The Shining of Moses' Face: A Case Study in Biblical and Ancient Near Eastern Iconography," in *In the Shelter of Elyon. Essays on Ancient Palestinian Life and Literature in Honor of G. W. Ahlström,* ed. W. B. Barrick and J. R. Spencer (JSOTSup 31; Sheffield: JSOT, 1984), pp. 159–173.

23 On the presence of both the elements of fear and awefulness, expressed in the absolute inapproachability of the *tremendum,* alongside the concepts of attraction and fascination, expressed in the power of the *fascinans,* as aspects of the experience of the *mysterium tremendum,* see R. Otto, *The Idea of the Holy* (New York: Oxford University Press, 1958), pp. 12–40.

manner. Beginning with the command to observe the Sabbath (35:1–3; cf. 31:14–17), the account proceeds to the assemblage of the people and the call for materials (35:4–9), followed by a summary of the cultic implements to be prepared (35:10–20). In response to the call, the people provide the materials necessary for the preparations (35:21–29), and the master artisans, Bezalel of Judah and Oholiab of Dan, are named (35:30–36:1). The people supply such an excess of materials that the craftsmen have to ask Moses to instruct them to stop (36:2–7). All of this provides the background for the construction of the Tabernacle (36:8–38), the cultic symbol of Yahweh's presence. Exod 38:9–39:31 recounts the completion of the orders, containing summaries of the materials used and the implements prepared (38:21–31; 39:32–43).[24]

Now, on the first day of the first month of the second year upon leaving Egypt, Moses was directed to erect "the Tabernacle, the Tent of Meeting" (*miškan 'ōhel mô'ēd;* 40:1–2; cf. v. 17). This work is completed in vv. 3–11 and is followed by the command to sanctify Aaron and his sons (vv. 12–15). Through their anointing they will be qualified as an "eternal priesthood for their generations" (*kĕhunnat 'ôlām lĕdōrōtām;* v. 15). All that Yahweh commanded, Moses fulfilled (v. 16), completing the arrangement of the cultus and, hence, the preparations for the "presence of Yahweh" in vv. 17–34. Now, to symbolize Yahweh's presence in a manner similar to Exod 24: 15–18 and 33:9–10, the cloud covered the Tent "and the glory of Yahweh filled the Tabernacle" (*ûkĕbôd yhwh mālē' 'et-hammiškān;* 40:34). Unlike in previous accounts (cf. 33:7–11), Moses was now unable to enter the Tent when the cloud of the presence was covering it, suggesting a possible shift in the role of Moses to a more "priestly" guise (cf. Lev 9:23).[25] This notice sets the stage for the sanctification of the community by way of the institution of the ritual activities that would guide it through its existence.[26]

---

[24] Despite the fact that the account in 35:1–39:31 contains a nearly verbatim repetition of the orders in 25:1–31:18, there are some significant differences. The command concerning the keeping of the light is not fulfilled until Lev 24:1–3, most probably because it can be completed only by Aaron and his sons in their roles as priests. Related to this, and in part explanatory for it, is the fact that the ordination of Aaron and his sons, commanded in 29:1–46, is not completed until Lev 8:1–36, no doubt because this ritual could not be conducted until the instructions for sacrifice, an important part of the ordination, had been delivered. In addition, the fulfillment of the commands about the atonement money (30:11–16) and the preparation of anointing oil and special incense (30:22–38) is not noted. Hence, while 35:1–39:31 displays an intimate knowledge of 25:1–31:18, it represents a deliberate reordering of a number of elements of the former.

[25] B. S. Childs, *The Book of Exodus*, p. 638.

[26] J. Milgrom points out that Exod 40:36–38, which notes that the divine cloud will lead Israel through its wilderness journey, is intrusive and is repeated in more detail in Num 9:15–23.

II. Sanctifying the Community:
Creating a "Kingdom of Priests" and a "Holy Nation"

The process of sanctification is one that requires a specific, divinely outlined ritual performance, for sanctification itself is the process of "making holy" (L. *sanctifico*). This fact is clearly presented by the structure of the book of Leviticus, for the major portion of the book is composed of speeches of Yahweh that Moses delivers to the congregation of Israel. In terms of command and fulfillment, the pattern in Leviticus follows that which was established in Exodus 25–31 and 35–40.[27] What is presented in the divinely directed ritual commands of Leviticus is complete Israelite conformity to the deity's will. The concept of rebelliousness that dominates the center of Exodus 25–40 is completely absent in Leviticus. This book presents the ritual performances that create the boundaries that separate Israel from all other nations and by which other peoples will identify the chosen people of God.

While the modern consensus is that the entirety of Leviticus belongs to the group known as the Priestly school, the book is commonly divided into at least two strata, one designated as the "Priestly" source, contained mostly in Leviticus 1–16, the other as the "Holiness" source, found in chapters 17–27. The relation of the two remains debated, though there seems to be a growing consensus that the "Holiness" source might be later than the "Priestly" source and may have constituted the "redactor" of these materials.[28] What is clear from the book itself is that a number of related issues, e.g., sacrifice, priesthood, purity, impurity, etc., all deriving from the technical world of the cultus, have been collected and edited here to form a particular ideal of how "Israel" was to serve Yahweh and how it was to preserve itself as a sanctified, separated people.[29] The requirements placed

---

As it stands, however, the Exodus passage creates a frame with its counterpart in Numbers and brackets all of the materials contained in Lev 1:1–Num 9:14, i.e., the account of all of the laws given to Moses (*Leviticus 1–16*, p. 61).

[27] For details on this pattern, see J. E. Hartley, *Leviticus* (WBC 4; Dallas: Word, 1992), pp. xxx–xxxi.

[28] The arguments for these positions are detailed by I. Knohl, "The Priestly Torah Versus the Holiness School: Sabbath and the Festivals," *HUCA* 58 (1987) 65–118, and, more recently, *The Sanctuary of Silence*, pp. 100–103, 200–203; and J. Milgrom, *Leviticus 1–16*, pp. 13–63. While both of these scholars argue that the "H" redaction of the Priestly material occurred in the pre-exilic period, it seems, nonetheless, clear that it did not take its place in the final Tetrateuchal or Pentateuchal narrative until a much later period. If this is the case, then there must have been at least one additional redactor for the final form of Leviticus.

[29] There are a variety of ways of understanding the final redactional structure of Leviticus. For a presentation and discussion of the standard analyses of the literary structure of the book,

upon "Israel" and the cultic prescriptions that constitute the life of the Tabernacle and nation are, by the testimony of Leviticus itself, *ideals.* This is a datum that has escaped the attention of the majority of commentators. From the historical critical standpoint it is certainly legitimate to reconstruct sources, assign them to particular historical/cultural contexts, and then describe the redactional process that led to their present form. Likewise, from a literary perspective, it is legitimate to analyze the final text of Leviticus as a whole and to determine the literary structures and patterns that characterize it. Yet neither of these two approaches addresses the major *religious* functions and implications of the texts in the context in which they most probably took their final form. Rather than finding in Leviticus the collected priestly prescriptions for the service at either the pre- or post-exilic Jerusalem Temple, one might begin to approach the materials from the context in which the final author(s) of Leviticus placed them—in the wilderness Tabernacle.[30] It is precisely this idealized retrogression into the period of "Israel's" sojourn in the "wilderness" that provides the clues for understanding the nature of the materials in Leviticus.

Leviticus describes the rituals that created and defined the people "Israel" at Mount Sinai, serving Yahweh in perfect obedience before the Tabernacle which represented his presence among his chosen people. The book describes the cultus and the rituals that *should* define Israel "forever." This, I suggest, is a crucial point that has been overlooked by scholars. While it is certainly possible that the prescriptions contained in Leviticus *might* have reflected actual historical actions performed by the priests in some particular cultic sanctuary at some particular time and in some specific setting, in their context in Leviticus, they occur in the wilderness at Sinai, within the setting of the Tabernacle administered by the Aaronid priesthood. They do not necessarily describe how things were; rather, they

---

see J. H. Hartley, *Leviticus,* pp. xxxii–xxxv. M. Douglas, following a structuralist approach to Leviticus, understands the shape of the book in terms of a circular structure by which the parallelism of the elements of the book balances and integrates the diversity of themes presented ("The Forbidden Animals in Leviticus," *JSOT* 59 [1993] 9–12).

30 As E. Leach has noted with respect to the biblical accounts in Leviticus, the ". . . ethnographical context is mythological: the Israelite Tabernacle, as described in the text, is culturally, architecturally, and archaeologically an impossibility." The details set forth in the accounts, however, may contain reflections of the procedures actually used during the period in which the work was written ("The Logic of Sacrifice," in *Anthropological Approaches to the Old Testament,* ed. B. Lang [IRT 8; Philadelphia: Fortress, 1985], p. 141; originally published in *Culture and Communication* [Cambridge: Cambridge University Press, 1976], pp. 81–93).

explain how things *ought* to be.[31] The very continuity between the "Israel" that was created at Sinai and the "Israel" that returned from "exile" and "restored" the true temple cultus of Yahweh in Jerusalem is one created by way of the narrative and social flexibility of the symbol "Israel" to create connections that may form part of a "shared history" by which a group identifies itself.[32]

Despite the variety of sources, traditions, histories, etc., that might have been used in the creation of the final narrative of the Tetrateuch and, ultimately, the Pentateuch, several factors seem to be apparent. The major Pentateuchal themes, i.e., the promises to the patriarchs, deliverance from Egypt, the revelation at Sinai, the wilderness wanderings, and the guidance into the land,[33] occur in this account as connected parts of a traditional history that presents the common past of the people for whom it was created. In ethnic and religious terms, then, it is this final "history" that provides "Israel" with the idealized descriptors by which it might establish, maintain, and recreate itself through a variety of challenges and situations. Embedded in these ideal views of what should be might also be some functional indicators of what might have been for the particular group or groups who chose to "share" this historical past.

The directions of Leviticus, presented as though occurring at Sinai, bring the movement of the narrative account of the deliverance of "Israel" from Egypt and the fulfillment of the promise of the land to a complete standstill. From the viewpoint of the narrative account, "Israel" will not come into existence apart from the creation and maintenance of the priesthood and cult. These would provide "Israel" with the means for becoming a "kingdom of priests" and "a holy people" (Exod 19:6). One essential element in the process is the institution of sacrifice. The directions concerning the proper methods by which these services are to be conducted constitute the topic of Lev 1:1–7:38. While the traditions concerning the origins

---

31 In order to understand the variety of ways in which one might reenvision the cultus or might reconstruct the image to which Israel should conform, one need only compare the cultus described in Leviticus with that detailed in Ezekiel 40–48, which presents itself as a vision, not as a description of how things actually might have been. A similar understanding of this aspect might be understood by considering the descriptions of the cult found in the Temple Scroll. The extensive consideration of ritual purity laws contained in the Mishnah and the Talmud illustrates most vividly the ways in which idealized statements may be maintained and emphasized through the generations.

32 A. P. Royce argues that to maintain and recreate ethnic identity, symbols must be highly flexible (*Ethnic Identity: Strategies of Diversity*, p. 82).

33 M. Noth, *A History of Pentateuchal Traditions*, pp. 46–62.

of Israel clearly "recollect" a time when sacrifices could be offered at any number of sacred sites by selected, special personages, e.g., Noah, Abram, Jethro, Moses, etc., this possibility ends with the legislative pronouncements of Leviticus. After this point, the sacrificial cult is to be performed by the priests, Aaron and his sons, at a specific sacred place, the Tabernacle/Tent.

Despite the tendency of modern critical scholarship to emphasize what is understood as the "prophetic critique" of the cult over the importance of the cultic rituals of the Temple,[34] there are several facts that should not be overlooked. In the first instance, it is quite clear that the ritual of sacrifice was the central service conducted by the priesthood at the Temple. One might even argue that the maintenance of the sacrificial cultus was the most important role that the priesthood played in Israel. This was most probably true in the periods of both the Solomonic Temple and the Second Temple. Second, Israel's sacrificial system shared a common pattern with the systems of the surrounding cultures, as is illustrated by both practice and terminology. Third, Israel's sacrificial system emerges full-blown in the descriptions of Leviticus, Numbers, and Deuteronomy. While all of the legislative materials concerning the proper performance of the ritual (and the performance must be proper in order to be efficacious) are presented as though given for the first time in the wilderness and followed from that time forward, such must be understood as anachronistic. The sacrificial rituals associated with the Priestly and deuteronomic materials reflect a highly sophisticated, temple-centered, priestly-dominated theory of sacrifice that presumes some extended period of development.[35]

---

34 Even a brief survey of some of the standard works on the Hebrew bible illustrates this propensity. To confirm this, one need only check such works as G. von Rad's *Old Testament Theology*, 2 vols. (San Francisco: Harper & Row, 1965); W. Eichrodt's *Theology of the Old Testament*, 2 vols. (Philadelphia: Westminster, 1967); G. Fohrer's *History of Israelite Religion* (Nashville: Abingdon, 1972); H. Ringgren's *Israelite Religion* (Philadelphia: Fortress, 1966); H. H. Rowley's *Worship in Ancient Israel* (Philadelphia: Fortress, 1962); H.-J. Kraus' *Worship in Israel* (Richmond: John Knox, 1965). Even the monumental study of Israelite institutions by R. de Vaux devotes a mere 43 pages to sacrifice, its history and development, and its significance in ancient Israel (*Ancient Israel, Vol. 2*, pp. 414–456). An even greater indictment of modern historical critical scholarship might be found in a brief survey of the major introductory text books that are used in university courses on the Hebrew bible.

35 As with most religious rituals, the origins of sacrifice remain debated. As W. Burkert notes, however, animal sacrifice constitutes the oldest documented form of religious ritual (*Homo Necans: The Anthropology of Ancient Greek Sacrificial Ritual and Myth* [Berkeley: University of California Press, 1983], p. 13). Burkert finds the origins of sacrifice in the transition from the hunt to the ritualized slaughter of domesticated animals. In contrast to this theory, R. Girard understands the ritual of sacrifice as a way of dispersing and diffusing an innate

If it is correct that the entire sacrificial prescription, like much of the religious legislation contained in the Hebrew bible, is anachronistic, then it might be useful to note how this might be effective in the effort to recreate and redefine an emerging ethnic group. Within the setting of the Persian "restoration" community, such a religio-mythological charter would have been vital to establishing the position of the cultus that was seeking to claim priority over the Temple in Jerusalem.[36] Likewise, given the Persian emphasis on the codification of indigenous "traditional" religious and legal systems, a compilation of the guidelines by which the temple service was to be conducted would provide the group that was able to promulgate such a code with an authoritative set of credentials. This would be even more impressive if that same group were to have the endorsement of the Persian crown. Perhaps the best indicator of some such action is to be found in the narrative presentations of Nehemiah and Ezra, two figures directly descended from the exiles who returned in official capacities with the full endorsement of the Persian court.[37] In the final analysis, there should exist little doubt that the production of the texts that now constitute the Hebrew bible is to be attributed to some such group of priests and/or scribes closely associated with the temple complex and claiming direct descent from the Priestly lines associated with the pre-exilic temple cultus. The emphasis placed on genealogies during this period further suggests the attempts of those supported by the Achaemenids to legitimate their claims to the land (cf. Ezra 2:1–64; Neh 7:5b–72a; 1 Chronicles 1–9).

While these documents may be understood in terms of their functions within the group that produced them, they also fulfill another important role in the life of the community. Unlike other sacrificial systems which, by definition, are the purview of the priesthood and which were often kept secret from the general populace, this one is to be taught to Israel.[38] Moses is instructed by Yahweh from the Tabernacle to address these

---

human tendency toward violence and aggression (*Violence and the Sacred* [Baltimore: Johns Hopkins University Press, 1977]). A brief summary of these positions and their relationship to sacrifice in Israel is presented by W. W. Hallo, "The Origins of the Sacrificial Cult: New Evidence from Mesopotamia and Israel," in *Ancient Israelite Religion,* pp. 3–5.

36 P. D. Hanson's analysis of Trito-Isaiah and the inner community debates over the "true" remnant of Israel and participation in the cultus of the Temple gives adequate illustration of the fact that the emergence of the temple cultus during the Persian period occurred as a process rather than as a simple one-time restoration (*The Dawn of Apocalyptic,* pp. 46–208).

37 On some of the problems associated with the accounts of Nehemiah and Ezra, see above, Chap. 2, pp. 30–33.

38 J. Milgrom, *Leviticus 1–16,* p. 143.

matters concerning the various types of sacrifices to the Israelites as a whole (Lev 1:1–2). In the initial instructions concerning sacrifice, emphasis is placed on one of the major functions that sacrifice plays in the Israelite cultus—reestablishing the proper balance in the divine-human relationship.[39] An important distinguishing aspect of the sacrificial materials provided in the initial seven chapters of Leviticus is the individual character associated with the sacrifices involved. In nearly every case, Lev 1:1–7:38 addresses sacrifices to be offered by individuals who have in some way failed to fulfill their role in the relationship with Yahweh.[40] The regular, cultic sacrifices prescribed for daily services and for festival days are not given until a later point in the narrative (Lev 23:1–44; Num 28:1–30:1), revealing the necessity for providing the people with a way in which the relationship with the deity could be maintained on their personal initiative as members of this select community.

However one analyzes the mythological functions of sacrifice, several of the symbolic aspects of the act seem to dominate in the biblical materials. On the most general of levels, sacrifice may be understood as an attempt to bridge the liminal space that denotes the mythic overlap between the profane realm of the human, hence ordinary, and the sacred realm of the divine, hence non-ordinary. The cultic activity itself occurs in this liminal area of overlap and is performed by special functionaries, i.e., the priests.[41] The priesthood, then, who will be purified and installed in Lev 8:1–36, will conduct the first public sacrifices in 9:1–24. The non-ordinary role of the priests is stressed throughout the guidelines for sacrifices for, though it appears that any Israelite could slaughter the animal presented to Yahweh, only the priests could enter the area of the sanctuary and perform the actual offering of the sacrifice, its suet, or its blood at the altar. The sacred space created by the presence of Yahweh in his sanctuary, then, represented the

---

[39] For discussions of the variety of theories concerning the symbolic function of the act of sacrifice, see J. Milgrom, *Leviticus 1–16*, pp. 440–443; G. A. Anderson, "Sacrifice and Sacrificial Offerings (OT)," *ABD* V, 871–873; and the literature cited therein. What is clear, given the variety of theories concerning sacrifice, is that the act must be understood in terms of a multivalent symbol of the relationship between the human and divine realms.

[40] Even in the case of the "sacrifice of well-being" (*zebaḥ šĕlāmîm;* 3:1–17; 7:11–21), a major purpose of which is to provide meat for the family table (J. Milgrom, *Leviticus 1–16*, p. 221), the suet of the sacrifice is to be offered with the burnt offering on the altar, indicating that a portion must be dedicated to the deity. Likewise, the fact that the offerer is to lean his hand on the head of the beast before slaughtering it (3:2, 8) suggests that some symbol of transference is involved in the action.

[41] For a schematization of this model, see E. Leach, "The Logic of Sacrifice," p. 138.

area of "overlap" between the two religio-mythic realms. Because of his role in this process of reinforcing or repairing the relationship between the community and Yahweh, the priest functioned as an intermediary in the same manner as did the prophet.[42] The role of the priest in the Israelite cult, at least as it is presented in the Hebrew bible, was just as critical, if not more so, as that of the prophet. As is clear from those passages describing the cultic calendar (Lev 23:1–44; Num 28:1–30:1), the sacrifices offered by the priesthood constituted the foundation of the communal relationship between Yahweh and his people. From the ideological position of the temple priesthood, the cessation of the sacrificial cultus could result in the destruction of the relationship. When individuals failed to fulfill Yahweh's directions, membership in the community could be called into question. This would create, in turn, a kind of social crisis that required some type of redress, either in terms of reintegration of the one who had failed or that person's expulsion from the group. By way of the appropriate sacrifice, the priest, serving as a special intermediator able to operate within the realm of the sacred that was forbidden to the person seeking reintegration into the sacred community, was able to assist in the resolution of such crises. The failure to understand the critical role of the priest in the religious and mythological world of Israel, then, would be failure to perceive a major portion of the nature of the divine-human relationship.

While it seems clear that no single generalization will suffice to explain the symbolic nature of Israelite sacrifice *in toto,* it might be possible to provide a general summary statement of the function of the cultic action in terms of the identity and life of the community that participates in, and supports, this ritual practice. Israelite sacrifice may be understood as a ritual activity that, by offering either certain prescribed animal or cereal gifts to the deity in accord with a divinely revealed outline, reinforces the relationship of the community as a whole with Yahweh or reintegrates into the faithful community those individual members who have inadvertently failed in their duties toward the deity. From the standpoint of the Priestly groups associated with the Tabernacle/Temple, sacrifice and covenant were inseparable.[43]

---

[42] The role of the prophet as an intermediator able to bridge the "gap" between the divine and human realms in crisis situations so as to effect a resolution for the community, not only in Israel, but in cross-cultural terms, has been documented by R. R. Wilson, *Prophecy and Society in Ancient Israel,* pp. 28–32.

[43] As D. Davies has noted, the Israelite concept of morality is directly connected to the sacrificial system, and both are embedded in the concept of covenant ("An Interpretation of Sac-

If the sacrifices described in Leviticus 1–7 are understood as ritual actions whereby certain types of ruptures in the covenantal relationship might be repaired, then the instructions for the performance of these actions might be understood as a necessary step in the preparation of the people to become the "kingdom of priests" and the "holy nation" that was their ideal destiny (Exod 19:6). The materials connect directly with the erection of the Tabernacle and cultic paraphernalia concluding with the presence of Yahweh descending upon the Tent (Exod 40:34–35) from which he gave the directions for sacrifice to Moses (Lev 1:1–2).[44] The prescriptions for the sacrifices themselves are presented in a very structured manner and, as I shall argue in the following sections, are divided to provide the necessary directions for actions that are necessitated by the movement of the narrative at large.[45] Lev 1:3–3:17 concerns three types of "free-will" offerings that are presented to Yahweh. These sacrifices are general in that they are not presented in response to any particularly designated offense or breach of the covenantal relationship. Lev 1:1–17 presents the prescriptions for the ʿôlâ, or whole burnt offering, which was to be presented at the entrance of the Tent. The specifics cover three types of ʿôlôt, those from the herd (vv. 3–9), those from the flock (vv. 10–13), and those from the birds (vv. 14–17). The initial section, then, provides the information on the types of animals acceptable for offering an ʿôlâ to Yahweh. Lev 2:1–16 addresses the guidelines concerning the "cereal offering" (minḥâ), only a portion of which was offered, the remainder going to the priests. Finally, Lev 3:1–17 outlines the special "sacrifice of well-being" (zebaḥ šĕlāmîm), where only the suet is

---

rifice in Leviticus," in *Anthropological Approaches to the Old Testament*, pp. 152–160 [first published in *ZAW* 89 (1977), 388–398]).

44 The terminology of the sacrificial system is very diverse and, at many points, obscure. In general, I follow the translations for the various designations of sacrifice given by J. Milgrom, *Leviticus 1–16*, passim. For discussions of the various types of sacrifices, see the commentaries and the literature cited therein.

45 The implications of this are important for understanding the manner in which the various sources might have been utilized by the scribal groups producing the Tetrateuch. It might not be too much to speculate that the bulk of the technical materials concerning sacrifice would be derived from a common archival source. This is not to assert that all the sacrificial materials belonged to the Priestly or the Holiness Codes, or any single document. Rather, it is to suggest that such sacrificial guidelines would have come from some sources associated with the active priesthood, the only group who would have had a need for them. Regardless of what form such archives might have taken and irrespective of whether they were embedded within a continuous narrative (which seems most unlikely), in their present form the sacrificial materials have been divided up to provide ritual and liturgical stages by which the narrative may sacralize the actions being recounted.

offered on the altar with the *ʿôlâ*. The flesh of this sacrifice, taken either from the herd (vv. 1–5) or from the flock (vv. 6–16), belonged to the offerer of the sacrifice and provided meat for special occasions. The section on the burnt offerings concludes with the notice of an "eternal ordinance" (*ḥuqqat ʿôlām*) binding upon Israel: "you may not eat any suet or blood" (*kol-ḥēleb wĕkol-dām lōʾ tōʾkēlû;* 3:17). The blood of the sacrifice, which contained the source of life, had "always" been forbidden for consumption (Gen 9:4; cf. Deut 12:16, 23); to that injunction was now added the fatty parts of the sacrificial animal, for those belonged to Yahweh.

From the general sacrifices that might be offered on various occasions, the instructions move to the "purification" offerings (*ḥaṭṭāʾt*) which were required when "anyone sins inadvertently" (*nepeš kî-teḥĕṭāʾ bišgāgâ;* 4:2) by breaking one of Yahweh's commands (4:1–35). Unlike the previous sacrifices, which were equally applicable to the population of Israel as a whole, these sacrifices are described in terms of the status of the person who has committed the sin, thus creating a crisis in the divine-human relationship. The list begins with the sacrifice to be offered by a priest who has sinned (4:3–12). Since the priests, as noted above, serve as the only group who were able to intercede between the human and divine realms in the sacrificial ritual, a failure by the priesthood would bring obvious negative consequences. The seriousness of this situation is illustrated by the special way in which the blood of the bull is taken inside the Tabernacle and sprinkled seven times against the veil of the sanctuary, placed on the horns of the altar of incense, and then poured out at the base of the altar of burnt offerings. Breaches of the covenantal relationship endanger the community, because the consequence of such sins is the contamination of the sanctuary itself, an act that threatens the continued presence of Yahweh in the midst of the people. All of the suet is then offered on the altar, and the remainder of the animal is burned in a pure place (*māqôm ṭāhôr*) outside of the camp.[46] If any member of the community sins inadvertently, the same procedure is to be followed (4:13–21). In this case, the group would be represented in the ritual by the "elders of the assembly" (*ziqnê hāʿēdâ;* 4:15). Following the communal situation, provision is made for inadvertent sins by the

---

[46] J. Milgrom, *Leviticus 1–16*, pp. 256–261. On the camp and Tabernacle as representatives of cosmological space and the necessity of maintaining its purity, see E. Leach, "The Logic of Sacrifice," pp. 140–144. The centrality of the idea of purity to the priestly world is presented by P. P. Jenson, *Graded Holiness: A Key to the Priestly Conception of the World* (JSOTSup 106; Sheffield: JSOT, 1992), pp. 56–88.

prince/chief (*nāśî*) of the people (4:22–26). This case involves a different procedure, for only a goat is offered, and its blood is placed on the horns of the altar of burnt offering and the remainder poured out at its base. In this instance, the priest does not enter the sanctuary. This same procedure is followed in the case of a common person who commits an inadvertent sin and presents a female goat as the purification offering (4:27–35).

Such general procedures for the purification offerings for the entirety of the community are followed by a series of four offenses that require purification sacrifices (5:1–13). "Whenever a person sins" (*wěnepeš kî-teḥěṭāʾ*) by failing to act as a witness, or by becoming unclean by contact with either animal or human uncleanliness, or by blurting out a rash oath (5:1–5), acts which result in a "feeling" of guilt (*ʾāšēm*), that person must "confess" (*hitwaddâ*) his misdeed and bring a "reparation offering" (*ʾāšām*)[47] so that the priest might effect expiation for his sin. This offering should be a she-lamb or she-goat (5:6), but if this is too much, the person may present two doves, one as a purification offering, the other as a burnt offering (vv. 7–10). If the doves are not affordable, then an offering of one-tenth of an ephah of fine flour (*sōlet*), with oil but not frankincense, is acceptable (vv. 11–13). The following section, 5:14–16, specifies that any person inadvertently sinning against something "sanctified to Yahweh" (*qodšê yhwh;* v. 15) must present a reparation offering of a ram that is valued at twenty per cent more than the value of the sanctified item.[48] This same reparation offering, a ram or its value, is also required for anyone who unknowingly violates any "one of Yahweh's prohibitive commands" (*ʾaḥat mikkol-miṣwōt yhwh ʾăšer lōʾ tēʿāśênâ;* 5:17). This section on the reparation offerings concludes with the sacrifices required of anyone who acts in contradistinction to an oath that involved a deposit or pledge or commits robbery or extortion against "his fellow" (*ʿămîtô;* 5:21). As with the case of one violating materials sanctified to Yahweh, the guilty party must present a ram or its value plus twenty per cent of the valuation of the property that was lost. In this way, the priest might effect expiation for the person. Hence, the reparation offering provides a way in which individuals in the community might repair inadvertent breaches in the human-divine and the human-human realms of relationships. Through the sacrificial rituals, the community could reintegrate those

47 On the meaning of the *ʾāšām*, or "reparation offering," see the discussion in J. Milgrom, *Leviticus 1–16*, pp. 339–345.

48 For a discussion of whether the value in silver of this offering could be substituted for the actual sacrifice, see J. Hartley, *Leviticus*, pp. 80–82.

individuals whose failings with respect to Yahweh or their fellow Israelites were inadvertent. Not all situations, however, could be repaired so easily.

With the major directions having been provided for the various sacrifices that Yahweh would require, the divine address turns to the instructions for the order of the sacrifices and the portions that will be dedicated to the priesthood (6:1–7:38). This section is addressed directly to "Aaron and his sons" (6:2), since they will be in complete control of the sacrificial cultus once they have been installed as priests. The initial directions concern ritual activities associated with the perpetual fire that is to be maintained on the altar as part of the "ritual for the burnt offering" (*tôrat hāʿôlâ;* vv. 2–6).[49] Since the *ʿôlâ* is offered as a complete burnt offering, nothing of it went to the priests. The "ritual for the cereal offering" (*tôrat hamminḥâ;* vv. 7–11) follows, with a portion given to the priests for their service at the altar as assigned by Yahweh (vv. 9–11). After the instructions for the priests' cereal offering (vv. 12–16), the "ritual for the purification offering" (*tôrat haḥaṭṭāʾt;* vv. 17–23) and the "ritual for the reparation offering" (*tôrat hāʾāšām;* 7:1–6) are presented. With respect to the portions given to the priests, one set of instructions for both the purification and reparation sacrifices is described (7:1–10).

The greatest detail is presented for the "ritual of the well-being sacrifices" (*tôrat zebaḥ haššĕlāmîm;* 7:11–21). The added emphasis is due, no doubt, to the fact that the "well-being" sacrifices are divided into three sub-types: the "thanksgiving offering" (*zebaḥ tôdâ;* 7:12–15), the "votive offering" (*neder*), and the "free-will offering" (*nĕdābâ;* 7:16–19). Even though the major purpose of the "well-being" offering was to provide meat for common familial consumption, the eating of the flesh of the offering was governed by certain cultic guidelines. In the case of the "thanksgiving offering," the flesh of the sacrifice was to be eaten on the day it was offered. None was to remain until the morning (7:15). In the case of the "votive" or "free-will" offerings, the sacrifice could be eaten over two days, but what was left on the third day was to be burned (7:16). The importance of observing these guidelines is presented in terms of purity and contamination (7:19b-21). The "well-being" sacrifices may be eaten by anyone who is ritually clean (*ṭāhôr;* v. 19b). Anyone who is not ritually pure and who eats

---

49 J. Milgrom (*Leviticus 1–16,* pp. 382–383) cites fourteen sets of instructions for ritual procedures designated as *tôrôt* that occur in Leviticus and Numbers (Lev 6:2, 7, 18; 7:1, 11; 11:46; 12:7; 13:59; and 14:54–57; 14:2 and 32; 15:32; Num 5:29–30; 6:21; 19:2 and 14; and 31:21).

sacrificial meat, whatever the source of his impurity, "that person will be cut off from his people" (*wĕnikrĕtâ hannepeš hahīw' mē'ammêhā;* vv. 20, 21). Clearly, the failure to abide by the priestly legislation regarding the eating of sacred food would result in exclusion, in one form or another, from the community of Israel.[50] While the cultic and social origins of the concepts of clean and unclean remain debated,[51] it seems clear that the legislative aspects of Leviticus use its particular expressions of these ideals as boundaries for defining Israel over against the "nations" and the Israel obedient to Yahweh over against the disobedient Israel that presents a danger to the divine presence and protection. To mediate this potentially dangerous situation, the ritual acts of sacrifice enable the people to make expiation for their failures and to render themselves acceptable before Yahweh.

Such a connection is made explicit by the section dealing with the suet and blood of sacrificial animals (7:22–27; cf. 17:13–14). Because the suet constituted Yahweh's portion (v. 23), anyone eating the suet would be cut off from his people, as would any who ate any flesh with blood (7:25–27; cf. 7:20–21). This warning concerning forbidden portions for the populace is concluded with a summary of the priests' portion of the "well-being" sacrifices (7:28–36) which designates the breast and the right thigh as portions given to the priest who offers the sacrifice, but carefully notes that the suet and blood are presented in the fashion required by the divine directives. The rights of the priests were to be understood as an "eternal prescription" (*lĕḥōq-'ôlām;* v. 34). The concluding summary concerning the sacrificial instructions is critical to understanding the formation of the people Israel in the context of their ancestral mythologies. The distinctive, separate identity of "Israel" was formulated not in the land of Judah or Israel and not under the great monarchic rule of David or his son Solomon. Rather, "Israel" as a special people, separate from all others, bound by covenant in a unique relationship with Yahweh, its personal god, received this special nature in the wilderness, after leaving Egypt. Hence, it is only proper that the author(s) of the early portions of this "primary history" depicted the instructions for the sacrificial cult as having been delivered by Yahweh to Moses on Mt. Sinai and as having been followed by "Israel" while in the "wilderness of Sinai."

---

50 Cf. above, Chap. 6, n. 62. The exact meaning of this phrase remains debated.

51 For discussions of the variety of terms used for "purity" and "impurity" and the numerous forms they take in the Hebrew materials, see the discussion and bibliography presented by D. P. Wright, "Unclean and Clean (OT)," *ABD* VI, 729–741, and P. P. Jenson, *Graded Holiness,* pp. 43–53.

These instructions, though part of the national mythology, also fit well into the overall narrative pattern, for they supply the background instructions necessary to complete the installation of Aaron and his sons to the active priesthood (8:1–36; cf. Exod 29:1–46). This section initiates Israel's life of service to Yahweh and the sanctification of its identity, all of which, by the Priestly orientation of these materials, revolves around the leadership of the priesthood and the ritual performances of the sacrificial cult. In response to Yahweh's directions, Moses takes Aaron and his sons, the priestly vestments, sacrificial animals, and anointing oil, and assembles "all the congregation" (*kol-hā'ēdâ*) before the Tabernacle (8:1–4). He then washes Aaron and his sons and clothes Aaron in the priest's vestments (8:6–9). The significance of this act is two-fold: special clothing serves as a special status marker within a community and, in religious and cultic settings, provides some type of special "protection" for the individual who mediates between the human and divine realms.[52] Moses performs the specified anointing rituals (vv. 10–12) before dressing Aaron's sons in their priestly garments. Then, most intriguingly, Moses offers the bull as the purification offering (vv. 14–17), one of the rams as a burnt offering (vv. 18–21), and the other ram as an ordination sacrifice (vv. 22–28). Each of these sacrifices by Moses is offered in conjunction with the sacrificial directions provided in the text (cf. 1:10–13; 4:3–12; 14:14, 17, 25, 28).[53] When the installation ceremony was completed (vv. 29–32), Moses directed Aaron and his sons to remain in the Tabernacle area for seven days (cf. Exod 29:30, 35–37) and to observe Yahweh's commands "so that you will not die" (*wĕlō' tāmûtû;* 8:35), a notice which stresses the critical nature of following the cultic directions of Yahweh. Contact with the sacred, in Israel's cultic ideology, as with most other religious constructs, requires special status and preparation. When these deeds are concluded as specified (8:36), those who have been through such rites of passage are acceptable as intermediators between the differing ontological realms.[54]

With the conclusion of the seven-day installation ceremony (9:1), Moses summoned Aaron, his sons, and the elders of Israel to participate in

---

52 R. A. Oden, Jr., *The Bible Without Theology,* pp. 100–101.

53 As A. Cody notes, Moses plays a unique role in this narrative by virtue of his acting as the priest who offers the sacrifices necessary to render Aaron and his sons ritually acceptable as mediators in the Tent and at the altar. The priesthood is here represented as having its origins with Moses, as did almost all of Israel's religious institutions (*A History of Old Testament Priesthood* [AnBib 35; Rome: Pontifical Biblical Institute, 1969], p. 42).

54 For a diagram of this type of "rite of passage," see E. Leach, "The Logic of Sacrifice," p. 138.

what is one of the most important transformative events in the history of the constitution of Israel as a people. Three types of sacrifice are prescribed: a calf as a purification offering and a ram as a burnt offering for Aaron and his sons, a he-goat for a purification offering and a calf and a sheep for a burnt offering for Israel, and an ox and a ram for a well-being offering, plus a cereal offering. The proper performance of these sacrifices was the prelude to the assurance that Aaron, the priesthood, and Israel were acceptable to Yahweh, whose presence would be in their midst, "for today Yahweh will appear to you" (*kî hayyôm yhwh nir'â 'ălêkem;* 9:4; cf. v. 6). With "all the congregation" (*kol-hā'ēdâ;* 9:5) gathered at the front of the Tent, Moses directed Aaron to offer the requisite sacrifices to make atonement on his behalf and on behalf of the people (v. 7). With these directions, the priestly powers were transferred from Moses to Aaron and his sons. Sacrifice, as well as matters of purity, would be their responsibility. In conformity to the proper ritual procedures, Aaron and his sons offered the sacrifices (9:8–21). After entering the Tent, Moses and Aaron exited and blessed the people (v. 23). The "glory of Yahweh" (*kĕbôd-yhwh*) then appeared to Israel as promised (9:23; cf. vv. 4, 6). The presence of Yahweh was confirmed by the fact that, as the people rejoiced over the theophany, fire came forth and consumed the sacrifices (9:24). Ritually, Israel was now bound to Yahweh and stood as a people ready to realize the goal of becoming a "kingdom of priests" and a "holy nation," i.e., to realize their ideal identity.[55]

But in the realities created by Hebrew narrative, such idealistic situations as a community standing in a perfected relationship with Yahweh do not constitute the only scenario presented. Nor do they present one that endures for too long in the present. Just as both priest and people appear

---

55 An aspect of these rituals that is generally overlooked is the public nature of the sacrifices and the participation of the populace as a whole in their performance. While some of the materials contained in these accounts may be quite ancient, dating to the period of the Solomonic Temple or earlier, the public sacrifices described here are not what one might expect at a royal sanctuary, given the evidence of surrounding cultures. Likewise, the association of the cultic sacrifices with matters of purity and Torah also suggest that what is described here might better be understood in the context of the Second Temple period, when the emphasis of the cult was not on the support of the ruling dynastic house, but rather on the construction and maintenance of a particular identity for the people by which they might remain separate from the surrounding (and competing) cultural groups. Yet, since the texts themselves place these actions in neither the Solomonic nor the Persian era cultic rituals, but rather in the wilderness at Sinai, it might not be too far-fetched to suggest that the rituals and prescriptions provided here are to be understood in mythological terms as ethnic and religious charters which function, on at least the ideological level, to provide boundaries for the definitions of "Israel" and "Israelite."

acceptable before Yahweh, an emergency threatens the community. Two of Aaron's sons, Nadab and Abihu, for reasons never divulged by the text, brought "strange fire" (*'ēš zārâ;* 10:1), on which they offered incense in the presence of Yahweh. Their action is summarized by the notice that what they had done was something that "had not been commanded" (10:1). In response, "fire came forth from before Yahweh and consumed them" (10:2; cf. 9:24). The presentation of the punishment leaves no doubt that the same divine fire that had accepted the sacrifices earlier now destroyed the priests who had failed to follow the prescribed ritual. Notably, whenever the priests might disobey the rules of holiness, they would be slain by the divine, and the community could be held liable for punishment. In this case, the immediate execution of Nadab and Abihu results in the aversion of the punishment of the people.[56] In this manner Yahweh would display his holiness, both to the priests and to the peoples (10:3).

The complete rejection of Nadab and Abihu is emphasized by the command to Aaron to continue in his duties at the Tabernacle, disallowing him from mourning for his sons who had failed in their priestly duties.[57] Immediately following this episode, Yahweh directly addresses Aaron (10:8), another indicator of the change in status that was brought about through the installation ceremony.[58] This address defines the tasks of the priesthood in a very broad manner. They must avoid strong drink when serving at the Tabernacle, a caution that seems only loosely connected with the context at best. The first task announced to Aaron is that he is to distinguish "between the holy and the profane" (*bên haqqōdeš ûbên haḥōl*) "and between the impure and the pure" (*ûbên haṭṭāmē' ûbên haṭṭāhôr;* 10:10). This important element of the priestly task provides the foundation on which the concept of a "nation of priests" might be erected, for it places the priesthood in the

---

[56] P. Segal, "The Divine Verdict of Leviticus x 3," *VT* 39 (1989) 94. An interesting possibility for understanding the background of this text is suggested by J. C. H. Laughlin. He argues that the story represents a Priestly polemic against the Zoroastrian practice of the fire ritual in which sacred fire is enshrined in a special temple. Since for the author(s) of Leviticus the altar fire was continual (Lev 6:1–6), any fire brought into the sanctuary's precincts could be considered "strange fire" and would have been condemned ("The 'Strange Fire' of Nadab and Abihu," *JBL* 95 [1976] 563–565).

[57] On the etiological level, this story explains why the line of Aaron, and hence the Zadokite priesthood, was traced through Eleazar and Ithamar instead of Aaron's elder sons, Nadab and Abihu.

[58] As J. Hartley has noted (*Leviticus,* pp. 134–135), this is the only place in Leviticus where Yahweh speaks directly to Aaron (cf. Num 18:1, 8, 20). Normally when Aaron is addressed, it is along with Moses (cf. Lev 11:1; 13:1; 14:33; 15:1).

mediatorial role of defining those realms that were acceptable for Israel and those that were to be avoided. Israel, in ideal terms, was to define itself through its holiness and its purity. Whenever there might be doubt about the ritual or cultic status of something, the decision lay with the Aaronic priest-hood.[59] Their decisions, however, were not to be kept to themselves, for the next part of their service was to teach to Israel "all the ordinances which Yahweh spoke to them through Moses" (*kol-haḥuqqîm 'ăšer dibber yhwh 'ălêhem bĕyad-mōšeh;* v. 11). From the perspective of the priesthood, the in-terpretation of Torah, and hence, intermediation between Israel and Yahweh in its ongoing relationship, belonged solely to Aaron and his sons.

The identity of "Israel" and the boundaries that would define the people would be interpreted and preserved by those who were charged with the services of the cult. But this "Israel" that is being recreated and maintained by the cultic directions in Leviticus is never defined in self-contained terms. Rather, "Israel" is conceived through its relationship with Yahweh. It is this constant relationship with the divine that necessitates the emphasis on purity and the ritual removal of impurity. While matters in the priestly world can be divided into four categories, sacred, profane, pure, and impure, the sacred must always be protected against impurity. The role of the priests in instructing the people in matters of purity and impurity is one that aims at decreasing the impurity that would threaten the community.[60] Hence, a dual emphasis upon both the instructions for purity and for purification of impurity characterizes priestly responsibilities. To apply the vocabulary of "social drama" to the cultus, the cultic activity provides a way to reintegrate what has become contaminated back into the realm of the pure, thus making it acceptable within the realm of the sacred. In this way, "Israel" could com-plete its role in the developing relationship with its god.

It is possible to understand the placement of the section on purity regulations in this context (11:1–15:33). Because the task of the priests is to educate the people in these matters, it seems only reasonable that the author(s) would take the opportunity to provide selected examples upon which the priesthood could expound. One of the most obvious examples of

---

[59] The emergence of the Zadokite line as the more aristocratic and primary priestly level above the more general "Levitical" priesthood would clearly find this account of the death of Nadab and Abihu and the elevation of their "ancestor," Eleazar, to the status of successor to Aaron (Num 20:24–29) useful in the attempt to gain control of the temple services during the Achaemenid era. For a discussion of the variety of reconstructions of the origins of the Zadokites, see A. Cody, *A History of Old Testament Priesthood*, pp. 156–174.

[60] J. Milgrom, *Leviticus 1–16*, pp. 616–617.

"Israelite" ethnic particularity is to be found in its dietary regulations. Few factors can set a people apart in ethnic terms as empirically as can a specially selective diet.[61] As. A. D. Smith has argued, ". . . the greater the number of differentiating cultural ties and/or unique cultural traits, the more intense the sense of separate ethnicity, and the greater the chances of ethnic persistence."[62] Most considerations of the dietary regulations presented in Lev 11:1–47 fail to take into account the role played by the construction of ethnic identity in the formulation and maintenance of these particular practices.

Moses and Aaron are instructed to present these regulations to the Israelites (11:1–2a), with Aaron fulfilling the command to teach Israel the difference between sacred and profane, impure and pure (10:10). The distinctions between clean and unclean quadrupeds (11:2b–8), fish (11:9–12), birds (11:13–19), and flying insects (11:20–23) are followed by the instructions for purification rituals (involving washing) for anyone who might be contaminated by contact with an impure creature. Following these ritual aspects is a short list of abominable swarming things (11:41–43). The entire section is followed by a clear statement of the reason for the necessity of purity:

> "For I am Yahweh your god; you shall sanctify yourselves (*wĕhitqaddištem*) and be holy (*wihîtem qĕdōšîm*) for I am holy. . . . For I, Yahweh, am the one leading you up from the land of Egypt to be your god (*lihyôt lākem lēʾlōhîm*). You will be holy, for I am holy" (*wihyîtem qĕdōšîm kî qādôš ʾănî*; 11:44–45).

61 A similar argument can be made concerning the roles of clothing and ritual activities as empirically constructed means by which a community can form boundaries around itself to maintain its distinctiveness in the face of other ethnic groups. Equally important is the fact that such efforts also make the group identifiable by outsiders; it is not simply an ascribed or internal trait, but is an actual observable phenomenon. With respect to the dietary laws of ancient Israel, the bibliography is extensive and, in my opinion, not entirely convincing with respect to either the symbolic value or the origins of these practices. Among some of the more recent attempts to explain the Israelite food laws, see M. Douglas, *Purity and Danger* (London: Routledge & Keegan Paul, 1966), pp. 41–57, and, more recently, her revised attempt in "The Forbidden Animals in Leviticus," pp. 3–23. An extensive treatment of the dietary regulations, including a critique of the various theories, especially those of Douglas, is presented by J. Milgrom, *Leviticus 1–16*, pp. 691–742. Milgrom does agree with Douglas' association of the food laws with the various divisions of the social world of ancient Israel (cf. p. 722, Fig. 13; p. 725, Fig. 14). For additional bibliography, see J. Hartley, *Leviticus*, pp. 147–148. An extended review of the history of explanations for the food laws is also provided by W. Houston, *Purity and Monotheism: Clean and Unclean Animals in Biblical Law* (JSOTSup 140; Sheffield: JSOT, 1993), pp. 68–123.

62 *The Ethnic Origins of Nations*, p. 28.

With this brief statement, the entirety of the sacrificial and purity systems is placed within the context of the Exodus/Sinai themes and united by the concept of Israel's unique identity created and maintained by its relationship with Yahweh. By following these guidelines and the purification procedures specified in the event of failures, Israel would be able to become the "kingdom of priests" and the "holy nation" that was to be its destiny (Exod 19:6).[63] The brief summary of the laws in 11:46–47 concludes the regulations regarding this clear ethnic distinguisher that would become part of Israelite distinctiveness and remain so.

Lev 12:1–15:33 presents an equally distinctive set of instructions designed to illustrate a variety of types of uncleanliness to which the community might be susceptible and the means of ritual purification in the event that such contamination occurs. Lev 12:1–8 describes the purification process necessary after childbirth, distinguishing between the state of blood purity resulting from the birth of a male (v. 4), to be circumcised on the eighth day (v. 3), and that resulting from the birth of a female (v. 5).[64] In Lev 15:1–33, the procedures to be followed after the occurrence of genital discharges are provided for both men and women. In that context, the necessity of observing the directions for purity are emphasized by the notice that "You shall make a sacred separation of Israel from its impurity that they not die through their impurity by polluting my Tabernacle (*běṭammě'ām 'et-miškānî*) which is in their midst" (15:31). Israelite purity and the continued presence of Yahweh are inextricably connected. These two sections dealing with birth and blood (life and death) construct a frame for the variety of forms of scale disease that might be encountered.[65] First

---

63 J. Milgrom argues that the idea of holiness with respect to Israel as a whole represents a future ideal that the Priestly writers of Leviticus envisioned as a desired state, but not as an actual status obtained by the people. It was the author of Deuteronomy (Deut 7:6; 14:2, 21; 26:19; 28:9) who designated Israel a "holy people" as a reality (*Leviticus 1–16*, p. 358). If one begins with the possibility that the deuteronomic materials might pre-date the Tetrateuchal materials, in terms of their written forms, then the future orientation of Leviticus might be seen as providing the background for their envisioned fulfillment in Deuteronomy. How one views the relationship between the date for the composition of the Tetrateuch and that of the deuteronomic corpus will also determine how one relates the shorter rendition of the food laws in Deut 14:3–21 to the materials in Lev 11:1–47.

64 These regulations regarding blood and various types of skin diseases are not without parallel in other cultures. What is special about them in terms of Israelite ethnicity is that they constitute a unique combination that is designed to separate Israel from all other groups by the way in which it conducts its life in all areas.

65 On the nature and meaning of *ṣāra'at*, see J. Milgrom, *Leviticus 1–16*, pp. 774–776, 816–826. Deut 24:8 notes that Israel is to follow the teaching of the Levitical priests with re-

are provided the procedures by which the priests are to make the determination of the afflictions and the ways in which the people with such ailments are to live (13:1–44), dwelling outside the camp (13:46) to avoid contaminating the rest of the community. Notably, impurity could affect inanimate objects also, like fabrics (13:47–59) or even houses (14:33–52). Consistent with the efforts to maintain the possibility of reintegration into the community, the prescriptions for identifying and dealing with these afflictions also contain the sacrifices necessary for reintegration after purification (12:6–8; 14:10–32; 15:13–15, 28–29). The priestly performance of the purification and sacrificial rituals provides the basis by which Israel might maintain itself in its proper relationship with Yahweh and remain a people separated from other groups by this religious and ethnic distinctiveness.

All of these regulations recounted since the erection of the sanctuary in Exodus 40 have been included to provide the necessary cultic background for Leviticus 16 and the instructions for the Day of Atonement. Since this ritual provides for the purging of uncleanliness and sin from the community of Israel, emphasizing a national/communal ceremony rather than an individual one, it serves as an excellent transition to the materials concerning holiness which follow. Also, as it constitutes the middle of the book of Leviticus, it also, naturally, occupies the central place in the Pentateuch as a whole.[66] Through Moses, Yahweh gives the instructions for the annual ritual to be celebrated on the tenth day of the month of Tishri (v. 29; contrast Ezek 45:18–20). The activities associated with this celebration require special preparations and sacrifices, since this constitutes the one and only day in the year that Aaron is allowed to enter into the most holy part of the Tabernacle before the Ark upon which Yahweh appeared (16:2). Since this brings the priest directly into the presence of the divine, the priest must take special care for his performance of the ritual, a fact that no doubt explains why the message to Moses is here connected with the deaths of Nadab and Abihu (10:1–6) for their failure to act in the proper way. Aaron is to wash himself and dress in his priestly vestments and present both purification and burnt offerings on his own behalf and for his household (vv. 3–4). Two male goats as a purification offering, along with a ram for a burnt offering, are to be taken from the community (v. 5). Aaron makes his purification of-

---

spect to scale disease (*negaꞌ-haṣṣaraꞌt*). It is possible that Leviticus represents an expansion on this text, which contains the only reference to this disease in Deuteronomy.

66 J. Hartley, *Leviticus*, p. 217.

fering (v. 6) and takes the two goats before the Tent, where he casts lots to select one goat for Yahweh and one for Azazel.[67] One goat is offered to Yahweh as a purification offering; the other is driven into the desert as an offering to Azazel (vv. 9–10, 21–22).

Obviously, given the fact that the second goat is to be the carrier of "all of their iniquities" (*kol-'āwōnōtām;* v. 22), the ritual preparations for its expulsion are quite extensive and symbolic. The slaughtering of both his and the people's purification offerings and the performance of the pre-scribed rituals with incense and the blood of the sacrifices constitute the expiation for the holy place of the Tabernacle necessitated by Israel's impu-rity, rebellious deeds, and sins (vv. 11–17). Aaron then performs the expi-ation ritual for the altar (vv. 18–19). The removal of the impurity of the community concludes with the completion of the ritual of the goat to be offered to Azazel (vv. 20–22). The priest lays both hands on the head of the goat and confesses all of Israel's impurities, rebellious deeds, and sins (vv. 21) before sending the goat out into the wilderness. After a ritual bathing, he offers the burnt offerings on his own behalf and on behalf of the people, along with the suet of the purification offerings.

After the prescriptions for the purification of the person who released the goat for Azazel are given (vv. 26–28), the regulations for the annual celebration of the ritual are presented as an "eternal ordinance" (*ḥuqqat 'ôlām;* vv. 29, 34). Both native born and resident aliens are to observe the day as a day of Sabbath rest, a notice indicating that the ritual purification of the people is to be all inclusive (vv. 29–34). The impure status of all Israel is to be expiated on this day. The proper completion of this ritual, noted in 16:34b, gives the entirety of the Israelite camp a new ontologi-cal status. Israel would now be a holy people in a holy relationship with its god. The purity/impurity regulations and the ritual means of purification outlined in the preceding chapters provide Israel with the means, on an individual level, of redressing the religious and social crises created by fail-ure to obey all of the divine commands. Now, where human failures have occurred, reintegration, not only into the profane sphere of the community at large, but also into the sacred relationship with Yahweh, is possible.

---

[67] For a discussion of Azazel and the "scapegoat" tradition in Israel and the ancient Near East, see D. P. Wright, *The Disposal of Impurity: Elimination Rites in the Bible and in Hittite and Mesopotamian Literature* (SBLDS 101; Atlanta: Scholars Press, 1987), pp. 15–74.

III. Encircling the Camp in Holiness:
The Moral Precepts of Cultic Propriety

As Leviticus 1–16 has provided the "how" to the community for their becoming a "kingdom of priests" and a "holy nation," Leviticus 17–27 concentrates on the "why."[68] With Leviticus 17 the emphasis of the addresses begins to broaden beyond the area of the individual Israelite or Aaronid priest. Now the community becomes the focus of many of the injunctions, for with the cultic and ritual prescriptions in place and the community purified by their performance, the concern becomes the development and maintenance of a holy camp in which Yahweh's presence might continue to dwell. These efforts begin with the prohibition of any profane slaughtering of quadrupeds (*šôr, keśeb,* or *ʿēz*) that are permissible to be used as sacrifices at any place other than at the Tent/Tabernacle. Anyone who failed to obey this injunction would be cut off from his people (17:3–4). In this way, all potential sacrificial blood could be properly handled, thus avoiding any kinds of apostate practices and bringing an end to sacrificing "in the open field" (*ʿal-pĕnê haśśādeh;* vv. 5–7). Such directions on the slaughtering of animals clearly presume the centralization of the cultus that was proscribed by the deuteronomic authors (cf. Deut 12:13–14).

This "eternal ordinance" (*ḥuqqat ʿôlām;* 17:7) is extended not only to the native Israelite, but also to the resident alien (*gēr*) who dwells in the land with them. In accord with the basic priestly ideals of purity that are operative throughout these materials, all who dwell in the camp/land are susceptible to impurity and, since the ideal is a "holy nation," all must follow the directives that regulate the purity of the people and of the land. In addition to the slaughter of certain animals, the injunction against eating blood is extended to the resident alien as well, since the life-force is in the

---

68 Chapters 17–27 are commonly designated as the "Holiness Code" ("H") and are regarded as having had a separate origin from chapters 1–16. J. Hartley presents a solid overview of the history of research on the "Holiness Code" along with its major characteristics (*Leviticus,* pp. 247–260). Overall, it would be accurate to note that there exists little scholarly agreement concerning the materials assigned to "H" beyond the fact that these materials differ in vocabulary and emphasis from chapters 1–16 (17). The status of chapter 17 remains debated since it seems to share more characteristics with 1–16 than with 18–27. It is also not clear whether "H" ever existed as an independent collection apart from its present shape in the final redaction of Leviticus. For the arguments that the writers responsible for "H" were also the final redactors of the "Priestly" materials in Leviticus, see I. Knohl, "The Priestly Torah Versus the Holiness School: Sabbath and the Festivals," pp. 65–118, and *The Sanctuary of Silence,* pp. 68–71.

blood and all life belongs to Yahweh (17:10–12). When an Israelite or resident alien slaughters acceptable game, he must pour out the blood and
cover it (vv. 13–14). Anyone violating the rules concerning the proper disposition of blood will be cut off from his people (vv. 10, 14).[69] Clearly, the
purity of the land and the proper handling of the blood containing the life
were related in the priestly view of the world. On the economic level, it
must also be remembered that the prescribed portions of selected sacrifices
went to the priests as their food and livelihood. Hence, the regulations on
the slaughter of certain animals fulfilled dual roles.

As the blood symbolically conveys the ideas of both death and life,
it is natural that the regulations regarding the killing of animals should
be followed by prescriptions addressing the creation of life. Lev 18:1–30
addresses the appropriate sexual relations for Israel. As is characteristic of these sections, stress is placed on the fact that the authority underlying these instructions is Yahweh.[70] Israel's life is to be set apart distinctly
from the customs of the people surrounding them. They are not to live "as
the custom of the land of Egypt" (*kĕmaʿăśēh ʾereṣ-miṣrayim*), out of which
they had come, nor "as the custom of the land of Canaan" (*kĕmaʿăśēh ʾereṣ-
kĕnaʿan*), to which they were going (18:3). Rather, they were to follow in
Yahweh's judgments and decrees, for in these was life (vv. 4–5). With these
prefatory remarks emphasizing Israel's special nature over against all other
groups, the divine address focuses on the basic unit of Israelite society, the
patrilineal nuclear family, and develops those sexual relationships that are
permissible (18:6–18).[71] Additional sexual unions are included (vv. 19–23),
emphasizing the impartation of impurity and focusing on forms of inter-

69 Interestingly, Lev 17:15–16 permits the eating of the flesh of an animal that has died or
been killed by predators, noting that it does impart uncleanliness that requires washing. According to Deut 14:21, such flesh is strictly forbidden for Israelites to eat, though it may be
given to a resident alien or sold to a foreigner.

70 Two recurrent phrases emphasize this stress on the divine authority: "I am Yahweh"
(*ʾănî yhwh;* Lev 18:5, 21; 19:12, 14, 16, 18, 28, 30, 32; 21:12; 22:2, 3, 8, 30, 31, 33; 26:2, 45)
and "I am Yahweh your God" (*ʾănî yhwh ʾĕlōhêkem;* Lev 18:4, 30; 19:3, 4, 10, 25, 31, 34; 20:24;
23:22, 43; 25:55).

71 It has often been noted that there are certain omissions in the list of forbidden relationships, most particularly relationships with one's daughter, sister, grandmother, step-sister, etc.
According to S. Rattray, this is because the purpose of the list is to emphasize *"who else"* is forbidden, in addition to those included in the nuclear family that would be considered "close kin"
(*šěʾēr bĕśārô;* 18:6 ["Marriage Rules, Kinship Terms and Family Structure in the Bible," SBLSP
26; ed. K. H. Richards (Atlanta: Scholars Press, 1987), 537–544]). A chart of forbidden relationships, accompanied by the punishments for breaking these rules, is given by Rattray on
p. 543.

course that fail to produce offspring. Any sexual activity that might be seen as a threat to the family unit is forbidden.[72] The necessity of purity and separateness is emphasized by the frame created by 18:3–5, noted above, and 18:24–30. Israel is not to defile itself in any of these ways (18:24) since this was the way in which all of the nations which Yahweh was going to drive out from before them had become defiled (*niṭmě'û*). This had rendered the land unclean so that it "vomited out" (*wattāqî'*) its inhabitants (v. 25). These sexual ordinances, like those regarding blood, are binding upon both native and resident alien (18:26). Failure to follow them would result in Israel's also being "vomited out" of the land (v. 28). Naturally, anyone failing to observe these rules of sexual propriety would be cut off from his people (v. 29).

The purity of the land was directly dependent upon the activities of the people in every aspect of their lives. The theme of "holiness" constitutes the ideal of the identity of this people being created by the defining characteristics of Leviticus. To maintain the holiness of the community, proper relationships must be maintained among all its members. Israel is to attempt to align itself with the exhortation, "You will be holy because I, Yahweh your god, am holy" (*qědôšîm tihyû kî qādôš 'ănî yhwh 'ĕlōhêkem;* 19:2; cf. 11:44, 45; 20:7, 26). Lev 19:3–32 presents a highly varied collection of directions aimed at securing the type of relationship within the community that would preserve the social structure of Israel. Most notable among these materials are 19:18b, which instructs the people to love their neighbors as themselves, and 19:33, which admonishes Israel to treat the resident alien like oneself, "because you were sojourners in Egypt." All these instructions are connected to the act of Yahweh in forming his special people through his act of deliverance: "I am Yahweh your God who led you out of the land of Egypt. You will observe all my ordinances (*kol-ḥuqqōtay*) and all my laws (*kol-mišpāṭay*) and you shall do them. I am Yahweh" (19:36b–37). Israel's confession of the exodus event as the foundation of its origins and its special selection by its god provides the basis for the claims placed by Yahweh upon them. Likewise, their adherence to these divinely originating directives will create the distinctly ethnic entity that will be "Israel."

When the goal of the social structure is to insure purity, and hence the divine presence, it is necessary for the group to have ways of resolving the

---

[72] Included in this list is the prohibition against offering one's child to Molech (18:21; cf. 20:2). Why it is contained in this list that is otherwise concerned with sexual relationships is not clear. For an extensive bibliography and a discussion of the practice of offering sacrifices to Molech, see J. Hartley, *Leviticus,* pp. 333–337.

crises that develop when rules are broken and purity and presence are threatened. As with the preceding materials regarding social relationships that will determine the nature and destiny of the community as a whole, these are addressed to both Israelite and resident alien (*gēr;* 20:2). It is not simply the individual that must remain pure, because the failures of the people as a group could pollute the land (cf. 18:24–30). One of the major functions of the sacrificial system was to provide a way in which inadvertent failures to follow Yahweh's instructions could be rectified without endangering the community. Not all failures, however, could be purged by way of ritual expiation. In some cases, like those recounted in Lev 20:2–16, the people who committed the deeds would have to be executed. Anyone who offered a child to Molech (cf. 18:21) was to be executed by stoning, for such actions were understood as "defiling my sanctuary and profaning my holy name" (*ṭammē' 'et-miqdōšî ûlĕhallēl 'et-šēm qodšî;* 20:3). In the event that the people failed to carry out the death sentence, Yahweh himself would cut off that person and his family (20: 4–5). The same fate would await anyone who engaged in any type of sorcery or consultation with the spirit world (v. 6). Yahweh's instructions for Israel were clear: "You will sanctify yourselves and become holy (*wĕhitqaddištem wihyîtem qĕdōšîm*), for I am Yahweh your god" (20:7; cf. 19:2).

Because Israel had been informed of Yahweh's requirements, they could be held responsible for such actions that could not be reintegrated into the social fabric by sacrifice. Hence, cursing one's parents, adultery, incest with one's mother or daughter-in-law, and homosexuality, among other sexual acts (vv. 9–16), were punishable by death. Other sexual activities that were prohibited, e.g., marrying one's sister or having sexual relations with an aunt, would also result in punishments ranging from bearing the responsibility to being cut off from the community (20:17–21). The ability to remain in the land to which they were destined required purity and adherence to the directions of Yahweh (20:22; cf. 18:25–28). By these particular cultural rules Israel would distinguish itself from others, for it was Yahweh "who separated you from the peoples" (*'ăšer-hibdaltî 'etkem min-hā'ammîm;* 20:24). Following Yahweh's ordinances, distinguishing between the pure and impure, making reparation wherever possible, and purging the evil from the community would create the nation that could continue to possess the land. This destiny was the one intended by Yahweh when he separated Israel to be his own (20:26).

As would be expected, if the social world of the common Israelite were to be governed by special norms, so too would that of the priesthood. All of

Israelite society was to be structured by the ritual actions associated with the fulfillment of Yahweh's commands. This means that the priesthood, in its role as interpreter of these laws (10:10–11), was constantly reinterpreting the social fabric of the people in accord with the reinterpretation and reapplication of their understandings of Yahweh's will. Because of the priesthood's role as intermediary between the human and divine realms, actions which brought them into direct contact with the sanctuary and its sacred precincts, their ritual purity had to be specially protected. Hence, there were special restrictions on the priests regarding contact with the dead (21:1–6). Even more strict in this regard were the regulations placed on the leading priest (21:10), since it was he who entered the most sacred part of the Tabernacle on the Day of Atonement. As to the common Israelite, special marriage rules pertained to the priesthood (21:7, 13–15), and the regulations regarding life extended even to the family (21:9).

While Aaron and his male offspring had been installed as Yahweh's selected priests, not every descendant could meet the requirements of the position. Lev 21:17–23 provides details on those descendants of Aaron who bore certain physical imperfections which made them ineligible for presenting offerings to Yahweh.[73] Like the animals acceptable for ritual slaughter at the Tabernacle, the priests who were allowed to approach the altar and the curtain before the sacred precincts (21:23) had to be free from any physical imperfections. Since, however, they were members of the priestly line, those who were ineligible for presenting sacrifices were still allowed to eat the dedicated meat along with their brothers, the active priests (21:22). A natural complement to these instructions is provided by those which follow immediately (22:1–16) and detail the care with which the priests must handle the sacrificial offerings. The overarching concern with purity emerges again clearly, for any priest who presented offerings to Yahweh while in a ritually impure state would be cut off from Yahweh's presence (22:3). In short, failure to maintain the proper degree of purity would result in expulsion from the priestly activities. Analogously, the priests had to exercise extreme caution in eating the specified offerings (vv. 4–8), for failure to follow the instructions faithfully could result in death (v. 9). The sanctified meat of the offerings was forbidden to the

---

[73] The regulations regarding animals acceptable for sacrifice are detailed in 22:17–33 and illustrate the complexity of the sacrificial system. While all burnt offerings had to be acceptable males without defect, and all well-being sacrifices had to be without blemish (vv. 18b–22), certain deformities were permissible in animals presented as free-will offerings, but not for vows (v. 23). Other defects for which animals were to be excluded are noted in 22:24–25.

common Israelite (v. 10), though certain people associated with the priestly clan could partake of such food. All of these priestly rules were aimed at insuring that the sacred materials were not profaned. Understood in terms of their social ramifications, such rules were designed to maintain the distinctions between profane and sacred, between the commoner and the priest, and between the nations and Israel. At every turn and in every way, care had to be taken to avoid profaning the name of Yahweh, the god who brought them out of Egypt (22:32–33).

The interplay between the ritualization of Israelite life through the cult and its sacrifices and the formation of the Israelite ethnic identity is further illustrated by the festivals that regulated the Israelite year, thus sacralizing time as well as space.[74] These celebrations are designated as "Yahweh's appointed feasts" (*môʿădê yhwh*), i.e., "sacred convocations" (*miqrāʾê qōdeš;* 23:2), to be proclaimed and observed by Israel. In many ways the most distinctive appointed time was the Sabbath, the regulations for which begin the sacralization of the year (23:3).[75] This festival was celebrated in the home, bonding the nuclear family together as an ethnically distinct unit. Likewise, because no other group observed this ritual performance, it separated Israel from others, providing a type of objectifiable evidence, internal and external, of Israel's distinctiveness among the nations. This one weekly celebration reinforced Israel's identity on both the familial and communal levels. The second festival prescribed, that of Passover and Unleavened Bread (23:4–8), is a sacrificial ritual that centers upon the communal aspects of eating the sacrificial lamb and celebrating the origins of the community by commemorating Yahweh's destruction of the Egyptians and his deliverance of his people.[76]

---

74 In addition to the cultic calendar of festivals found in Lev 23:1–44, festival calendars are also contained in Exod 23:14–17; 34:18–26; Deut 16:1–17; Num 28:1–30:1; and Ezek 45:18–25. As is well known, there are significant differences among the names and descriptions of the festivals presented in these materials, demonstrating that the final redaction of the Hebrew bible incorporated a number of contrasting traditions that suggest that cultic practices in ancient Israel were quite dynamic. For a discussion of these calendars, see R. de Vaux, *Ancient Israel, Vol. 2*, pp. 470–474, and below, Chap. 9, pp. 306–308.

75 The origins and antiquity of the Sabbath celebration remain obscure. As G. F. Hasel concludes after surveying modern attempts to explain the origins of the Sabbath, "No hypothesis whether astrological, menological, sociological, etymological, or cultic commands the respect of scholarly consensus. Each hypothesis or combination of hypotheses has insurmountable problems" ("Sabbath," *ABD* V, 851).

76 In noting that the Israelite Passover festival concentrates on the communal aspect of sacrifice, it is important to stress that there is also an expiatory side to the slaughter of the lamb, since the blood placed on the door-posts provides protection against harm for those participat-

In anticipation of the settlement in the land, Israel is instructed to celebrate the Feast of Weeks (23:9–22) and to present the designated sacrifices to Yahweh. As described earlier, the Day of Atonement is to be celebrated on the tenth day of the seventh month (23:26–32). Finally, on the fifteenth day of that same month, the festival of Sukkoth (Booths) is to begin (23:33–36, 39–43). Excepting the Sabbath celebration, each of the cultic rites involves the presentation of sacrifices to Yahweh. Apart from the Passover (and Unleavened Bread) festival, these festivals involve both the priesthood and the central sanctuary, since all sacrificial animals must be offered at the altar of the Tabernacle (cf. 17:3–4). The logic of presentation here is quite intentional, moving from the familial Sabbath and Passover celebrations to the national pilgrimage days which solidify the identity of the community through its participation in the sacrificial rituals at the prescribed times of the year. Whatever the origins of individual celebrations might have been, now they are completely disengaged from the agricultural or pastoral year and regulated by a calendar that is maintained by the priests and the central sanctuary. The purity of the community can now be regulated by the priesthood through the standardized sacrifices performed in such a manner as to sacralize people, place, and time.[77]

In terms of the classification of sacred and profane, pure and impure, there are no middle grounds. Such a system reflects the ideals that would be contained in a world-view that was formulated around what we have called "absolute justice." The state to be desired and striven for by all Israel was the state of ritual purity that would allow the sacred to remain in its midst. But, as noted above (cf. 20:1–27), explicit legislation was also necessary to address failures in these areas. Lev 24:10–16 addresses the sanctity of the divine name via the story of the blasphemous utterance by the son of an Israelite woman and an Egyptian man. Cursing the name of god required the death penalty and led to the formulation of a general rule on blasphemy that was to be applied to both native Israelite and resident alien (23:16).

---

ing in the rite. On the important structural dichotomy of the ideal types of "communion" and "expiatory" sacrifices, see N. Jay, *Throughout Your Generations Forever: Sacrifice, Religion, and Paternity* (Chicago: University of Chicago Press, 1992), pp. 17–29. Jay's observations concerning gender and sacrifice will become apparent in the next chapter, when the community of Israel is structured genealogically by patrilineal descent, a characteristic that will become the basis for the religious and social structure of the "Israel" of the restoration era.

77 On the importance of ritual in the sacralization of people, space, and time, see F. H. Gorman, *The Ideology of Ritual: Space, Time and Status in the Priestly Theology* (JSOTSup 91; Sheffield: JSOT, 1990), pp. 13–38, 55–60.

Maintaining the community meant regulating claims of personal injury, e.g., 23:17–21, on a one-to-one basis, noting again that there was to be one law for all dwelling in Israel's precincts (v. 22).

The inclusion of the resident alien (*gēr*) along with the native born Israelite (*'ezrāḥ*) in these formulations is critical, for it emphasizes that Israel's identity was inextricably tied to the land. All those who dwelt in Israel's midst, i.e., in the land promised by Yahweh, had to observe the same regulations with respect to purity. Failure to do so could endanger the presence of the divine in Israel's midst, since purity and impurity are not states that distinguish among ethnic or national lines. Rather, purity had to be maintained in the idealized areas surrounding the Tabernacle, i.e., the area on which Israel is settled, be that the wilderness camp or the land itself. All those living within those borders were subject to these rules. Thus, the sanctity of the land itself occupied an essential place in the vision of this sacralized community, a position clearly emphasized by the regulations regarding the Sabbatical and Jubilee years.[78]

The idea that the land, like the people themselves, was to participate in a periodic period of rest from its labors (25:2–7) included it in the process of the maintenance of the sacred sphere. Like all of the other structures associated with the identity of Israel, these two distinctive ideals were given "on Mt. Sinai" (25:1; cf. 26:46), projecting the practices of the future back into the mythic times of origin. But the Sabbatical year itself was part of a larger method of calculating the use of the land that culminated in the celebration of the Jubilee (*yôbēl*) every fiftieth year (25:10). According to the legislation associated with the Jubilee, all family territories which had been sold during the period since the last Jubilee year were to be returned to the family that had originally owned it. This special set of regulations had both economic and social ramifications. At the economic level, the years left until the celebration of the next Jubilee, and hence the number of harvests that could be anticipated from a parcel of land, were critical for calculating the cost of buying or selling family property (25:13–17). Family lands were

---

[78] Not unlike the weekly Sabbath celebration, the origins and antiquity of the Sabbatical and Jubilee years remain obscure. For discussions of these two events, along with proposals on their origins, see S. Hoenig, "Sabbatical Years and the Year of Jubilee," *JQR* 59 (1969) 222–236; N. P. Lemche, "The Manumission of Slaves—the fallow year—the sabbatical year—the jobel year," *VT* 26 (1976) 38–59; M. Greenburg, S. Safrai, and A. Rothkoff, "Sabbatical Year and Jubilee," *EncJud* 14 (1971) 574–586; C. J. H. Wright, "Jubilee, Year of," *ABD* III, 1025–1030, and "Sabbatical Year," *ABD* V, 857–861; and J. A. Fager, *Land Tenure and Biblical Jubilee: Uncovering Hebrew Ethics through the Sociology of Knowledge* (JSOTSup 155; Sheffield: JSOT, 1993), pp. 24–37.

not to be sold permanently because the land itself belonged to Yahweh alone. Israel was a resident alien on the land provided by the divine landlord Yahweh (25:23–24). To insure that such sales of land were only temporary, detailed prescriptions regulated the process of redeeming, i.e., buying back, land which had been sold. All land, however, automatically reverted to the original owning family in the year of the Jubilee (25:25–34).

In this manner, Israel, ideally, recreated its tribal holdings every fiftieth year, continually recreating its social world as at the beginning. With the announcement of the Sabbatical and Jubilee year requirements, the issue of familial property was only a distant promise to be fulfilled after the end of the Tetrateuchal and Pentateuchal materials. But this placement clearly plays an important conceptual role in the ways in which claims might be placed upon the land. It takes little imagination to see how functionally effective a legal tradition like that of the Jubilee year might have been to a group of immigrants "returning" from "exile" to restore their family property and holy city, knowing full well that the land to which they laid their claim was in possession of others, and had been for at least a full generation. Just as Israel's identity was connected directly to the land promised by Yahweh, so too was its claim to the possession of that land and the manner in which it was to be possessed. Just like the inalienability of the land, according to the traditions associated with the Jubilee year, the freedom of native Israelites who had been forced into slavery because of economic hardship was to be automatically restored during that time (25:39–43). Native Israelites were not to be sold or treated like regular slaves, for Yahweh proclaimed that "they are my slaves (*kî-'ăbāday hēm*) whom I brought out of the land of Egypt" (v. 42; cf. v. 55). Because of this, all Israelite slaves were to be redeemed, even those sold to non-Israelites (vv. 47–55). Within the legislation of the Jubilee year, the status of Israel and the allotment of its land to the originally intended tenants was continually, and ideally, renewed.

The essential nature of the commands that have been presented in association with Sinai to the existence of Israel and its relationship with Yahweh is underlined in Lev 26:1–46. Here Israel is again invoked to faithful worship of Yahweh to the exclusion of all others (26:1–2). Immediately following this call is presented a list of blessings and curses which provide the basis for understanding the status of the parties involved in this divine-human relationship.[79] Lev 26:3–23 contains the blessings that Yahweh will

---

[79] On the traditional nature of these blessings and curses within the setting of ancient Near Eastern treaties, see K. Baltzer, *The Covenant Formulary in Old Testament, Jewish, and Early*

insure "if" ("and only if"?) Israel obeys Yahweh's statutes and commands. In 26:4–10, the results described would transform the land into a paradisial place. The Tabernacle would be in its midst (v. 11), and Yahweh proclaims that "I shall walk about among you; I will be your god and you will be my people" (*wĕhithallaktî bĕtôkĕkem wĕhāyîtî lākem lēʾlōhîm wĕʾattâ tihyû-lî lĕʿām;* 26:12).[80] Obedience to Yahweh insures Yahweh's presence and Israel's identity.

Failure to follow Yahweh's commandments, the "if not," would obviously result in the punishment prescribed by the curses (26:14–39), which would destroy Israel and exile it from the land. Israel would be punished with a "sword which exacts the vengeance of the covenant" (*ḥereb nōqemet nĕqam-bĕrît;* 26:25) seven-fold for their sins (vv. 18, 21, 24, 28). Yet even this punishment suddenly seems to stop short of a complete and absolute destruction of Israel, for Yahweh announces that "if they confess their iniquity" (*wĕhitwaddû ʾet-ʿăwōnām*) and humble themselves, "then I will remember my covenant" (*wĕzākartî ʾet-bĕrîtî*) with Jacob, Isaac, and Abraham (26:40–42). The failure to follow Yahweh's commands would bring undeniably stern punishment and even the possibility of complete rejection. But this ever-present threat of destruction is suddenly tempered with the contradictory nature of the divine paradox: even though Yahweh will bring about *all* of the curses of the covenant, will disperse Israel among the nations and render the land desolate, he will not destroy them completely, nor will he break his covenant with them. Though Israel may fail to realize the ideal of holiness that forms the basis of its identity and its special relationship with Yahweh, Yahweh will remain steadfast in his commitment to his people.

The final chapter of Leviticus addresses the issue of vows dedicating various gifts, including personal devotion, to Yahweh, and the manners by which the value of such vows is to be determined (27:1–34). These prescriptions which regulate the redemption of those things that have been dedicated to Yahweh complete the instructions necessary for the community

---

Christian Writings (Philadelphia: Fortress, 1971), p. 154, and D. Hillers, *Treaty-Curses and the Old Testament Prophets* (Biblica et Orientalia 16; Rome: Pontifical Biblical Institute, 1964), pp 40–42.

80 As K. Baltzer points out, the formula "I will be your God and you shall be my people" presents the clearest definition of the divine relationship with Israel. In addition to the occurrence of the formula in Lev 26:12, see also Exod 6:7; Deut 27:9; 29:12; Jer 7:23; 11:4; 13:11; 24:7; 30:22; 31:33; 32:38; Ezek 11:20; 14:11; 36:28; 37:23, 27; Zech 8:8 (*The Covenant Formulary*, p. 37, n. 90).

to regulate its social structure and to address the issues of purity and sacrality while living in an impure and profane world. It is only fitting that these instructions should all be given at Mt. Sinai, where the people could encounter their god in his sacred appearances and not be contaminated by the nations that would threaten the maintenance of their special identity. The concluding verse of Leviticus notes, with reference to the whole of the divine instruction that began in Exod 20:1, "These are the commandments which Yahweh commanded Moses for Israel on Mt. Sinai" (27:34). All that Yahweh had commanded, Moses had reported to Israel and to the priesthood. For the author(s) of Leviticus, it was the duty of this priesthood, then, to teach all of these commandments to Israel (10:11). Yet the instructions presented, detailed though they often are, do not constitute a complete cultic code that can be applied consistently without continued interpretation, as can be seen clearly in the later rabbinical developments in the Mishnah and the Talmud. The didactic aspect of the priesthood to select, present and instruct, and interpret the laws of Yahweh, set the priestly group at the head of the Israelite camp, as the one group that had the potential to realize Yahweh's goal of being a "kingdom of priests." As the human intermediators able to expiate and purge Israel of impurity, the priests became the group responsible for maintaining Yahweh's presence among his people. The legislative materials of Leviticus, as applied by the priests, formed the boundaries that could create and identify Israel as a "holy nation." All depended, however, on the maintenance of purity and faithfulness to the covenant.

⟶ 8 ⟵

TOWARD THE LAND:
THE RECONSTRUCTION OF THE COMMUNITY

I. Constructing the Ideal Camp: The Contours
of the Community and the Preparations for the Journey

As the materials in Leviticus began constructing the cultic boundaries
that would separate Israel from all other peoples, a distinction that was created by the presence of Yahweh in its midst, the accounts in the book of
Numbers both continue and reorient those cultic and ritual elements. The
book itself may be divided into three distinct sections: Num 1:1–10:10
describes the preparations for the journey from Sinai; Num 10:11–20:29
narrates the movement from Sinai to Kadesh, concluding with the death of
Aaron; and Num 21:1–36:13 describes the beginning of the conquest of the
land, concluding with the arrival on the plains of Moab. Though the narratives presented are diverse in nature, they are connected by two themes: the
instructions for the community at Sinai and the movement of Israel toward
its land.

Certainly one might observe that a "holy nation" requires a land, and
that membership in that ethnic and religious community might not be extended in the same manner to all. The very existence of the community
might be connected with the ability of the group to maintain the proper relationship with Yahweh as part of the aspect of separateness and holiness. In
the case of Numbers, it is notable that the work addresses two entirely different generations of "Israelites": the generation that left Egypt, but that
failed to be faithful to Yahweh and was condemned to die in the wilderness (14:20–35; 26:64–65), and the generations born in the wilderness and
defined in the second census list (Numbers 26). Only Caleb and Joshua

would prove to have been faithful enough to bridge the gap between the
generations.

The continuation of the Tetrateuchal narratives in Numbers addresses
these issues in an uneven narrative style.[1] In nearly every story recounted,
the proper maintenance of the relationship between Israel and Yahweh provides the focus. Essential for maintaining the human side of the relationship
was Israel's complete faithfulness to Yahweh's revealed instructions, especially with respect to the establishment of the sacrificial cultus and the
maintenance of ritual purity. All of this begins with Israel's arrival at Sinai,
the mount of Yahweh's personal revelation, and continues until Israel de-
parts from the mountain. Hence, the preparation for the journey and the
issue of the continuing revelation of the divine will provide additional emphases to be developed. Because of the mixing of narrative accounts and
descriptions of cultic prescriptions and activities, the narrative connectors
are often difficult to determine.[2] As suggested previously, however, this presents a problem to the investigator only if it is presumed that the text was
intended to be read as an integral whole. In the case of the variety of materials in Numbers, it might be much more productive to analyze each section
in terms of its possible didactic functions and its contributions toward the
formation of boundaries for the community.

In the second month of the second year after the departure from Egypt,
Yahweh directs Moses and Aaron to take a census of "all the congregation
of Israel" (*kol-ʿădat-bĕnê-yiśrāʾēl;* 1:1–2). What has been implicit throughout much of the Tetrateuchal narrative to this point now is made explicit:
the census of the entire congregation will include "every male, by their
heads" (*kol-zākār lĕgulgĕlōtām;* v. 2), who is twenty years old or older and

---

[1] The unevenness of the narrative accounts presented in Numbers is commonly attributed
to the redactional efforts of the Priestly writers who are credited with the editorial disruption of
the JE materials in order to incorporate their own sources into the previously existing whole.
The reconstruction of the process of redaction, however, is far from clear. For discussions of
the sources involved in Numbers and the ways in which the Priestly materials reorient the JE
materials, see G. B. Gray, *Numbers* (ICC; Edinburgh: T. & T. Clark, 1903), pp. xxix–xxxix, and
B. A. Levine, *Numbers 1–20* (AB 4; New York: Doubleday, 1993), pp. 48–71.

[2] A clear description of one way in which the narratives of Numbers may be connected is
presented by J. Milgrom, "Numbers, Book of," *ABD* IV, 1146–1148. This has been more fully
developed by M. Douglas, who argues that the "rung structure" of Numbers is created by the
arrangement of thirteen sections which alternate between story/narrative and legal materials.
According to her analysis, Numbers is a tightly conceived, highly structured composition (*In the
Wilderness: The Doctrine of Defilement in the Book of Numbers* [JSOTSup 158; Sheffield:
JSOT, 1993], pp. 102–126).

eligible for military service (1:3). In neither of the census accounts of Numbers 1 or 26 are women included. The effects of this on the nature and structure of the society and religion cannot be overestimated. It is clearly beyond the bounds of the present book to attempt to explain the origins of this uneven patriarchal dominance, legitimated and maintained through the religious institutions that provided the ethnic distinctiveness for the community. Nonetheless, it might be appropriate to suggest several possible ways of approaching the issue.

While the origins of patriarchy, sacrifice, and purity laws are intriguing areas for speculation, theories describing these stand quite outside the realm of confirmation. What does seem clear is that Israel incorporated each of these common religious phenomena and adapted it to the needs and contours of its own situation. At the same time, one must not lose sight of the fact that the descriptions of the sacrificial cultus or the laws of purity are *not* descriptions of the general religious practices of the common Israelite. Rather, the Tetrateuchal narratives, like the Hebrew bible as a whole, are the products of a particular segment of that religious society and represent the materials selected by that group as functional descriptions of their particular visions of reality.[3] What becomes clear in the descriptions of both the cult and its functionaries is that the "congregation of Israel" who will constitute the "kingdom of priests" and the "holy nation" will be male. If one extends N. Jay's arguments concerning sacrifice to the materials in Leviticus and Numbers, the cultus described therein might be understood as a foundation myth of the constitution of a male-dominated religious group.[4] Yahweh's presence among his people was directly related to the proper maintenance of the covenantal obligations, realized most completely in the sphere created through ritual purity and sacrifice, and participation in the sacred precinct associated with Yahweh's presence was restricted to the male-only priesthood. Additionally, membership in this priesthood was determined by lineage, i.e., the priests who conducted the cultus of the sanctuary were restricted to the sons of Aaron.[5]

---

3 It is essential to distinguish between the understanding of a text as serving a functional need for a group and a text as an accurate description of the religious views of a particular group. In the case of ancient societies, only the former is open to any type of demonstration. The latter is, and will always be, quite unknowable.

4 *Throughout Your Generations Forever,* esp. pp. 1–40.

5 On the basis of the materials presently available, it is impossible to write a history of the priesthood in ancient Israel. It is clear that sometime during or after the "exilic" period, a group who claimed descent from Zadok, through Aaron, became the dominant priestly clan, and the

If, as Jay has argued, one functional aspect of the sacrificial cultus is to reinforce descent, then the male-only priesthood was essential for the maintenance of the identity of Israel that was traced through its male-oriented genealogies. This type of ritual cultus guarantees more than simply a stable line of descent. Jay notes, as a type of "common" sacrificial principle,

> . . . that it is by participation in the rule-governed (moral, not biological) relatedness of father and son in a ritually defined social order, enduring continuously through time, that birth and death (continually changing the membership of the "eternal" lineage) and all other threats of social chaos may be overcome.[6]

Constructed through the ritualization of all communal life around the issues of purity and obedience to the priestly administration of the service of the Tabernacle was a separate, eternal, moral world which guaranteed the presence and blessings of the deity who had revealed himself as their deliverer. The antiquity of the entire set of cultic prescriptions, set as they are in the "original" revelation at Sinai/Horeb, establishes the foundational mythological and ritual pattern for the structuring of the ideal community "Israel."

Such an ideal, it must be remembered, would always remain just that. Yet even as such it possesses important functional aspects. As products of the priestly and scribal guilds, professions open only to males in this instance, the stories support the major concerns of that gender in particular and those two sub-groups specifically. If the production of these stories that contribute to the overall ideal vision presented in the Tetrateuchal narratives is located in the period of the Persian restoration of Jerusalem and the establishment of its "ancestral" cultus, then the emphasis on descent lineage is readily intelligible. Further, those Babylo-Persian trained functionaries "returning" from the East to reclaim their familial lands would find some legitimizing claims to the land to be to their advantage. As is commonly noted in works on the Hebrew bible, the "legitimate" restoration community was formed by those who "returned" from the exile in Babylon. The tendentiousness of this claim is generally overlooked. Instead, as P. R. Davies has suggested,

---

Levitical priestly group was subjugated to them. Beyond this, little else is known with any real certainty. For a discussion of the various traditions associated with Israel's priesthood, see A. Cody, *A History of Old Testament Priesthood* (AnBib 35; Rome: Pontifical Biblical Institute, 1969).

6 *Throughout Your Generations Forever,* p. 39.

To explain the existence of the biblical literature, we must conclude that the creation of what was in truth a *new* society, marking a definitive break with what had preceded, was accompanied by—or at least generated—an ideological superstructure which denied its more recent origins, its imperial basis, and instead indigenized itself. Its literate class (drawn from those who had come from Babylonia) created an identity continuous with the kingdoms that had previously occupied that area, of whom some memory, and probably some archival material, will have remained within Palestine. These wrote into the history of Yehud an 'Israel' which explained their own post-'exilic' society and the rights and privileges of the immigrant élite within that society.[7]

How much of what might have been the religion and culture of the Judah or Israel that inhabited Palestine prior to the destruction of those national states by the Assyrians and Babylonians has yet to be determined. What might be described with some degree of confidence, however, is how some of these narratives provided boundaries for the community which developed and attempted to apply them, both to legitimize their claims to ancestry and to establish their particular religious program on the inhabitants over whom they had control. Allegiance to the shrine/Tabernacle/Temple and to the priesthood who served at it develops as a major focus of the materials.

The covenant mediator, Moses, and the ancestor of the priesthood, Aaron, were to be assisted in their census of those who constituted the people by the leaders of the twelve tribes (1:4–15), the critical social unit for the description of the people.[8] The census of the twelve tribes is then given, numbering the males of military age for each of the twelve units, for a total of 603,550 (1:46; cf. 11:21; Exod 12:37).[9] Notably, the tribe of Levi is not included in the figure (vv. 47, 49), since its members will be assigned the task of service to the Aaronid priesthood and will serve as guards and transporters of the Tabernacle (Numbers 3–4). As the organization of the

---

[7] *In Search of 'Ancient Israel'*, p. 84.

[8] It is obvious that the organization of the people into tribal groups is an anachronism. While the origins of the tribes remain debated, it seems clear that they were connected not only with lineage groups, but also with geographical areas. This latter factor makes it clear that the retrojection of this unit into the wilderness stories is a literary and ideological factor. For details, see J. A. Soggin, *An Introduction to the History of Israel and Judah*, rev. ed. (Valley Forge, PA: Trinity Press International, 1993), pp. 169–170.

[9] Numerous attempts have been made to explain away the impossibly high number that is given in the text. As G. B. Gray has estimated, the figure given here would indicate a total population of at least two to two and one-half million people (*Numbers*, p. 13). A survey of the major attempts to explain the origin of the total is provided by P. J. Budd, *Numbers* (WBC 5; Waco, TX: Word, 1984), pp. 6–9.

people is presented here, the Levites, noted for their devotion to Yahweh (Exod 32:25–29), are described as completely subjugated to the "sons of Aaron," who had been consecrated and set apart as the only legitimate priesthood in Leviticus.

The emerging structure of the community is provided by the assignment of the various tribal groups to specific locations with respect to the Tabernacle, which was at the center of the camp (2:1–34).[10] The account provides for both the arrangement of the people when encamped and the order of march when they would move (cf. 9:15–23). Judah, accompanied by Issachar and Zebulun, would encamp to the east of the Tent and would lead the march (vv. 3–9). To the south would be Reuben, Simeon, and Gad, who would follow (vv. 10–16). At the center of the marching order was the Tent, carried by the Levites (v. 17). Following this came Ephraim, Manasseh, and Benjamin, who would camp to the west of the Tent (vv. 18–24) and would precede the final tribal unit composed of Dan, Asher, and Naphtali, whose encampment would be on the northern side (vv. 25–31). The arrangement of the camp was in accord with Yahweh's command (v. 34). The deity provided the prescriptions for the formation of the sacred space that formed the locus for his continued presence among his people.

Having already noted the separate status of the Levites (1:47, 49; 2:33), the author(s) provide a description of the hierarchical arrangements that would characterize the priesthood. Care is taken to distinguish between the offspring of Aaron (and Moses) while at Sinai[11] and the Levites, who are given over to the charge of Aaron "to perform the work of the Tabernacle" (*laʿăbōd ʾet-ʿăbōdat hammiškān;* 3:7). The status of the Levites is interesting, for while they are clearly subordinated to the Aaronid priests (vv. 6–9), they are also separated from the remainder of the congregation and given assignments in the sacred precincts associated with the Tabernacle. The reason for this special status is provided: the Levites are to stand in service as substitutes for the first-born of Israel (3:12; cf. 8:16–19; Exod 13:2, 13–14; 34:19–20; Deut 15:19–23). As the first-born belong to Yahweh (v. 13), so the Levites will stand in their place to represent the fulfillment of Yahweh's commands.

10 For a diagram of the layout of the camp and a comparison of the tribal allocations here with those in Ezek 48:30–35, see J. Levenson, *Theology of the Program of Restoration of Ezekiel 40–48* (HSM 10; Missoula, MT: Scholars Press, 1976), pp. 118–121.

11 As will be confirmed in Num 26:64–65 (cf. 14:26–35), none of the people included in the census at Sinai would be included in the census taken in Moab (Numbers 26), except Caleb and Joshua. Notice is given here also of the deaths of Nadab and Abihu (vv. 3:2–4; cf. Lev 10:1–3) because of their cultic impropriety.

In order to fulfill both the description of the status of the Levites and the redemption of the first-born of Israel, it was necessary to take a census of the Levitical families. Every Levite male of the age of one month and older (contrast 1:3) was to be numbered (v. 15) according to membership in the house of either Gershon, Kohath, or Merari. As with the arrangement of the tribes of Israel around the perimeter of the camp, each of the clan groups of the Levites was assigned a particular camping location: the Gershonites encamped on the west side of the Tabernacle (v. 23), the Kohathites on the south side (v. 29), and the Merarites on the north (v. 35). Moses, Aaron, and the sons of Aaron would encamp on the east of the Tabernacle (v. 38). In accord with the census, the responsibilities of each group in the transportation of the Tabernacle were prescribed (vv. 25–26, 31, 36–37). The total muster of the Levites is given as 22,000 even (3:39).[12]

The census of the Levites is followed by the order to take a muster of the first-born of Israel who were one month old or above (3:40–43), the total of which was 22,273. This creates the necessity for the redemption of the 273 first-born of Israel not replaced by Levites. The redemption price of each individual was set at five shekels, to be given to the priests (3:46–48), for a total of 1,365 shekels (v. 50). Such an ordinance clearly emphasizes the centrality of the priesthood and sanctuary in the maintenance of the structure of the social world of those who defined themselves in accord with these laws. A second muster of the Levites was necessary, however, to determine the number eligible for the service of the transportation of the Tabernacle whenever the camp moved. In this census, those Levites aged thirty to fifty were included.[13] Census figures, accompanied by an elaboration of the duties of each of the Levitical groups, are provided in 4:4–33. The resulting figure of Levites old enough to work at the Temple was 8,580 from the clans of Kohath, Gershon, and Merari. It would be they who would do the work of transporting the Tabernacle after it was dismantled by

---

12 When one adds the totals given for each clan in vv. 22, 28, and 34, the total is 22,300. As 3:40–51 makes clear, 22,000 seems to be the total intended. It is possible that the error is the result of an haplography in 3:28, where "six hundred" (*šēš*) has replaced the original "three hundred" (*šēlōš*), a mistake that would bring the totals into agreement (cf. G. B. Gray, *Numbers*, p. 28). Such a possibility is suggested by the reading "three hundred" in G[L] (*BHS*). Why this has not been corrected remains unexplained. Interestingly, Rashi notes that the three hundred Levites not accounted for in the census total were themselves first-born and did not, thus, serve as substitutes for other Israelites.

13 Notably, Num 8:24–25 states that the age of the Levites who serve at the Tabernacle is to be between twenty-five and fifty years old. A third tradition, reflected in 1 Chr 23:24, 27; 2 Chr 31:17; and Ezra 3:8, indicates that the service of the Levites began at twenty and had no upper limit. For a brief discussion of the problem, see G. B. Gray, *Numbers*, pp. 32–33.

the Aaronid priests. Contact with the most holy portions of the Tabernacle by the Levites would result in death (4:15). The various realms of sanctification required differing levels of consecration and status.

It is precisely this concern with sanctification that prepares the way for the materials dealing with the purity of the camp. With the Tabernacle as its center, the camp of Israel became Yahweh's earthly abode. For him to remain in their midst, however, it was necessary that the ritual purity of the camp be maintained at all times. This is specified by the notice that those who were unclean must be sent outside the camp (vv. 2–3), "so that they will not defile their camp in which I am dwelling" (*wĕlō̉ yĕṭammĕ̉û ̉et-maḥănêhem ̉ăšer ̉ānî šōkēn bĕtôkām;* 5:3). Purity, however, for the Israelite writer(s), required more than physical purity. The concept of a "holy nation" required allegiance to the instructions of Yahweh in actions as well as by physical separation from impurity. Hence, connected to the previous instructions are those dealing with various types of misdeeds (*maʿal;* 5: 5–10) committed by members of the community. Such misdeeds required both a confession and restitution plus a penalty (v. 7).

Each of these sets of rules operates on the basis of some empirical knowledge of purity and righteousness. Sometimes, however, it is not completely clear whether or not a person has committed some kind of misdeed that might endanger the camp or the familial unit. Such might be exemplified by the case of a wife suspected by her husband of infidelity. With no witness or confession, all that existed was suspicion. In such a case, the priest placed the woman under oath as part of a ritual ordeal that was designed to determine her guilt or innocence (5:11–31).[14] What seems most important about this unique "trial by ordeal" is that it provides a way to determine the guilt or innocence of a person with respect to a misdeed that could not have been inadvertent. Understood in this way, it provides an example for other cases that could arise in a community with respect to suspected actions that could only have been performed deliberately.

This concept of deliberateness connects these issues of the purity of the camp and community with the following section introducing the vows and obligations of the Nazirite (6:1–21). Such vows, which restricted certain behaviors on the part of the participant, were voluntary and, in a sense, "beyond the call of duty." Anyone who took such a vow was obligated to

---

14 B. A. Levine provides an extended discussion of this trial by ordeal that places it within the context of ancient Near Eastern legal traditions, emphasizing especially the parallels from Mesopotamian materials (*Numbers 1–20*, pp. 200–212).

refrain from any product of the vine (especially strong drink), to refrain from cutting the hair, and to avoid all corpse contamination (vv. 3–7).[15] The special status of the person taking the vow of a Nazirite is indicated by the fact that "he is consecrated to Yahweh" (*qādōš hû' layhwh*) for the duration of the vow (v. 8). Because of the holiness associated with the vow, it was necessary to provide special instructions for the fulfillment of the oath in the event of a sudden death that contaminated the Nazirite. Likewise, as in many instances which involve changes in religious status, the fulfillment of the vow was to be marked with special offerings (vv. 13–21). It is clear from the offerings indicated that such vows were quite exceptional and were engaged in only in very special situations.

All these episodes recounted in the opening of Numbers have addressed the organization of the people, the camp, the order of march, the responsibilities of the Levites, the necessity for purity, and the special status that might be obtained through vows. These diverse matters provide the general guidelines for the idealized camp to be maintained to preserve Yahweh's presence among his people. Because of the obedience of the people to the commands, Yahweh provides a blessing for Aaron to pronounce over Israel (6:22–27).[16] The obedient, organized community, gathered about the sanctuary cared for by the priests, the sons of Aaron, was now sanctified by Yahweh, preparing the way for the consecration of the Tabernacle (7:1–89).

The truly episodic nature of the narrative becomes clear at this point. Though there is a natural progression within the narration of events and instructions offered, it is obvious that much of the organization is superficial and that the episodes or accounts might also be used separately from each other. The consecration of the Tabernacle is set chronologically at the completion of its erection (Exod 40:9–11; Lev 8:10), a vivid example of the temporal overlapping that characterizes much of the material in these sections (7:1). Detailed descriptions are provided for the offerings from the leaders of the tribes (cf. 1:5–15) given to the Levites for the maintenance of the Tabernacle (7:2–9) and for the offerings to be given for the dedication of the altar (vv. 10–88). After these offerings were provided by the tribal

---

15 It should be noted that this final requirement is similar to the restriction regarding contact with the dead that was placed upon the high priest (Lev 21:1–4), an indication of the sacrality of the vow.

16 For a discussion of this blessing, see P. D. Miller, Jr., "The Blessing of God. An Interpretation of Numbers 6:22–27," *Int* 29 (1975) 240–251. A discussion of the benediction discovered at Kateph Hinnom and its relationship to the benediction in Numbers is provided by B. A. Levine (*Numbers 1–20*, pp. 236–244).

leaders in prescribed order, the account notes that Yahweh would speak directly with Moses from above the Ark whenever Moses entered the Tent (7:89). In the effort to establish the sanctity of the community, the authors have provided a way to insure that the maintenance of the priesthood and Tabernacle was the responsibility of each tribal unit. Likewise, the Tabernacle itself becomes the central symbol for the people, since its consecration leads to the beginning of the cultic life of the community.

Despite the ideal that the whole community was to become a "kingdom of priests," not just any Israelite held the status necessary to approach the sacred precincts of the Tabernacle, an issue that will be developed in the stories associated with the rebellions of Korah, Dathan, and Abiram (chaps. 16–17). The Tabernacle itself was to be guarded by the Levites, who are now dedicated and able to perform their duties (8:5–26; cf. 3:1–51). Their special status is confirmed by the notice that they are to be separated from the midst of Israel to belong to Yahweh alone. They are to be "completely dedicated" (*nĕtûnîm nĕtûnîm*) to Yahweh as substitutes for the first-born of Israel (cf. 3:9–12; Exod 13:2; 34:19–20; Deut 15:19–23). With the completion of this dedication ceremony, the camp is one step closer to being ready to move, since provisions for the safe transportation of the Tabernacle have been concluded.

The episodic nature of the narration becomes quite apparent with the notice in 9:1 that the upcoming events occurred in the first month of the second year after the Israelites left Egypt. That places the celebration of the Passover (vv. 2–14) a full month *earlier* than the events recounted in Numbers 1–8, the beginnings of which were placed in the second month of the second year (1:1). Rather than to assume that the final editors simply erred in the dating of this section, since it is obviously out of place *vis-à-vis* the other events narrated, one might understand it as another episode, connected to an otherwise synchronic narrative which itself understood the divine revelation at Sinai to be somewhat simultaneous. For the modern critic reading these stories as though they were meant to be read together and their various data compared, this is problematic. From another perspective, the effort to dissolve chronology into mythography fits the religious functions of the writers quite well.[17] In response to Yahweh's command, Israel celebrates the Passover on the fourteenth day of the first month (9:2–4).

Interestingly, simultaneity does not mean that all remains static. As becomes clear in 9:6–14, it is possible to modify the "original" regulations

---

17 As Rashi emphasizes in his commentary on this verse, "there is no chronological order in Torah" (*'ên sēder mûqdām ûmĕ'ûḥār battôrâ; cf. b. Pesaḥ* 6b).

regarding the celebration of the Passover (cf. Exodus 12) to provide for those unable to participate at the specified time due to some type of unavoidable cultic impurity, e.g., contact with a corpse. Such modifications, however, are presented within the context of the continuation of Yahweh's revelation through Moses. Before he is able to answer, Moses directs those who have requested that some provision be made in special situations to "stay here until I hear what Yahweh commands concerning you" (*'imdû wĕ'ešmĕ'â mah-yĕṣawweh yhwh lākem;* v. 8). Whatever his exalted status in the community, Moses remains simply an intermediator between Yahweh and the various elements composing the people. The new legislation allows for the celebration of the Passover by those unclean or on a distant journey on the fourteenth day of the second month (9:10–12). Modified in this way, the instructions would be binding on both resident alien and native born (9:14). Additionally, the placement of this section in non-chronological order allows for the passage of time in the previous narrative so that all of Israel might have had the opportunity to celebrate the only Passover observed during the period in the wilderness.

Fittingly, the celebration of the Passover in Numbers is a precursor to the journeying forth of the camp from Sinai, a function that parallels its role and placement in the story of the exodus. Further preparations for initial movement away from Sinai are given in 9:15–23, which returns to the narrative description of Yahweh's presence descending upon the newly erected Tent (Exod 40:36–38; cf. Num 7:1). Whenever the "cloud" (*'ānān*), which appeared over the Tent at night "like the appearance of fire" (*kĕmar'ēh-'ēš;* v. 15), would move, Israel would embark; whenever it stopped, Israel would encamp. The movement of the camp would be completely subjected to the movements of Yahweh. Ultimately, it would be he who would lead them along the way to their land,[18] since the movement of the cloud is equated with "the order of Yahweh" (*'al-pî yhwh;* 9:18 [2x]; 20 [2x]; 23 [3x]). All that remained to be completed before the journey began was to make two silver trumpets to assemble the people for the march (10:1–6). These would signal the camp to move out in the specified formation. They were also to be sounded in battle once the people entered the land, so that Yahweh might remember his people and deliver them (10:9), as well as on important festival days (v. 10).

---

[18] Earlier in the narratives, this role has been played by the "messenger" (*mal'āk*) of Yahweh (Exod 14:19; 23:20, 23; 32:34; 33:2). Prior to the erection and consecration of the Tent/Tabernacle, Yahweh himself did not dwell in the midst of the people. With the completion of the instructions at Sinai, Yahweh's presence replaced the need for an intermediary figure.

II. From Sinai to Kadesh: The Community Disintegrates

On the twentieth day of the second month of the second year after they
left Egypt (10:11), a mere nineteen days after the census was taken (1:1)
and less than two months after the erection of the Tabernacle (Exod 40:17),
the cloud moved from upon the Tent, signifying the beginning of the
journey toward the land. From Sinai, Israel journeys to the "wilderness of
Paran" (Num 10:12)[19] in accord with the order of Yahweh and in conformity with the descriptions given in Numbers 2–4. The action returns to pick
up the account of the exodus itinerary that had ended with the arrival at
Sinai in the third month after the exodus (Exod 19:1).[20] Moses' actions in
the tradition contained in Num 10:29–36 give a sudden suggestion that the
idealized camp and its relationship to Yahweh might be less than perfect.
Moses, the divinely selected intermediary and leader of Israel, asks Hobab,
his Midianite father-in-law,[21] to accompany them to the land Yahweh had
promised and to act as their guide, since "you know our encampments

19 As is commonly recognized, the itinerary is extremely difficult to follow, especially
with respect to the traditions associated with Kadesh. According to B. A. Levine, the confusion
is created by the geographical terminology introduced by the final editor of the materials (P).
Accordingly, northern Sinai is designated the "Wilderness of Paran," while the southern part
of the peninsula is called the "Wilderness of Sinai." Kadesh-Barnea, however, is located in
the "Wilderness of Zin" in the southern Negeb. Through what Levine calls "geographical 'fudging,'" the final redactors were able to have Kadesh located both in Paran and in
Zin. In this way, the P writers were able to keep Israel in the Sinai region, i.e., in the area of the
sacred mountain, for nearly the entirety of the forty-year wilderness period (*Numbers 1–20*,
pp. 53–57). Alongside this chronology is that of the other stories ("sources" [?]) that suggest
that Israel went directly to Kadesh and remained there for only a very short period (Deut 1:19,
46; 2:14). For a discussion of the various theories that have been developed concerning the relationship between the Sinai and Kadesh materials, see R. de Vaux, *The Early History of Israel*
(Philadelphia: Westminster, 1978), pp. 419–425.

20 It is widely held that the traditions associated with the stay at Sinai (Exod 19:1–Num
10:10) have been inserted into an earlier existing narrative. This older tradition would have had
a more simple itinerary: from Egypt to Kadesh, then to the promised land (J. A. Soggin, *An Introduction to the History of Israel and Judah*, p. 130).

21 As is well known, the identity of Moses' father-in-law is debated due to the differences
in the texts themselves. In Exod 2:18 his name is Reuel, while Exod 3:1; 18:1; etc. call him
Jethro. To complicate the matter further, Judg 4:11 refers to him as Hobab the Kenite. M. Weinfeld argues that Hobab the Kenite is the ally of Moses and Israel, noting that Judg 1:16 reflects
such an alliance between the Kenite/Midianite tribes and Israel. Weinfeld further supports
his theory by repointing the strange phrase *'ap ḥōbēb 'ammîm*, "also he (Yahweh) loves the
peoples," in the old poem in Deut 33:3a to read *'ap ḥōbāb 'immām*, "also Hobab was with them"
("The Tribal League at Sinai," in *Ancient Israelite Religion*, pp. 306–308). See also Chap. 6,
n. 32, and below, n. 26.

in the wilderness and you could serve as our eyes" (*yādaʿtā ḥănōtēnû bammidbār wĕhāyîtā lānû lĕʿênāyim;* 10:31). That Moses would suggest a human leader through the wilderness to the land could be understood as a rejection of Yahweh's leadership (cf. Exod 40:34–38; Num 9:15–23), though this possibility is not developed in the text. Interestingly, Hobab refuses, electing to return to his own land instead of accompanying Israel.

This brief scene ends abruptly, moving directly to the description of their journey from Sinai. Led by "the cloud of Yahweh" (*ʿănan yhwh;* 10:34; cf. Exod 40:38) and accompanied by the Ark, Israel set out on a three-day journey to find a place to camp (v. 33). Instead of developing the account of this journey, the writer(s) place the "Song of the Ark" (10:35b-36) here, noting that it was sung "whenever the Ark journeyed forth" (v. 35a).[22] The situation dissolves immediately, showing that the stability of the relationship that had been characterized by Israel's obedience from the "golden calf" incident (Exod 32: 30–35) until the present (Num 11:1–3) was only a short-lived matter. "Now the people continued complaining" (11:1), though about what, precisely, is not immediately revealed. It is clear from the divine response, which was to send a devouring fire that destroyed those on the edge of the camp (v. 1), that Yahweh was not going to tolerate a continuation of the "murmurings" that had characterized the journey to Sinai (cf. Exod 14:11–12; 15:24; 16:2–3; 17:2–3). In response to the people's cry, Moses entreated Yahweh, and the fire went out (v. 2). The entire episode forms an etiology for the place, Taberah (*tabʿērâ*), for there the fire of Yahweh "had blazed" (*bāʿărâ*) at them (v. 3). One is left to wonder what would have happened to the people had Moses not interceded with Yahweh on their behalf.[23]

This brief etiology provides a fitting introduction to the stories that follow, since they address the actions of the generation that will not be allowed to enter the land toward which they are moving. The rebelliousness

---

[22] Verses 35–36 are separated in the Masoretic text from the rest of the text by a set of inverted *nuns*. This suggests that the Masoretes understood these verses as having been cited from some other source. For a discussion of this, see S. Z. Leiman, "The Inverted *Nuns* at Numbers 10:35–36 and the Book of Eldad and Medad," *JBL* 93 (1974) 348–355, and B. A. Levine, "More on the Inverted *Nuns* of Num 10:35–36," *JBL* 95 (1976) 122–124.

[23] R. C. Culley finds a punishment pattern present in the following five accounts contained in Numbers: Num 11:1–3; 11:4–35; 12:1–16; 20:1–13; and 21:4–9. Though there are variations in the roles played by the variety of characters in these stories, the pattern of wrongdoing followed by punishment is characteristic of all five ("Five Tales of Punishment in the Book of Numbers," in *Text and Tradition: The Hebrew Bible and Folklore,* ed. S. Niditch [SBLSS; Atlanta: Scholars Press, 1990], pp. 25–34).

of the people, already suggested by the request to Hobab that he be Israel's guide, is now developed more fully. In Num 11:4–35, two important themes regarding the nature of the community are combined: the issues of obedience and authority. The "rabble" (*'ăsapsūp*) of the people began wishing for meat (v. 4), since all they had now was manna (v. 6; cf. Exod 16:1–36). Naturally, upon hearing the complaints that centered on how much better things had been in Egypt (v. 5), Yahweh became angry with the people (v. 10; cf. 11:1). Unlike the previous incident where the punishment was immediate, a new element is introduced. Though one might have expected some notice of punishment followed by intercession by Moses, what is recorded is a spirited complaint from Moses himself, asking that Yahweh slay him if he is not willing to help and relieve the burden from his shoulders (vv. 11–15; cf. Exod 18:13–26; Deut 1:9–18). In response to this protest, Yahweh directs Moses to gather seventy elders and officers of Israel at the Tent. There he will take some of the spirit that was upon Moses and place it upon them so that they will be qualified to help (11:17).[24]

Before this event is recounted, a transition is made back to the previous episode. The people are to be sanctified so that Yahweh may give them meat in response to their request (v. 18). That this is not the response the "rabble" had desired is indicated by Yahweh's decree that the people would eat meat "until it comes out of your nose" (*'ad 'ăšer-yēṣē' mē'appěkem;* v. 20). This is because the people had rejected Yahweh by asking why they had left Egypt, the single event that had established Yahweh's claim upon them and had given them the opportunity to become a special people. Two very important roles concerning authority are emphasized here: the claim and power of Yahweh over his people and the role and importance of Moses. Certainly Yahweh could have endowed the seventy with some degree of his spirit without taking it from Moses. Instead, because Moses' spirit is shared with them, the emphasis is placed on the abundance of Yahweh's spirit which Moses had been granted. Not surprisingly, when Yahweh placed some of Moses' spirit upon the seventy, "they began to prophesy, but did not continue" (*wayyitnabbě'û wělō' yāsāpû;* v. 25). Clearly, the possession of the spirit brought about a sudden change in status that had a visible effect upon the activities of the actors.[25]

24 The reference to the bestowal of a portion of the spirit upon the seventy selected men is important in that it makes clear that the controlling fact in the authority of all—priest or prophet—is the presence and power of Yahweh, a fact that will be developed in the following episodes.

25 Critical to the concept of prophecy is that the prophet acts in ways that are associated with the very role and status of the prophet. For cross-cultural examples of the importance

The power ascribed to Yahweh reaches beyond the immediate environs of the Tabernacle where the people had been convened (vv. 16, 24). Two of the seventy, Eldad and Medad, who had stayed in the camp, also received some of the spirit and "began to prophesy in the camp" (*wayyitnabbĕ'û bammaḥăneh;* v. 26). When Joshua asked Moses to stop them, Moses replied with the wish that Yahweh would put his spirit on all the people and make them prophets (*nĕbî'îm;* v. 29). Far from being jealous for his position, Moses was zealous for his god and his people. Through the spirit could come sanctification, and that would lead to the insurance of Yahweh's presence, which, in turn, would lead to sanctification. Thus, a nation of people specially endowed with the spirit of Yahweh would be able to become a "holy nation" and a "kingdom of priests."

With the resolution of Moses' problem concerning governance, the narrative returns to the complaint that had raised Yahweh's ire. Yahweh provides the people with meat, again in the form of quail (11:31–32). He was still angry with them because of their rebelliousness and struck down a large number of them, thus creating an etiology for the place name, Qibroth Hattavah, "the graves of craving" (*qibrôt hatta'ăwâ*), after those buried there (v. 34; cf. v. 4). The journey then is resumed. The points of the story are clear: obedience brings rewards; rebellion brings punishment. The community has returned to the types of actions that typified the human-divine relationship of failure to obey and trust Yahweh that had become a characteristic before Sinai. Would they reform on the journey or would the paradoxical nature of the relationship between Yahweh and Israel continue?

This incident of the failure of the people is followed immediately by the account of another challenge to Moses, this time from Aaron and their sister Miriam (cf. Exod 15:20), with respect to his Cushite wife.[26] It is interesting to speculate as to the reasons for noting that Moses' wife was from outside the circle of Israel. While it is clear from other materials (Ezra, Nehemiah) that such exogamous relationships were forbidden, there also existed traditions that allowed for their occurrence, such as those reflected

---

of such stereotypical behavior, see R. R. Wilson, *Prophecy and Society in Ancient Israel,* pp. 62–66.

26 Exactly what the issue concerning Moses' marriage to the Cushite woman was is never given. It is unclear if she is to be identified with Zipporah, his Midianite wife. F. M. Cross, however, argues that the term *kūš* originally applied to one group within what he designates the "Midianite league" and, along with the byform *kūšān,* is used to designate a south Transjordanian district. Hence, Cross suggests that the woman is to be identified with Zipporah and that the issue being addressed is the "mixed" blood of the Mushite branch of the priesthood (*Canaanite Myth and Hebrew Epic,* p. 204). See also Chap. 6, n. 33.

in Ruth. The issue here, however, is one of divine mediation, not marriage. If there is an endogamy/exogamy issue underlying this story, it has been re-placed by another issue. The challenge is clear: "Has Yahweh spoken only with Moses? Has he not also spoken with us?" (12:2). The issue, one might note, is two-fold. First of all, the preceding story of the prophetic activities of the seventy males selected from Israel demonstrates that divine revela-tion was not restricted to Moses. Despite the fact that Miriam herself could bear the designation "prophetess" (Exod 15:20), her status, like that of the seventy, was different from that of Moses. What would distinguish Moses from the others is the mode of revelation. While Yahweh might reveal his will and directions through various intermediaries, only with Moses did he speak directly, i.e., "mouth to mouth" (*peh 'el-peh;* v. 8), a closeness re-inforced by the notice that Moses "looks upon the likeness of Yahweh" (*těmūnat yhwh yabbîṭ;* v. 8).

The special status of Moses, standing as he does as the paradigm of the prophet (Deut 18:18–22), is defended beyond doubt. What remains is the punishment to be administered by Yahweh for the challenge of his interme-diator. Miriam, and not Aaron, is afflicted immediately with scale-disease, and, despite Moses' intercession on her behalf, Yahweh declares that she must be separated from the camp for seven days, as was anyone who was found to be unclean (vv. 11–14).[27] As noted above with the census, it is ap-parent that the major roles in the development and leadership of the com-munity were to belong to males.[28] The priesthood, led by the paradigmatic Aaron, escapes punishment, just as it had in the case of the "golden calf," despite his apparent central role in the crisis.

Despite the interludes in the movement of the people, the basic thrust of this section of Numbers deals with the motion toward the promised land. The way in which the fulfillment of this promise will be affected by this continually rebellious group is exemplified by the story presented in 13:1–14:45, which illustrates the complete dissolution of the relationship between Yahweh and the exodus generation. To prepare the way for the entry into the land, an act that would complete the process of developing the ethnic identity of the people, since ethnicity, like nationhood, is tied

[27] A recurring motif that ties a number of episodes together is the anger of Yahweh that characterizes his response to the variety of failures on the part of Israel (11:1, 10, 33; 12:9; 25:3; 32:10; 32:13).

[28] A strong case can be made that Miriam may once have played an important leadership role in the traditions associated with the wilderness. For references, see R. J. Burns, "Miriam," *ABD* IV, 869–870.

closely to the concept of land, Moses dispatched twelve spies (13:1–16).[29] After a forty-day investigation, they returned to the people in the Wilderness of Paran at Kadesh (v. 26)[30] and gave their report (vv. 27–29). The initial report tells of the strength of the inhabitants of the land and their fortified cities. When Caleb urged an immediate attack, the other spies disagreed and gave a report designed to discredit the land's desirability (vv. 30–33). The people immediately went into mourning (14:1) and again began to murmur against Moses and Aaron, wishing that they had died in Egypt, a place to which they even expressed the desire to return (14:2–4). Upon hearing the people's response, Moses, Aaron, Joshua, and Caleb themselves mourn.

Now Joshua and Caleb insist that this bounteous land can be conquered since Yahweh is with them, thus turning the issue into one of obedience to Yahweh's demands (14:7–9). Israel, however, acted in a manner that can only be understood as a complete rejection of the leadership that had been appointed by Yahweh. They decided to stone them and, no doubt, would have if Yahweh's glory had not suddenly appeared over the Tent (14:10). Given the patterned response of rebellion followed immediately by punishment that characterized the preceding stories, one expects the same here. This is threatened, but in a different form. Yahweh proclaims that because the people continue to reject him and refuse to believe in him, despite all the wondrous deeds he has performed on their behalf (14:11), he will send a plague upon them and "I will dispossess him" (*wĕʾôrīšennû;* v. 12). But of Moses he proclaims, "And I will make you a great nation, stronger than he" (*wĕʾeʿĕśeh ʾōtĕkā lĕgôy-gādôl wĕʿāṣûm mimmennû;* v. 12).[31] The paradoxical nature of the divine is again clearly revealed, for no sooner does he determine to end his relationship with this people whom he has

[29] The freedom of the author(s) to manipulate the materials they were constructing to address their needs is revealed by the reference in 13:16 to Moses' renaming Hoshea, son of Nun, the spy selected from Ephraim (13:8), Joshua. A reflection of this tradition is found in Deut 32:44, where reference is made to Hoshea, son of Nun. Prior to this, Joshua has been mentioned only seven times in the Tetrateuchal materials (Exod 17:9, 10, 13; 24:13; 32:17; 33:11; Num 11:28).

[30] On the geographical problems associated with locating Kadesh in the Wilderness of Paran, see above, n. 19.

[31] It is interesting to note that the promise to Moses here appears to be a combination of the earlier promise recounted in Exod 32:10b, "I will make you into a great nation" (*wĕʾeʿĕśeh ʾōtĕkā lĕgôy gādôl*), and the reference to that event in Deut 9:14, where Yahweh is quoted as saying "I will make you into a nation mightier and more numerous than he" (*wĕʾeʿĕśeh ʾōtĕkā lĕgôy-ʿāṣûm wārāb mimmennû*).

chosen, but who are unwilling to trust in his direction or follow his word, than Moses intercedes, convincing him not to carry out his pronouncement (14:13–19).

Yahweh's pronouncement, however, reveals a way to maintain his covenantal relationship with Israel while punishing the entirety of the people for their failure. According to Moses' request, he forgives the people for their deed (vv. 19–20), but swears by his own name that none of those who witnessed his great deeds and signs in Egypt or in the wilderness and who tested him "these ten times" (zeh ʿeśer pĕʿāmîm, 14:22) would be allowed to see the land which he had promised to their fathers (14:24). The entirety of that generation, excepting Caleb (14:24) and Joshua (14:30), would die in the wilderness. Yahweh simply decided that "this evil congregation" (ʿēdâ hārāʿâ hazzōʾt; v. 26) would perish and that their children would inherit the land which they had rejected (14:31). To insure that this would happen, the group would be forced to wander in the wilderness for forty years, one year for each day the spies had spent in the promised land (14:33–34; cf. 13:25). Those spies who had argued against Joshua and Caleb (13:30–33) were killed by a plague in the presence of Yahweh (14:36–38).

To emphasize further the failure of this generation to understand that their very existence and identity were dependent upon Yahweh's protection and presence, and that this was directly connected to their obedience to all that had been given them at Sinai, the people acted in a totally inappropriate manner to the proclamation and decided to launch an attack to enter the land (14:40). Though they mourned when Moses announced Yahweh's decision (v. 39), and though they admitted that they had sinned ("for we have sinned" [kî hāṭāʾnû; v. 40]), they clearly failed to understand the implications of their misdeeds. Moses warned them that Yahweh would not be with them in their attack because it was in violation of his command (14:41–43), but the people attacked anyway without Moses or the Ark (v. 44). They were beaten all the way back to a place called Hormah, "Destruction" (ḥormâ).[32]

The complete rejection of the generation that was included in the census of Numbers 1 constitutes what may be understood as a unified episode that could stand independently of its surrounding narrative. Its heuristic value, especially for the generation "returning" from "exile" and claiming a

---

32 Hormah appears again in Num 21:1–3, where Israel defeats its Canaanite king. There, however, the battle is a defensive one that they are able to win, because, in contrast to the present account, there they behave in accord with Yahweh's commands.

right to the land, should not be overlooked. Jerusalem and Judah, though less densely populated after the "exile," were far from uninhabited. Certainly those who had remained in the land those fifty to sixty years, and their ancestors, felt that they had a claim to the land also. Yet it was the people who had not been taken into "exile" who represented the generation whose sinful actions had been responsible for the loss of the Temple and the city. What more powerful way to convey the rejection of an entire generation of people, while retaining one's select status, than to show how Yahweh himself had once rejected an entire generation, transferring his promise to another.

As though to begin preparing this next generation, the story of the rejection of the original group is followed by a series of cultic instructions which, though somewhat varied, present an interesting contrast with the rebellion accounts. In 15:1–16, instructions are given for cereal offerings and libations that were required with animal sacrifices to be performed when they entered the land, making it very clear which generation is being addressed. The offerings to accompany the first fruits were also directed toward the entry into the land (15:17–21). Sacrifices to atone for inadvertent offenses, both communal and individual, were delineated (15:22–31), with the notice that anyone who acted "in defiance" (*běyād rāmâ*) would be "cut off" from his people (vv. 30–31).[33] This had been the sin and would be the fate of the exodus generation. The sacrality of Yahweh's commands is further underlined by the episode of the man caught violating the Sabbath (15:32–36), a sin that brought the death penalty. Finally, to remind Israel constantly of "all Yahweh's commandments" (*kol-miṣwōt yhwh;* v. 39) and so that "you might be holy to your god" (*wihyîtem qĕdōšîm lēʾlōhêkem;* v. 40), all Israelites were to wear tassels of purple thread at the corners of their garments (15:37–38).

For purposes of instruction, there can never be too many examples that clarify the divine selection of one group over another. Such is the case with the account of the rebellion of Korah, Dathan, and Abiram (16:1–35), the results of which are recounted in 17:1–28.[34] Korah, a Levite from the clan

---

[33] For a discussion of the variety of interpretations given to this punishment and a list of the crimes for which this is prescribed, see above, Chap. 6, n. 62, and Chap. 7, n. 50.

[34] The standard source analysis of this story uncovers two originally separate accounts that have been edited into the present composite narrative. The account of a rebellion of Dathan and Abiram and the Reubenites (cf. Deut 11:6) originally belonged to the JE epic. Korah's rebellion was taken from the "Priestly" materials. In the former, the challenge was directed at Moses, while the latter was a challenge to the authority of Aaron. According to F. M. Cross, the

of Kohath, along with Dathan and Abiram, from Reuben, gathered some two hundred and fifty "chiefs of the congregation, selected by the assembly, men of renown" (*něśî'ê 'ēdâ qěrî'ê mô'ēd 'anšê-šem;* 16:2), and assembled them against Moses and Aaron (16:3). Their complaint seems to be composed of several parts. First, they seem to have reacted against the purity/ holiness requirements mentioned in 15:40, when they assert that "all the congregation, all of them, are holy/sanctified" (*kol-hā'ēdâ kullām qědōšîm;* 16:3), noting that the proof of this is that Yahweh is in their midst. By requiring more, Moses and Aaron have gone too far. But, as the rebels have failed to understand, the states of holiness and purity are determined not by humans but by Yahweh. If Moses and Aaron are exalted in the community, it is because of Yahweh's choice, not because of anything innately special about them. The results of the rebellion make it clear that challenges to the priestly line selected and established by Yahweh would bring only disaster.

In response to the claim of holiness, Moses answers that Yahweh would reveal who was holy (*haqqādôš*) and who would be allowed to draw near his presence in service (16:5). The central role of service at the sanctuary, i.e., access to the divine will, constitutes a second area of the rebels' complaint. The group was to assemble on the next day with firepans and incense at the Tent; there Yahweh would choose which one was "holy" (16:7). Because they were seeking the priestly status reserved for Aaron and were rejecting the special Levitical status they already enjoyed, their acts were understood as a challenge to Yahweh (vv. 8–11). Dathan and Abiram introduce a third complaint, this one aimed explicitly at Moses and at the truthfulness of Yahweh's promise of the land. Refusing to appear when summoned, Dathan and Abiram accuse Moses of leading them out of a land "flowing with milk and honey" (*zābat ḥālāb ûděbaš;* v. 13)[35] and of failing to provide them with the promised inheritance (v. 14). Moses, naturally,

---

underlying theme of a conflict between the Mushite and Aaronid priesthoods has been pushed into the background in the final redaction of the two accounts (*Canaanite Myth and Hebrew Epic*, pp. 205–206). In its present form, it is a challenge to both Moses and Aaron. However one chooses to regard the reconstruction of independent stories, it must be admitted that the present text conveys a very different message than either of the reconstructed accounts.

35 This phrase is normally applied to the land promised by Yahweh to Israel (Exod 3:8, 17; 13:5; 33:3; Lev 20:24; Num 13:27; 14:8; 16:13–14; Deut 6:3; 11:9; 26:9, 15; 27:3; 31:20). That the rebels would apply it to the land of Egypt demonstrates the way in which they have totally misunderstood the obligations of the human-divine relationship and have abrogated their rights to be included among those who would inherit the promise.

pleads his innocence before Yahweh (16:15). Clearly, the following events vindicate Moses and Aaron from such a variety of challenges.

When the groups had assembled at the Tent as directed, "the glory of Yahweh appeared to the whole congregation" (v. 19). The resolution of the issue would be public in nature. When Yahweh instructs Moses and Aaron to separate themselves from the group so that he might destroy them instantly (16:20–21), Moses and Aaron intercede, asking if the entire group should be the object of his wrath when only one person had sinned.[36] Apparently, Yahweh had not completely forgotten the possibility of destroying this group and transferring his promise over to Moses (14:11–12). Again, Yahweh yields to the intercessory pleas and relents, instructing the group to retreat from the area of the tents of Korah, Dathan, and Abiram (vv. 22–24). In accord with the punishment that was announced through Moses (16: 28–30), the earth opened up and swallowed the rebels, along with all their family and belongings (16:31–34), and fire issued forth from Yahweh and devoured the two hundred and fifty followers who had offered incense. All that remained were the firepans that had been sanctified by virtue of their presentation before the deity. These were to be hammered into sheets of plating for the altar as a memorial so that no stranger, defined as "one not descended from Aaron" (*lō² mizzera² ²ahărôn;* 17:5), should ever approach Yahweh as had Korah and his group (17:1–5).

When the social fabric of a group disintegrates, there is little to provide stability. This is evidenced by the general rebellion that faces Moses and Aaron as a result of the punishment of the rebels by Yahweh. "The whole congregation of Israel" (*kol-²ădat bĕnê-yiśrā²ēl*) gathered against them with the complaint: "You have slain the people of Yahweh" (*²attem hămittem ²et-²am yhwh;* 17:6). At stake is the issue of defining the boundaries of the people, Israel. Would the people make these boundaries, deciding when and how they should be "holy," or would these decisions be made by Yahweh and enforced through his acts and those of his chosen leaders? Would this generation finally recognize that by breaking the relationship established at Sinai, it was the one ultimately responsible for the punishments it received? Again, Yahweh reveals himself to Moses and Aaron at the Tent and announces his intention to destroy the congregation (*hā²ēdâ*) at once (17:7–9).

---

[36] This, along with the question of the possibility that the righteous might play some vicarious role in the preservation of the community, was an important theme developed during the exilic period. Some of the same issues are addressed in Gen 18:23–32 (J. Van Seters, *Abraham in History and Tradition,* pp. 214–215).

So intent was Yahweh on punishment that he had already sent a plague upon the people (v. 11).

Aaron, following the directions of Moses, made expiation for the people, thus stopping the plague, but not until it had already killed 14,700 in addition to those who had died with Korah (17:11–14). It was through the actions of Aaron, i.e., the priest, that Israel had been saved from complete destruction. The following story concerning the selection of the rod of Levi which bore the name of Aaron focuses upon the divine designation of Aaron and his offspring as the only priests acceptable to Yahweh (17:16–28). Aaron's rod was to be placed in the Tent in order to remind anyone who might act rebelliously of the consequences of such deeds (vv. 27–28). These additional stories of rebellion and the continued divine affirmation of Moses and Aaron as the co-leaders of the community reinforce the order and structure given to the people at Sinai. To become a "nation of priests" and "a holy people" required a divinely designated and properly trained priesthood to instruct the people and to intercede for them when the sacrality of time and space was endangered. Without the priesthood, proper purity could not be maintained and the presence of Yahweh among his people would be threatened. The well-being of the entire community rested upon the proper performance of the cultic rituals by the sons of Aaron. It should occasion no surprise that the author(s) of these materials would reemphasize the matter of the communal obligation to support the priests and Levites with their offerings (18:1–32). Now, however, as the action begins to focus on the land and the movement toward possessing it, a new element is introduced. Unlike the other units constituting the community, neither the Aaronid priests nor the Levites would receive a portion (*ḥēleq*) or inheritance (*naḥălâ*) in the land. Rather, Yahweh and the offerings presented by the people would be their portion in the land (18: 20, 23–24).

Two important issues have been raised in the context of the continued rebellions and the punishments which have been pronounced and those that have been carried out. Would the condemnation of the entire exodus generation to die in the wilderness include Moses and Aaron? The answer to this would be given very soon (20:2–13). First, however, the issue of the danger to the purity of the camp through the actual deaths of the characters in the story needed to be addressed. In anticipation of the deaths of Miriam and Aaron (20:1, 28), and the necessity of the purification of those who would contact their bodies, the ritual of the "red heifer" for the removal of corpse contamination is described.[37] Num 19:1–10 describes the preparation of the cow and the production of the ashes that were necessary to restore the purity of those who were contaminated by contact with a corpse. The performance of the purification process follows in vv. 11–22. Failure to purify such contaminants would "defile the Tabernacle of Yahweh" (*'et-miškan yhwh timmē'*; 19:13), and any person who did so would be "cut off" from the people.

With these instructions completed, the action returns to the deeds of the people and the resolution of the issues noted above. In the first month of what evidently was to be understood as the fortieth year, the people came to the Wilderness of Sin and dwelt at Kadesh/Meribah (cf. Num 27:14; Deut 32:51; Ezek 47:19; 48:28). There Miriam died and was buried.[38] This event introduces the story of the exclusion of Moses and Aaron from the promised land that constitutes a clear parallel to an earlier story of the rebellious nature of the people (Num 20:2–13//Exod 17:1b-7). When the people find that there is no water, they bring to Moses their now common complaint about being brought out into the wilderness to die. They even express the wish that they had died with their kinspeople (vv. 3–5). Yahweh instructs Moses with respect to the appropriate actions, and, in a completely uncharacteristic manner, Moses does not follow the divine directions (20:8–11). As a result, Moses and Aaron are denied entry into the land (v. 12), providing an apt etiology for the place name, Meribah, "Place of Strife" (*mĕrîbâ;* 20:13; cf Exod 17:7).[39] The way for this had already been prepared with the references in 14:28–38 that of the entire exodus group, only Caleb and Joshua would be allowed to enter the land promised to the ancestors.

With these questions now resolved, the narrative resumes its movement toward the land. The preparations for the entry begin with the request

---

[37] For a discussion of this ritual as a form of purification offering, see J. Milgrom, "The Paradox of the Red Cow (Num xix)," *VT* 31 (1981) 62–72, and *Leviticus 1–16*, pp. 270–278.

[38] The lack of any elaboration on the death of Miriam is interesting, given the fact that there is evidence suggesting that she had played an important role in Israel according to some traditions. For a discussion of these, see P. Trible, "Bringing Miriam Out of the Shadows," *BibRev* 5 (1989) 14–24, 34. Similarly, however, there is no extended treatment of the death of Aaron.

[39] The question of Aaron's sin is interesting, for he seems to have been condemned here purely by association. W. H. Propp notes that in this way an explanation was provided for Aaron's failure to enter the land while, at the same time, Aaron himself remained free of any misdeed against the divine ("The Rod of Aaron and the Sin of Moses" *JBL* 107 [1988] 19–26).

for passage through the land of Edom which is emphatically denied by the
Edomite king (20:14–21).[40] Unable to gain permission, the group journeys
around Edom, moving from Kadesh, the site at which they had arrived
in Num 13:26 (called *midbar pā'rān*)[41] to Mt. Hor. There Aaron died and
was buried; the priesthood passed to his son Eleazar (20:23–28). There
would be no disruption in the priestly line. The sons of Aaron would preserve the purity of the people and the sanctity of the Tabernacle. All that
remained now was the completion of the story with the movement into the
promised land.

III. From Kadesh to Moab: Preparations for the Conquest

How Israel would take the land promised to them now becomes a more
pronounced focus of the narratives. With the cultus given shape and the
priesthood established (now into a second generation), the people could
begin to delineate their identity in more definitive terms *vis-à-vis* the land.
An example of the power of Yahweh's presence is provided by the story
of the defeat of the Canaanite king of Arad, who attacked the Israelites and
took some of them captive (21:1–3). When Israel made a vow to Yahweh
that they would completely destroy the cities of the king if Yahweh would
give them victory, they were successful, destroying them and their cities
and providing an etiology for the place name Hormah, "Destruction."[42]
Israel's success, now as always, would be dependent upon its relationship
to Yahweh. It was this that provided the foundation and definition of the
people and its destiny.

That this somewhat anecdotal account should be followed by another
simply drives home the point concerning Israel's dependence upon Yahweh and his appointed leader, Moses (21:4–9). On their journey around
Edom the people reiterate their complaint against Yahweh and Moses for
bringing them into the wilderness to die from a lack of food and/or water
(21:4–5; cf. 16:13; 20:5). In response to their rebelliousness, Yahweh sends

40 J. Van Seters has suggested that this section, like Num 21:21–35, is a Yahwistic expansion on a deuteronomistic original ("The Conquest of Sihon's Kingdom: A Literary Examination," *JBL* 91 [1972] 182–197, and, more recently, *The Life of Moses*, pp. 383–404).

41 On the geographical problems associated with the narratives, see above, n. 19.

42 Note that in Num 14:40–45, there is reference to Hormah in the unsuccessful attempt to
enter the land. As G. Coats notes, the present story does not form a part of the conquest traditions, but is simply an incident associated with the wilderness journey ("Conquest Traditions in
the Wilderness Theme," *JBL* 95 [1976] 183).

snakes among them, causing many to be bitten and die (v. 6). When the people admit their sin and ask Moses to intercede, Yahweh provides him with instructions that will lead to the deliverance of the people (vv. 7–9).[43] The didactic quality of the story seems clear: rebellion brings punishment and death; obedience, life and deliverance. The possession of the land promised to the fathers would be subject to the same criteria.

These lessons having been presented, the narrative returns to the journey, taking the people through the Transjordan until they arrive on the other side of the Arnon, which separated the border of Moab from the Amorites (21:10–20).[44] The journey provides the introduction to another request for passage, this time through the territory of the Amorite king Sihon (21: 21–35; cf. 20:14–21).[45] When Sihon attacks Israel at Jahaz, Israel is victorious, seizing his territory from the Arnon to the Jabbok as far as the border of Ammon, settling in Heshbon and its villages (21:23–25, 31).[46] At Edrei, Og of Bashan came out to battle against Israel and was annihilated (21:33–35; cf. Deut 3:1–3). An obedient Israel would be rewarded by Yahweh not only with victory in war but also with the land of those enemies who dared to battle against Yahweh.

---

[43] 2 Kgs 18:4 notes that Hezekiah destroyed the bronze serpent that had been made by Moses. As J. Van Seters notes, it is difficult to see how Num 21:4–9 might serve as an etiology for an image made by Moses that was subsequently destroyed in a cultic reform that received the full support of the deuteronomistic writer (*The Life of Moses*, pp. 225–226).

[44] The itinerary is interrupted by two poetic fragments, the first from the "Book of the Wars of Yahweh" (*sēper milḥāmōt yhwh;* 21:14–15), and the second, the "Song of the Well" in 21:17b-18. For a reconstruction and interpretation of the former, see D. L. Christensen, "Num 21:14–15 and the Book of the Wars of Yahweh," *CBQ* 36 (1974) 359–360. For a discussion of the itinerary, which cannot be traced with any confidence, see R. de Vaux, *The Early History of Israel*, pp. 562–564.

[45] The difficulties of establishing any criteria by which one might determine sources used in the final production of the Tetrateuchal narratives are amply illustrated by the debates over the relationship between the account of the conquest of Sihon and Og in Numbers and the account in Deuteronomy. J. Van Seters has argued strongly that the account in Num 21:21–35 is dependent upon Deut 2:24–3:11 and Judg 11:19–26 ("The Conquest of Sihon's Kingdom," 182–197; *The Life of Moses*, pp. 383–404). J. R. Bartlett, on the other hand, offers a critique of Van Seters' position and concludes exactly the opposite relationship among these texts ("The Conquest of Sihon's Kingdom: A Literary Re-examination," *JBL* 97 [1978] 347–351). As I suggest in the next chapter, the critical factor in making such judgments is not the literary evidence, but rather the model by which one makes the decisions.

[46] The "Song of Heshbon," contained in 21:27–30, contains a taunt against Moab that has occasioned much discussion. For a reconstruction of the song and a discussion of its numerous textual problems, see P. D. Hanson, "The Song of Heshbon and David's *NÎR*," *HTR* 61 (1968) 298–310. J. Van Seters emphasizes the relationship of this passage to the parallel in Jer 48: 45–46 and finds little reason to regard the song as archaic (*The Life of Moses*, pp. 398–402).

Now encamped on the plains of Moab on the other side of the Jordan from Jericho, Israel was poised for its conquest of the land (Num 22:1; cf. Deut 1:1–5). Not every king, however, chose war as the best way to deal with the threat that this massive group presented. Balak, king of Moab, chose instead to place a curse upon the very Israel whom Yahweh had blessed. For this purpose, he summons Balaam, son of Beor, to come and curse Israel for him (22:2–7).[47] Clearly unknown to Balak is Balaam's allegiance to Yahweh and Yahweh's control over the events that were to unfold. Before Balaam would answer the summons of Balak, he consulted with Yahweh (22:8), foreshadowing the fact that the role he was about to play was not that of a professional diviner but, rather, that of a Yahwistic prophet.[48] Initially, Yahweh instructs him not to go (22:9–14), telling him that "he [Israel] is blessed" (*kî bārûk hû̕;* 22:12). When Balak sends another group to summon him, Balaam informs them that no matter what Balak might offer him, he can do only what "Yahweh my god" (*yhwh ̕ĕlōhāy;* v. 18) instructs him to say (22:15–21). Clearly, for Balaam and the author(s) of these materials, Yahweh is in control of all the ensuing activities (22:8, 13, 19; 23:5–6, 12, 16).[49]

This time when Balaam consults Yahweh (22:19), he is instructed to go, "but you may do only what I tell you" (*wĕ̕ak ̕et-dābār ̕ăšer-̕ădabbēr ̕ēlêka ̕ōtô ta̕ăśeh;* v. 20). Under these divine constraints, Balaam accompanies them to Moab and toward his encounter with Israel.[50] As soon as Balaam meets Balak, he informs him that he will speak only what God puts

47 P. J. Budd presents a balanced overview of the variety of attempts to analyze the sources comprising the Balaam cycle in Numbers 22–24 and their lack of unanimity (*Numbers,* pp. 256–265). Whatever its origins, this collection of stories is connected to the present context of the itinerary and not by any necessary connection to the previous events. Though Deut 23: 5–6 reflects a tradition of Yahweh's changing Balaam's attempt to curse Israel into a blessing, the deuteronomic writer does not connect this with the events narrated in Deut 2:24–3:11 (cf. Josh 24:9–10; Neh 13:2). Num 31:8, 16 links Balaam to the apostasy at Peor (Num 25: 1–19), while Josh 13:22 associates his death with an Israelite battle with Midian.

48 Compare Num 22:8, 18, 19, 20, 35, 38; 23:3, 5, 12, 15, 16, 17, 26; 24:13 with the depiction of the prophet in Deut 18:18–22.

49 The late eighth-century BCE texts discovered at Deir ʿAllā, which contain references to the pronouncements of one Balaam, son of Beor, who is called a "seer of the gods" (*ḥzn ̕lhn*), indicate that there might have been an east Jordanian tradition associated with the figure of Balaam. They do not suggest, however, that the tradition is old, but only that it was known to other cultural groups. On the Balaam tradition at Deir ʿAllā, see J. A. Hackett, "Some Observations on the Balaam Tradition at Deir ʿAllā," *BA* 49 (1986) 216–222.

50 The story of Balaam's ass (22:22–35) interrupts the flow of the story and seems to contradict the commission from Yahweh to go to Moab. While it is possible to regard it as a conflation from another source or a supplement from a later period, it might also be possible to

in his mouth (22:38), preparing the way for the introduction of the oracles he will deliver.[51] Three times Balaam prepares to receive an oracle, offering sacrifices to the deity (23:1–6, 13–17; 23:27–24:2). Only after the third oracle is the patterned presentation broken (24:10–14) when it returns to reiterate the words addressed to the messengers in 22:18 (24:12–13) that he would be able to do only what Yahweh commanded. These actions are broken by four short oracles, each of which places a blessing upon Israel (23:7–10, 18–24; 24:3–9, 15–24). In his final pronouncement, Balaam foretells the subjugation of Moab by Israel "in the latter days" (*bĕʾaḥărît hayyāmîm;* 24:14) before he returns to his home. From the perspective of the stories of Balaam, Israel had been singled out by Yahweh as his special possession which he had blessed. No human agency could change that against the will of the divine. Even the foreigner, Balaam, is presented as recognizing this.

No sooner is the special nature of Israel reemphasized than an account is presented underlining the importance of fulfilling the obligations placed upon Israel by Yahweh. Israel now is depicted as "playing the harlot" (*znh*) with the women of Moab and taking part in the worship of Moabite gods (25:1–2).[52] That Israel had chosen to yoke itself to the Baal of Peor (or Baal Peor), thus rupturing the covenantal alliance completely, led to Yahweh's immediate anger (25:3). To avert the divine wrath, Moses is commanded to execute[53] "all the leaders of the people" (*kol-rāʾšê hāʿām;* 25:4), clearly indicating that those who were to be responsible for the people had failed in the duties entrusted to them. Moses then orders the execution of all those who had "yoked themselves to Baal of Peor" (25:5; cf. v. 3).

---

understand it as a variation on the stories associated with Balaam, preserved here to be used as those who were responsible for presenting the texts desired.

51 For a presentation of the numerous textual problems associated with the oracles of Balaam and an attempt to reconstruct the text, see W. F. Albright, "The Oracles of Balaam," *JBL* 63 (1944) 207–233. Though Albright regarded the oracles as very archaic, their date remains debated among scholars. What is clear is that whatever traditional materials might be contained in the oracles, in their present context they date from a time much later than that in which they are placed. As with the earlier materials relating to Edom (Num 20:14–21), the account concerning a kingdom of Moab presupposes a time much later than that presumed by the chronology of the narrative.

52 The connection between sexual activity with non-Israelite women and the worship of foreign gods is implied by such passages as Deut 7:3–4, Exod 34:15–16, and Lev 20:5–6. The possibility of religious apostasy presents a consistent threat to the ideological boundaries constructed by the author(s) of these materials.

53 The precise meaning of the verb *yāqaʿ* remains unclear. It occurs in a similar context in 2 Sam 21:6, 9. For discussions of the possible meanings, see the commentaries.

Some insight into the nature of the people's misconduct is provided by
the story of Zimri, the Simeonite, and Kozbi, a Midianite woman, that is
related in 25:6–19. When Phineas, son of Eleazar, discovered Zimri and
Kozbi engaged in an act of intercourse at the Tent of Meeting, he took his
spear and ran the two of them through, stopping not only their activity but
also the plague that had begun among the people (25:6–9; cf. 17:13).
Clearly, the divine punishment had begun immediately, for as Moses was
ordering the execution of those who had sinned, a plague had already
broken out, killing some twenty-four thousand before it was stopped by
Phineas' act.[54] For this, Phineas and his offspring were granted an "eternal
covenant of priesthood" (*bĕrît kĕhunnat ʿôlam;* v. 13), an act on Yahweh's
part that both exonerates the priesthood of Aaron from any misconduct
in this matter and insures the continuation of the line through Eleazar's offspring. Though the community might continue to fail to fulfill its responsibilities in the relationship between Israel and Yahweh, the priesthood
remained as the key to leadership over the people.

But such a severe breach of the covenantal obligations as the worship
of other gods required more than simply a plague from Yahweh.[55] It required the reestablishment of the community as a whole. This would be performed through the completion of another census (26:1–56). Like the initial
one, this muster included all those males of military age, i.e., twenty years
and up (26:2; 1:3), of which there were a total of 601,730 (26:51; compare
603,550 of 1:46). It would be to the members of this new generation that
the land would be allotted according to tribal size (vv. 52–56). A second
Levitical census, totalling 23,000, was also taken (26:57–65; cf. 3:1–51).
Crucial to understanding the complete expiration of the generation that left
Egypt is the notice in 26:63–65 that not one single member of the group
numbered by Moses and Aaron at Sinai was included, apart from Moses,
Caleb, and Joshua.

As with the former census, the implication is clear that those who
would inherit the rights of ownership of the land would be male. The story
of the five daughters of Zilophehad of Manasseh raises the question of
females' rights to inherit land (27:1–11). Their father had died without leaving any male offspring. In order to preserve the name of their father, the
daughters came to Moses and Eleazar and all the congregation at the Tent

[54] The tradition of a plague at Peor is reflected in Ps 106:28–31.

[55] Despite the numerous instances of positive relationships between Israel and Midian, the
actions of Kozbi occasion the proclamation of war against the Midianites (25:16–18), an event
narrated in Num 31:1–54.

of Meeting (27:1–2) and requested that they be given a possession (*'ăḥuzzâ;* v. 4) among their father's brothers.[56] After consulting Yahweh, Moses pronounced the ordinance that when a man dies with no sons, the inheritance goes to his daughter (27:8). If there is no daughter, then it goes to his brothers (v. 9); if there are no brothers, then it goes to his father's brothers (v. 10). If none of these conditions exists, then the inheritance should go to the nearest kin of the deceased (v. 11). Thus, the divine pronouncement made clear allowance for the inheritance of property by females, but only with restrictions. This possibility is further curtailed in the final chapter of Numbers, where the story is continued. In 36:1–13 the heads of the tribe of Manasseh address Moses and the leaders of the people in response to the decision given in 27:1–8. At issue is the potential loss of tribal holdings if the woman should marry outside of her clan.[57] Moses, by Yahweh's command, agrees with their concerns (36:5) and adds the resolution that the daughters of Zilophehad are free to marry whomever they choose, but *only* within their father's tribe. In this way the inheritance of the Israelite tribes would not be transferred from one to another (36:5–9) and tribal integrity would be maintained. The daughters of Zilophehad concede to these directions, and the possessions of Manasseh are retained (vv. 10–12). As noted earlier, the rights given to women in Israel were at all points subject to the approval and restrictions of the male power structure.[58]

Immediately following the initial decision concerning inheritance rights, the narrative turns to the issue of Moses' successor (27:12–23).

---

[56] It is interesting to note the reference to the fact that their father had not taken part in the rebellion of Korah but rather had died for his own sins, i.e., as part of the exodus generation (27:3). According to J. Weingreen, it is possible that such a profession of innocence was part of the legal process of the transfer of property ("The Case of the Daughters of Zilophehad," *VT* 16 [1966] 518–522).

[57] On the difficulties associated with this section, see N. K. Gottwald, *The Tribes of Yahweh,* pp. 265–267.

[58] No clearer indicator of this secondary status could be provided than that contained in 30:2–17, which addresses the issue of vows taken by an Israelite woman. Since the fulfillment of vows obligated the person making the vow to present certain offerings to Yahweh (cf. Lev 7:16; Num 15:3; 29:39), the act of taking vows entailed certain financial responsibilities. In the case of widows or divorced women, the vows were binding, as was the case with a man's vows (30:3, 10). If, however, the woman was still living with her father or was married, the binding nature of the vow was determined by the male. In these two cases, the father or husband had the right of accepting or of invalidating the vows taken by the dependent woman (30:4–14). On the role of religious vows in the lives of women in the ancient Near East, see K. van der Toorn, *From Her Cradle to Her Grave: The Role of Religion in the Life of the Israelite and the Babylonian Woman* (The Biblical Seminar, 23; Sheffield: JSOT, 1994), pp. 97–99.

Moses is commanded to go up on Mt. Arbaim to see the land that Yahweh has given Israel. After he sees the land, he will die, as did Aaron (27:13; cf. 20:23–29). In 27:15–21, Yahweh oversees the appointment of Joshua to succeed Moses. While one expects the account of Moses' death to follow immediately upon the appointment of his successor,[59] such is hardly the case. Before that event will be narrated, a number of addenda are appended to the narrative (chapters 28–36), as well as the majority of the book of Deuteronomy. Their present position in the book seems to suggest very strongly that the author(s) of this section, at least, were quite unconcerned with constructing any kind of narrative coherence. Instead, since there were matters of importance to be included, they were arranged in simple consecutive fashion, further suggesting that they were never intended to be understood as constructing a unified, consistent narrative account.

Num. 28:1–30:1 presents a supplemental list of offerings following yet another variation of the yearly cultic calendar.[60] These commands are addressed to the entire community and have been placed here to insure their Mosaic authority alongside other such lists (28:6). The centrality and importance of the Temple is underlined by the financial responsibilities that the community would bear for the upkeep of the cultus once they were in the land. This section concentrates on those offerings that were to be presented in addition to the daily sacrifices that were required and listed in vv. 3–8. The special offerings for each of the major religious celebrations are enumerated: Sabbath (vv. 9–10); the first day of the month (vv. 11–15); Passover (vv. 16–25); First Fruits/Weeks (vv. 26–31); the first day of the seventh month (Trumpets; 29:1–6); Day of Atonement (vv. 7–11); and Tabernacles (vv. 12–38).

Another clear addendum to the text is the account of the war with Midian that was alluded to in 25:16–18 but not recounted.[61] The account addresses two areas: the conduct of holy war and the disposition of the spoils taken in battle. The latter point relates directly to the issue of provi-

---

59 That the death of Moses is not recounted until Deuteronomy 34 is an important clue in unraveling the problem of the composition of the Tetrateuch. It is clear that the narrative requires the death of Moses to follow quickly upon the account of the commissioning of Joshua. If one reconstructs continuous narrative sources as the underlying documents from which the final redaction of the Pentateuch was performed by an element of the "Priestly" group, as is common, then it is clear that the death of Moses has been transposed to the end of Deuteronomy (32:48–52; 34:1, 7–9). For a discussion of this, see J. Blenkinsopp, *The Pentateuch*, pp. 229–232.

60 Compare Exod 23:10–19; 34:18–26; Lev 23:1–44; Deut 16:1–17.

61 On the section dealing with the issue of vows taken by women (Num 30:2–17), see above, n. 58.

sions dedicated to the Temple and the support of the priesthood. Moses is ordered by Yahweh to avenge Israel against the Midianites because of their luring Israel away from Yahweh (cf. 25:6–19).[62] In this story, the war is commanded by Yahweh and directed by the priesthood in the person of Phineas (31:6). In the course of the war, Israel killed every adult Midianite male, including the five Midianite kings and Balaam (31:7–8). Everything else they took as spoil and returned to their camp (vv. 9–12). There they were met by an angry Moses for their failure to carry out what evidently was the order of the battle: to kill every Midianite male and every non-virgin Midianite female. In accord with Moses' instructions, the oversight was corrected (vv. 13–20).

Since this section has a distinct Priestly cast to it, it is of no surprise that the issue of corpse contamination should be addressed, since the warriors had certainly become polluted in the battle (31:19–20; cf. Lev 11:32; Num 19:18–19). The captured spoil was also purified and then divided among the warriors and the congregation (vv. 25–31). Of the great abundance captured, prescribed amounts were to be provided to the sanctuary and priesthood. Because this had been a war commanded by Yahweh and directed by the priesthood, portions of the wealth were dedicated to Yahweh, the priests, and the Levites (31:32–47), an illustration of the proper way in which war was to be conducted and the community maintained. The power of Yahweh in their midst is underlined by the notice that the leaders reported to Moses that not one single warrior had been lost in the battle (31:49), a rather phenomenal occurrence.

As a result of the victories that had been won in the Transjordan, the opportunity arose for some tribal groups to settle there. Num 32:1–42 recounts the manner in which Reuben, Gad, and half of the tribe of Manasseh settled in the area around Yazer.[63] When Reuben and Gad saw how suited Yazer (cf. 21:32) was for grazing sheep and cattle, they requested

[62] A war with five Midianite kings that was also associated with the death of Balaam is recounted in Josh 13:21–22, where it is recounted in the context of the defeat of Sihon. That the account in Numbers appears to be redactionally out of place is clear from the notice in 31:2b to Moses that he is to avenge Israel and "afterwards, you will be gathered to your people" (ʾaḥar tēʾāsēp ʾel-ʿammêkā), suggesting that an account of Moses' death was at some point associated with these events.

[63] Interestingly, Manasseh is not mentioned alongside Reuben and Gad until 32:33, though it is clearly a participant in the proceedings. It is possible that the reason for this is to be found in the fact that the mention of the "half tribe of Manasseh" (ḥāṣî šēbeṭ mĕnaššeh) clearly presumes the Cisjordanian settlement, which is not detailed until the narratives in Joshua. It is possible that this reference to that group is to be understood either as a late gloss on the present account or as an anticipation of the deuteronomistic reference.

that it be given to them (32:1–5). Moses, interestingly, was incensed at the request, understanding it as an expression of their unwillingness to cross over the Jordan and participate in the conquest of the land with their brothers. He compared their actions to those of the spies who had contributed to the loss of an entire generation by their actions (vv. 8–13; cf. 13:25–33). But Reuben and Gad replied that they were most willing to cross the river and battle for the land for the sake of their brothers. Their only request was that they be allowed to build cities to protect the women and children and cattle folds for their herds (32:16–19). In response, Moses declared that if they were to do this, then they might have these Transjordanian holdings (vv. 20–22), but if not, they would have sinned against Yahweh (v. 23). When Reuben and Gad agreed, Moses, who would not be allowed to enter the land and who would have no role in its apportionment, directed Eleazar, Joshua, and the heads of the tribes to see that they would receive these lands once they had helped their brothers in the conquest of Canaan (vv. 28–30). The story places its emphasis upon the necessity of unified action on behalf of the whole of the people, even when it does not directly concern a single tribal group. For the future of the people, at whatever time this story might be applied, the lesson is clear.[64]

A further addendum to the narratives is found in the wilderness itinerary of Num 33:1–49, which traces the stages of the journey from Egypt, beginning with Ramesses, and ending with the arrival at Shittim (vv. 3, 49), a journey which mentions some forty-two places.[65] This list of stations is followed by instructions for the possession and allotment of the land that is to take place (Num 33:50–56; compare Deut 7:1–6; 12:2–3; Exod 34:10–16). To maintain their distinctiveness and the status as a "holy nation," they are to eliminate "all the inhabitants of the land" (*kol-yōšĕbê hāʾāreṣ;* 33:52) and to destroy all their images and places of worship. With this emphasis placed on the land, it is not surprising that the account includes a

---

[64] Source criticism has found little consensus in its attempts at analyzing this particular passage. For a discussion of the composite nature of the story, see P. J. Budd, *Numbers,* pp. 337–342.

[65] Israel will remain at Shittim until they cross the river, an event that is not recounted until Josh 3:1–5:12. The problematic nature of the composition of the itinerary is illustrated by the contrasting analyses of F. M. Cross and J. Van Seters. Cross argues that Numbers 33 is the document from which the Priestly writer restructured the older JE epic narrative found in Exodus-Numbers (*Canaanite Myth and Hebrew Epic,* pp. 308–317, 321). Van Seters, on the other hand, argues that this chapter can be understood only as a late post-P text that presumes the entirety of the Pentateuch in its present form (*The Life of Moses,* pp. 153–164). One is tempted to suggest that the criteria used to make such distinctions are simply not effective.

description of the boundaries of the land of Canaan (34:1–29).[66] In preparation for the imminent conquest, the names of those who would divide the land alongside Joshua and Eleazar were given (vv. 16–29).

As far as the Tetrateuchal narrative might be envisioned, little else remained to be recounted except the actual conquest of the land. One legal matter did remain, however, and that was the establishment of the provision for cities of refuge and the cities which were to be given to the Levites, who otherwise would be given no inheritance in Canaan (35:1–34).[67] From Israel's inheritance, six cities of refuge were to be established and forty-two cities were to be provided to the Levites (35:6–8). Dimensions for the pasturage areas outside the city walls were delineated (vv. 4–5) for the legal purpose of establishing the exact extent of the city's power of possession. This was necessary for the establishment of the laws associated with the cities of refuge (35:9–34; cf. Exod 21:12–14; Deut 19:1–13; Josh 20:1–9). Anyone who had committed an accidental murder might flee to one of these six cities for safety from blood revenge and be protected there until the death of the high priest or until judgment was passed upon him by the congregation (35:9–25). The person was confined to the legal boundaries of the city, and, should he venture outside of them, he might be slain legally by the blood avenger of the murdered person (35:26–27). All of these legal provisions were to be obeyed for the simple religious reason that spilled blood pollutes and can be atoned for only by blood (35:31–33). Such pollution cannot be allowed to occur because that would endanger the presence of the divine—"for I Yahweh dwell in the midst of the Israelites" (*kî ʾănî yhwh šōkēn bĕtôk bĕnê yiśrāʾēl;* 35:34). This creates and maintains the special identity of this people now poised on the edge of the land that was promised to them. What would be expected to follow immediately is the account of the possession of that land. Instead, the reader encounters the whole of Deuteronomy.

---

66 As was the case with the previous two chapters, there is little if any agreement over the sources from which this section might have drawn or of its relative date. For the various views, see the discussion of P. J. Budd, *Numbers,* pp. 363–366.

67 For the evidence that Num 35:1–34 is dependent upon the text of Joshua 14–21 and its description of the cities to be given to the Levites, see A. G. Auld, *Joshua, Moses and the Land: Tetrateuch-Pentateuch-Hexateuch in a Generation Since 1938* (Edinburgh: T. & T. Clark, 1980), pp. 79–85.

──── ꙮ 9 ꙮ ────

Deuteronomy and the Tetrateuch: Redefining Community

I. The Death of Moses and the Creation of a Primary History?

At the conclusion of the book of Numbers, a new "Israel" that was formed by the descendants of those who had departed from Egypt stood on the plains of Moab, across from Jericho, and waited for the divine command to cross over and take the land that had been promised to their ancestors. Such a command does not occur, however, until Josh 1:1–9. As it presently stands, then, and as has frequently been recognized, the Tetrateuchal narrative is incomplete, since one would expect that it would end with the conquest of the land and the fulfillment of the promises made by Yahweh.[1] If, however, the Tetrateuch and the deuteronomistic history are joined together as a "primary history," then the issue of the non-fulfillment of the promise is resolved, since the latter contains a complete account of the conquest of Canaan. This issue provides the focus for the present chapter.

As I have argued in the previous chapters, the literary and chronological relationships among the various sources and the redactional layers that form the books of Genesis through Kings depend more upon the model from which the analyst begins than upon the evidence itself. In terms of the classical position of the documentary hypothesis, the Tetrateuchal sources

---

[1] For this reason, many scholars maintain that the sources that were used in the composition of the Tetrateuch or the Pentateuch continue into Joshua, thus forming the Hexateuch. For a classic statement of this, see the comments on the composition of Joshua by S. R. Driver, *An Introduction to the Literature of the Old Testament* (Cleveland, OH: Word Publishing Co., 1967 [orig. published 1913]), pp. 103–116.

and narrative clearly predate the deuteronomic materials. Yet, as the recent work of J. Van Seters demonstrates,[2] a cogent and plausible argument for the opposite position, based upon the same data, may be developed. It might not be an overstatement to suggest that the premises upon which both positions are based are ambiguous.[3] Despite the seeming incompatibility of these two stances, they do share a common presupposition: the biblical accounts contained in the materials under consideration were intended by their original authors to form a continuous narrative account that could be read as a unified whole. Each position also explains gaps in the narrative, or the lack of unified narrative flow, as the result of later editing by any number of redactors. As I have suggested throughout this study, there is another perspective from which these materials may be understood.

One way to avoid some of the problems created by the documentary hypothesis, in whatever form it is presented, might be illustrated by a consideration of Josh 1:1–9 and some of its implications for understanding the related narratives. It begins with the chronological notice, "after the death of Moses" (*wayhî 'aḥărê môt mōšeh*), an event recounted in Deut 34:1–7. As noted in the previous chapter, however, the narrative account of the installation of Joshua in Num 27:12–23 (cf. Deut 31:14–15, 23) suggests that Moses' death should be recounted in that context. Obviously, however, it is not. The account of Moses' death presents some clues to a way out of the documentary dilemma.

With the death of Moses, the command is given to Joshua to lead the people across the Jordan to begin the conquest of the land (Josh 1:2–6). But here a new element is introduced: the success of the conquest will be directly dependent upon the people's allegiance to the written "book of the Torah" (*sēper hattôrâ*) which had been given by Moses (1:7–9). As argued

---

2 *Prologue to History* and *The Life of Moses.* Van Seters is not the first to observe that what is commonly designated as the Yahwistic narrative displays a dependence upon the deuteronomistic and prophetic materials. On this position, see also the work of H. H. Schmid, *Der sogenannte Jahwist.* M. Rose offers a careful analysis of some of the major instances of the literary primacy of the deuteronomistic texts over those associated with the Yahwistic accounts in *Deuteronomist und Jahwist, passim.*

3 The heated exchange between J. Van Seters and R. Friedman over the former's reconstruction of the Yahwistic narrative that takes a peculiarly personal tone suggests that it is unlikely that either position is very much interested in actually attempting to understand the other ("Scholars Face Off Over Age of Biblical Stories: Friedman vs. Van Seters," pp. 40–44, 54). It may be the case that the most basic premises with which each of these scholars begins his analysis of the formation of the Pentateuch are simply incompatible. See above, Chap. 1, n. 12.

in Chap. 2, this *tôrâ,* in its context in Joshua, referred to the deuteronomistic edition of the book of Deuteronomy, and not to the Pentateuch as
a whole.[4] But, in its final canonical form, *tôrâ* most clearly does refer to the
whole of the Pentateuch.[5] Again, the way in which the death of Moses is
understood might suggest how this shift occurred and the context to which
it might be attributed.

The way in which one addresses the problem of the account of the
death of Moses is indicative of the manner in which one understands the development of the Pentateuchal traditions. Most commentators agree that the
account of the installation of Joshua in Num 27:12–23 comes from the hand
of the Priestly writer.[6] This section consists of two distinct parts: the imminent death of Moses (vv. 12–14) and the installation of Joshua (vv. 15–23).
The appointment of Joshua as the successor to Moses is also contained in
Deut 32:48–52, while the death of Moses is recorded in Deut 34:1–12. Both
of the passages in Deuteronomy belong to the deuteronomistic framework
which created the connecting links between Deuteronomy and the national
history contained in Judges through Kings.[7] When the narrative of Numbers
is read with the presupposition that there was, at one time, an underlying
account that was intended to be read as a whole, with few if any major narrative interruptions, which is the perspective of all of the various documentary theories, it seems reasonable to note that the death of Moses would
follow naturally at the end of the narrative in Num 20:1–13, which re-

---

[4] Since the groundbreaking analysis of M. Noth, it has been recognized that Deut 1:
1–4:43, 31:1–13, and portions of chapter 34 were directly related to the deuteronomistic history and formed a frame for the "older" deuteronomic law, the basic form of which is found in
Deut 4:44–30:20 (*Überlieferungsgeschichtliche Studien*). Since Noth's original thesis, a general
consensus has been reached among scholars that Deut 4:44–28:66 constituted the more "original" form of Deuteronomy. The remainder of the book is understood as the work of the deuteronomistic author plus various supplements. As M. Weinfeld has noted, Deuteronomy 1–3
corresponds to 31:1–8, while 4:1–40 corresponds to 30:1–10 (*Deuteronomy 1–11* [AB 5;
New York: Doubleday, 1991], pp. 1–14). For further discussion of the various layers of tradition
history that have been reconstructed for Deuteronomy, see A. D. H. Mayes, *Deuteronomy*,
pp 41–55.

[5] As noted above in Chap. 2, pp. 50–55, this designation had occurred by the end of the
first century CE at the latest. Note the reference to the five books of Moses which comprised
the law and the traditional history from the creation until the death of Moses in Josephus (*Ag.
Ap.* 1 § 39).

[6] See, for example, the discussion of M. Noth, *Numbers* (OTL; Philadelphia: Westminster,
1968), p. 213.

[7] See above, n. 4.

counted the sin at Meribah and the death of Aaron.[8] Obviously, this narrative connection no longer exists.

The delay in the recounting of the death of Moses is further complicated by the interesting chronology involved. While Num 31:2 makes it clear that Moses is to conduct the war against Midian before his death, there is an amazing lack of chronological information provided in the materials stretching from Numbers 27 to Deuteronomy 34. Related to this is the fact that according to the chronological scheme of Deuteronomy, the entirety of the speeches given by Moses takes place on the final day of his life.[9] In short, the events and materials contained in the literature stretching from Num 28:1 to Deut 34:1 seem to take place on one day. Here the basic presupposition concerning the nature of the narratives themselves comes into play. If it is presumed that the accounts of the Pentateuch constitute a unified narrative whole, then there are clearly problems with the present shape of the text and its contents. If such a presupposition is not made, then the problem is dissipated, though still not resolved. At issue is not simply the literary relationship of the various stories to one another and to the Pentateuchal narrative as a whole, but also the chronological relationships of those stories to each other.

Another way of phrasing this issue might be to ask, simply, when does Moses die? The answer developed by biblical scholars is anything but simple and is generally dependent upon a division of the text into sources and redactional rearrangements. For M. Noth, ". . . only (Num) 27.12–14 belonged to the original version of the P-narrative and was later repeated in Deut. 32.48–52 and that, on the other hand, 27.15–23 was added only when the Pentateuch was linked to the Deuteronomistic work. . . ."[10] Embedded in Noth's analysis, and accepted by most, is the understanding that "originally," Deuteronomy was separate from the Tetrateuch and was inserted at a later point to form the Pentateuch. This view is based on the recognition that in the "original" form of the Priestly narrative contained in the Tetrateuch, Moses' death was an event that occurred along the way (Num 27:12–23), as were the deaths of Miriam (20:1) and Aaron (20:22–29).

---

8 This is the position taken by Noth (*Numbers,* p. 213) and followed by most. A question remains, however, concerning the nature of the Priestly source. There seems to be little consensus as to whether P was a continuous narrative or simply a collection of texts that have been woven into a pre-existing narrative to form a new work by some later Priestly redactor who was responsible for creating the Pentateuch in its final form.

9 J. Blenkinsopp, *The Pentateuch,* p. 237.

10 *Numbers,* p. 213.

When Deuteronomy was added to the Tetrateuch, it was necessary to transpose the commissioning of Joshua and the death of Moses from their "original" positions in the narrative to the end of Deuteronomy.[11]

If this position concerning the relationship between the corpus of materials contained in the Tetrateuch and the book of Deuteronomy is accepted, then the question concerning the "original" ending of Deuteronomy must be addressed before returning to the possible shape of the "original" account of the death of Moses to be reconstructed in the context of Num 27: 12–23. According to the analysis of J. Van Seters, the basic account of the death of Moses in Deuteronomy 34 belongs to the deuteronomistic historian, but has been through a number of "redactional additions." For Van Seters, the earliest ending to the deuteronomic materials is to be found in 34:1a (minus the Priestly additions),[12] 5 (without the P addition of *'al-pî-yhwh*), 6a, and 7a (?). This text would have been followed immediately by Joshua 1 and would have yielded the following narrative:[13]

> [1a]And Moses went up to the top of Pisgah [5]and Moses the servant of Yahweh died there in the land of Moab. [6a]And he buried him in the valley in the land of Moab before Beth-Peor. [7a(?)]Now Moses was one hundred and twenty years old when he died. [Joshua 1:1]Now after the death of Moses, ...

A survey of commentaries on Deuteronomy reveals that this reconstruction of the account of the death of Moses is generally accepted.

If this did represent the "original" ending of Deuteronomy, however, the next question to be addressed is the issue of the redactional incorporation of that book into the Tetrateuchal narrative. At this point consensus dissolves. The problem involves several areas of dispute regarding the relative "age" of the sources and the process of redaction. For A. D. H. Mayes, Deut 34:1–6 was the basic work of the deuteronomistic historian, who had anticipated these events in 3:27.[14] J. Van Seters, however, offers a radically different view of 34:1–6, arguing that the description of the land contained in vv. 1b–3 does not belong to the deuteronomistic writer.[15] He further as-

---

[11] J. Blenkinsopp, *The Pentateuch*, pp. 229–231.

[12] Most source analyses recognize that the phrases "from the plains of Moab to Mt. Nebo" (*mē'arbōt môāb 'el-har nĕbô*) and "which is opposite Jericho" (*'ăšer 'al-pĕnê yĕrēḥô*) are characteristic of the Priestly source. Cf. S. R. Driver, *Deuteronomy*, 3rd ed. (ICC; Edinburgh: T. & T. Clark, 1973 [orig. published 1895]), p. 417.

[13] *The Life of Moses*, pp. 452–455.

[14] *Deuteronomy*, p. 411.

[15] *The Life of Moses*, pp. 453–455. Van Seters argues that the description of the region shown to Moses in terms of tribal territories is completely anachronistic and occurs nowhere

serts that the description of the land contained in the MT, which begins with
the notice of Yahweh "showing" the land to Moses (v. 1bα) and concludes
with the reference that he had "shown" him the land, but he would not be
allowed to enter it (v. 4), is to be attributed to the Yahwistic narrative, rather
than to the deuteronomistic writer, upon whose narrative account the Yahwist built.[16]

Van Seters' argument does not stop here. He continues his analysis of
Deut 34:1–12 by arguing that the reference to the fact that no one knows the
place of Moses' burial (v. 6b) might also belong to this Yahwistic author.
The problem here might be illuminated by taking S. R. Driver's observation
concerning this chapter into account. Driver notes that while the general
source analysis seems clear, there are "one or two places where the phraseology displays so little that is characteristic that it might have been used by
any narrator."[17] Clearly this is the case with 34:6b. Van Seters also assigns
vv. 7b–8 and vv. 10–12 to this Yahwistic writer, whose work represents a
second layer of tradition reflected in the present texts.[18] What is most important about the assignment of these materials to the Yahwistic narrative is
the implication it carries for the analysis of the formation of the Pentateuch
itself. As M. Noth pointed out, in the case of Deuteronomy 34, we are dealing not with the redactor of the Pentateuch, but rather with the redactor
responsible for connecting the Pentateuchal narrative with the beginning
part of the deuteronomistic history.[19]

There are, then, at least two possibilities for understanding the account of the death of Moses. The first approach, and this is the position of
the standard presentation of the documentary hypothesis, recognizes that in
its present form, Deut 34:1–12 is a combination of at least three different
versions of the death of Moses (JE, P, D, and later expansions).[20] What

---

else in the deuteronomistic history. Likewise, he points out that the Samaritan Pentateuch contains quite a different description of the land (cf. *BHS*), which is probably closer to the original
ideal than might have been contained in the deuteronomistic version.

16 *Ibid.*

17 *Deuteronomy*, p. 417.

18 *The Life of Moses*, p. 455.

19 *A History of Pentateuchal Traditions*, p. 16. For Van Seters, the process of composition
is completed by the Priestly embellishments in v. 1a and at the end of v. 5, along with the whole
of v. 9. The geographic changes encountered in the description of the land in vv. 1b–3 are understood as late post-P additions (*The Life of Moses*, p. 455).

20 See, for example, the statement of R. Friedman, who recognizes the independent character of Deuteronomy from the Tetrateuchal material and states that its incorporation into the
narrative was simply a matter of moving the JE and P stories about Moses' death to the end of

is critical to understanding the importance of the reconstructions in this instance is the recognition of the order of the redactional activity. For S. R. Driver, the text is the result of the combination of a basic JE narrative, contained in 34:1b-5a, 6, and 10, plus a redactional gloss in v. 1a from P, and a deuteronomic ending in 34:11–12.[21] An alternate account of the redactional growth of this unit is offered by A. D. H. Mayes, who argues that 34:1–6 (omitting the P addition in v. 1) belongs to the deuteronomistic historian; 34:7–9 belongs to P, and 10–12 represents a post-deuteronomistic addition to the text.[22] This analysis agrees, in part, with that of J. Blenkinsopp, who attributes 34:1, 7–9 to the "Priestly narrative" and 34:2–6 to an expansion "in Deuteronomic style."[23] These approaches presuppose that the account of the death of Moses reveals a three-fold redactional history. The deuteronomistic account of Moses' death has been supplemented by a Priestly account, which has been transposed from its original setting in Numbers, and this new account has been further expanded by secondary editorial activity.

When these differing versions of the redactional growth of the account of the death of Moses are considered together, it becomes clear that there exist no solid criteria by which to assign passages to any particular source. What Mayes regards as the work of the deuteronomistic historian in 34:1–6, Blenkinsopp regards as, in large part, an expansion, though in deuteronomic style. Driver, however, assigned the majority of these same verses to JE, a position closer to that of Van Seters than to Mayes or Blenkinsopp. The basic incompatibility of these arguments occurs with the reconstruction of the redactional stages. Even were the above critics in accord with their assignment of these verses to their "original" sources, they still would not agree over the order of the redactional layers. For Mayes, the classical position of the documentary hypothesis still holds true: the narrative allusions in Deuteronomy are directly dependent upon the older narrative history contained in the JE materials.[24] Blenkinsopp, however, offers another reconstruction that posits the formation of the Pentateuch from two

---

the book of Deuteronomy (*Who Wrote the Bible?*, p. 231). Friedman analyzes the account as follows: 34:1–6 belongs to E (JE?); 34:7–9, to P; and 34:10–12, to Dtr1 (p. 275). This agrees, in the main, with the older analysis of O. Eissfeldt, who attributes 34:1*, 7–9 to P; 34:1*, 2–6 to J; and 34:10–12 to D (*The Old Testament: An Introduction* [Oxford: Blackwell, 1965], pp. 189, 200, 230).

21 *An Introduction to the Literature of the Old Testament*, p. 72.

22 *Deuteronomy*, p. 411.

23 *The Pentateuch*, p. 230.

24 See the position of S. R. Driver on this arrangement (*An Introduction to the Literature of the Old Testament*, pp. 79–81).

major sources, Deuteronomy, the "Priestly history," and a deuteronomistic/
deuteronomic editing of the story stretching from Abraham to Moses that is
more extensive than the documentary hypothesis envisions.[25] For Blenkinsopp, the traditional J and E sources, at least in some portions of the Pentateuch, largely evaporate, at least as continuous narratives.[26]

For Van Seters, the traditional positions on J and E are likewise unten-
able, but for very different reasons. Van Seters, like many modern source
critics, finds little evidence for an Elohistic narrative, preferring to regard
the traditional E materials as secondary additions to the Yahwistic account.[27]
More importantly, Van Seters regards the Yahwist as "an ancient historian
who tried to present the antiquarian traditions about the origins of Israel in
the context of both Eastern and Western traditions about primeval times."[28]
Hence, this ancient writer produced a continuous narrative of Israel's past.
While on one level this might be understood as consistent with the position
held by the standard documentary hypothesis, on another, it is quite incompatible with it. For Van Seters, this Yahwistic history was produced not as an
independent history, but rather as an intentional supplement to the national
history that had already *been* produced by the deuteronomistic historian.
When understood in this way, the major narrative line in the Tetrateuch becomes a post-deuteronomistic, pre-Priestly supplement to the national history contained in the deuteronomistic version of Deuteronomy plus Joshua
through Kings.[29] For Van Seters, then, the Yahwistic supplementation of the
deuteronomistic history created a type of "primary history" that presented
Israel's story of its past from the creation to the beginning of the exile. Understood in this way, the Yahwist must be dated to the time of the exile.[30]

---

25 *The Pentateuch*, pp. 233–239.

26 Blenkinsopp takes the following position: "If we continue to use the designations J and
E, it will be more to maintain continuity in the scholarly tradition than for the reasons for which
they were postulated in the first place, for we have seen that the criteria according to which these
two sources are identified have proved to be generally unsatisfactory" (*The Pentateuch*, p. 130).

27 See especially his treatment of the Abraham traditions and the reconstructed sources
from which they were composed in *Abraham in History and Tradition*. A convenient summary
of the materials in Genesis is provided on p. 313.

28 *The Life of Moses*, p. 1.

29 *Ibid.*, pp. 457–458.

30 While the date of the composition of the deuteronomistic history remains debated, it is
clear that in its final redaction it can date no earlier than the exile. For a discussion of the exilic
dating of that work, see my *Narrative History and Ethnic Boundaries*, pp. 37–47. For a review
of the various positions taken with respect to the composition and date of the deuteronomistic
history, see. S. L. McKenzie, *The Trouble with Kings*, pp. 1–19.

The implications of these discussions are problematic to any attempt to reconstruct the history of the composition of the Pentateuch as a whole. Following Van Seters, one would understand that the creation of a "primary history" was the result of the Yahwistic historian. It would have been the redactional activity of the Priestly school that separated the Pentateuchal materials from that larger unit and created a "Torah." But, if one follows Blenkinsopp, the reconstruction takes quite another twist. Blenkinsopp regards Deuteronomy, along with its accompanying interpretive history, as part of an early "canonical" corpus that included selected prophetic materials.[31] The major narrative history recounting the stories stretching from the creation to the erection of the wilderness sanctuary at Shiloh and the allotment of the tribes by Joshua and Eleazar (Joshua 18–19) was contained in what Blenkinsopp designates as the "Priestly history," composed during the Babylonian exile.[32] If one takes these two contrasting positions as indicative of the state of the field, then one might conclude that there is little unambiguous evidence that might be mustered in support of any of the reconstructions of the account of the death of Moses, let alone of the Pentateuch as a whole. It might be pointed out that neither of these positions is compatible with the traditional position of the documentary hypothesis.

If the intention is to try to establish a consensus position from which to work, the following might serve as a starting point. We must take seriously the suggestion of R. Rendtorff that it is doubtful that the Pentateuch ever existed as an independent entity without Deuteronomy or apart from a connection with the deuteronomistic history.[33] If this is accurate, then the puzzle becomes the relationship between the Tetrateuchal materials and the deuteronomistic history. For the standard documentary hypothesis, there is no ambiguity here: *"JE alone formed the basis of Dt."*[34] But, as noted above, this position has come under severe criticism that cannot be ignored.[35] Clearly, the composition of the Tetrateuch and of the deuteronomistic history, not to mention the "old core" of Deuteronomy, must be

---

31 *The Pentateuch*, p. 235.

32 *Ibid.*, pp. 237–239.

33 *The Problem of the Process of Transmission in the Pentateuch*, p. 200.

34 S. R. Driver, *An Introduction to the Literature of the Old Testament*, p. 81 [italics in the original].

35 To the scholars holding the priority of the deuteronomistic materials over the Tetrateuchal narratives cited above in n. 2 should be added, among others, R. Rendtorff, *The Problem of the Process of Transmission in the Pentateuch;* A. D. H. Mayes, *The Story of Israel between Settlement and Exile,* p. 148; and R. N. Whybray, *The Making of the Pentateuch,* pp. 222–225.

understood as separate phenomena. If one accepts the position that the "original" form of Deuteronomy has been edited by the deuteronomistic historian and given a new beginning and ending, thus incorporating Deuteronomy into its national history as a foundational document of sorts,[36] then the beginning of Joshua, the first "historical" work following Moses' farewell speech to Israel, requires that the deuteronomistic ending of Deuteronomy provide an account of Moses' death.

On this point we may note a consensus among scholars. However, when the attempt is made to reconstruct this deuteronomistic ending, the consensus dissolves. The majority of scholars agree that the story of Moses' death has been edited in light of a source or sources *later* than the deuteronomistic form of chapter 34 to give it its present shape. Additionally, it is recognized by most that some of the editorial changes to the "original" deuteronomistic ending of Deuteronomy are to be associated with the same hand responsible for the account of the investiture of Joshua in Num 27:12–23 (P). The remainder of the additions to the "original" continue to be debated. From this, then, we can conclude that the process of the formation of the Pentateuch as a whole, as well as of the "primary history," which would result in the combination of the Tetrateuch with the deuteronomistic history, was, in and of itself, a complex one that probably involved more than one redactional layer. One possibility for resolving this dilemma might be to look at some of the parallels between the accounts of Israel's past contained in the deuteronomistic sections of Deuteronomy and those found in the Tetrateuchal materials.

II. Deuteronomistic and Tetrateuchal Traditions of the Past

In an analysis of the probable relationships between the deuteronomic corpus and the Tetrateuchal materials, two major areas of comparison may be isolated: the common references to events in the two corpora and the parallel sets of religious and cultic materials.[37] Deuteronomy contains two major sections which present narrative accounts paralleling events in the Tetrateuch: Deut 1:6–3:29, which reflects the journey from Mt. Horeb to the arrival in Moab, and Deut 9:8–10:11, which recounts the events associated with the golden calf and the events which followed. To anticipate the

---

[36] On the role of Deuteronomy in the formation of the national and ethnic identity of Israel, see my *Narrative History and Ethnic Boundaries*, pp. 32–37.

[37] Rather complete lists of these may be found in S. R. Driver, *Deuteronomy*, pp. iv–vii, xiv–xv, and *Introduction to the Literature of the Old Testament*, pp. 73–75, 80–81.

problems that might influence the results of such an inquiry, it is of note that scholarship is divided into two diametrically opposed camps. One side, following the classical exposition of the documentary hypothesis, notes that the deuteronomic materials are directly dependent upon the JE narrative in the Tetrateuch,[38] while some recent critics argue exactly the opposite.[39] Each group bases its position on precisely the same criteria applied to the identical texts.

As a beginning point, we might note the reference in Deut 1:9–18 concerning the appointment of judges over the people. According to those who insist that the deuteronomistic materials are dependent upon the Tetrateuchal narratives, this account is understood as parallel to, and derived from, the stories contained in Exod 18:13–23 and Num 11:11–17.[40] In a different manner, Van Seters argues that Deut 1:9–18 can be explained completely by appeal to the deuteronomic corpus (e.g., Deut 16:18, 17:8–13), with no dependence whatsoever upon the Tetrateuchal narratives.[41] A third possibility has been argued by M. Noth, who suggests that these accounts were derived from some common tradition that allowed a variety of motifs to be combined in different ways.[42] Such radically differing perspectives on the same materials invite investigation. Though there are indications of a possible literary relationship among these three texts, the direction and history of such are debated.

The following passages are commonly noted as parallels: Deut 1:9b, 10, 12 and Num 11:14, 17b; Deut 1:15, 17b, 18 and Exod 18:20, 21b, 22a, 25, 26.[43] The first set of parallels concerns Moses' complaint that he is unable to bear the burdens of the people alone.[44] In Deut 1:9–18, the

---

38 For example, see S. R. Driver, *Introduction to the Literature of the Old Testament*, p. 81, or, more recently, M. Weinfeld, *Deuteronomy 1–11*, p. 19.

39 In this case, the works of H. H. Smend, A. D. H. Mayes, N. Whybray, J. Van Seters, among others, all assert that the materials in the so-called JE portions of the Tetrateuch are expansions upon the deuteronomic materials.

40 See, for example, M. Weinfeld, *Deuteronomy 1–11*, pp. 139–140; A. D. H. Mayes, *Deuteronomy*, 118; etc.

41 *The Life of Moses*, pp. 214–219.

42 *A History of Pentateuchal Traditions*, p. 128, nn. 360–362, and p.163. More recently, this position has been argued by M. Rose, *Deuteronomist und Jahwist*, pp. 238–244.

43 A. D. H. Mayes, *Deuteronomy*, p. 118.

44 Deut 1:9b reads: "I am not able to bear you alone" (*lō-ʾûkal lĕbaddî śēʾēt ʾetkem*) and is paralleled closely by Num 11:14a: "and I am not able to bear all of this people alone" (*lō-ʾûkal ʾānōkî lĕbaddî lāśēʾt ʾet-kol-hāʿām hazzeh*). The reference in 11:14b to the fact that the burden is too great for him might be taken as a parallel to Deut 1:10, which notes that Yahweh had increased the number of the people beyond counting. The gathering of seventy of the elders of the

appointment of tribal leaders (*rā'šê šibṭêkem;* vv. 13, 15) to act as officers (*šōṭĕrîm;* cf. v. 15) and judges (*šōpĕṭîm;* cf. v. 16) is clearly intended to alleviate the problem of Moses' burden. Notably, the deuteronomistic writer places the appointment of these figures prior to the departure from Sinai, i.e., within the context of the reception of the revelation at the sacred mount. Here, it is Moses who initiates the idea, while in Exodus 18, it is Jethro who conceives the move, and in Numbers 11, Yahweh provides the impetus for the appointment.[45] The instructions given to the judges in Deuteronomy concern impartiality in the court (1:17), a set of guidelines missing in the accounts in Exodus and Numbers.[46] Careful investigation of these three texts reveals that despite a common thematic content, there are also great discrepancies among them. Since there are no distinctive literary characteristics that would demand that priority be given to any of the accounts, I suggest that no such determination can be made until some firm criteria are established.

---

people to serve as officers (*šōṭĕrîm;* Num 11:16) who would receive part of the spirit placed upon Moses resulted in their acting as judges with Moses, "so you will not bear it alone" (*wĕlō'-tiśśā' 'attâ lĕbaddĕkā;* 11:17b). That these passages involve direct literary parallels is clear. Problematically, the parallels do not contain any distinctive vocabulary or grammatical constructions. Since there is nothing unusual about any of the phraseology that would be suggestive of an "original" source, it is impossible to determine which set of materials might have been dependent upon the other. The same situation exists with the second set of parallels. Deut 1:15 contains a description of the qualifications of the men to be selected. They are to be "wise and experienced men" (*'ănāšîm ḥăkāmîm wîdū'îm;* note that 1:13 adds "discerning" [*nĕbōnîm*] to the list of qualifications) who would be made "chiefs of thousands, chiefs of hundreds, chiefs of fifties, and chiefs of tens, and officers of your tribes" (*śārê 'ălāpîm wĕśārê mē'ôt wĕśārê ḥāmiššîm wĕśārê 'ăśārōt wĕšōṭĕrîm lĕšibṭêkem*). Exod 18:21 describes the men appointed as judges as "men of distinction, who fear god, men of truth, who hate illegal gain" (*'anšê-ḥāyil yir'ê 'ĕlōhîm 'anšê 'ĕmet śōnĕ'ê bāṣa'*). It would be this group who would be divided into chiefs in a manner paralleling Deut 1:15. Such designations for leadership, however, are extremely common and reveal little if anything about the direction of dependence, if any, between the texts. Likewise, while both Deut 1:17 and Exod 18:22 describe the way in which these judges are to lessen the burden on Moses, bringing only the most difficult cases before him, there is enough linguistic variation between them to make a determination of dependence impossible.

45 The account of the appointment of seventy elders in Numbers 11 seems to be a secondary addition to the story of the request for meat by Israel. As M. Noth argued, the basic narrative is to be found in vv. 4–13, 18–24a, 31–34, into which a later hand has inserted vv. 14–17 and 24b–30 (*Numbers,* p. 83). These passages in Numbers are concerned more with the sharing of the spirit placed on Moses and shared with the elders, who then prophesy, than with the administration of a system of justice in the camp.

46 For additional discrepancies among the three accounts, see M. Weinfeld, *Deuteronomy 1–11,* pp. 139–140. Weinfeld notes that the Samaritan Pentateuch places Deut 1:8–19 after Exod 18:24 (p. 140), a dislocation of the text based, quite clearly, on the similarities between the two.

To do this, then, it is necessary to continue the investigation of those parallel materials to ascertain whether scholarship has established any testable criteria that might resolve the direction of literary dependence. Immediately following the account of the organization of judges, Deut 1:19 notes that the people left Horeb and went to Kadesh, fulfilling the command given in 1:7. This move introduces the deuteronomistic account of the spying out of the land and the resulting failure of the people to conform to Yahweh's demands (1:20–46), an account which has numerous parallels with the stories in Numbers 13–14. As with the previous material, however, the direction of literary dependence remains debated. The account in Numbers, commonly understood as predominantly a Yahwistic composition with Priestly editing,[47] is generally regarded as the earlier, and hence, the source for the story in Deut 1:19–46. This position, however, has not gone unchallenged.[48] As was the case with the narratives concerning the appointment of judges, the accounts of the spying out of the land and the abortive conquest attempt display a number of similarities, but also many differences. Though it is possible that they are ultimately related in a literary manner, they now tell rather different stories in very different contexts.

The most effective way of evaluating the potential relationship between the two accounts is to review the major instances of parallels that the stories contain and see what, if anything, they reveal about the composition of the accounts. From the very beginning, it is important to note two major distinctions between the accounts. In the story in Numbers (13:1–2), it is Yahweh who commands Moses to send out the spies, while the account in Deuteronomy makes this a request by the people (1:22). The mission in Numbers has a two-fold purpose: to see if the country is "good or bad" and to collect military information about the strength of the inhabitants (13:18–20). In Deuteronomy, the spies' purpose is to find the best route for attack (1:22).[49] The major functional differences in the narratives should not be overlooked in an analysis of the possible relationships between the two.

An important point of departure for the comparison is the geographical locale from which the spies are dispatched. Deut 1:19 gives Israel's location as Kadesh-Barnea, while Num 13:3 locates the people in the "wilderness of

[47] For an analysis of the composition of Numbers 13–14, see B. A. Levine, *Numbers 1–20*, pp. 347–349.

[48] For arguments that the deuteronomistic account is the primary one, see the arguments of J. Van Seters (*The Life of Moses*, pp. 370–377) and M. Rose (*Deuteronomist und Jahwist*, pp. 264–294).

[49] M. Weinfeld, *Deuteronomy 1–11*, pp. 144–145.

Paran" (*midbar pāʾrān*). Num 32:8, however, notes that the spies were sent
out from Kadesh-Barnea, which suggests quite strongly that the account
in Numbers 13–14 has been edited by a later writer.[50] The critical reference
here is found in Num 13:26, which recounts that the spies returned from
their mission to "the wilderness of Paran, at Kadesh" (*midbar pāʾrān
qādēšāh*).[51] The probability of later editing makes the process of comparison even more difficult. The entire issue of the spies, as noted earlier, is
introduced in radically different ways. In Num 13:1–2, Yahweh directs
Moses to send men to spy (*twr*) out the land. "One man of each patrilineal
tribe" (*ʾîš ʾeḥād lemaṭṭēh ʾăbōtāw;* v. 2) is to be sent, a number that agrees
with the account in Deuteronomy (*ʾîš ʾeḥād laššābet;* 1:23b). In Deut 1:22,
the people ask Moses to send out spies to search (*ḥpr*) out the land and to
bring a report on "the way by which we should go up" (*hadderek ʾăšer
naʿăleh-bāh*), a request that is in direct response to the injunction that they
"go up, take possession . . . do not fear nor be dismayed" (*ʿălēh rēš . . . ʾal-
tîrāʾ wĕʾal-tēḥat*).

Similarly, the commission given to the spies differs greatly between
the accounts. In contrast to the request that the spies are to seek out a route
for the attack, Num 13:17–20 provides them with explicit instructions to
go through the Negeb into the hill country (*hāhār;* 13:17), to ascertain if the
people there were weak or strong, few or many, to determine if the land was
good or bad, and to scout the defenses of the cities (vv. 18–19). In evaluating the prosperity of the land, they were to bring some of its fruit back with
them (v. 20). Deut 1:24 notes that the spies went up to "the hill country"
(*hāhārāh;* cf. 1:7, 19) and came to the Wady Eshkol, in the vicinity of Hebron, and spied (*rgl*) upon it. From there they brought back some fruit and
a report on the nature of the land: "The land that Yahweh our god is giving
us is good" (*ṭôbâ hāʾāreṣ ʾăšer-yhwh ʾĕlōhênû nōtēn lānû;* 1:25). The parallel in Num 13:21–24 is more detailed than this, using the command to
bring some fruit (13:20) as the basis for an etiology of Eshkol (vv. 23–24).
Additionally, Num 13:22 notes that three descendants of Anaq, Ahiman,

50 Literary critics have long noted that the Yahwistic materials in this section have been
supplemented by the Priestly writer. For the various divisions of the materials, see, among
others, B. A. Levine, *Numbers 1–20,* pp. 347–49; P. J. Budd, *Numbers,* pp. 141–144, 150–153;
and J. Van Seters, *The Life of Moses,* pp. 366–370.

51 B. A. Levine argues that the geographical ambiguity here is produced by the Priestly
rewriting of the JE tradition, which originally contained specific reference to Kadesh as the
place from which the spies were sent. The confusion is the result of the Priestly writer's efforts
to keep Israel at Sinai as long as possible (*Numbers 1–20,* pp. 53–57).

Sheshai, and Talmai, lived at Hebron. Interestingly, Josh 15:13–15 associates these same three descendants of the Anaq with the area of Hebron (cf. Judg 1:10). Deut 1:28 notes that the people refused to go up to take the land because the Anaq were there.[52] One of two options would seem to face the interpreter: either the Tetrateuchal writer(s) have expanded on the deuteronomistic account, or the deuteronomistic writer has condensed the Tetrateuchal story. What is lacking to this point are any reliable criteria by which to make the decision.

The mission in Numbers lasts some forty days, after which time the spies return to Moses and Aaron with their report. Deuteronomy makes no notice of the length of the mission. The report in Deut 1:25 is quite short, but is amplified by the people's explanation for their refusal to proceed with the attack in 1:28. Israel grumbled that Yahweh had led them out of Egypt only to give them into the power of the Amorites, who would destroy them (1:27). Despite the injunctions by Moses that the people be brave (1:29; cf. v. 21), the people blamed the spies for destroying their courage by telling them that they had seen "a people greater and taller than we, large cities fortified to the heavens, and even descendants of the Anaq" (1:28). The report of the spies in Num 13:27–29 presents a similar assessment of the land. Rather than noting simply that the land was "good" (Deut 1:25), the spies note that it was a land "flowing with milk and honey" (*zābat ḥālāb ûděbaš*), and display some of the fruit to demonstrate their assessment (13:27). To this they add that the people of the land are "strong" (*ʿaz*), that the cities are "fortified and very large" (*běṣûrôt gědōlōt měʾōd*), and that they also saw descendants of the Anaq there (13:28). This clearly reflects an assessment close to that which was attributed to the spies by the people in Deut 1:28.[53]

---

[52] References to the Anaq/Anaqim are not uncommon in Deuteronomy (1:28 2:10, 11, 21; 9:2) and in the deuteronomistic history (Josh 11:21, 22; 14:12, 15; 15:13, 14; 21:11; cf. Judg 1:10). Outside of the deuteronomic corpus, reference to this people occurs only in Numbers 13:22, 28, 33.

[53] Despite the obvious parallels, there are some significant differences to note. While Deut 1:28 says "a people greater and taller than we" (*ʿam gādôl wārām mimmennû*), the parallel in Num 13:28 notes only that they were "strong" (*ʿaz*). The references to the fortified nature of the cities are very similar. Deut 1:28 notes that they had seen "great cities, fortified to the heavens" (*ʿārîm gědōlōt ûběṣûrōt baššāmāyim*), while the spies report in Num 13:28 that "the cities are fortified and very large" (*heʿārîm běṣûrôt gědōlōt měʾōd*). Interestingly, this is the only such reference to "fortified cities" (*ʿārîm běṣûrôt*) in the Tetrateuch, while such designations are common in the deuteronomistic history (Deut 1:28; 3:5; 9:1; Josh 14:12; 2 Sam 20:6; 2 Kgs 19:25). As pointed out in the previous note, references to the descendants of the Anaq are common in the deuteronomic corpus and occur only in this chapter of Numbers in the Tetrateuch.

The description of the inhabitants of the land and their distribution (Num 13:29) has no parallel in the account in Deuteronomy.[54] That the two appear to be related in literary terms is clear, but the assignment of priority cannot be determined on any clear evidentiary grounds.

Num 13:30 presents another new element of the story with the speech by Caleb, who urges the people to attack the land immediately. This seems to provide a parallel to Moses' address in Deut 1:29–33, in which he attempts to assure the people of Yahweh's presence and his power in fighting on their behalf. The spies who had accompanied Caleb in the investigation of the land disagree with his assessment, however, and note that the people in the land are "too strong for us" (*ḥāzāq hûʾ mimmennû;* 13:31). They now change their original report on the nature of the land (13:27–29) and, in its place, offer an "unfavorable report" (*dibbâ*), noting that all the inhabitants of the land are "giants" (*ʾanšê middôt*), members of the Nephilim, descendants of the Anaq, before whom Israel is like grasshoppers (13:32–33).[55]

The complexity of the literary relationship is compounded by the presence of Caleb in the spy tradition. In response to this new report, the people began complaining against Moses and Aaron and expressed their desire to return to Egypt (14:1–4). Their decision is addressed by Joshua and Caleb, who assure them that Yahweh would help them take the land and that they should avoid rebelling against him (vv. 6–9). Just as the people were prepared to stone them, the presence of Yahweh appeared at the Tent of Meeting to announce his judgment on them (14:10). In contrast to this, Deut 1:34–39 presents Yahweh's response immediately following Moses' attempt to urge the people to attack the land (1:29–33). Moses announces that Yahweh had sworn that not one member of "this evil generation" (*haddôr hāraʿ hazzeh*) would see the land that he had sworn to their ancestors (1:35), with one surprising exception. Caleb would be allowed to enter the land "because he was completely loyal to Yahweh" (*yaʿan ʾăšer millēʾ*

---

54 This listing of five ethnic designators, Amalekite, Hittite (Sam/LXX, Hivite), Jebusite, Amorite, and Canaanite, is reminiscent of the numerous lists of ethnic groups that were traditionally associated with Palestine in the biblical materials and which, despite the variations in presentation, constituted the "seven nations greater and stronger than you" (*šibʿâ gōyīm rabbîm waʿăṣûmîm mimmekâ;* Deut 7:1). R. Boling notes that there are some twenty-one of these somewhat stereotyped lists (Gen 10:15–18=1 Chr 1:13–16; 15:19–21; Exod 3:8, 17; 23:23; 33:2; 34:11; Deut 7:1; 20:17; Josh 3:10; 9:1; 11:3; 12:8; 24:11; Judg 3:5; 1 Kgs 9:20=2 Chr 8:7; 1 Chr 1:13–16; 2 Chr 8:7; Ezra 9:1; Neh 9:8 [*Joshua* (AB 6; New York: Doubleday, 1982), p. 165]).

55 The Nephilim (*nĕpîlîm*) are mentioned elsewhere only in Gen 6:4 and are associated with the Anaq only here.

ʾaḥărê yhwh; 1:36). Since such an exception would not be granted to Moses, who also belonged to that generation (1:37), this verse seems to be intrusive. In Num 14:20–23, Yahweh announces his condemnation of all those who had seen his wonders and had yet rebelled against him, noting that there would be one exception—Caleb. Caleb now stands for the next generation, for it would be his offspring who would inherit the land (14:24), because he, according to Yahweh, possessed a different spirit and "was completely loyal to me" (*waymallēʾ ʾaḥărāy*).

There can be little doubt that the similarities between the reasons given for Caleb's exemption suggest that there is some literary relationship between the two accounts. This is further suggested by the fact that in 14:30, the exemption granted to Caleb is extended to Joshua, with no explicit reason given. For the account in Numbers, quite clearly, Joshua, one of the spies (cf. 13:16), belonged to the generation that had been in Egypt. The deuteronomistic history, however, seems to associate Joshua with the next generation, i.e., with the children of those who had left Egypt, and gives no indication that he was one of the spies. Instead, Joshua would lead Israel to possess the land (Deut 1:38), thus replacing Moses as leader.[56] One further reference in this section suggests that the two accounts are related. In Deut 1:40, Moses orders the people to turn and march "through the wilderness, toward the Reed Sea" (*hammidbārāh derek yam-sûp*). Similarly, in Num 14:25, immediately following the notice of the special status of Caleb, Moses directs the people to turn and march "to the wilderness, toward the Reed Sea" (*hammidbār derek yam-sûp*). It seems clear that either these two accounts are directly related or are derived from a common literary source. At the level of their functional usage, however, it is important to note that they contain conflicting information if one presumes that they were intended to be read together. If, on the other hand, they are understood as representing two variant renditions of a particular set of traditions, one a summarizing history (Deuteronomy 1–3) and the other an expansive narrative (Exodus-Numbers), each of which could be used for didactic purposes, then the problem of inconsistencies in the accounts becomes less troublesome.

After Moses commanded them to turn and journey toward the Reed Sea (Deut 1:40), the people publicly recognized their sin and announced

---

56 J. Van Seters argues that the Caleb tradition is completely secondary in Deut 1:36 and is to be attributed to a later scribe who was attempting to bring this account into conjunction with the one in Numbers (*The Life of Moses*, pp. 377–379).

their intention to attack the land as Yahweh had commanded (1:41). In the account in Numbers, this decision to attack (Num 14:40) is separated from the command to journey into the wilderness (Num 14:25) by a lengthy speech by Yahweh, announcing the condemnation of the rebellious group (14:26–35), and the notice of the death by a plague of those spies who had brought the negative report (14:36–38). In both accounts, Moses warns the people not to go up in battle, because Yahweh is not with them.[57] Instead of obeying, they launched an attack into the hill-country, only to be routed by its inhabitants and defeated at Hormah (Deut 1:43–44; Num 14:44–45).[58]

The next set of parallel accounts that may be considered addresses the deuteronomistic tradition of Israel's Transjordanian conquests (Deut 2:1–3:11 and Numbers 20–21).[59] The deuteronomistic account contains five distinct episodes. Deut 2:3–7 recounts the order to march through Edom; 2:8–9, 16–18 pertains to their crossing through Moab; 2:19 reflects the journey toward Ammon; 2:24–37 describes the conquest of Sihon's kingdom; and 3:1–7 concerns the conquest of Og. The latter two events are summarized in 3:8–11. The accounts concerning Edom and the defeat of Sihon and Og indicate that there are clear contacts between the deuteronomistic and Tetrateuchal materials (Num 20:14–21; 21:21–35), though there are numerous differences in the accounts as they presently stand. The direction of the dependence, as in the cases above, remains disputed. One of the clearest indicators of a literary relationship is found in a comparison of Num 21:4 and Deut 2:1: "And they journeyed from Mt. Hor by way of the Reed Sea to go around the land of Edom" (*wayyisʿû mēhōr hāhār derek yam-sûp lisbōb ʾet-ʾereṣ ʾĕdôm;* Num 21:4); and "And we turned and journeyed through the wilderness by way of the Reed Sea . . . and we went around Mt. Seir" (*wannēpen wannissaʿ hammidbārāh derek yam-sûp . . . wannāsob ʾet-*

---

57 Deut 1:42 reads, "I am not in your midst" (*ʾênennî bĕqirbĕkem*), while Num 14:42 reads, "for Yahweh is not in your midst" (*kî ʾên yhwh bĕqirbĕkem*). The variation is to be explained by the difference in direct and indirect speech. Most interesting is the fact that these two warnings end with the identical statement: "lest you be defeated by your enemies" (*lōʾ tinnagĕpû lipnê ʾōyĕbêkem*). The account in Numbers notes further that neither Moses nor the Ark accompanied them into battle (14:43), a notice that is not found in Deuteronomy. It should be observed that for the deuteronomic tradition, the Ark served another purpose (cf. A. D. H. Mayes, *Deuteronomy*, pp. 203–205).

58 Deut 1:44 notes that it was the Amorites who inhabited the hill-country and who defeated Israel, while Num 14:43, 45 designates the ones defeating them as Amalekites and Canaanites (cf. 13:29).

59 For a discussion of the basic unity of Deut 2:1–3:11, see J. Van Seters, *The Life of Moses,* pp. 384–386.

har śēʿir; Deut 2:1). In each case, these relate to the fulfillment of commands presented earlier in the narratives (cf. Num 14:25 and Deut 1:40).[60]

Despite these similarities, there are also numerous differences in the accounts that contribute to the lack of agreement concerning the directions of literary dependence. While Num 20:14–21 contains an account of the encounter with the Edomites, it differs markedly from the account in Deut 2: 3–7. In Deut 2:4, the command is given to "pass through" (ʿābar) the borders of "your kinspeople, the sons of Esau" (ʾăhêkem běnê-ʿēśāw), who live in Seir. They are not to engage them in battle, for Yahweh had given Mt. Seir to them as their inheritance (yěruššâ; 2:5). To provide for their needs, they would purchase food and water from the Edomites (2:6). Num 20:14–17 begins with the notice that Moses sent messengers to the king of Edom asking for permission to pass through Edom on the King's Highway.[61] Edom denies the request and threatens war if Israel tries to pass through its territory, forcing Israel to turn away (20:18–21).[62]

Deut 2:8–9 and 2:19 reflect traditions related to those found in 2: 4–5. The land of Moab and Ammon are not to be part of Israel's conquest, for each of these was an inheritance for the sons of Lot (2:9, 19; cf. Gen 19: 30–38). Notably, Deut 2:14 points out that the journey from Kadesh to the Transjordan area took thirty-eight years, the period of time needed for the rebellious generation to die. The conquest of the land begins following this, with the command to cross the Wadi Arnon and battle against the Amorite, Sihon of Heshbon (2:24–25).[63] The literary relationship between

---

[60] For a discussion of the materials in Numbers that interrupt the account of the journey, see above, Chap. 8, pp. 263–271.

[61] The deuteronomistic characteristics of the "historical credo" in 20:14b-16 have been noted by S. Mittmann, who concludes that it is derived from Deut 26:5–9 ("Num 20:14–21: eine redaktionelle Kompilation," in *Wort und Geschichte*, ed. H. Gese and H. P. Rüger [AOAT 18; Neukirchen-Vluyn: Neukirchener Verlag, 1973], pp. 146–147); see also J. Van Seters, *The Life of Moses*, p. 389.

[62] J. Van Seters argues that Num 20:14–17 is a combination of materials constructed on the basis of Deut 2:4–9 and Judg 11:12–28. It is also clear, according to his analysis, that 20:14–17 is related to Num 21:21–35, which is also dependent upon deuteronomistic materials (*The Life of Moses*, pp. 393–404).

[63] The problem of the conquest of the Transjordan is interesting since, in the Tetrateuchal sources, this area seems not to have been considered a part of the promised land. Additionally, for the Tetrateuchal narratives, the sojourn at Kadesh seems to have been the last stage of the wilderness journey, while the deuteronomic sources note it as the beginning. Likewise, because the Tetrateuchal material does not reflect the tradition of the journey through Edom and Moab to the border of the Amorites, the itinerary in Numbers is much more complex (20:22–29; 21:10–20).

the accounts concerning the Israelite defeat of Sihon and Og has generated much debate.

As P. J. Budd notes, recent analyses of these traditions have argued strongly that Num 21:21–35, like Num 20:14–21, is almost entirely deuteronomistic in form.[64] As presented by J. Van Seters, this section is almost entirely dependent upon Deut 2:26–37, 3:1–7, and Judg 11:19–26.[65] While there can be little dispute that these accounts are related, if not to one another, then to a common tradition shared by all,[66] the exact nature of the interrelationship remains debatable. When these parallel accounts of the journey from Sinai to Kadesh and the encounters with the peoples in the Transjordan are compared, one is forced to conclude that while it is clear that there is a literary dependence among the accounts, the direction of that dependence is determined not by any set of agreed-upon literary criteria, but rather by a previous commitment to a model of interpretation.[67] This situation, then, requires us to search further.

The story of the golden calf contained in Exodus 32 presents clear parallels with the materials contained in Deuteronomy 9–10 and 1 Kings 12. As with the other materials considered, there exists no real consensus among scholars beyond the recognition that a literary relationship exists among these accounts. It should be noted that the account of Jeroboam's erection of the calf images at Dan and Bethel, contained in 1 Kgs 12:28–33, is a part of the deuteronomistic history, and is to be attributed to the same author responsible for Deut 9:7–10:11. Hence, the problem of the literary relationship among the texts concerns the relationship of the account in Exodus 32 to that constructed by the deuteronomistic school. While it is possible that the texts reflect historical actualities, the accurate recording of

64 In the accounts of the conquest of the territory of Sihon, see, for example, the following parallels: sending of messengers to Sihon (Num 21:21; Deut 2:26; Judg 11:19); request for passage (Num 21:22; Deut 2:27; Judg 11:19); refusal of request (Num 21:23a; Deut 2:30a; Judg 11:20); battle and Israelite victory (Num 21:23b-24; Deut 2:32–33; Judg 11:20–21); Israel's possession of Amorite territory (Num 21:25; Deut 2:34; Judg 11:22); etc.

65 *Numbers,* pp. 143–44, and bibliography cited there, to which should be added J. Van Seters, *The Life of Moses,* pp. 393–404, and the literature noted therein.

66 See, for example, the arguments of J. R. Bartlett, "The Conquest of Sihon's Kingdom: a Literary Re-examination," pp. 347–351, and W. A. Sumner, "Israel's Encounters with Edom, Moab, Ammon, Sihon and Og according to the Deuteronomist," *VT* 18 (1968) 216–228.

67 A similar literary dilemma is encountered in the analysis of the relationship of the Transjordanian settlement of Reuben and Gad, recounted in Num 32:1–42 and Deut 3:12–20. Compare the treatment of J. Van Seters, *The Life of Moses,* pp. 441–450, with that of A. D. H. Mayes, *Deuteronomy,* pp. 145–146, or that of P. J. Budd, *Numbers,* pp. 337–342.

such was not the only, nor even necessarily the primary, function of the materials. In each of these accounts, the materials serve as didactic stories which instruct the community in the necessity of allegiance to Yahweh and Yahweh alone as the basis for the maintenance of the group.[68]

According to modern analysis, Exod 32:1–35 is an extremely complex interweaving of materials.[69] Several parallels make it clear that this account is intimately related to the deuteronomistic story, most notably, vv. 7–14, which many regard as deuteronomistic additions to the exodus account.[70] Despite the apparent connections among the texts, notice must also be given to the many differences. The golden calf episode in Exod 32:1–35 forms an integral part of the literary complex stretching through chapters 33 and 34[71] and develops a specific episode in which Yahweh's relationship with Israel is threatened and then restored. In Deut 9:7–10:11, this event constitutes one of several instances in the past when Israel angered Yahweh by rebelling against him and was threatened with annihilation. Additionally, the deuteronomistic account is presented as part of an admonition by Moses, reminding Israel that the land they were about to take possession of was theirs only because of Yahweh's promises to their ancestors (9:1–6).

A clear parallel is presented between the two accounts with the categorization of Israel as a "stiff-necked people" (*'am qĕšēh-'ōrep;* Deut 9:6, 13; Exod 32:9; 33:3, 5; 34:9; cf. Deut 10:16; 31:27), a description that accounts for their continuous rebellions against Yahweh. According to Deut 9:7, Israel had been "rebelling against Yahweh" (*mamrîm . . . 'im-yhwh*) from the day they left Egypt until that very day. The account of the apostasy in Deut 9:9–21 begins with the notice that these events had occurred while

---

[68] For the ways in which the narratives in the deuteronomistic history serve this purpose, see my arguments in *Narrative History and Ethnic Boundaries,* esp. pp. 266–281. These "sins of Jeroboam which he sinned and which he caused Israel to sin" (*ḥaṭṭô't yārob'ām 'ašer ḥāṭā' wa'ăšer heḥĕṭî' 'et-yiśrā'ēl;* 1 Kgs 15:26, 30; 15:34; 16:19; 16:26; 16:31; 22:53; 2 Kgs 3:3; 10:29; 13:6; 13:11; 14:24; 15:9; 15:18; 15:24; 15:28) form an important structural device in the presentation of the accounts of the kingdom of Israel which culminates in 2 Kgs 17:20–23, where these sins are presented as the reason for the destruction of Israel.

[69] For analyses of the compositional structure of this passage, see B. S. Childs, *The Book of Exodus,* pp. 557–562; W. I. Toews, *Monarchy and Religious Institution in Israel under Jeroboam I,* pp. 123–135; J. Van Seters, *The Life of Moses,* pp. 290–295; etc.

[70] J. Blenkinsopp suggests that the entire episode is "a D composition," thus conforming to his concept of a deuteronomistic editing of the Tetrateuchal materials. Additionally, since Exodus 32–34 conforms to the frequent deuteronomistic pattern of sin, punishment, and forgiveness, Blenkinsopp suggests that the entire section is deuteronomistic (*The Pentateuch,* pp. 192–194).

[71] B. S. Childs, *The Book of Exodus,* p. 562.

Moses was on the mountain for forty days and nights (cf. Exod 34:28), receiving "the tablets of the covenant" (*lûḥōt habběrît;* 9:9; cf. Exod 31:18)[72] which had been "written by the finger of God" (*kětûbîm bě'eṣba' 'ĕlōhîm;* 9:10; cf. Exod 31:18b).

Yahweh then instructed Moses to descend quickly from the mountain because the people "have made themselves a molten image" (*'āśû lāhem massēkâ;* 9:12). Here, the Exodus account provides a much fuller description of the people's acts than the deuteronomistic one. Exod 32:1–6 explains the people's actions: Moses' delay in coming back down the mountain led the people to request that Aaron make a god/gods (*'ĕlōhîm*) for them since they did not know what had happened to Moses (32:1).[73] Aaron conceded to their wishes and constructed the image of a calf from the gold that the people had brought (vv. 2–4), built an altar, and proclaimed a festival to Yahweh (v. 5). On the next day, the people offered sacrifices and celebrated, actions interpreted as the worship of the calf image (32:8).[74]

The role of Aaron in the narrative has occasioned much discussion, especially given his positive role in an act that was understood universally as a violation of Yahweh's will (cf. esp. 32:21–25). B. S. Childs is clearly correct in noting that the negative view of Aaron, who was unable to restrain Israel from committing this misdeed, draws attention back to Moses, the mediator powerful enough to restrain Yahweh from his anger (32:9–14).[75] Deut 9:20, however, notes that Yahweh was angry enough with Aaron to destroy him, but that it was Moses' intercession that saved him also.[76] In conjunction with this intercessory role of Moses is Yahweh's decision

---

[72] On the carefully patterned structure of this section, built on the references to forty days and forty nights, see M. Weinfeld, *Deuteronomy 1–11*, pp. 426–428.

[73] See above, Chap. 7, n. 14.

[74] F. M. Cross notes the numerous polemical aspects of this account and concludes that it is to be understood as a reapplication of an original etiology concerning the cultic installation at Bethel, that now contains a strongly negative tone in light of the cultic actions taken by Jeroboam (*Canaanite Myth and Hebrew Epic*, pp. 73–75).

[75] *The Book of Exodus*, p. 570.

[76] A. D. H. Mayes suggests that this verse, like 10:6–9, is a later addition by the Priestly writer, who was attempting to bring this section into correspondence with material dealing with Aaron found in Numbers 20 and 33 (*Deuteronomy*, pp. 200, 205–206). Interestingly, M. Weinfeld also notes that this constitutes an independent unit, as is indicated by the reference "in that time" (*bā'ēt hahîw'*), a phrase added in the Samaritan Pentateuch to Exod 32:10 and found in the Qumran text of Exod 32:10–30 (4QpaleoEx^m) (*Deuteronomy 1–11*, p. 411). While it is difficult to evaluate the significance of the latter, the flexible nature of the textual tradition should not be overlooked. Clearly, editorial changes were possible in the materials into the second century BCE.

with respect to Israel: in Deut 9:14 he announces his decision to destroy Israel completely, but proclaims to Moses that "I will make you into a nation stronger and more numerous than he" (*wĕ ʾeʿĕśeh ʾôtĕkā lĕgôy-ʿāṣûm wārāb mimmennû*), a transfer of the ancestral promise that is also contained in Exod 32:10 (*wĕ ʾeʿĕśeh ʾôtĕkā lĕgôy gādôl*). Deut 9:15–17 recounts Moses' descent from the mountain and his breaking of the tablets (cf. 32:19). Only here does the account identify the image as a calf (*ʿegel;* 9: 16; cf. 21). Because of the people's sin, Moses prostrated himself before Yahweh (9:18; cf. v. 9), fearing that he would fulfill his threat to destroy Israel. The very nature of the "divine paradox" is underlined, since Yahweh could promise to give Israel the land sworn to the ancestors (9:5) and then determine to destroy them completely, and, presumably, give the promise to another. The necessity of intercession for a people who would not learn constitutes a major emphasis of the account.

In each of the narratives, Moses' intercession before Yahweh is successful. Problematical, as might be assumed by now, is the nature of the potential literary relationship between the two accounts. Several clear parallels exist between them: Deut 9:26, 29 and Exod 32:11; Deut 9:27 and Exod 32:13; and Deut 9:28, Num 14:16, and Exod 32:12 all contain parallel constructions.[77] Clear also are the parallels that exist between the two accounts of Moses' destruction of the image (Deut 9:21; Exod 32:20).[78] The preceding discussions regarding the parallel accounts contained in these selected sections of Deuteronomy and the Tetrateuchal materials suggest that there can be little reasonable doubt that some literary connection exists among the variety of materials under consideration. Despite the efforts of commentators, no reliable criteria have been developed by which one might demonstrate the direction of such connections. For those who argue for the classical form of the documentary hypothesis, it is clear that the accounts in

---

[77] In Deut 9:26, Moses implores Yahweh not to destroy his people "whom you led out from Egypt with a strong hand" (*ʾăšer-hôṣēʾtā mimmiṣrayim bĕyād ḥăzāqâ*), a sentiment further expanded in v. 29, which notes that the people were delivered "by your great power and your outstretched hand" (*bĕkōḥăkā haggādôl ûbizroʿăkā hannĕṭûyâ*), expressions that are clearly paralleled by Exod 32:11, "with great power and a strong arm" (*bĕkōaḥ gādôl ûbĕyād ḥăzāqâ*). Similarly, in Deut 9:27 Moses implores Yahweh to "remember (*zĕkōr*) your servants, Abraham, Isaac, and Jacob," while Exod 32:13 recounts the plea to "remember (*zĕkōr*) Abraham, Isaac, and Israel, your servants." Deut 9:28 contains Moses' appeal to Yahweh's pride, asking him not to destroy the people because Egyptians would attribute their destruction to Yahweh's inability to bring the people into the land, a sentiment reflected also in Exod 32:12 and Num 14:16.

[78] For a comparison of these two verses, see M. Weinfeld, *Deuteronomy 1–11*, pp. 412–414.

the Tetrateuch are primary and that the deuteronomistic materials are summarizing and condensing them for a different purpose. Those who regard the deuteronomistic materials as primary argue then that the Tetrateuchal writers have chosen to supplement the accounts in Deuteronomy, thus introducing a variety of parallel accounts. As I have been suggesting, however, a third approach, which does not share the presupposition that the texts were originally intended to be read as a whole, might provide a way out of the dilemma.

III. The Cultic Legislation—Some Comparisons

Contained in the Pentateuchal materials are five different cultic calendars, assigned traditionally to each of the major Pentateuchal sources: Exod 23:14–18; Exod 34:18–23 (J or JE); Deut 16:1–17 (D); Lev 23:1–43 (H & P); Num 28:1–29:39 (a late appendix to P [?]). While a number of types of offerings and cultic activities are detailed in these texts, they share a common focus in their presentation of the three major festivals celebrated during the Hebrew year: Passover (*pesaḥ*)/Unleavened Bread (*maṣṣôt*); Weeks (*šĕbūʿôt*); and Booths (*sukkôt*). While one might be willing to allow for regional variation, traditional changes over time, etc., one might still expect that, in the final edition of a work that was intended to be read and understood as constituting a unity, the festival calendar would be regularized. This, however, is not the case. It is the very lack of regularity, together with the assignment of certain descriptions of the festivals to particular sources in the Pentateuch, which plays an essential role in the formation and maintenance of the documentary hypothesis.[79] The assurance with which such analyses of the materials were performed and their editorial relationships expounded that once dominated the field can no longer be maintained.

It is generally agreed that the calendar contained in Exodus 23, along with the parallel in Exodus 34, represent the earliest forms of the traditions recounting the celebration of these festivals and that these precede the calendars found in Deuteronomy 16, Leviticus 23, and Numbers 28–29.[80]

---

79 See the classic discussion of these festivals in J. Wellhausen, *Prolegomena to the History of Ancient Israel*, pp. 83–120.

80 B. S. Childs, *The Book of Exodus*, p. 483; S. R. Driver, *Deuteronomy*, p. 118; etc. According to the analysis of R. de Vaux, Exod 23:14–18 is Elohistic; Exod 34:18–23 is Yahwistic; Deut 16:1–17 is deuteronomic; Leviticus 23 belongs to the Holiness Code; and Numbers 28–29

Because there are a number of differences among these calendars, it is best to treat the festivals in the order in which they are presented and then move to some generalized statements about the possible relationships among these texts. The most problematic of the three festivals is the presentation of the rituals of Passover and Unleavened Bread. Exod 23:14 begins with the notice shared by all of the texts: "Three times during the year you shall celebrate a feast to me" (*šālōš rĕgālîm tāḥōg lî baššānâ;* cf. Deut 16:16), a command that all males were required to obey (*kol-zĕkûrĕkā;* 23:17). The first festival listed is the "feast of Unleavened Bread" (*ḥag hammaṣṣôt*), a seven-day festival during which *maṣṣôt* was to be eaten. This feast was to be held in the month of Abib (*ḥōdeš hāʾābîb*, "for in it you went out of Egypt" (*kî-bô yāṣāʾtā mimmiṣrayim;* 23:15; cf. 13:4; 34:18). It is further noted that no person should appear before Yahweh without offerings.[81]

Remarkably absent from this calendar, however, is any reference to the Passover, with which the festival of *maṣṣôt* was already associated in Exod 12:1–13:16.[82] To complicate the picture, it must be noted that major portions of these materials are commonly assigned to the Priestly source, which would then suggest that the connection between Passover and Unleavened Bread might be secondary.[83] This connection between Passover

---

comes from Priestly circles and provides a commentary on Leviticus 23 (*Ancient Israel: Vol. 2*, pp. 471–474). With respect to the latter, see the discussion of I. Knohl, who argues that Leviticus 23 (and Numbers 28–29) reflects the work of two Priestly groups, PT, the Priestly Torah (Knohl's designation for the P materials), and the later HS, or Holiness School, who put these chapters into their present form (*The Sanctuary of Silence*, esp. pp. 8–45).

[81] B. S. Childs notes that this calendar is part of the section known as the "Book of the Covenant" but gives every indication of being an originally independent unit (*The Book of Exodus*, p. 483).

[82] Explanations for this absence, like that of J. I. Durham, who states that the lack of any reference to Passover is "entirely logical" because the point of reference in the calender in 23:14–17 is the agricultural feast from which the festival of *maṣṣôt* was to be taken, are less than convincing.

[83] For discussions of the assignment of these materials, see the commentaries. It is interesting that B. S. Childs assigns 12:2–23, 27b, 29–34, 37–39 to J; 12:24–27a, 13:3–16 to D; 12:35–36 to E; and the remainder of 12:1–13:6 to P. He offers no defense of this division (*The Book of Exodus*, p. 184). In contrast, J. Van Seters argues that all of 12:1–28, 43–50 and 13:1–2 belong to the Priestly source, hence making them part of the latest strata of traditions contained in the Pentateuch. This means that 12:29–39 and 13:3–16 are parts of the J account, which was then supplemented by P. This would suggest, then, that Passover had no role in J. Instead, J emphasized the celebration of *maṣṣôt* and the redemption of the first-born (13:3–16; *The Life of Moses*, pp. 114–123).

and Unleavened Bread is presumed in both the calendars in Lev 23:4–8 and in Num 28:16–25.[84]

The problem that arises, then, is the relationship of these materials to the Passover/Unleavened Bread materials contained in Deut 16:1–8.[85] According to this calendar, the feast of Passover is to be celebrated in the month of Abib (16:1), i.e., at the time which Exod 23:15 designates for the festival of Unleavened Bread, which is connected with the Passover in Exod 12:1–13:16 and 34:25. The passage in Deuteronomy, however, creates a problem with its requirement in 16:2 that the Passover sacrifice be made "in the place where Yahweh chooses to make his name dwell" (*bammāqôm 'ăšer-yibḥar yhwh lĕšakkēn šĕmô šām*).[86] In contrast to the familial celebration of the rite described in Exod 12:1–14, Passover becomes in Deuteronomy a pilgrimage festival, a deuteronomistic tradition reflected in the accounts of the celebration of the festival in Josh 5:10–11 and 2 Kgs 23:21–23.[87] Deut 16:4b notes that the flesh of the sacrifice must be eaten

---

[84] A major innovation in the presentation of these festivals that characterizes the Priestly materials is their connection to specific dates. Hence, the Passover is to begin on the fourteenth day of the first month, while the feast of *maṣṣôt* begins on the fifteenth (Lev 23:5–6; Num 28: 16–17). This dating also occurs in the Priestly materials in Exod 12:2–6, 18–19. A further development is found in Num 9:9–14, where provision is made for the celebration of the Passover on the fourteenth day of the second month for those who were either ritually unclean via corpse contamination or on a lengthy journey and unable to celebrate the festival in the first month. See above, Chap. 8, pp. 258–259.

[85] The problem of the origins of the various festivals is not important in the present context. While numerous studies have been devoted to the origin and evolution of both the Passover and Unleavened Bread festivals, there is as yet little agreement among scholars. For an overview of the major positions, see the bibliography and discussion in J. E. Hartley, *Leviticus*, pp. 363–365, 376–383.

[86] In the deuteronomistic history, this place is to be understood as Jerusalem, the city which Yahweh had chosen, and the site of the Temple. For other occurrences of this and related phrases, see M. Weinfeld, *Deuteronomy and the Deuteronomic School*, pp. 324–325. The utility of this phraseology is often overlooked, for with the loss of Jerusalem and the Temple, the possibility of sacrifice at a shrine could be reapplied within changing circumstances and needs. Hence, from the perspective of exiled Judahites in the Diaspora, the possibility of fulfilling the commands of Deuteronomy, even with respect to sacrifice, remained a reality.

[87] In Josh 5:10–11, the Israelites celebrated the Passover in Gilgal, the base camp for the conquest. Josh 5:10 notes that the festival was held on the fourteenth day of the month, in the evening. Josh 5:11 states that "on the morrow of the Passover" (*mimmoḥŏrat happesaḥ*), i.e., on the next day, they ate some of the produce of the land, including *maṣṣôt* and parched grain. The temporal reference is missing in the LXX (cf. *BHS*), and could either be original or indicate a later gloss to connect the eating of the *maṣṣôt* with the Priestly materials in Exod 12:15–20, etc. Whether this indicates that the narrative intends a connection between Passover and *maṣṣôt* is ambiguous from the context. The account in 2 Kgs 23:21–23 recounts the Passover celebrated

before the morning (cf. Exod 23:18; 34:25). Deut 16:5–6 explicitly prohibits the offering of the Passover sacrifice apart from the divinely designated central sanctuary. Verse 7 commands that the offering be eaten at the designated place and that on the next morning the people are to return to their tents.[88] In examining the sections in Deut 16:1–8 that address the celebration of the Passover, it would seem quite clear that the celebration in Deuteronomy is envisioned as a one-day pilgrimage to a specified shrine at which an evening sacrifice was offered and eaten to commemorate the people's exodus from Egypt (vv. 1–2, 6). In the deuteronomic account, the celebration of the Passover takes on a national ethnic ideal, for the whole of the nation was to gather at the sanctuary and commemorate their ancestors' exodus from Egypt, while in the other Tetrateuchal materials, it is the familial associations with the ritual that are emphasized. I shall argue below that these two emphases stand in tension with each other, but are not necessarily mutually exclusive.

Also embedded in this text are commands concerning the celebration of the festival of *maṣṣôt*. In contrast to the calendars contained in Exod 23:15, 18; 34:18, 25; 12:1–14, 15–20, which maintain a distinction between the festivals of *maṣṣôt* and *pesaḥ,* Deut 16:1–8 combines the two into a single ritual celebration.[89] In combining them, the deuteronomic legislation creates an internal tension between the two celebrations. Now, the one-day pilgrimage festival of *pesaḥ* is combined with the seven-day celebration of *maṣṣôt,* transforming the latter into a pilgrimage celebration also. One must surely question whether it would be likely that many Israelites would be able to journey to Jerusalem, or another centralized shrine, celebrate the Passover in Abib, at the time of the barley harvest, return home the next day (16:7), and then return for an assembly on the seventh day of *maṣṣôt* (16: 8). At the very least, the deuteronomic version of *pesaḥ/maṣṣôt* modifies

---

according to the "book of the covenant" (*sēper habbĕrît*) during the time of Josiah. The only other details given note that no such celebration had occurred since the time of the Judges and that this one was held in Jerusalem in the eighteenth year of Josiah's reign (vv. 22–23). No mention is made of *maṣṣôt* or of the day of the month on which it was held. Both texts, however, do presume a communal celebration of the feast at a central sanctuary in accord with deuteronomic prescriptions.

88 It has long been noted that Deut 16:7 commands that the Passover offering be boiled (*biššēl*), an order that directly contradicts the Priestly instructions in Exod 12:9. Why the Passover sacrifice is extended to cattle, or is allowed to be cooked as any other offering, remains obscure.

89 M. Weinfeld, *Deuteronomy 1–11,* p. 23.

completely the domestic aspects of the festival and transforms them into national/ethnic ideals.[90]

With respect to the literary relationships among these texts, especially those in Exodus and Deuteronomy, there are a number of intriguing problems. When one compares Deut 16:3–4, 8 with Exod 23:15, 18; 34:18, 25; and 13:3–6, it appears that the texts are related.[91] As with the materials considered in the previous section, what is far from clear is the direction of dependence among these texts. The situation can be easily illustrated by juxtaposing two contrasting interpretations. According to M. Weinfeld, the deuteronomic calendar is dependent upon the laws contained in the "book of the covenant" (Exod 21–23), which were revised in accord with deuteronomic ideology which was intended to replace the older legislation.[92] A part of this position is the presupposition that both the festivals of *pesaḥ* and *maṣṣôt* are ancient, predating the monarchic period. In direct contrast to this is the position of J. Van Seters, who argues that the earliest statement concerning the Passover is in Deut 16:5, where it originally had no connection with Unleavened Bread. This means that the references to *maṣṣôt* contained in Deut 16:3–4, 8 are late, secondary glosses to Deuteronomy, not deuteronomic borrowings of earlier materials. The celebration of *maṣṣôt* was an exilic development, arising from the destruction of the Temple and the loss of a legitimate place to offer the Passover sacrifice. Only later, at the hands of the Priestly writer, were the two connected as closely as they are in the present texts.[93]

90 For the deuteronomic writer, as for the Priestly authors, all sacrifice was to be offered at the central shrine. A difference arises between the two, however, in the consideration of the sacral aspect of the slaughter of animals. From the perspective of the Priestly tradition, more particularly the "Holiness School," comes the idea that all slaughter, excepting only game animals, was a sacred act that required that the blood of the animal be sprinkled on the altar (Lev 7:1–7). Even the blood of game animals, which were not allowable as sacrifices, was to be covered with dust, since all blood was conceived of as possessing a sacral quality (Lev 17:13–14). The deuteronomic legislation allowed, on the other hand, for profane slaughter outside of Jerusalem, noting that the blood might be poured on the ground like water (Deut 12:15–16, 20–24), while maintaining the prohibition against eating blood (M. Weinfeld, *Deuteronomy and the Deuteronomic School*, pp. 213–214).

91 A convenient chart comparing these texts is given by S. R. Driver (*Deuteronomy*, p. 192).

92 *Deuteronomy 1–11*, p. 19.

93 *The Life of Moses*, pp. 119–127. Van Seters also argues that the connection of the offering of the first-born with the tenth plague and the exodus, reflected in the stipulations of Exod 34:19–20 (cf. Exod 13:11–16), is a post-deuteronomistic development that he assigns to his reconstructed Yahwist. Deut 15:19–23 presents the deuteronomic prescriptions for the first-born, but without connection to the exodus stories (pp. 120, 124).

While it must be admitted that Van Seters' reconstruction of the literary history of the texts is somewhat idiosyncratic, it must also be pointed out that it is such *only* when placed alongside the regnant paradigm in the field. It should be noted that there is no reason *not* to accept the well formulated arguments of Van Seters, based on the evidence available. The evaluations of the relationship between the festivals of *pesah* and *massôt*, then, suffer from the same problems encountered earlier: there are no clear criteria on which to base informed judgments concerning the relationship of the texts to each other. While the materials could conceivably be pre-exilic, they may just as likely date to the Persian period or later. The accounts of the other two pilgrimage festivals offer no clearer picture.

The second and third pilgrimage festivals noted in Exod 23:16 are the "feast of the harvest" (*hag haqqāṣîr*) of the first-fruits and the "feast of ingathering" (*hag hāʾāsîp*). The latter was to be celebrated at the end of the year (*běṣēʾt haššānâ*), while no date is established for the former. The "feast of the harvest" probably refers to the celebration at the completion of the grain harvest in June, while the "festival of ingathering" is held at the completion of the grape/olive season in September, a calendar that clearly presumes a Fall New Year.[94] The parallel text in Exod 34:22 notes: "You shall observe a feast of weeks (*hag šābūʿōt*), the first-fruits of the wheat harvest (*bikkûrê qěṣîr ḥiṭṭîm*) and the feast of ingathering (*hag hāʾāsîp*) at the turn of the year (*těqûpat haššānâ*)." Exod 23:16 and 34:22 agree on the

---

[94] B. S. Childs, *The Book of Exodus*, pp. 483–484. The period during which Israel's calendar shifted to a Spring New Year is not certain. Since none of the biblical texts provides a complete description of the length of the year or the exact time from which its beginning was reckoned, the matter remains debated. For a discussion of the available data, see R. de Vaux, *Ancient Israel, Vol. 1*, pp. 190–193. To complicate the matter further, it must be noted that there is a distinct possibility that different calendars might have been employed to calculate different types of events. This is clearly the case reflected in the Mishnah (*m. Roš Haš*; Neusner translation):

    1:1 A. There are four new years:
          B. (1) the first day of Nisan is the new year for kings and festivals;
          C. (2) the first day of Elul is the new year for tithing cattle.
          D. R. Eleazar and R. Simeon say, "It is on the first day of Tishre."
          E. (3) The first day of Tishre is the new year for the reckoning of years, for Sabbatical years, and for jubilees,
          F. for planting [trees] and for vegetables;
          G. (4) the first day of Shebat is the new year for trees, in accord with the opinion of the house of Shammai.
          H. The House of Hillel says, "On the fifteenth day of that month [is the new year for trees]."

designation and time of the "feast of ingathering" (*ḥag ḥā'āsîp*), but differ in their designation for the festival associated with the wheat harvest.

In Exod 34:22, the festival of the first-fruits of the wheat harvest is designated as "the feast of Weeks" (*ḥag šābū'ōt*), which would correspond to the "feast of the harvest"(*ḥag haqqāṣîr*) noted in Exod 23:16. This festival is clearly agricultural in origin and intent, since its celebration is determined by the beginning of the wheat harvest. According to the deuteronomic tradition, which also calls this celebration "the feast of Weeks" (*ḥag šābū'ōt;* 16:10, 16; Ezek 45:21), the time of its celebration is set at "seven weeks" (*šib'â šābū'ōt*) after the beginning of the harvest of the standing grain (16:9). The notice of this festival in Lev 23:15–16 adds some precision to the dating, but also introduces a new problem. Lev 23:15 designates the celebration of the festival as beginning fifty days after the offering of the sheaf, which was performed on the day after the Sabbath on the festival of Passover (cf. 23:11). Hence, according to the Priestly tradition, the "feast of Weeks" was celebrated fifty days after the Passover, hence, the designation Pentecost (*hē pentēkostē hēmera=ḥǎmiššîm yôm*).[95]

In addition to these two festivals, the various calendars add a third. This one is designated "the festival of ingathering" (*ḥag ḥā'āsîp*) in Exod 23:16 and 34:22. Interestingly, Deut 16:13, 16 and Lev 23:39 call it the "festival of Booths" (*ḥag hassukkôt;* cf. Ezra 3:4; Zech 14:16, 18–19; etc.). Lev 23:16 refers to it as the "feast of Yahweh" (*ḥag yhwh*), while elsewhere it is called simply "the feast" (*heḥāg;* 1 Kgs 8:65; 2 Chr 7:8; Neh 8:14; Ezek 45:23, 25). The celebration of this festival is associated with the harvest at the end of the year in Exod 23:16 and 34:22. Deut 16:13 notes that the festival lasts seven days, is associated with the ingathering of the vintage, and is located, as the others, in the place that Yahweh chooses (16:15). None of these three texts associates the festival in any way with the exodus from Egypt. Such an association is made in Lev 23:42–43, where the construction of booths is interpreted as a commemoration of the dwellings used in the wilderness. In Leviticus this festival also lasts seven days, but, as is

---

95 The phrase "on the morrow of the Sabbath" has caused a great deal of debate. The Sadducees understood it literally, and this meant that the festival always fell on a Sunday. The Pharisees, on the other hand, interpreted "Sabbath" as the first day of Passover (which was a Sabbath) so that the festival always falls on the fifty-first day from the first day of Passover. The Qumran community seems to have interpreted "Sabbath" as the Sabbath after the end of the Passover. Because they had a fixed solar calendar, this "Sabbath" always fell on the twenty-sixth of Nisan, so the festival always landed on Sunday, the fifteenth of Sivan (Louis Jacobs, "Shabuot," *EncJud* 14:1319). It is interesting to note that Ezekiel does not mention this festival.

the custom in that calendar, the date is fixed to the fifteenth day of the seventh month (23:34) rather than being associated with the activities of the harvest.

It is clear, then, that despite a number of similarities among the calendars, there are also significant differences. Likewise, while it is clearly possible to discern among these texts a process of standardization that allows for the study of the evolution of the traditions, as did J. Wellhausen,[96] this is not the only way in which the materials associated with the festivals might be read. Much of the interpretation of the parallel accounts depends upon the starting point of the interpreter. If one begins with the standard assumption that the texts of the Pentateuch must be taken as a whole, and read *only* in light of that whole, then one might be inclined to adopt a position like that of M. Weinfeld, when he notes that the author of Deuteronomy, the last book of the Pentateuch, utilized the legal traditions contained in the earlier Tetrateuch and intended his laws to replace those.[97] One might then infer that the "later" Priestly writer, in supplementing the materials available to him with a new account, also intended to replace traditions that ran counter to his position.

There may be, however, another way of approaching the issue that is related to the method used earlier. One of the major questions that the standard approach to the interpretation of these materials has not been able to answer is the underlying reason for duplicating materials, thus creating extensive conflicts among traditions, rather than a simple editing out of contradictory materials. Some scholars, following S. Sandmel, argue that the authors of the biblical narratives were hesitant to change the received text and instead practiced the "process of neutralizing by addition"[98] to explain conflicts present in the text. Such an explanation suggests that the biblical texts had received some type of canonical status at an early point in the history of their composition. This would certainly go against the evidence for textual modifications that are implied by the diverse chronological traditions found among the MT, LXX, and Samaritan Pentateuchs.

But the contents of the materials in the Tetrateuch, while not displaying the degree of thematic unity once supposed,[99] do reflect one clear probability. They represent religious and cultural traditions that have been drawn

---

[96] *Prolegomena to the History of Ancient Israel*, pp. 83–120.

[97] *Deuteronomy 1–11*, p. 19.

[98] "The Haggada within Scripture," *JBL* 80 (1961) 120.

[99] R. Rentdorff, *The Problem of the Process of the Transmission in the Pentateuch*, esp. pp. 178–206.

from a number of sources. Likewise, it seems most probable that the present shape of the Tetrateuch, if not the Pentateuch as a whole, is the result of at least one literary supplementation, and probably more. This is not to suggest that the various sources reflect ancient traditions. It is also not to suggest that the Tetrateuchal materials ever existed in a basic continuous narrative account prior to the authorial activities that might have been initiated during the Persian period.[100] This is not, however, to adopt the explanation offered by Sandmel. While it does seem probable that supplementation to an existing text or texts must be argued, it does not mean that the supplementation occurred out of a desire to "neutralize" any previously existing account or prescriptions.

The problem of accounting for parallel materials, duplicate stories, contradictory laws, etc.[101] has been greatly increased through the adoption of a very ancient rabbinic understanding of the texts: they are divinely inspired and, hence, contain no contradictions. The texts we have, as is well known, do indeed contain contradictions and contrasting accounts of the same events. J. Levenson suggests that the solution to such a quandary is either to act arbitrarily and choose one text over its parallel, or to assign equal sanctity to all of the materials, contradictions notwithstanding.[102] It might be argued that such problems that develop when the texts are read as a whole, which presupposes in a sense the theological position noted above, seem less problematic when this presupposition is dropped. It would hardly be original to suggest that the standard literary critical approach to understanding the composition of the Tetrateuch, Pentateuch, or, for that matter, any biblical text, represents a modern, European book view that is most probably a misrepresentation of the ways in which literature was produced in the

---

100 While it might be possible to equate this late version of a Tetrateuchal narrative with what J. Van Seters designates as the "Yahwist," I am hesitant to do so on the basis of the arguments above that suggest that sufficient criteria for such distinctions among "Yahwistic," "Elohistic," and "Priestly" materials do not exist. For a critique of the standard criteria, see R. N. Whybray, *The Making of the Pentateuch*, pp. 43–126.

101 See the discussion by M. Weinfeld, *Deuteronomy 1–11*, pp. 19–24, 30–35.

102 *The Hebrew Bible, the Old Testament, and Historical Criticism*, p. 3. Levenson notes that it is the latter that allows the texts to address modern concerns: "By harmonizing inconcinnities, the tradition presents itself with a timeless document, one that appears to speak to the present only because the historical setting of the speaking voice or the writing hand has been suppressed, and all voices and all hands are absorbed into an eternal simultaneity" (*Ibid.*). For a presentation of the development of the concept that Torah is both eternal and preexistent, see Warren Harvey, "Torah," *EncJud* 15:1236–1238.

ancient Near East.[103] What might be novel would be to suggest that scholars break away from the "book view" completely in attempting to understand the possible functions of the completed work of the Tetrateuch/Pentateuch/ primary history. Instead of attempting to construct a theory that explains why an editor or author supplemented a document with a variation on the same story or the like, there may be many insights to be gained by suggesting another approach to understanding the variety of arguments that have been used to support the standard theories of sources underlying the Pentateuch and the history of their formation.

IV. Tetrateuch, Pentateuch, and Primary History:
Some Conclusions

Rather than rehearsing the litany of reasons for rejecting the standard interpretation of the materials constituting the Pentateuch that have been mentioned in the preceding pages, I would like to suggest some of the parameters that might be used to frame a new model for approaching these documents. A beginning place is the recognition that the community that produced the biblical materials was not the only religious community claiming descent from the variety of traditions associated with the defunct nation-state of Judah. Likewise, the shapes that various forms of early Judaism took were not always the same and did not develop in the same directions or with the same speed in every locale. Clearly, the religious communities of Elephantine and Samaria suggest the variety of competing ways in which the connections to the traditions associated with Judah could be adopted and adapted. Into the search for a single theory to account for the growth of the textual traditions must be inserted the recognition of the plurality of groups that might have constituted the intended audience for the materials.

Thanks to the emphasis on centralization that forms a critical part of the deuteronomistic corpus, Jerusalem emerged as a potential unifying sym-

---

103 I. Engnell phrased it in this way: "It is not necessary for a person to have a very profound understanding of the similarities between the various cultures of the ancient Near East to be able to see that the whole literary-critical system is based upon a complete misunderstanding of the actual situation. It reflects a modern, anachronistic *book view*, and attempts to interpret ancient biblical literature in modern categories, an *interpretatio europaeica moderna*" ("The Pentateuch," *A Rigid Scrutiny*, p. 53).

bol for Judaism in the Diaspora.[104] This was, in all probability, a result of the Persian decision to refortify Jerusalem, thus enhancing its importance in the area beginning in the mid-fifth century BCE.[105] With the reestablishment of Jerusalem as an important urban center, the cultic significance of the city could have been bolstered by the claims of the deuteronomistic materials that this was to be the only legitimate place of worship of Israel's only god, Yahweh. These same narrative accounts, as I have argued elsewhere, provided an outline of the social and ethnic identity of the people who would designate themselves, and be designated, by the ethnic descriptor, "Israelite/Hebrew."[106]

In addition to the deuteronomistic claims regarding Jerusalem and the Persian support of its status, another factor also made Jerusalem a central symbol for early Judaism as it emerged at that time throughout the Diaspora.[107] Despite the fact that different forms of Judaism took radically differing positions on the Temple in Jerusalem, it is clear that the concept of Temple continued to play a central role in Judaism during the Persian and Hellenistic periods. Indeed, it appears that very few Jewish groups of those eras had any vision of their religious traditions without a Temple, at least prior to its destruction by the Romans in 70 CE.[108] The Temple in Jerusalem and the professional staff which served there, priests and scribes, would have provided the locus for the production of the materials that would

104 The notable obvious exception here is the Samaritan movement, which rejected the claims of Jerusalem and instead viewed Shechem and Mt. Gerizim as central symbols for their movement. The reasons for such a development were clearly connected to the rivalry of claims that developed among such groups in the Second Temple period. Still, the symbolic power of the Jerusalem cultus should not be overlooked with respect to the Samaritans, for that sectarian movement itself chose to adapt the basic collection of texts created by the Jerusalem guild to its own uses.

105 For the biblical and archaeological evidence for the refortification of Jerusalem at this time, see H. G. M. Williamson, "Nehemiah's Walls Revisited," *PEQ* 116 (1984) 81–88. A survey of the variety of ways in which the missions of Nehemiah and Ezra have been placed within the context of Persian imperial policies is presented by K. G. Hoglund, *Achaemenid Imperial Administration in Syria-Palestine and the Missions of Ezra and Nehemiah*, pp. 207–240.

106 *Narrative History and Ethnic Boundaries*, pp. 55–85.

107 On the varieties of Judaism emerging in the Persian age, see the discussions of M. Dandamayev, *et al.*, "The Diaspora," in *The Cambridge History of Judaism, Vol. 1*, ed. W. D. Davies and L. Finkelstein (Cambridge: Cambridge University Press, 1984), pp. 326–399.

108 A variety of understandings of the role of the Temple in Diaspora Judaism are presented by J. A. Overman and W. S. Green in "Judaism (Greco-Roman Period)," *ABD* III, 1039–1041. As they point out, the Temple remained a central symbol and concern in the Mishnah, a document produced over a century after its destruction by the Romans (p. 1039).

become the present *TANAK*. Since this Temple had been rebuilt with Persian support and staffed by "exiles" that had been born and trained outside of the land, it should not be too great a leap of logic to suggest that the collection and writing of the traditions of the people might also have been related to Persian policies.[109] By placing the production of the Tetrateuch within the context of this complex of emerging traditions associated with these early forms of Judaism, we might begin to address the question of the relationships among Tetrateuch, Pentateuch, and a primary history.

To accomplish this, a major conceptual shift must be made from the dominant conception of Judaism that governed the development of the documentary hypothesis and which, all too often, guides discussions among biblical scholars today. The interpretive model of Judaism that dominated the nineteenth and most of the twentieth century was one that understood the Judaism represented by the Temple in Jerusalem as the normative point of development. A newer, more historically nuanced model, understands that the Judaism associated with the Jerusalem Temple represented one particular system of Judaism among many, and that the history of the development of Judaism must be understood in terms of the evolution of ideological systems over time. While such systems were historically related, they also involved significant and substantive changes.[110] Once it is understood that the biblical materials reflect the traditions gathered together by one particular system of early Judaism and that that particular Judaism was not the only one that claimed to be a/the legitimate descendant of the religious traditions of the now defunct nation-state of Judah, then the basic foundations of the documentary hypothesis crumble. In simple, historical terms, we are unable to trace one single line of growth of these traditions or one line of documentary development from the period of the monarchy to that of the Second Temple. This calls, then, for a new interpretive model to explain the emergence of the materials that constitute the books of Genesis through Kings in the Hebrew canon.

Since it is necessary to establish a starting point, I shall begin with a major presupposition that has become more common in the field, but which admittedly remains within the arena of conjecture. Following the suggestions made by a number of scholars, I propose that the deuteronomistic

---

109 See above, Chap. 2, pp. 23–25.

110 See, for example, G. Boccaccini, "Multiple Judaisms," *BibRev* 11 (1995) 38–41, 46, and the bibliography cited there.

history be considered the earliest written history produced by those who claimed Judahite descent.[111] This would mean, then, that the deuteronomistic work is to be understood as analogous to the historical tradition represented by works such as that of Herodotus, dating to the mid-fifth century BCE.[112] This early national history, which described the rise and fall of Israel and Judah in the land of Canaan, interpreted throughout by deuteronomic concepts of covenant,[113] provided both an explanation for the disaster that had befallen Judah and a blueprint for the maintenance of Judahite culture, religion, and ethnicity against the threat of complete cultural assimilation.[114] Based on the final narrative event contained in this history (2 Kgs 25:27–30), it may be stated with confidence that the history, in its present form, cannot antedate 561 BCE. This would require, then, that the composition of the Tetrateuch be placed at a later, exilic or post-exilic date, and that the older model, which understands the stories in the Tetrateuch to have been composed earlier than the deuteronomic materials, be rejected. If this position is accepted, then the Tetrateuch never existed apart from the deuteronomistic history, for which it serves as an introduction.[115]

By adopting this position, we might begin to understand the formation of these materials in terms of their functional aspects. While the deuteronomistic history had presented an interpretation of the history of the nation, the addition of the Tetrateuchal materials resulted in the creation of a new category of history.[116] Now, the national history of Israel and Judah is traced back to the origins of the earth and of all peoples, creating a history that conformed to a known pattern that became a standard long after what is normally considered the "biblical period," and which is paralleled by such

---

111 Among others, see the works of J. Van Seters, *Prologue to History,* p. 332, and *The Life of Moses,* p. 457; M. Rose, *Deuteronomy und Jahwist,* pp. 316–328; J. Blenkinsopp, *The Pentateuch,* pp. 233–237; A. D. H. Mayes, *The Story of Israel between Settlement and Exile: A Redactional Study of the Deuteronomistic History,* p. 141; H. H. Schmid, *Der sogenannte Jahwist,* pp. 168–169; R. N. Whybray, *The Making of the Pentateuch,* p. 225; etc.

112 It is interesting to note that S. Mandell and D. N. Freedman have argued recently that Herodotus was familiar with and influenced by the primary history produced in Judah, i.e., by Genesis-Kings (*The Relationship between Herodotus' History and Primary History, passim*).

113 On the deuteronomic origins of the covenantal ideal, see L. Perlitt, *Bundestheologie im Alten Testament,* p. 232.

114 See my *Narrative History and Ethnic Boundaries, passim.*

115 See above, Chap. 3, pp. 62–71.

116 As has long been recognized, both the Tetrateuch and the Pentateuch, in terms of historiographic traditions in the ancient Near East, exist in a kind of limbo. They simply are without parallels (R. N. Whybray, *The Making of the Pentateuch,* p. 241).

works from the Hellenistic period as the *Babyloniaka* of Berossus and the *Aigyptiaka* of Manetho.[117] What is most important about such parallels is not just that they provide a literary context for understanding the Israelite "primary history," but that each of them was written in response to a particular cultural and historical situation. Both of these histories were written in response to the threats of assimilation and loss of national religious and cultural traditions that were presented by the conquests of the Greeks. Israel's "primary history" might also be understood as a response to the threats provided by the conquests by the Babylonians and Persians.

The older deuteronomistic history, which had centered on the possession and loss of the land, had also conceived of the national identity in terms of the monarchy of David.[118] It soon must have become clear that the restoration of a national monarchic state on the model of the older dynastic ideal represented by the traditions associated with David was not to be realized. The complete absence of the figure of Zerubbabel from the coronation scene in Zech 6:9–15 suggests that this model was lost in the official expectation and the messianic ideal was pushed into the future by those groups who maintained it. Likewise, the manner in which this same text, in its present corrupt form, moves the crown to Joshua, the high-priest, is illustrative of a significant ideological shift precipitated by the historical realities of the Second Temple period. While the visions of Ezekiel had replaced the king with a secular prince, secondary in importance to the Zadokite priesthood, now even this princely ideal was lost, leaving only the leadership of the priesthood associated with the Temple.[119]

Such a shift in the basic cultural patterns of the community's structure would have effected a corresponding change in the manner in which the community envisioned itself and its identity. No longer could conquest provide the best explanation for their claim to the land, for it was they who had now been conquered and resettled under the auspices of their new suzerains. But a strong claim to the land could be made by adjusting some already existing traditions. In the form given it by the deuteronomistic

117 J. Blenkinsopp, *The Pentateuch*, p. 41.

118 It was the reign of David that constituted Israel's "golden age," in terms of the development of its national and ethnic mythology. The deuteronomistic writers also presented a pattern and program for the restoration of that ideal. For a discussion of how the deuteronomistic writers perceived of these issues, see my *Narrative History and Ethnic Boundaries*, pp. 209–286.

119 On the official organization presupposed by Ezekiel's vision in chapters 40–48, see J. Levenson, *Theology of the Program of Restoration in Ezekiel 40–48*, pp. 111–158.

writer, Deuteronomy had provided the introduction to the subsequent history. Part of the rhetoric of Deuteronomy is its frequent emphasis upon the fact that Yahweh had promised the land to Israel's ancestors.[120] This emphasis created the basis for constructing a new sense of identity based on claims to genealogical descent which were grounded now in the original one to whom the unconditional promise had been granted, Abram/Abraham. Membership in the community could now be traced by ancestry,[121] and the promise of the land would be claimed by this group.

In addition to the promise of the land, Deuteronomy provides a number of additional frameworks that could be filled in by supplementation.[122] Israel's escape from bondage in Egypt, its covenant with Yahweh at his sacred mount, and the journey from Sinai to Moab, along with notice of the hardships and rebellions encountered, are all recounted in the narrative sections of Deuteronomy. The Tetrateuch develops these accounts and, in doing so, reshapes many of the stories and patterns established in Deuteronomy. Most importantly, it is the narratives associated with Mt. Sinai that provide new contours for the community associated with the Second Temple. One of the most pressing issues that the new Jerusalem temple cultus would face would be the issue of priestly legitimacy (cf. 1 Chr 5:27–41, etc.). Interestingly, Deuteronomy places little emphasis upon the priesthood, a fact that should occasion little surprise, since the book does not stress sacral institutions to any great degree.[123] The accounts of Leviticus and Numbers,

---

120 J. Van Seters notes the extremely complex problems associated with the theme of the promise of the land and its occupation. According to his reconstruction of the traditions of the land, the earliest idea was that the land belonged to Yahweh and possession of it was dependent upon obedience to Yahweh. The land was given to Israel after the exodus and was taken by conquest. Alongside this theme of national origins was another, i.e., the idea that the land had been promised to the eponymous ancestors, and the land had been unconditionally given to them quite apart from the traditions associated with the exodus. For Van Seters, it was the post-deuteronomistic, pre-Priestly exilic Yahwist that combined these two traditions to form the one that now dominates the Tetrateuch (*Prologue to History*, pp. 227–245).

121 The special emphasis placed upon genealogy and community is exemplified in the lists given in Ezra 2:1–64 and Neh 7:5b–72a. The near repetition of the Ezra list in Nehemiah was intended to serve as the basis for an expanded census that would contribute to the repopulation of Jerusalem and as identifying that group as one community which was defined by its allegiance to the law of Yahweh (J. Blenkinsopp, *Ezra-Nehemiah* [OTL; Philadelphia: Westminster, 1988], p. 45).

122 See above, pp. 293–306.

123 M. Weinfeld, *Deuteronomy 1–11*, p. 29. Deut 18:1–8 specifies that the priesthood should come from the tribe of Levi. Aaron, the ancestor from whom all priests, as contrasted with Levites, were to be descended according to the materials in Leviticus, is mentioned in only three places in Deuteronomy (9:20 [2x]; 10:6; 32:50), and never in connection with the priesthood.

which do provide precisely the structure of Israel's sacral institutions and which address the needs for ritual purity, reenvision the configuration of this new ethnicity, "Israel." It would be a mistake to suggest that the Tetrateuchal narratives represented simply a collection of materials intended to supplement the ideals expressed in Deuteronomy. Rather, these accounts, varied as they are, functioned to create a new and competing vision of the identity of Israel that built upon the ideal perspectives presented in Deuteronomy. Instead of focusing upon the image of the "law of the king" and the role of the Torah there (Deut 17:14–20), the Tetrateuchal narratives emphasize the cultus as the guarantee of the presence of Yahweh in accord with its revelation at Sinai/Horeb.

Such shifts of emphasis and changes in structures of leadership, and the effects which these things have upon group self-identities, are to be expected among groups that have been exiled from their homelands.[124] Such changes would be expected even more if, as suggested earlier, the very claims by those repopulating and reestablishing Jerusalem to stand in line of descent from those who had been exiled were ideological creations.[125] What does seem most certain concerning the "restoration" of a temple cultus in Jerusalem is that it was performed by subjects of the Persian government who had been commissioned by that government to repopulate Jerusalem and who had been identified, and identified themselves, as descendants of the ancient city of Jerusalem and the older national state of Judah. To support their claims to legitimacy and to provide the necessary ethnic descriptors to recreate their Judahite lineage, they claimed descent from the line of Jacob/Israel and, thus, inheritance of the divinely promised right to the land that had been given to their ancestors.

In recreating a variety of stories that complemented the deuteronomistic corpus, these writers inadvertently (?) created an Israelite "primary history" that stretched from the creation of the earth to the end of Israel's national existence. Whether this was done before the earliest such Greek histories or whether it was in imitation of them will remain debated for some time. It did, most probably, occur during the mid-fifth to fourth centuries BCE, and, most probably, took place in a manner quite different from that presumed by the commonly accepted models for the composition of such a history. As P. R. Davies has correctly argued, the explanation for the compilation of the biblical materials must begin with the recognition that it

---

124 See above, Chap. 1, p. 12.
125 See the discussion above, Chap. 3, pp. 62–71.

is to be attributed to "the society created in Judah in the Persian period."[126] What is often overlooked, however, is the inevitable diversity of such a society, even though it might have represented an ethnic group that was identified with the previous society associated with the state of Judah and the city of Jerusalem. It is precisely here that the documentary hypothesis, as well as the standard paradigm for understanding the development of the religions of ancient Israel and Judah, fails. Whatever group may have populated the scribal school established in Jerusalem, and it would have been imperative for the Persian administration that there be one, would have represented a number of diverse specialties.[127] Likewise, in compiling a document or set of documents that could be used by the priestly groups in defining the identity of "Israel" and in instructing the people in that identity, these scribes most probably utilized diverse traditions, e.g., regional, local, or otherwise divergent instructions concerned with the celebration of the festivals. That one cultic calendar should specify a festival in terms of an agricultural event and another in terms of a set calendar need mean only that there were different traditions associated with the celebration of that feast, not that there was any diachronic evolution of the practice. The same may be stated about the variations in divine names and doublets of stories contained in the Tetrateuch. They need not represent ancient, variant traditions reflecting differing sources. They may only represent a collection and collocation of variant regional traditions, at best. At worst, they may have been the result of a series of redactional layers laid one upon the other over a relatively brief period of scribal activity.

Such an approach as this brings the idea of the inception of the Tetrateuchal materials into line with some literary processes which we can begin to trace. While there still remains much to be debated about the process of the creation of the Mishnah and the Talmud, there do seem to be several generally established points. Each of these works may contain accurate reflections of ancient traditions, but in their present form, they also include a number of newly created positions that have, by virtue of their literary presentation, been set forth as ancient and traditional. Also, despite the traditions associated with the adaptation and utilization of each of these documents, they do not represent the culmination of a lengthy period of traditional literary growth. Rather, they are the result of the activity of specific scholarly scribal schools that, in a relatively brief period of time, recreated

---

126 *In Search of 'Ancient Israel'*, p. 94.
127 For a discussion of such, see P. R. Davies, *Ibid.*, pp. 115–117.

the traditions of the past to sustain and shape the present.[128] Despite the fact that these two works are some four to eight centuries later than the period in which the biblical materials were created, they nonetheless represent the best parallels we have for understanding the formation of the biblical accounts.

Hence, I suggest that the formation of the Tetrateuch be understood as an attempt to redefine the structure of the community in terms of a genealogically related group who understood themselves in terms of a specific cultic pattern, i.e., a community that defined itself by reference to the special covenantal relationship in which it stood with its deity, Yahweh. The identity of this people "Israel" was to be created and maintained through its cultus, one which stressed the necessities of moral and ritual purity to insure the presence of Yahweh in its midst. The ways in which these were to be maintained were through the continued proper cultic performance of sacrifice and adherence to the instructions of the priesthood. In terms of their material culture, kingship and national identity had been replaced by hierocratic home-rule and a new concept of ethnic identity. With the change in the physical and political structures of these new "Judahites" came, as would be expected, the creation of a new superstructure to support and maintain the identity of the people in its new world.[129]

In creating the Tetrateuchal materials as a complement to the materials in Deuteronomy and, in the course of development, recreating Moses as the central actor in the account, Deuteronomy was detached from its position as the foundational document which provided the ideological frame for the subsequent deuteronomistic history. While one result of the addition of the Tetrateuch to the deuteronomistic history was the creation of an Israelite "primary history," it is uncertain how this document functioned in the life of the cultus. At the same time that this "primary history" was created, the basis for redividing it was also conceived. At some point in the functional life of the "primary history," possibly at the time that the prophetic

---

[128] The composition of the Mishnah may provide another parallel with the writing of the biblical texts under consideration. According to J. Neusner, the Mishnah was a rabbinical response to the disasters of the two defeats at the hands of the Romans that intended to address the issues of Jewish oppression (*Judaism: The Evidence of the Mishnah* [Chicago: University of Chicago Press, 1981], pp. 282–283). Documents such as the Temple Scroll (11QT) or 4QMMT clearly suggest that both the Mishnah and the Talmud, despite their late compilations, stand in a lengthy line of tradition concerning the discussion and application of selected portions of the Torah and also attest to the wide diversity evident in the various forms of Judaism in their day.

[129] On the relationships existing among infrastructure, structure, and superstructure within cultural groups, see M. Harris, *Cultural Materialism*, pp. 51–55.

books were being assembled,[130] Deuteronomy was incorporated into the Tetrateuch through a modification of the tradition that Moses' death had been one of many events that had occurred along the journey in the wilderness to make it coincide with the completion of Moses' farewell address in Deuteronomy. The effect of this was to gather all of the material associated with Sinai/Horeb and the reception of the Torah into one narrative account. In response to the Achaemenid impetus to consolidate subject ethnic groups by supporting the collection and codification of their "traditional" laws and customs, the Pentateuch was produced by the scribal groups established in the rebuilt city of Jerusalem and its central religious shrine, the Temple.[131]

The Pentateuch that was created by these priests and scribes had as its central focus the materials associated with Sinai (Exod 19:1–Num 10:28), an episode that represents nearly one-fifth of the entire work.[132] Contained herein are the collected traditions that form not only the major elements of a national myth of ethnic identity, ranging from stories of origins, ancestry, golden age and its loss, to the promise of regaining that ideal moment. Such could have provided a supplement to the deuteronomistic history, but instead it served to reinvent the identity of the group. No longer did the monarchy represent the ideal; the proper maintenance of the cultus and its concomitant requirements of moral and ritual purity are now the visions to be initiated. To sanctify the land in a manner that would insure the presence of Yahweh, the god of heaven, in their midst, thus establishing themselves as a "kingdom of priests" and as a "holy nation" (Exod 19:6), required that they diligently follow the instructions and rituals detailed in the revelation at Sinai. While Moses had provided the model for prophecy in the deuteronomistic literature, the newly formed Pentateuch redirected the channels of authority, establishing Moses as the primary mediator of Yahweh's revelation of his will, but Aaron, the ancestor of the priesthood, as the functionary who would maintain those traditions. This shifting emphasis in the identity of the people is given literary expression with the missions of Nehemiah and Ezra, Persian officials who helped reestablish

130 The process of the collection and the function of the prophetic materials that are presently contained in the Hebrew bible stand beyond the boundaries of the present work. Several points are clear, however. Whatever the antiquity of the traditions reflected in the books attributed to the so-called "writing prophets," the present sayings have been edited to include more recent interpretive oracles. Additionally, it is clear that the final compilation of the materials was rather late, probably no earlier than the later Persian or early Hellenistic period. Tentatively, I would suggest that the group responsible for the final form of the prophetic books was related to, if not identical with, the group that created the Tetrateuchal narratives.

131 See above, Chap. 3, nn. 83–84.

132 J. Blenkinsopp, *The Pentateuch*, pp. 135–136.

Jerusalem and define the people in terms of the priestly functions associated with the instructions of the "book of the law of the god of heaven," Yahweh.

There can be little doubt that the priestly and scribal groups resettled in Judah by the Persians represented a diversely trained collection of persons. Likewise, this group most probably represented a number of widely divergent traditions associated with the pasts of the ancestral groups that they represented. Once they were resettled by the Achaemenid rulers and given the task of collecting and consolidating the traditions associated with "Israel," they no doubt took into account the variety of "traditional" forms which the religion had taken among the populace into whose midst they had been resettled. It would have been from this amalgam of materials, some potentially ancient, others probably fabricated, that the stories constituting the Pentateuch were created. Tensions among various stories attest to the fact that the Pentateuch was never intended to be read or analyzed as a whole, but rather to represent a general collection of materials, paratactically sequenced, from which parts could be extracted for a variety of reasons, religious, political, didactic, etc.

This approach, admittedly, would force scholars to abandon the idea that the sources underlying the Pentateuch date back in an unbroken chain to Israel's national origins during the time of David and Solomon.[133] I suggest that the advantages of such an approach far outweigh the disadvantages. By recognizing that the appropriate paradigm of Judaism is one that recognizes that religion's great diversity from its earliest time, one can understand the variations of materials more easily. The scribal groups responsible for the production of the Pentateuch chose to be as inclusive as possible in their efforts at collecting and preserving the "traditions" that would become sacred to this ethnic and religious community now reinvented and reenvisioned as "Israel." The connections are tenuous, the historical realities, fragile, the final work, monumental. But, it must always be remembered, even with its eventual canonization, it was not the culmination of the religious tradition. Rather, it was only one stage of development that represented one aspect of the traditions and literatures of one type of Judaism of its day. To lose perspective on this historical datum is to return to the mistaken paradigm of monolithic growth that has characterized the analysis of the Pentateuchal materials to the present day.

---

[133] For a detailed discussion of this shift, and the variety of positions that have developed, see G. N. Knoppers, "The Vanishing Solomon: The Disappearance of the United Monarchy from Recent Histories of Ancient Israel," *JBL* 116 (1997) 19–44.

⸺ ᴤ 10 ᴂ ⸺

Postscript: Recreating a Community

The previous chapters have argued that the various materials contained in Genesis through Kings may be understood as providing a narrative foundation for the reformulation and maintenance of "Israelite" ethnic and national identity in the Second Temple period. In presenting this argument, I have suggested that a new model for understanding the role and functions of the materials in the Tetrateuch and the Pentateuch might lead us to a new understanding of the formation of these compositions.[1] This approach seriously challenges several positions commonly assumed by modern researchers and argues that some of these should be abandoned altogether. One such position is the general attitude taken toward the understanding of these materials as "scripture." While I have not attempted a systematic investigation of the process of the formation of the Hebrew scriptures, I have suggested throughout that this must be understood as a cultural process that attributes authority to selected texts within specific historical and sociological situations. It is clear that this process was under way by the early second century BCE and was not complete until the end of the first century CE at the earliest. It is also apparent that though selected texts were beginning to be treated as "scripture" by this point in time, the text itself was not unchangeable.[2] Hence, even during the period of the selection of materials that would be treated as scriptural, the process of composition continued.

A second argument that has been developed is that while the standard Judaism based upon the Mishnah and the Talmud clearly identified the Torah with the Pentateuch, it is highly doubtful that any of the biblical references to the Torah made this identification. As our investigation suggests,

---

[1] The ways in which the "deuteronomistic history" functions to provide ethnic descriptors and boundaries are presented in my *Narrative History and Ethnic Boundaries*, pp. 32–37.

[2] Cf. J. Blenkinsopp, *The Pentateuch*, pp. 47–50.

the identification of Torah and Pentateuch belongs to the process of canon
formation and not to the period of the composition of the books composing
the Hebrew bible. A third area we have investigated concerns the manner in
which these texts might have been used. The prevailing approach to the
Tetrateuchal and Pentateuchal materials presumes that these accounts were
intended as a unified literary whole that was directed at an audience that
was literate enough to read the text as a whole. I have argued a very different position. In functional terms, the texts would have been read aloud and
interpreted for the general populace (cf. Neh 8:1–8), possibly at pilgrimage
festivals (Deut 31:11–13) or some other public event. In this way, the ruling
elite of the Second Temple would have been able to unite the populace by
the public reformulation of ethnic identity based upon the application of
certain selected texts. This "Israel" would have been recreated, not through
reading these texts as a whole, but by hearing portions of them interpreted
and applied to their present situations.

Additionally, while many of the traditions contained in the final form
of the Tetrateuchal and Pentateuchal stories might be ancient, the written
form in which we have them is no earlier than the Persian period. Hence,
this interpretive model for analyzing the formation of the Hebrew scriptures
focuses upon the restoration community of the Second Temple period. It
should occasion no surprise that the biblical materials began taking form
during this era, since the mid-Persian and Hellenistic periods were times of
major literary activity in early Judaism.[3] It was also a period when the
issues of religion and ethnicity were critical to the survival of the restored
Jerusalem community.

However one reconstructs the religion of ancient Israel and Judah, it
seems obvious that the religious traditions established by the post-exilic
community differed from those that had preceded them. The monarchy,
which had provided the support for the national religion of Judah in the pre-
exilic period, was no longer a living reality. Instead, the cultus established
after the exile developed as a "temple community," with little or no emphasis upon kingship. This alone necessitated modifications to the religious
traditions that had preceded them. Such changes directly affected the issue
of ethnic identity, for this restoration community was not a homogeneous

---

[3] For general overviews of the literature produced during this period, see M. E. Stone,
ed., *Jewish Writings of the Second Temple Period: Apocrypha, Pseudepigrapha, Qumran Sectarian Writings, Philo, Josephus* (CRINT; Assen/Philadelphia: Van Gorcum/Fortress, 1984),
and G. W. E. Nickelsburg, *Jewish Literature Between the Bible and the Mishnah: A Historical
and Literary Introduction* (Philadelphia: Fortress, 1981).

group. While many claiming Judahite descent returned from exile with the support of the Persian court, many more had remained in the vicinity of Jerusalem and also claimed legitimate descent from the pre-exilic ancestors. Control of the Temple and, hence, the land could be decided on the basis of the demonstration of continuity with the past. It was within the process of the formation of the Tetrateuch and the Pentateuch that the boundaries for ethnic identity were created and the foundations for the development of early Judaism laid.

By developing the argument in this way, I am suggesting that a new model for interpreting these materials might yield some highly instructive conclusions. It is clear that the consensus once claimed by the documentary hypothesis has disappeared. The model developed here makes no claim to address the major problems associated with this loss of consensus. Rather, it refocuses the issues and addresses them in a different manner. Instead of concentrating upon possible sources and redactional layers, this approach begins with the biblical texts that we possess and analyzes how they might have functioned *vis-à-vis* the assumptions outlined above. Following the lead taken by a number of other scholars, I have argued that the Tetrateuchal materials were composed as supplements to the deuteronomistic materials, rather than adopting the more common position that the deuteronomistic materials are built upon the Tetrateuchal traditions. The materials of the Tetrateuch, then, may be understood as constructing a full ethnic mythography, placing "Israel's" origins in space and time in the remote past, providing them with a particular genealogy, recounting the stories of migration, oppression, and liberation, and, most importantly, defining the unique aspects of this particular people.[4]

The variety of materials of various genres that constitute the Tetrateuch provide the foundations for the social and religious construction of "Israel's" identity. Utilizing these materials, the priesthood of the Temple could select those sections that were most appropriate to the needs of the community to develop those defining characteristics, both internal and external, that constructed "Israel's" ethnic boundaries. At some point in the formation of the Tetrateuchal materials, Deuteronomy, which had provided much of the basis for the development of the traditions contained in the Tetrateuch, was separated from the deuteronomistic history and added to the Tetrateuch, thus forming the Pentateuch.

[4] The major parts constituting a fully developed ethnic myth are given by A. D. Smith, *The Ethnic Origins of Nations*, p. 192.

This redactional shift, possibly occurring as early as the fifth century BCE, created a new work, a "primary history," that recounted the whole of "Israel's" history from the creation of the world until the beginning of the Babylonian exile. This "primary history" provided a complete myth of ethnic and national origins. It also supplied the basis for recreating and maintaining the ethnic distinctiveness of the group that was resettled in Jerusalem and who claimed the right to the land. Only at a much later time, as part of the process of canonization, was the Pentateuch separated from this "primary history" and accorded the status of Torah.

A central focus of this "primary history" is the distinctive character of "Israel" that was determined by its relationship with Yahweh. What separated the ideal "Israel" created in these materials from all other peoples was established at Mt. Sinai/Horeb. There, "Israel" received the divine instructions that would establish them as "Yahweh's possession," "a kingdom of priests and a holy nation" (Exod 19:5–6). The fulfillment of these instructions would insure that the camp would be sanctified and pure, leading to the presence of Yahweh in "Israel's" midst. This divine presence would be the uniquely distinguishing factor that would separate "Israel" from all other nations on the earth. This factor alone helps explain the extensive, diverse materials gathered in this complex that address issues of purity/impurity and holiness/profaneness. Centering on the Tabernacle, the site of Yahweh's presence, the cultus, under the leadership of the sons of Aaron, was responsible for maintaining the purity and holiness of the people. An essential part of this was the sacrificial ritual, for it was the correct performance of the prescribed sacrifices that enabled the reintegration into the community of members who had become unclean. Hence, not only was the Tabernacle/Temple cultus an essential element of the idealized community, but it was also the only legitimate method of maintaining the community in conjunction with the Torah received at Sinai/Horeb.

The narrative accounts of the past, containing as they do the instructions from Yahweh that provide divinely established boundaries for the people, constitute the idealized boundaries by which "Israel" was to understand its role in the midst of the nations. I have argued throughout that this method of analyzing the materials contained in the Tetrateuch and the Pentateuch allows scholars to develop an understanding of the role and function of these various literary pieces both in the construction of the distinctive cultural identity of "Israel" and in the development of early Judaism. While it is clear that there are many questions that have not been addressed by this study, there is much to be learned about the various ways in which ethnic, religious groups draw upon the traditions of their past, either real or creatively imagined, to create their identities and maintain themselves over time. One of the major advantages of the approach is that it allows us to utilize the data before us, i.e., the texts contained in the Hebrew bible, without the necessity of postulating separate written sources that have been combined by various hands at different periods. Though it leaves many of the questions associated with the transmission of the traditions unanswered, it does address a number of issues not confronted by the historical critical approach as it is commonly practiced. This model allows for the investigation of the ways in which the texts might have been used by various communities in different cultural and historical periods. In this it hopes to make a contribution to the field of the study of religions in general and the analysis of the Hebrew bible in particular. Utilizing the highly flexible ethnic symbol "Israel," the narratives of the Tetrateuch and the Pentateuch provided the basis for the recreation, bounding, and maintenance of an historical group as it faced a variety of threats to its ethnically and religiously distinctive understanding of itself.

SELECTED BIBLIOGRAPHY

Aberbach, M. and L. Smolar. "Aaron, Jeroboam, and the Golden Calves." *JBL* 86 (1967) 129–40.

Ackroyd, P. R. "The Written Evidence for Palestine." Pp. 207–20 in *Achaemenid History IV: Center and Periphery* (Proceedings of the Groningen 1986 Achaemenid History Workshop). Ed. by H. Sancisi-Weerdenburg and A. Khurt. Leiden: Nederlands Instituut voor het Nabije Oosten, 1990.

Ahlström, G. W. *Who Were the Israelites?* Winona Lake, IN: Eisenbrauns, 1986.

Albright, W. F. "The Oracles of Balaam." *JBL* 63 (1944) 207–33.

———. "Jethro, Hobab, and Reuel." *CBQ* 25 (1963) 1–11.

Anderson, G. A. "Sacrifice and Sacrificial Offerings (OT)." *ABD* V:870–86.

Auld, A. G. *Joshua, Moses & the Land: Tetrateuch-Pentateuch-Hexateuch in a Generation Since 1938.* Edinburgh: T. & T. Clark, 1980.

Aune, D. E. "On the Origins of the 'Council of Javneh' Myth." *JBL* 110 (1991) 491–93.

Baltzer, K. *The Covenant Formulary in Old Testament, Jewish, and Early Christian Writings.* Philadelphia: Fortress, 1971.

Barth, F. "Introduction." Pp. 9–37 in *Ethnic Groups and Boundaries: The Social Organization of Culture Difference.* Ed. by F. Barth. Boston: Little, Brown, 1969.

Bartlett, J. R. "The Conquest of Sihon's Kingdom: A Literary Re-examination." *JBL* 97 (1978) 347–51.

Bechtel, L. "What if Dinah is not Raped? [Genesis 34]." *JSOT* 62 (1994) 19–36.

Berger, P. and T. Luckmann. *The Social Construction of Reality: A Treatise in the Sociology of Knowledge.* New York: Doubleday, 1966.

Bledstein, A. J. "Was Eve Cursed? [or Did a Woman Write Genesis?]." *BibRev* (1993) 42–45.

Blenkinsopp, J. *A History of Prophecy in Israel: From the Settlement in the Land to the Hellenistic Period.* Philadelphia: Westminster, 1983.

———. "The Mission of Udjahorresnet and Those of Ezra and Nehemiah." *JBL* 106 (1987) 409–21.

———. *Ezra-Nehemiah.* OTL; Philadelphia: Westminster, 1988.

———. "Temple and Society in Achaemenid Judah." Pp. 22–53 in *Second Temple Studies: 1. Persian Period.* Ed. by P. R. Davies. JSOTSup 117; Sheffield: JSOT, 1991.

———. *The Pentateuch: An Introduction to the First Five Books of the Bible.* New York: Doubleday, 1992.

Bloom, H. *The Book of J.* With a translation of "J" by David Rosenberg. New York: Grove Weidenfeld, 1990.

Boccaccini, G. "Multiple Judaisms." *BibRev* 11 (1995) 38–41, 46.

Boling, R. *Joshua.* AB 6; New York: Doubleday, 1982.

Boorer, S. "The Importance of a Diachronic Approach: The Case of Genesis-Kings." *CBQ* 51 (1989) 195–208.

Briant, P. "Social and Legal Institutions in Achaemenid Iran." Pp. 517–28 in *Civilizations of the Ancient Near East,* Vol. I. Ed. by J. M. Sasson. New York: Scribner's, 1995.

Brichto, H. C. *Toward a Grammar of Biblical Poetics: Tales of the Prophets.* New York/Oxford: Oxford University Press, 1992.

Brook, G. J. "Power to the Powerless: A Long Lost Song of Miriam." *BARev* 20 (1994) 62–65.

Budd, P. J. *Numbers.* WBC 5; Waco, TX: Word, 1984.

———. "Holiness and Cult." Pp. 275–98 in *The World of Ancient Israel: Sociological, Anthropological and Political Perspectives.* Ed. by R. E. Clements. Cambridge: Cambridge University Press, 1989.

Burkert, W. *Homo Necans: The Anthropology of Ancient Greek Sacrificial Ritual and Myth.* Berkeley: University of California Press, 1983.

Burns, R. J. "Miriam." *ABD* IV:869–70.

Campbell, A. F. and M. A. O'Brien. *Sources of the Pentateuch: Texts, Introductions, Annotations.* Minneapolis: Augsburg/Fortress, 1993.

Carr, David M. "Controversy and Convergence in Recent Studies of the Formation of the Pentateuch." *RelSRev* (1997) 22–31.

Carroll, R. "Israel, History of (Post-Monarchic Period)." *ABD* III:567–76.

Cassuto, U. *The Documentary Hypothesis and the Composition of the Pentateuch.* Jerusalem: Magnes, 1961.

Charlesworth, J. H., et. al. *The Dead Sea Scrolls: Hebrew, Aramaic, and Greek Texts with English Translations, Vol. 1: Rule of the Community and Related Documents.* Tübingen: Mohr/Louisville, KY: Westminster/John Knox, 1994.

Childs, B. S. *The Book of Exodus.* OTL; Philadelphia: Westminster, 1974.

Christensen, D. L. "Num 21:14–15 and the Book of the Wars of Yahweh." *CBQ* 36 (1974) 359–60.

Clifford, R. J. "The Tent of El and the Israelite Tent of Meeting." *CBQ* 33 (1971) 221–27.

Clines, D. J. A. *Ezra, Nehemiah, Esther.* NCBC; Grand Rapids, MI: Eerdmans, 1984.

———. *The Theme of the Pentateuch.* JSOTSup 10; Sheffield: JSOT, 1986 [originally published 1978].

Coats, G. W. *Rebellion in the Wilderness.* Nashville: Abingdon, 1968.

————. "Conquest Traditions in the Wilderness Theme." *JBL* 95 (1976) 177–90.

————. *Genesis, With an Introduction to Narrative Literature.* FTOL 1; Grand Rapids, MI: Eerdmans, 1983.

————. *Moses: Heroic Man, Man of God.* JSOTSup 57; Sheffield: JSOT, 1988.

Cody, A. *A History of Old Testament Priesthood.* AnBib 35; Rome: Pontifical Biblical Institute, 1969.

Collins, J. "Dead Sea Scrolls." *ABD* II:85–101.

————. "Historical Criticism and the State of Biblical Theology." *The Christian Century* 110 (1993) 743–47.

Conrad, E. W. "Heard But Not Seen: The Representation of 'Books' in the Old Testament." *JSOT* 54 (1992) 45–59.

Coote, R. B. *Early Israel: A New Horizon.* Minneapolis: Augsburg/Fortress, 1990.

————. *In Defense of Revolution: The Elohist History.* Minneapolis: Augsburg/Fortress, 1991.

———— and D. R. Ord. *The Bible's First History.* Philadelphia: Fortress, 1989.

———— and D. R. Ord. *In the Beginning: Creation and the Priestly History.* Minneapolis: Augsburg/Fortress, 1991.

Cowley, A. *Aramaic Papyri of the Fifth Century B. C.* Oxford: Clarendon, 1923.

Cross, F. M. *The Ancient Library of Qumran,* rev.ed. New York: Doubleday, 1961.

————. *Canaanite Myth and Hebew Epic.* Cambridge: Harvard University Press, 1973.

Culley, R. C. "Five Tales of Punishment in the Book of Numbers." Pp. 25–34 in *Text and Tradition: The Hebrew Bible and Folklore.* Ed. by S. Niditch. SBLSS; Atlanta: Scholars Press, 1990.

Dandamaev, M. A., *et al.* "The Diaspora." Pp. 326–400 in *The Cambridge History of Judaism, Vol. 1.* Ed. by W. D. Davies and L. Finkelstein. Cambridge: Cambridge University Press, 1984.

———— and V. G. Lukonin, *The Culture and Social Institutions of Ancient Iran.* English ed. by P. L. Kohl; Cambridge/New York: Cambridge University Press, 1989.

Davies, D. "An Interpretation of Sacrifice in Leviticus." Pp. 151–62 in *Anthropological Approaches to the Old Testament.* Ed. by B. Lang. IRT 8; Philadelphia: Fortress, 1985; first published in *ZAW* 89 (1977) 388–98.

Davies, P. R. *In Search of 'Ancient Israel'.* JSOTSup 148; Sheffield: JSOT, 1992 [reprinted 1995].

Demsky, A. "Writing in Ancient Israel and Early Judaism: Part One: The Biblical Period." Pp. 2–20 in *Mikra.* CRINT, sec. 1. Assen/Maastrict/Philadelphia: Van Gorcum/Fortress, 1988.

De Vries, S. J. "A Review of Recent Research in the Tradition History of the Pentateuch." Pp. 459–502 in *SBLSP* 26. Ed. by K. H. Richards. Atlanta: Scholars Press, 1987.

Douglas, M. *Purity and Danger.* London: Routledge & Keegan Paul, 1966.

————. "The Forbidden Animals in Leviticus." *JSOT* 59 (1993) 3–23.

————. *In the Wilderness: The Doctrine of Defilement in the Book of Numbers.* JSOTSup 158; Sheffield: JSOT, 1993.

Driver, S. R. *An Introduction to the Literature of the Old Testament.* Cleveland, OH: Word Publishing Co., 1967; originally published 1913.

———. *Deuteronomy,* 3rd ed. ICC; Edinburgh: T. & T. Clark, 1973; originally published 1895.

Durham, J. I. *Exodus.* WBC 3; Waco, TX: Word, 1987.

Eichrodt, W. *Theology of the Old Testament.* 2 vols. Philadelphia: Westminster, 1967.

Eilberg-Schwartz, H. *The Savage in Judaism: An Anthropology of Israelite Religion and Ancient Judaism.* Bloomington/Indianapolis: Indiana University Press, 1990.

Eissfeldt, O. *The Old Testament: An Introduction.* Oxford: Blackwell, 1965.

Eliade, Mircea. *The Sacred and the Profane: The Nature of Religion.* New York: Harcourt, Brace, Jovanovich, 1959.

Engnell, I. "The Pentateuch." Pp. 50–67 in *A Rigid Scrutiny: Critical Essays on the Old Testament.* Nashville: Vanderbilt University Press, 1969.

Eph'al, I. "Syria -Palestine under Achaemenid Rule." *CAH*² IV:139–64.

Eslinger, L. "Freedom or Knowledge? Perspective and Purpose in the Exodus Narrative [Exodus 1–15]." *JSOT* 52 (1991) 43–60.

Fager, J. A. *Land Tenure and Biblical Jubilee: Uncovering Hebrew Ethics through the Sociology of Knowledge.* JSOTSup 155; Sheffield: JSOT, 1993.

Finkelstein, I. "Ethnicity and the Origin of Iron I Settlers in the Highlands of Canaan: Can the Real Israel Stand Up?" *BA* 59 (1996) 198–212.

Fishbane, M. *Biblical Interpretation in Ancient Israel.* Oxford: Clarendon Press, 1985.

Fohrer, G. *History of Israelite Religion.* Philadelphia: Fortress, 1966.

Fox, M. V., ed. *Temple in Society.* Winona Lake, IN: Eisenbrauns, 1988.

Freedman, D. N. "The Law and the Prophets." Pp. 250–65 in *VTSup* 9; Leiden: E. J. Brill, 1963.

———. "Canon of the Old Testament." *IDBSup:* 130–36.

———. "The Earliest Bible." Pp. 29–37 in *Backgrounds to the Bible.* Ed. by M. P. O'Connor and D. N. Freedman. Winona Lake, IN: Eisenbrauns, 1987.

Friedman, R. E. *Who Wrote the Bible?* Englewood Cliffs, NJ: Prentice Hall, 1987.

———. "Tabernacle." *ABD* VI:292–301.

———. "Torah (Pentateuch)." *ABD* VI:605–22.

———. "Review of J. Van Seters' *Prologue to History: The Yahwist as Historian in Genesis.*" *BibRev* 9 (1993) 12–16.

Gamble, H. Y. "Canon (New Testament)." *ABD* I:853–61.

Garbini, G. *History and Ideology in Ancient Israel.* New York: Crossroad, 1988.

Geertz. C. "Religion as a Cultural Symbol." Pp. 87–125 in *The Interpretation of Cultures.* New York: Basic Books, 1973.

Girard, R. *Violence and the Sacred.* Baltimore: Johns Hopkins University Press, 1977.

Gorman, F. H. *The Ideology of Ritual: Space, Time and Status in the Priestly Theology.* JSOTSup 91; Sheffield: JSOT, 1990.

Goshen-Gottstein, M. "Scriptural Authority (Judaism)." *ABD* V:1017–21.

Gottwald, N. *The Tribes of Yahweh: A Sociology of the Religion of Liberated Israel, 1250–1050 B.C.E.* Maryknoll, NY: Orbis, 1979.

————. *The Hebrew Bible: A Socio-Literary Introduction.* Philadelphia: Fortress, 1985.

Graham, W. *Beyond the Written Word: Oral Aspects of Scripture in the History of Religion.* Cambridge: Cambridge University Press, 1987.

Gray, G. B. *Numbers.* ICC; Edinburgh: T. & T. Clark, 1903.

Green, R. M. *Religion and Moral Reason: A New Method for Comparative Study.* New York: Oxford University Press, 1988.

Green, W. S. "Writing with Scripture." Pp. 7–23 in *Writing with Scripture,* by J. Neusner. Philadelphia: Fortress, 1989.

————. "The Difference Religion Makes." *JAAR* 62 (1994) 1191–1202.

Greenberg, M. "Moses." *EncJud* 12:378.

————, S. Safrai, and A. Rithkoff. "Sabbatical Year and Jubilee." *EncJud* 14:574–86.

Greenstein, E. "On the Genesis of Biblical Prose Narrative." *Prooftexts* 8 (1988) 347–54.

Gunn, D. M. "New Direction in the Study of Biblical Hebrew Narrative." *JSOT* 39 (1987) 65–75.

Hackett, J. A. "Some Observations on the Balaam Tradition at Deir ʿAlla." *BA* 49 (1986) 216–22.

Hallo, W. W. "The Origins of the Sacrificial Cult: New Evidence from Mesopotamia and Israel." Pp. 3–13 in *Ancient Israelite Religion: Essays in Honor of Frank Moore Cross.* Ed. by P. D. Miller, Jr., P. D. Hanson, and S. D. McBride. Philadelphia: Fortress, 1987.

Halpern, B. *The First Historians: The Hebrew Bible and History.* San Francisco: Harper & Row, 1988.

Hanson, P. D. "The Song of Heshbon and David's *NÎR.*" *HTR* 61 (1968) 298–320.

————. *The Dawn of Apocalyptic.* Philadelphia: Fortress, 1975.

————. "Rebellion in Heaven, Azazel, and Euhemeristic Heroes in 1 Enoch 6–11." *JBL* 96 (1977) 195–233.

————. "Israelite Religion in the Early Post-exilic Period." Pp. 485–508 in *Ancient Israelite Religion: Essays in Honor of Frank Moore Cross.* Ed. by P. D. Miller, Jr., P. D. Hanson, and S. D. McBride. Philadelphia: Fortress, 1987.

Haran, M. *Temples and Temple-Service in Ancient Israel: An Inquiry into the Character of Cult Phenomena and the Historical Setting of the Priestly School.* Oxford: Clarendon, 1978.

————. "Book-Scrolls in Israel in Pre-Exilic Times." *JJS* 33 (1982) 161–73.

————. "Book-Scrolls at the Beginning of the Second Temple Period: The Transition from Papyrus to Skins." *HUCA* 54 (1983) 111–22.

————. "More Concerning Book-Scrolls in Pre-Exilic Times." *JJS* 35 (1984) 84–85.

————. "The Shining of Moses' Face: A Case Study in Biblical and Ancient Near Eastern Iconography." Pp. 159–73 in *In the Shelter of Elyon. Essays on Ancient Palestinian Life and Literature in Honor of G. W. Ahlström.* Ed. by W. B. Barrick and J. R. Spencer. Sheffield: JSOT, 1984.

Harris, M. *Cultural Materialism: The Struggle for a Science of Culture.* New York: Random House, 1979.

Hartley, J. E. *Leviticus.* WBC 4; Dallas: Word, 1992.

Hasel, G. F. "Sabbath." *ABD* V:849–56.

Hayes, J. H. *An Introduction to Old Testament Study.* Nashville: Abingdon, 1979.

Headland, T. N., K. L. Pike, and M. Harris. *Emics and Etics: The Insider/Outsider Debate.* Frontiers of Anthropology 7; New York: Sage, 1990.

Hendel, R. S. "Of Demigods and the Deluge: Toward an Interpretation of Genesis 6:1–4." *JBL* 106 (1987) 13–26.

———. "The Social Origins of the Aniconic Tradition in Early Israel." *CBQ* 50 (1988) 365–82.

Hermann, S. *A History of Israel in Old Testament Times.* Philadelphia: Fortress, 1975.

Herr, M. D. "Oral Law." *EncJud* 12:1439–45.

Hicks, L. "Abraham." *IDB* I, 14–21.

———. "Isaac." *IDB* II, 728–31.

Hillers, D. *Treaty-Curses and the Old Testament Prophets.* Biblica et Orientalia 16; Rome: Pontifical Biblical Institute, 1964.

Hobsbawm, E. "Introduction: Inventing Traditions." Pp. 1–14 in *The Invention of Tradition.* Ed. by E. Hobsbawm and T. Ranger. Cambridge: Cambridge University Press, 1983.

Hoenig, S. "Sabbatical Years and the Year of Jubilee." *JQR* 59 (1969) 222–36.

Hoffmann, H.-D. *Reform und Reformen: Untersuchungen zu einem Grundthema der deuteronomistischen Geschichtsschreibung.* ATANT 66; Zürich: Theologischer Verlag, 1980.

Hofman, S. "Karaites." *EncJud* 10:761–85.

Hoglund, K. G. "The Achaemenid Context." Pp. 54–72 in *Second Temple Studies.* Ed. by P. R. Davies. JSOTSup 117; Sheffield: JSOT, 1991.

———. *Achaemenid Imperial Administration in Syria-Palestine and the Missions of Ezra and Nehemiah.* SBLDS 125; Atlanta: Scholars Press, 1992.

Horsley, R. A. "Empire, Temple and Community—But No Bourgeoisie! A Response to Blenkinsopp and Petersen." Pp. 163–74 in *Second Temple Studies.* Ed. by P. R. Davies. JSOTSup 170; Sheffield: JSOT, 1991.

Houston, W. *Purity and Monotheism: Clean and Unclean Animals in Biblical Law.* JSOTSup 140; Sheffield: JSOT, 1993.

Isaacs, H. R. "Basic Group Identity: The Idols of the Tribe." Pp. 29–52 in *Ethnicity: Theory and Experience.* Ed. by N. Glazer and D. P. Moynihan. Cambridge: Harvard University Press, 1975.

Jacobs, L. "Torah, Reading of." *EncJud* 15:1246–55.

Jacobsen, T. "The Graven Image." Pp. 15–32 in *Ancient Israelite Religion: Essays in Honor of Frank Moore Cross.* Ed. by P. D. Miller, Jr., P. D. Hanson, and S. D. McBride. Philadelphia: Fortress, 1987.

Janzen, W. "Land." *ABD* IV:143–54.

Jay, N. *Throughout Your Generations Forever: Sacrifice, Religion, and Paternity.* Chicago: University of Chicago Press, 1992.

Jenks, A. W. *The Elohist and North Israelite Traditions.* SBLMS 22; Missoula, MT: Scholars Press, 1977.

Jenson, P. P. *Graded Holiness: A Key to the Priestly Conception of the World.* JSOT-Sup 106; Sheffield: JSOT, 1992.

Knight, D. A. "The Pentateuch." Pp. 263–96 in *The Hebrew Bible and Its Modern Interpreters.* Ed. by D. A. Knight and G. M. Tucker. Philadelphia/Chico, CA: Fortress/Scholars Press, 1985.

Knohl, I. E. "The Priestly Torah Versus the Holiness School: Sabbath and the Festivals." *HUCA* 58 (1987) 65–118.

———. *The Sanctuary of Silence: The Priestly Torah and the Holiness School.* Minneapolis: Augsburg/Fortress, 1995.

Knoppers, G. N. "The Vanishing Solomon: The Disappearance of the United Monarchy from Recent Histories of Ancient Israel." *JBL* 116 (1997) 19–44.

Kraus, H.-J. *Worship in Israel.* Richmond: John Knox, 1965.

Kuhn, T. *The Structure of Scientific Revolutions,* 2d ed. Chicago: University of Chicago Press, 1970.

Kuhrt, A. "The Cyrus Cylinder and the Achaemenid Imperial Policy." *JSOT* 25 (1983) 83–97.

Lambdin, T. O. *Introduction to Biblical Hebrew.* New York: Charles Scribner's Sons, 1971.

Larsson, G. "The Chronology of the Pentateuch: A Comparison of the MT and LXX." *JBL* 102 (1983) 401–09.

Laughlin, J. C. H. "The 'Strange Fire' of Nadab and Abihu." *JBL* 95 (1976) 563–65.

Leach, E. "The Logic of Sacrifice." Pp. 136–50 in *Anthropological Approaches to the Old Testament.* Ed. by B. Lang. IRT 8; Philadelphia: Fortress, 1985 [originally published in pp. 81–93 of *Culture and Communication.* Cambridge: Cambridge University Press, 1976].

Le Déaut, R. "The Targumim." Pp. 563–90 in *The Cambridge History of Judaism, Vol. 2: The Hellenistic Age.* Ed. by W. D. Davies and L. Finkelstein. Cambridge: Cambridge University Press, 1989.

Leiman, S. Z. "The Inverted *Nuns* at Numbers 10:35–36 and the Book of Eldad and Medad." *JBL* 93 (1974) 348–55.

Lemche, N. P. "The Manumission of Slaves—the fallow year—the sabbatical year—the jobel year." *VT* 26 (1976) 38–59.

———. "'Hebrew' as a National Name for Israel." *Studia Theologica* 33 (1979) 1–23.

———. *Early Israel: Anthropological and Historical Studies on the Israelite Society before the Monarchy.* VTSup 37; Leiden: E. J. Brill, 1985.

———. *Ancient Israel: A New History of Israelite Society.* Sheffield: JSOT, 1988.

———. *The Canaanites and Their Land: The Tradition of the Canaanites.* JSOTSup 110; Sheffield: JSOT, 1991.

———. "Is It Still Possible to Write a History of Ancient Israel?" *SJOT* 8 (1994) 165–90.

Levenson, J. D. *Theology of the Program of Restoration of Ezekiel 40–48.* HSM 10; Missoula, MT: Scholars Press, 1976.

———. *Sinai and Zion.* Minneapolis: Winston, 1985.

―――. "The Sources of Torah: Psalm 119 and the Modes of Revelation in Second Temple Judaism." Pp. 559–74 in *Ancient Israelite Religion: Essays in Honor of Frank Moore Cross*. Ed. by P. D. Miller, Jr., P. D. Hanson, and S. D. McBride. Philadelphia: Fortress, 1987.

―――. *The Hebrew Bible, The Old Testament, and Historical Criticism*. Louisville: Westminster/John Knox, 1993.

Levine, B. A. "More on the Inverted *Nuns* of Num 10:35–36." *JBL* 95 (1976) 122–24.

―――. *Numbers 1–20*. AB 4; New York: Doubleday, 1993.

Lewis, B. *History—Remembered, Recovered, Invented*. Princeton: Princeton University Press, 1975.

Lichtheim, M. *Ancient Egyptian Literature, Vol. I: The Old and Middle Kingdoms*. Berkeley/Los Angeles: University of California Press, 1973.

―――. *Ancient Egyptian Literature, Vol. III: The Late Period*. Berkeley/Los Angeles: University of California Press, 1980.

Loewenstamm, A. "Samaritans." *EncJud* 14:725–58.

Loewenstamm, S. E. "The Making and Destruction of the Golden Calf." *Bib* 56 (1975) 237–46.

Lohfink, N. "Die Erzählung vom Sundenfall." Pp. 81–101 in *Das Siegeslied am Schilfmeer*. Frankfurt am Main: J. Knecht, 1965.

―――. *Die Väter Israels im Deuteronomium: mit einer Stellungnahme von Thomas Römer*. OBO 111; Freiburg, Switzerland: Universitätsverlag/Göttingen: Vandenhoeck & Ruprecht, 1991.

Maier, J. *The Temple Scroll*. JSOTSup 34; Sheffield: JSOT, 1985.

Mandell, S. and D. N. Freedman. *The Relationship between Herodotus' History and Primary History*. South Florida Studies in the History of Judaism 60; Atlanta: Scholars Press, 1993.

Mayes, A. D. H. *Deuteronomy*. NCBC; Grand Rapids, MI: Eerdmans, 1981.

―――. *The Story of Israel between Settlement and Exile: A Redactional Study of the Deuteronomistic History*. London: SCM, 1983.

McCarthy, D. J. *Treaty and Covenant: A Study in Form in the Ancient Oriental Documents and in the Old Testament*. AnBib 21a, rev. ed.; Rome: Biblical Institute Press, 1978.

McEvenue, S. E. "The Political Structure in Judah from Cyrus to Nehemiah." *CBQ* 43 (1981) 353–64.

McKenzie, S. L. *The Trouble with Kings: The Composition of the Book of Kings in the Deuteronomistic History*. VTSupp 42; Leiden: E. J. Brill, 1991.

Mendels, D. *The Rise and Fall of Jewish Nationalism*. New York: Doubleday, 1992.

Mendenhall, G. "Covenant Forms in Israelite Tradition." *BA* 17 (1954) 50–76.

Mettinger, T. N. D. *No Graven Images? Israelite Aniconism and Its Ancient Near Eastern Context*. ConBOT 42; Stockholm: Almqvist & Wiksell, 1995.

Meyers, J. *Ezra-Nehemiah*. OTL; Philadelphia: Doubleday, 1964.

Mihelic, J. L. and G. E. Wright. "Plagues in Exodus." *IBD* 3:822–24.

Milgrom, J. "The Paradox of the Red Cow (Num xix)." *VT* 31 (1981) 62–72.

————. *Leviticus 1–16.* AB 3; New York: Doubleday, 1991.

————. "Numbers, Book of." *ABD* IV:1146–55.

Miller, J. M. and J. Hayes. *A History of Ancient Israel and Judah.* Philadelphia: Westminster, 1986.

Miller, P. D., Jr. "The Blessing of God. An Interpretation of Numbers 6:22–27." *Int* 29 (1975) 240–51.

Mittmann, S. "Num 20:14–21: eine redaktionelle Kompilation." Pp. 143–49 in *Wort und Geschichte.* Ed. by H. Gese and H. P. Rüger. AOAT 18; Neukirchen-Vluyn: Neukirchener Verlag, 1973.

Moran, W. L. "The ANE Background of the Love of God in Deuteronomy." *CBQ* 24 (1963) 77–87.

Mullen, E. T., Jr. *The Assembly of the Gods: The Divine Council in Canaanite and Early Hebrew Literature.* HSM 24; Chico, CA: Scholars Press, 1980.

————. *Narrative History and Ethnic Boundaries: The Deuteronomistic Historian and the Creation of Israelite National Identity.* SBLSS; Atlanta: Scholars Press, 1993.

Neusner, J. "'Israel': Judaism and Its Social Metaphors." *JAAR* 55 (1987) 331–61.

————. *Scriptures of the Oral Torah.* San Francisco: Harper & Row, 1987.

————. *The Mishnah: A New Translation.* New Haven: Yale University Press, 1988.

————. "Understanding Seeking Faith: The Case of Judaism." *Soundings* 71 (1988) 329–46.

Nickelsburg, G. W. E. *Jewish Literature Between the Bible and the Mishnah: A Historical and Literary Introduction.* Philadelphia: Fortress, 1981.

Niditch, S. "The 'Sodomite' Theme in Judges 19–20: Family, Community, and Social Disintegration." *CBQ* 44 (1982) 365–75.

Noth, M. *Exodus.* OTL; Philadelphia: Westminster, 1962.

————. *Überlieferungsgeschichtliche Studien,* 3d ed. Tübingen: Max Niemeyer Verlag, 1967 [originally published 1943].

————. *Numbers.* OTL; Philadelphia: Westminster, 1968.

————. *A History of Pentateuchal Traditions.* Trans. by B. W. Anderson. Englewood Cliffs, NJ: Prentice Hall, 1972.

Oden, R. A., Jr. "Jacob as Father, Husband, and Nephew: Kinship Studies and the Patriarchal Narratives." *JBL* 102 (1983) 189–205.

————. *The Bible Without Theology: The Theological Traditions and Alternatives to It.* San Francisco: Harper & Row, 1987.

Oller, G. "Zaphenath-Paneah." *ABD* VI:1040.

Otto, R. *The Idea of the Holy.* New York: Oxford University Press, 1958.

Overman, J. A. and W. S. Green. "Judaism [Greco-Roman Period]." *ABD* III: 1038–41.

Peckham, B. *History and Prophecy: The Development of Late Judean Literary Traditions.* New York: Doubleday, 1993.

Pedersen, J. "Pessahfest und Pessahlegende." *ZAW* 52 (1934) 161–75.

Perlitt, L. *Bundestheologie im Alten Testament.* WMANT 36; Neukirchen-Vluyn: Neukirchener Verlag, 1969.

Pike, K. L. *Language in Relation to a Unified Theory of the Structure of Human Behavior,* 2d ed. The Hague: Mouton, 1967.

Polzin, R. *Moses and the Deuteronomist: A Literary Study of the Deuteronomic History.* New York: Seabury, 1980.

Porten, B. *Archives from Elephantine.* Berkeley: University of California Press, 1968.

———. "The Jews in Egypt." Pp. 372–400 in *The Cambridge History of Judaism, Vol. I: Introduction: The Persian Period.* Ed. by W. D. Davies and L. Finkelstein. Cambridge: Cambridge University Press, 1984.

———. "Elephantine Papyri." *ABD* II:445–55.

Preus, J. S. *Explaining Religion: Criticism and Theory from Bodin to Freud.* New Haven: Yale University Press, 1987.

Propp, W. H. "The Rod of Aaron and the Sin of Moses." *JBL* 107 (1988) 19–26.

Puech, E. "Fear of Isaac." *ABD* II:779–80.

Purvis, J. D. *The Samaritan Pentateuch and the Origins of the Samaritan Sect.* HSM 2; Cambridge: Harvard University Press, 1968.

———. "The Samaritans." Pp. 591–613 in *The Cambridge History of Judaism, Vol. II: The Hellenistic Age.* Ed. by W. D. Davies and L. Finkelstein. Cambridge: Cambridge University Press, 1989.

de Pury, A. "Yahwist ('J') Source." *ABD* VI:1012–20.

Qimron, E. "Miqṣat Maʿase Hatorah." *ABD* IV:843–45.

——— and J. Strugnell. *Qumran Cave 4.V, Miqṣat Maʿaśe Ha-Torah, DJD X.* Oxford: Oxford University Press, 1994.

Rabinowitz, P. "Truth in Fiction: A Reexamination of Audiences." *Critical Inquiry* 4 (1977) 125–30, 134–35.

Rattray, S. "Marriage Rules, Kinship Terms and Family Structures in the Bible." Pp. 537–44 in SBLSP 26. Ed. by K. H. Richards. Atlanta: Scholars Press, 1987.

Rendtorff, R. *Das Überlieferungsgeschichtliche Problem des Pentateuch.* BZAW 147; Berlin: de Gruyter, 1977.

———. "The 'Yahwist' as Theologian? The Dilemma of Pentateuchal Criticism." *JSOT* 3 (1977) 2–10.

———. *The Problem of the Process of Transmission in the Pentateuch.* Trans. by J. J. Scullion. JSOTSup 89; Sheffield: JSOT, 1990; German original, 1977.

Ringgren, H. *Israelite Religion.* Philadelphia: Fortress, 1966.

Römer, T. *Israels Väter: Untersuchungen zur Väterthematic im Deuteronomium und in dem deuteronomistischen Tradition.* OBO 99; Göttingen: Vandenhoeck & Ruprecht, 1990.

Roosens, E. E. *Creating Ethnicity: The Process of Ethnogenesis.* Frontiers of Anthropology 5; Newbury Park, CA: Sage, 1990.

Rose, M. *Deuteronomist und Jahwist: Untersuchungen zu den Berfhrungspunkten beider Literaturwerke.* ATANT 67; Zurich: Theologischer Verlag, 1981.

Ross, J. F. "The Prophet as Yahweh's Messenger." Pp. 98–107 in *Israel's Prophetic Heritage.* Ed. by B. Anderson and W. Harrelson. New York: Harper & Row, 1962.

Rowley, H. H. *Worship in Ancient Israel.* Richmond: John Knox, 1965.

Royce, A. P. *Ethnic Identity: Strategies of Diversity.* Bloomington/Indianapolis: Indiana University Press, 1982.

Sancisi-Weerdenburg, H. "Darius I and the Persian Empire." Pp. 1035–50 in *Civilizations of the Ancient Near East, Vol. II.* Ed. by J. M. Sasson. New York: Scribner's, 1995.

Sanders, J. A. *Torah and Canon.* Philadelphia: Fortress, 1972.

Sandmel, S. "The Haggada within Scripture." *JBL* 80 (1961) 105–22.

Sarna, N. M. "Bible." *EncJud* 4:814–36.

———. *Exploring Exodus: The Heritage of Biblical Israel.* New York: Shocken, 1986.

Schiffman, L. "Temple Scroll." *ABD* VI:348–50.

Schmid, H. H. *Der sogennante Jahwist: Beobachtungen und Fragen zur Pentateuchforschung.* Zürich: Theologischer Verlag, 1976.

Schwartz, R. M. "The Histories of David: Biblical Scholarship and Biblical Stories." Pp. 192–210 in *Not in Heaven: Coherence and Complexity in Biblical Narrative.* Ed. by J. P. Rosenblatt and J. C. Sitterson, Jr. Indiana Studies in Biblical Literature; Bloomington/Indianapolis: Indiana University Press, 1991.

Segal, P. "The Divine Verdict of Leviticus x 3." *VT* 39 (1989) 94.

Shanks, H. "For This You Waited 35 Years: MMT as Reconstructed by Elisha Qimron and John Strugnell." *BARev* 20 (1994) 56–61.

———. "Scholars Face Off Over Age of Biblical Stories: Friedman vs. Van Seters." *BibRev* 20 (1994) 40–44, 54 (with replies by J. Van Seters and R. Friedman).

Shutt, R. J. H. "Aristeas, Letter of." *ABD* I:380–81.

Skinner, J. *Genesis,* 2d ed. ICC; Edinburgh: T. & T. Clark, 1930 [1st ed., 1910].

Smith, A. D. *The Ethnic Origins of Nations.* Oxford: Blackwell, 1986.

Smith, D. L. *The Religion of the Landless: The Social Context of the Babylonian Exile.* Bloomington, IN: Meyer Stone Books, 1989.

Smith, J. Z. *Drudgery Divine: On the Comparison of Early Christianities and the Religions of Late Antiquity.* Chicago: University of Chicago Press, 1990.

Smith, M. *Palestinian Parties and Politics that Shaped the Old Testament.* London: SCM Press, 1987.

Smith, M. S. *The Early History of God: Yahweh and Other Deities in Ancient Israel.* San Francisco: Harper & Row, 1990.

Smith, W. C. *What Is Scripture? A Comparative Approach.* Minneapolis: Fortress, 1993.

Soggin, J. A. *An Introduction to the History of Israel and Judah,* rev. ed. Valley Forge, PA: Trinity Press International, 1993.

Speiser, E. A. *Genesis.* AB 1; Garden City, NY: Doubleday, 1964.

Stern, E. *Material Culture of the Land of the Bible in the Persian Period: 538–332 B.C.* Warminster/Jerusalem: Aris & Phillips/Israel Exploration Society, 1982.

———. "New Evidence on the Administrative Division of Palestine in the Persian Period." Pp. 221–26 in *Achaemenid History IV: Center and Periphery* (Proceedings of the Groningen 1986 Achaemenid History Workshop). Ed. by

H. Sancisi-Weerdenburg and A. Khurt. Leiden: Nederlands Instituut voor het Nabije Oosten, 1990.

Sternberg, M. *The Poetics of Biblical Narrative: Ideological Literature and the Drama of Reading.* Indianapolis/Bloomington: Indiana University Press, 1985.

Stone, M. E., ed. *Jewish Writings of the Second Temple Period: Apocrypha, Pseudepigrapha, Qumran Sectarian Writings, Philo, Josephus.* CRINT; Assen/Philadelphia: Van Gorcum/Fortress, 1984.

Sumner, W. A. "Israel's Encounters with Edom, Moab, Ammon, Sihon and Og according to the Deuteronomist." *VT* 18 (1968) 216–28.

Swete, H. B. *An Introduction to the Old Testament in Greek.* New York: KTAV, 1968.

Thompson, R. J. *Moses and the Law in a Century of Criticism since Graf.* Leiden: E. J. Brill, 1970.

Thompson, T. L. *The Historicity of the Patriarchal Narratives: The Quest for the Historical Abraham.* BZAW 133; Berlin/New York: de Gruyter, 1974.

———. *The Origin Tradition of Ancient Israel I. The Literary Formation of Genesis and Exodus 1–23.* Sheffield: JSOT, 1987.

———. *Early History of the Israelite People: From the Written and Archaeological Sources.* SHANE, 4; Leiden: E. J. Brill, 1992.

Tigay, J., *et al. Empirical Models for Biblical Criticism.* Philadelphia: University of Pennsylvania Press, 1985.

Toews, W. I. *Monarchy and Religious Institution in Israel under Jeroboam I.* SBLMS 47; Atlanta: Scholars Press, 1993.

Torrey, C. C. *The Composition and Historical Value of Ezra-Nehemiah.* BZAW 2; Geissen: J. Ricker, 1896.

Tov, E. "Textual Criticism (OT)." *ABD* VI:401.

Trible, P. "Bringing Miriam Out of the Shadows." *BibRev* 5 (1989) 14–24, 34.

Turner, V. "Social Dramas and Stories about Them." Pp. 137–64 in *On Narrative.* Ed. by W. J. T. Mitchell. Chicago: University of Chicago Press, 1981.

Ulrich, E., et al. *Qumran Cave 4: VII: Genesis to Numbers.* DJD XII; Oxford: Clarendon, 1994.

———. *Qumran Cave 4: IX: Deuteronomy, Joshua, Judges, Kings.* DJD XIV; Oxford: Clarendon, 1996.

———. *Qumran Cave 4: X: The Prophets.* DJD XV; Oxford: Clarendon, 1997.

Vander Kam, J. "Ezra-Nehemiah or Nehemiah and Ezra?" Pp. 55–75 in *Priests, Prophets and Scribes: Essays on the Formation and Heritage of Second Temple Judaism in Honor of Joseph Blenkinsopp.* Ed. by E. Ulrich, J. W. Wright, R. P. Carroll, and P. R. Davies. JSOTSup 149; Sheffield: JSOT, 1992.

———, E. Tov, *et al. Qumran Cave 4: VIII: Parabiblical Texts, Part 1.* DJD XIII; Oxford: Clarendon, 1994.

van der Toorn, K. *From Her Cradle to Her Grave: The Role of Religion in the Life of the Israelite and the Babylonian Woman.* The Biblical Seminar 23; Sheffield: JSOT, 1994.

Van Seters, J. "The Conquest of Sihon's Kingdom: A Literary Examination." *JBL* 91 (1972) 182–97.

————. *Abraham in History and Tradition.* New Haven: Yale University Press, 1975.

————. "The Religion of the Patriarchs." *Bib* 61 (1980) 220–33.

————. "Tradition and Social Change in Israel." *Perspectives in Religious Studies* 7 (1980) 96–113.

————. *In Search of History: Historiography in the Ancient World and the Origins of Biblical History.* New Haven: Yale University Press, 1983.

————. "The Plagues of Egypt: Ancient Tradition or Literary Invention?" *ZAW* 98 (1986) 31–39.

————. *Prologue to History: The Yahwist as Historian in Genesis.* Louisville: Westminster/John Knox, 1992.

————. *The Life of Moses: The Yahwist as Historian in Exodus-Numbers.* Louisville: Westminster/John Knox, 1994.

de Vaux, R. *Ancient Israel: Its Life and Institutions.* 2 vols. New York: McGraw-Hill, 1965.

————. "Ark of the Covenant and Tent of Reunion." Pp. 136–51 in *The Bible and the Ancient Near East.* New York: Doubleday, 1971.

————. *The Early History of Israel.* Philadelphia: Westminster, 1978.

von Rad, G. *Old Testament Theology,* 2 vols. San Francisco: Harper & Row, 1965.

————. "The Form-Critical Problem of the Hexateuch." Pp. 1–78 in *The Problem of the Hexateuch and Other Essays.* New York: McGraw-Hill, 1966.

Vorländer, H. *Die Entstehungszeit des jehowistischen Geschichtswerkes.* Europäische Hochschulschriften, Reihe 23, Theologie, Bd. 109; Frankfurt am Main: Verlag Peter Lang, 1978.

Waltke, B. "Samaritan Pentateuch." *ABD* V:932–40.

Weinberg, J. "Das *Bēit ʾābōt* im 6–4 Jh. v. u. z." *VT* 23 (1973) 400–14.

Weinfeld, M. "The Covenant of Grant in the Old Testament and in the Ancient Near East. *JAOS* 90 (1970) 184–203.

————. *Deuteronomy and the Deuteronomic School.* Oxford: Clarendon, 1972.

————. "The Tribal League at Sinai." Pp. 303–14 in *Ancient Israelite Religion: Essays in Honor of Frank Moore Cross.* Ed. by P. D. Miller, Jr., P. D. Hanson, and S. D. McBride. Philadelphia: Fortress, 1987.

————. *Deuteronomy 1–11.* AB 5; New York: Doubleday, 1991.

————. "Deuteronomy, Book of." *ABD* II:168–83.

Weingreen, J. "The Case of the Daughters of Zilophehad." *VT* 16 (1966) 518–22.

Wellhausen, J. *Prolegomena to the History of Ancient Israel.* Cleveland and New York: World Publishing Company, 1957; originally published 1883.

Wenham, G. J. *Genesis 1–15.* Waco, TX: Word, 1987.

Westermann, C. *The Promises to the Fathers.* Philadelphia: Fortress, 1980.

————. *Genesis 1–11: A Commentary.* Minneapolis: Augsburg, 1984.

————. *Genesis 12–36.* Minneapolis: Augsburg, 1985.

————. *Genesis 37–50.* Minneapolis: Augsburg, 1986.

————. *Basic Forms of Prophetic Speech.* Louisville: Westminster/John Knox, 1991 [German original, 1960].

de Wette, W. M. L. *Dissertatio Critico-Exegetica qua Deuteronomium a prioribus Pentateuchi libris diversum alius cujusdam recentioris auctoris opus esse monstratur.* Jena: Etzdorf, 1805.

Whitelam, K. W. "Israel's Traditions of Origin: Reclaiming the Land." *JSOT* 44 (1989) 19–42.

————. "The Identity of Early Israel: The Realignment and Transformation of Late Bronze-Early Iron Age Palestine." *JSOT* 63 (1994) 57–87.

Whybray, R. N. *The Making of the Pentateuch: A Methodological Study.* JSOTSup 53; Sheffield: JSOT, 1987.

Widengren, G. "The Persian Period." Pp. 489–538 in *Israelite and Judean History.* Ed. by J. H. Hayes and J. M. Miller. Philadelphia: Westminster, 1977.

Williamson, H. G. M. "Nehemiah's Walls Revisited." *PEQ* 116 (1984) 81–88.

————. "Palestine, Administration of (Persian)." *ABD* V:81–86.

Wilson, R. *Genealogy and History in the Biblical World.* New Haven: Yale University Press, 1977.

————. *Prophecy and Society in Ancient Israel.* Philadelphia: Fortress, 1980.

Wright, D. P. *The Disposal of Impurity: Elimination Rites in the Bible and in Hittite and Mesopotamian Literature.* SBLDS 101; Atlanta: Scholars Press, 1987.

————. "Unclean and Clean (OT)." *ABD* VI:729–41.

Würthwein, E. *The Text of the Old Testament.* Grand Rapids, MI: Eerdmans, 1979.

Yadin, Y. *The Temple Scroll.* 3 vols. Jerusalem: Israel Exploration Society, 1983.

Young, T. C., Jr. "The Consolidation of the Empire and Its Limits of Growth under Darius and Xerxes." *CAH²* IV:53–111.

————. "The Early History of the Medes and the Persians and the Achaemenid Empire to the Death of Cambyses." *CAH²* IV:1–52.

————. "Persians." Pp. 295–300 in the *Oxford Encyclopedia of Archaeology in the Ancient Near East,* Vol. IV. Ed. by E. M. Meyers. New York/Oxford: Oxford University Press, 1997.

Zvi, E. ben. "The List of Levitical Cities." *JSOT* 54 (1992) 77–106.

GENERAL INDEX

Printed in the United States
92400LV00003B/22/A

9 780788 503825